The Global Debate over Constitutional Property

The Global Debate over Constitutional Property

Lessons for American Takings Jurisprudence

GREGORY S. ALEXANDER

The University of Chicago Press
Chicago and London

Gregory S. Alexander is the A. Robert Noll Professor of Law at Cornell Law School. He is the author or coauthor of several books, including the award-winning *Commodity and Propriety: Competing Visions of Property in American Legal Thought, 1776–1970* (1997), also published by the University of Chicago Press.

The University of Chicago Press, Chicago 60637
The University of Chicago Press, Ltd., London

Printed in the United States of America

15 14 13 12 11 10 09 08 07 06   1 2 3 4 5

ISBN: 0-226-01298-0 (cloth)

Library of Congress Cataloging-in-Publication Data

Alexander, Gregory S., 1948–
The global debate over constitutional property : lessons for American takings jurisprudence / Gregory S. Alexander.
p. cm.
Includes bibliographical references and index.
ISBN 0-226-01298-0 (cloth : alk. paper)
1. Right of property—United States. 2. Eminent domain—United States. 3. Right of property—Germany. 4. Eminent domain—Germany. 5. Right of property—South Africa. 6. Eminent domain—South Africa. I. Title.

K721.5.A44 2006
343′.0252—dc22   2006002484

♾ The paper used in this publication meets the minimum requirements of the American National Standard for Information Sciences—Permanence of Paper for Printed Library Materials, ANSI Z39.48-1992.

To my children, Beth and Ted

CONTENTS

PREFACE

This book was written with two sets of readers in mind. The first are readers who are interested in the general normative question whether constitutionalizing property is desirable. The second are readers who are specifically interested in the constitutional property law of the countries discussed here, primarily the United States, Germany, and South Africa. Hopefully, both sets will comprise an international rather than strictly American audience. Because the intended audience is so diverse, not all chapters will be of interest to all readers. For example, American readers who are conversant with the Supreme Court's takings jurisprudence may wish to skip chapter 2, which is aimed at readers who know little or nothing about American takings law. Chapters 3 and 4, on German and South African constitutional property law, respectively, can be read as freestanding contributions, although they discuss themes that recur throughout the entire book. Chapter 1, which discusses why the issue of making property a constitutional right is so controversial, can also be read as a freestanding essay. Nevertheless, all of the chapters were written with the intent of constituting an integrated whole.

Several aspects of constitutional property law, including some that are of keen interest to comparativists, have been excluded. Notable among these exclusions is the status of property as an international human right. I do not discuss, for example, property under the European Convention on Human Rights (1950) or the Universal Declaration on Human Rights (1948). Nor do I discuss takings disputes under the North American Free Trade Agreement. Although these aspects of comparative constitutional property law are extremely interesting and important, limitations of space as well as my own lack of expertise in these areas made it seem prudent for me to leave these topics for other authors who are much more knowledgeable about international law than I am.

The discovery of an explicit social-obligation norm in other constitutional property clauses was what led me to write this book. Several years ago, I encountered the property clause of the German Constitution (more properly, the Basic Law). Having just completed work on a book that argued that property as the basis for "propriety," or the common social welfare, was a recurrent but underdeveloped theme in American legal thought, I was struck by the fact that the German constitutional property clause, unlike the takings clause of the American Constitution, expressly states that "[p]roperty entails obligations." The same section went on to specify, "Its use should also serve the public interest." I was interested in what differences, in rhetoric and reasoning if not in result, this social-obligation language might produce between American and German constitutional property law. So began my first undertaking in comparative law.

The idea of an explicit social-obligation norm in constitutional property law was also the basis for my interest in the property clause of South Africa's postapartheid constitutions. At an international conference on "Property Law on the Threshold of the 21st Century," which was held in Maastricht, The Netherlands, in 1995, I was first exposed to the intense debate then occurring in South Africa over whether property should be made a matter of constitutional protection in the newly democratic regime. South African scholars, all of whom were remarkably well-informed about both American and German constitutional property law, educated me about the unique aspects of the problem of constitutionalizing property in postapartheid South Africa. I was particularly struck by the way in which first the interim (1993) and later the final (1996) constitutions elaborated on the social-obligation norm far more extensively than the terse language of the German Basic Law's property clause. My interest kindled, I maintained contact with several of these scholars, particularly Andre van der Walt, over the following years and became better informed about the experiment that South Africa's constitutional property clause represents. A book that brought together the similarities and differences among the American, German, and South African approaches to constitutional property was a natural outcome of these experiences.

In a very real sense the book is also a natural successor to my earlier book, *Commodity and Propriety: Competing Visions of Property in American Legal Thought, 1776–1970* (1997). The idea of a social-obligation norm as a fundamental aspect of the constitutional right of property is an integral aspect of the vision of property as the material basis for promoting the common social good. While that book was intended to be strictly historical and descriptive, however, this book concerns modern law and is both descriptive and normative in its aims. Those aims are described more fully in the introduction, but it bears stating at this point that one of the book's main objectives is to encourage the development of an explicit social-obligation norm of American takings law. The experiences that other legal systems have had with such a norm seem to me a useful means of advancing that objective. That, at least, is the hope.

ACKNOWLEDGMENTS

This book has been in gestation for quite some time, and I have accumulated a number of debts in the process of working on it. I am indebted to the Max Planck Society for providing me with a grant to spend extended periods of time at the Max Planck Institute for Public Comparative and International Law, in Heidelberg, Germany, and to its past codirector, Professor Dr. Jochen Frowein, for encouraging my work during my stays there. A fellowship grant from the Stellenbosch Institute for Advanced Study, in Stellenbosch, South Africa, allowed me to spend time working through South Africa's new constitution and consulting with colleagues there. I am indebted to its director, Bernard Lategan. Generous research support also came from Cornell Law School. I am indebted to Dean Stewart Schwab for his support and encouragement. Finally, and most importantly, this book could not possibly have been completed without a year's sabbatical spent as a Fellow at the Center for Advanced Study in the Behavioral Sciences, in Stanford, California. I am indebted to the William and Flora Hewlett Foundation for funding my fellowship there and to Doug McAdam, the center's former director, for his encouragement and incomparable hospitality. The center provided a matchless environment for engaging in collaborative conversations with amazingly talented scholars about this project.

Portions of this book have been the subject of talks at several institutions, including the Max Planck Institute in Heidelberg, the University of Stellenbosch, the University of California at Berkeley, Santa Clara University, the University of Southern California, the University of Virginia, and Cornell University. I want to express my gratitude to those institutions and their members for their warm hospitality and encouraging comments. I am grateful to a number of people for helpful comments on various chapters. These readers include Annelise Riles, Steven Shiffrin, Trevor Morrison, Eric

Kades, Lauren Edelman, Martin Shapiro, Christopher Kutz, Ehud Brosh, Sia Akermark, Daniel Bell, Laura Underkuffler, and James Krier. Andre van der Walt, Hanoch Dagan, and two anonymous reviewers provided exceptionally helpful comments and suggestions on much of the book. Superb research assistance was provided by D. S. Pensley and Beth Golmar. I am deeply indebted to all of these individuals.

INTRODUCTION

Constitution making is in the wind. Since the 1980s, constitution making and constitution revision have occurred at an unprecedented rate around the world. Beginning with the end of apartheid in South Africa and the fall of communist states in central and Eastern Europe and continuing with constitutional revisions throughout Africa and South America, constitution making has proliferated in recent years. These events have led American constitutional lawyers and scholars to discover the field of comparative constitutional law.[1] A comparative approach was rare in American constitutional law scholarship just a decade ago, but today it is flourishing. Prompted perhaps by what Bruce Ackerman calls the "rise of world constitutionalism,"[2] American constitutional lawyers have increasingly turned their attention to the comparative study of a wide variety of topics, ranging from federalism to abortion to free speech.[3]

Despite comparative constitutional law's revival in the United States, American constitutional scholars have generally ignored the topic of property.[4] Whereas American constitutionalists have focused a great deal of comparative attention on individual constitutional rights such as equality and privacy, they have devoted very little attention to constitutional protection of property elsewhere in the world. This book is an attempt to fill that gap.

American comparative constitutional scholars' inattention to property is strange. One of the most controversial questions confronting modern constitution makers around the world has been whether to recognize property as an entrenched right. In postapartheid South Africa, for example, property was included in the interim and final constitutions, but only after a great deal of heated debate, as I will discuss in chapter 4. A similar debate raged in Canada (discussed in chapter 1) a few years ago when the federal government proposed a property clause for inclusion in the Charter of Rights, and the result was to reject constitutional property. And in Israel, 1992 legislation enacting a Basic Law on Human Dignity and Liberty has drawn sharp criticism for its inclusion of the right to property.[5] Similar disputes over constitutionalizing property have occurred elsewhere in the world as well.[6]

Why the Controversy?

Why has constitutional property been so controversial? Chapter 1 provides a fuller account of the arguments that have been made in debates around the world over the idea of a constitutional right of property, but a brief summary will be helpful at this point to set the stage for the entire book.

The modern debate about whether property should be made a constitutional right has tended to be less about economics than about politics. Specialists in economic development policy have debated the importance of clear property rights for economic growth,[7] but that debate has not played a major role in the constitutional debate over property. The issue for constitutionalists is not whether secure property rights are a necessary condition for economic development (although constitutionalists may and likely do care about that), but whether property should be made an entrenched right, one that enjoys a relatively high degree of immunity from the forces of ordinary democratic politics. The constitutionally salient concern is the impact of making property an entrenched right in a democracy, particularly in new democracies.

There is an old debate over the relationship between private property rights and democracy, and the modern constitutional debate has revived much of that debate. On the one hand, critics of property rights have long argued that property undermines democracy. To them, property rights are the source of inequality, of both wealth and political power, denying meaningful opportunity for political participation and self-governance. Property is a source of domination, not democracy.[8] On the other hand, some proponents of property have argued that private property rights support democracy, or at least certain versions of democracy. Cass Sunstein succinctly expresses this old view in stating that property "creates the kind of security that is indispensable to genuine citizenship in a democracy."[9]

For those who view property as the foundation of democracy, constitutional protection of property rights is very important as a tool for creating and maintaining a liberal democratic order, particularly in new democracies. As I will discuss further in chapter 1,[10] some commentators go so far as to argue that without constitutional protection, property rights are unlikely to achieve the degree of security and stability that is necessary for a properly functioning liberal democracy as well as for an efficient free market economy, or at least that there is a substantial risk that they will not do so.

This line of argument draws on the special place that property rights have long enjoyed in classical liberal thought. According to classical liberalism, constitutionalism is marked, as Frank Michelman puts it, by a "habitual, strong inclination toward a clear demarcation between politics and law, . . . between the supposed provinces of legislatures and of courts."[11] Classical liberals understand rights as constitutive of the private sphere whose inviolability against public action is the bedrock of personal autonomy and political liberty. They consider the right of property to be the template for all individual rights.[12] The greatest threat to property's protective role, according to this view, is democracy itself. Left unchecked, democracy degenerates into the tyranny of the majority, as legislatures persistently invade the property-based private realm with actions aimed at redistributing wealth. The "power of numbers," in Claus Offe's terms, will overwhelm the "power of property."[13] The only practical solution to this dilemma, property rights theorists surmise, is to insulate property from the forces of ordinary politics by taking it out of the province of the legislature and placing it exclusively (or nearly so) in the hands of courts.

From this perspective, constitutionalizing the right of property makes great good sense. Making property a matter of constitutional protection means that questions about property—how it is distributed, how it is used, and so on—are not subject to the pathologies of ordinary politics. Property becomes "Super Property." It is substantially (although not completely) isolated from the public sphere, thereby securing the integrity of the private sphere. Where property has been given constitutional status, the courts' only legitimate role is strictly enforcing individual property rights. Specifically, it is the job of courts to protect private property interests against legislative actions that redistribute property entitlements, actions that violate the strict separation between the public and private spheres. Liberals of this persuasion hold that property, conceived as the right of individual owners to exclusive possession, use, and control of desired and scarce resources, is the very foundation upon which liberalism's categorical separation of the public and private realms is based.

This version of liberalism is deeply flawed, as critics have pointed out. One of its defects is that it rests upon the old Blackstonian conception of ownership, which depicts ownership as "that sole and despotic dominion which one man claims and exercises over the external things of the world, in total exclusion of the right of any other individual in the universe."[14] As any number of scholars have pointed out, this conception of ownership has never actually existed, either in Blackstone's time or in ours.[15] It is simply a myth, but a myth that is very persistent.

The Blackstonian conception of ownership underscores classical liberalism's mistaken notion that property serves as the basis for the categorical separation of the private world from the public world. The whole notion that the private and public spheres can be kept categorically separate is a pernicious illusion. The public and private are inevitably interdependent. With respect to private property, a regime of legal property rights is simply not possible without the active engagement of the public sphere. As the American legal realists correctly pointed out, property rights are nothing more or less than allocations of the state's coercive power to individuals.[16] The enforcement of property rights requires exercise of the state's power to coerce others. In effect, then, no state, no property.

An allied theme in this critique stresses property's relational character.[17] Individual property rights are embedded in and in turn give structure to relationships. As Jennifer Nedelsky writes, rights are "a means of structuring the relations between individuals and the sources of collective power so that autonomy is fostered rather than undermined."[18] This relational view of rights is highly problematic for the argument that a constitutional right of property is necessary to maintain the liberal political order, which is defined as a regime in which individual interests are immune from invasions by the public will. Property's inherently relational character means that insofar as holdings are concerned, courts are inevitably in the business of redistribution. Indeed, strictly speaking, courts are constantly distributing, rather than *re*distributing, property because property, relationally understood, is always in flux. The sharp property boundaries required for the categorical separation of the private and public realms, the individual and the community, are simply not possible. Seen in this way, constitutional property is inherently distributional because property itself is inherently relational. Constitutionalization of property perpetuates the false belief that it is possible (and desirable) categorically to isolate private interests from public involvement. The cost of this illusion is a stunted form of democracy and "a system of institutions that allocates political power unequally and fails to foster political participation."[19]

Is Property a Special Case?

This problem with classical liberalism's theory of categorically separating the public and private sphere is not unique to the right of property. It is true of every individual constitutional right. If a strict or impregnable wall between the public and private realms is impossible, then no individual right can be made totally immune from collective action. The attempt to protect a right by making it a constitutional matter futilely sacrifices democracy for an illusion. Rather than eliminating the problem of collective power, the classical liberal strategy simply shifts the locus of collective control from one public body to another. It shrinks the sovereignty of the democratic legislature and expands that of unelected courts. Individual constitutional rights are protected not by removing them from the control of the state but by empowering one source of state power, the courts, over another whose legitimacy stems from the ordinary processes of democratic politics. In this respect, the decision whether to constitutionalize the right of property poses a problem that is inherent in all individual rights.

Still, property does pose a special problem for liberal constitutionalism. Property is special in two respects. First, property is inherently allocative in function. As Laura Underkuffler-Freund puts it, "[W]ith regard to property, *the giving to one person necessarily denies or takes from another.*"[20] Property rights "give to some what cannot be given to all: they allocate rights to particular individuals infinite, non-sharable resources."[21] To be sure, other individual rights, free speech, for example, may also have allocative effects, but the allocation of scarce resources is not one of the primary purposes of rights like free speech (at least not one of their commonly understood primary purposes). The allocation of scarce resources, however, is widely understood to be one of the core purposes of property rights. The inherently allocative feature of the right of property is one reason why it is so highly contentious.

Closely related to this first reason why property poses a special problem is a second. Property, not as a right but as the object of the right, or what one might call the stakes of property rights, is foundational.[22] At least some basic assets are necessary for the meaningful exercise of all other rights. Indeed, they are necessary for life itself. In this sense, property, as the access to subsistence necessities, is also foundational for the exercise of all political and constitutional rights. My rights to express dissenting political views and to vote in political elections are not very meaningful to me if I lack subsistence food and shelter. Precisely because the stakes of property rights are so high, the *right* of property, including the constitutional right of property, has been controversial. Both supporters and opponents of a constitutional right of property have tended to share the classical conception of the right of property. In its classical sense, the right of property is about *keeping,* not *getting* or *having,* access to resources, including basic subsistence resources. Those who believe that individuals should have a right to subsistence living support, which one might consider to be an aspect of the right to *life*,[23] have opposed granting constitutional status to property rights because they have assumed that a constitutional right of property is in this sense in tension with, if not fundamentally incompatible with, a right of access to foundational goods.

These two factors have made the stakes of constitutionalizing property seem very high. Entrenching the right of property means that adjustments between competing claims to the exclusive right to appropriate the same goods cannot be made through the processes of ordinary majoritarian politics. Critics of constitutional property worry that supermajoritarian protection of property will inevitably lead to an unacceptably high degree of inequality in the distribution of scarce resources or will reinforce an existing maldistribution of wealth, including the basic necessities for human existence. In subsequent chapters of this book, I will argue that the effect of constitutionalizing property on governmental redistribution of resources depends not simply on the mere fact of whether or not a constitutional property clause exists, but also on how the clause is interpreted. Interpretation, in turn, depends on, among other factors, the character and background of a country's community of constitutional interpreters.[24] The important point to be noted here, however, is that the constitutional right of property does pose special problems.

Text Does Matter

I have indicated that one of the core themes of this book is that interpretation matters. This is not to say that text is irrelevant. Hardly. Judicial interpretation of a constitutional property clause[25] turns on many factors, among which is its text. As I will argue throughout the book, this is especially true with respect to matters related to the social-obligation dimension of the constitutional property right. What kind of property clause (and in what kind of constitution) may well influence how property rights claims are interpreted.

Constitutional property clauses are not all identical, although there are certain features that all constitutional property clauses have in common. All recognize that the state may "expropriate" or "take" property.[26] Moreover, all of them place restrictions on the state's power to expropriate property. The two notable restrictions that nearly all constitutional property clauses share are, first, that expropriations are permitted only for "public purposes" or for "public use" and, second, that such expropriations must be compensated, at least to some degree.[27] Beyond these common features, certain important textual differences exist among some constitutional property clauses. Textual differences are important because they can and in some cases do influence the substantive reach of the social-obligation norm. Of these textual differences, by far the most important concerns the social-obligation norm itself. The American Constitution's property clause, the takings clause of the Fifth Amendment, contains no social-obligation provision as such. It acknowledges the limited character of the American constitutional right of property only indirectly, by permitting the state to expropriate property under particular circumstances. Beyond this, there is no formal textual recognition of the social obligation of property.

Some constitutions go further, however. They acknowledge, textually and affirmatively, that the constitutional right of property is limited by an overriding obligation that property serve the needs of society. The German Constitution, which I discuss in detail in chapter 3, is an example of such a constitutional property clause. It states, in relevant part, that "Ownership [*Eigentum*] entails obligations. Its use should also serve the public interest."[28] This social-obligation provision explicitly acknowledges, as the American takings clause does not, that owners of property have social responsibilities to society. Other national constitutions include similar language in their property clauses, and some, such as South Africa's, have textually extended the social-obligation provision beyond that of the German clause. As I will discuss in subsequent chapters, this text has facilitated judicial interpretations of both the German and South African property clauses that place significant limits on the scope and substance of the constitutional right of property. The absence of such a social-obligation textual provision in the American takings clause is one of the single most important differences between that clause and the other two property clauses that are the main examples studied in this book, the German and South African clauses. However, as I will argue in chapter 5, although the text of the American constitutional property clause lacks a social-obligation provision, its tradition does not, at least not entirely. The germ of the idea behind a social-obligation provision does exist in American takings jurisprudence. But the failure of courts expressly to acknowledge the social-obligation norm, hiding it under some murky rubric like "public-harm abating," has left it sorely underdeveloped. This is the real point separating American takings law from its German and South African counterparts. Chapter 5 proposes that American courts expressly recognize takings jurisprudence's hidden social-obligation norm and openly develop its exact contours.

Why a Comparative Approach?

Looking at constitutionalization of property from a comparative perspective is not an uncontroversial undertaking, for constitutional law or even for nonconstitutional law.[29] In recent years scholars and judges (including members of the United States Supreme Court) have debated the appropriateness of using constitutional materials and practices from other countries to study and resolve American constitutional questions.[30] Within this debate I am firmly in the camp of those who insist that American constitutional law needs to take the comparative turn. Many reasons have been offered for why a comparative approach is both appropriate and desirable for constitutional law, most of which are not unique to constitutional comparative law.[31] Some of these have motivated me to write this book.

One reason is self-knowledge and self-understanding.[32] The comparative method is dialogic and distancing. By providing distance from ourselves, comparative study reveals aspects of ourselves that were not previously apparent. It puts into question legal practices that we take for granted, sometimes yielding the insight that those practices are a "false necessit[y]."[33] Comparison provides purchase for critique and contingency.[34] A highly relevant question here is whether constitutional status is a necessary condition for a regime of stable property rights. Comparing our constitutional property experience with that of other countries provides us with some fresh insight into the claim made in some quarters (for example, the World Bank) that constitutional protection is required for secure property rights.[35] For example, as we will see in chapter 1, Canada's Charter of Rights lacks a property clause, but property rights in Canada enjoy a high degree of stability and security.

A highly important nonnecessitarian insight from comparative analysis concerns the impact of constitutionalization of property on government programs designed to redistribute private wealth. Does constitutional protection of property inevitably withdraw from the realm of political debate decisions about the proper distribution and use of valuable social resources? Does it substantially preclude collectively deliberated programs designed to promote equality of resources through redistribution? These have been the central questions involved in global debates over the propriety of including property in the ranks of constitutionally protected interests. Democracies that have decided not to constitutionalize property (or that have withdrawn property clauses from their constitutions) have done so primarily on the basis of their belief that to constitutionalize property means to end political debate over property and to entrench the extant (and presumably unjust) distribution of wealth. Those who urge that property no longer enjoys constitutional protection in other countries, notably in the United States, often share the same belief. Many legal commentators who are normatively opposed to constitutional property clauses believe that a virtually inevitable effect of making property rights a matter of constitutional protection is creating the minimal night watchman, antiredistributive state.[36] This argument is commonly stated in terms of the American *Lochner* era, when the U.S. Supreme Court adopted an activist stance against redistributive legislation. So, for example, opponents of India's now defunct constitutional property provision argued that the clause was inherently antiredistributive.[37]

A comparative perspective suggests that those commentators who believe that a constitutional property clause necessarily precludes substantial redistributive politics are mistaken. The effect that such a provision has on a society's distribution and use of valuable resources, including land, depends on its background political traditions and legal culture. While the clause clearly affects government redistributive policy, it does not, in and of itself, freeze or even substantially prevent collective redistributions of property. The relevant question is not whether there is or is not a property clause, but how the clause is interpreted. It is background nonconstitutional political and legal culture, not the constitutional property clause, that does the antiredistributive work.

A second reason for the comparative approach is that it sometimes discloses reasons for constitutional practices that we share with other countries but that are not part of our accepted explanations. In the case of American constitutional property law, the conventional American wisdom is that the takings clause serves two functions, commonly termed efficiency and fairness.[38] Property, according to this account, is about just two concerns: maximizing social wealth and treating people fairly. The experiences of other mature liberal democracies that have debated elevating property to constitutional status show that these are not the only purposes that might be served by constitutionalizing property. The Canadian story is an example of how constitutional property can have multiple valences, including valences that are not recognized in the standard American explanation. As we will see, in Canada, the drive to entrench property as a constitutional right was substantially based on concerns about federalism. Although it was ultimately rejected, the proposed property clause was basically understood as a device for maintaining federal unity, a very different function from those identified in American takings scholarship. The Canadian experience illustrates the fact that much American constitutional scholarship on the topic of takings misses the complexity of what constitutional property is all about.

Finally, a straightforwardly instrumental, or "functionalist,"[39] reason for studying constitutional law from a comparative perspective is to clarify and to move toward solving domestic legal problems. This seems especially true in the case of American constitutional property law. It is a commonplace among American legal scholars that American takings law is a "muddle."[40] *Is* American takings law a muddle? My reaction to the question is to ask, "Compared with what?" No one can (or at least should) critically evaluate the jurisprudence in the abstract. Some sort of benchmark is needed. The comparative approach provides one. By comparing American takings law with its counterparts in other liberal democracies, we will be in a much better position to decide whether the conventional wisdom about the sad state of our takings jurisprudence is warranted and, if it is, what factors have contributed to the problem. My judgment is that our takings law in fact *is* a muddle. American takings law is substantially less principled and less transparent than the constitutional property jurisprudence of some other countries, especially Germany. Chapter 3 will indicate the relevant respects in which Germany's constitutional property law is more transparent, if not more substantively principled than ours.

Along the same functionalist lines, the comparative approach may also disclose opportunities for legal systems to solve domestic problems by borrowing legal norms or practices from other jurisdictions.[41] Borrowing is perhaps the most commonly stated reason for engaging in comparative legal analysis. It is also a highly disputed practice. Among the problems with attempts to borrow legal practices, especially constitutional practices,[42] from other countries is one of the very factors that I emphasize in this book: the central importance of a nation's background legal and political culture and traditions to the meaning of the provisions of its constitution. The importance of background legal and political traditions and culture is one reason Justice Scalia has given for resisting the idea of constitutional borrowing.[43] This is not the appropriate occasion for fully responding to critiques like Justice Scalia's. I merely make two points here.[44] First, it matters a great deal what is being borrowed. Constitutional practices are not all of a piece. Some are more imbued with, or run counter to, deeply ingrained cultural meaning than others. An attempt to transplant into the American Constitution the German concept of objective human dignity, for example, would very likely encounter resistance or misunderstanding, given the American cultural tradition of rights as subjective in nature.[45] Second, sometimes the most deeply entrenched traditions and culture are what most need challenging. As William Forbath and Lawrence Sager have written, "What is 'deeply rooted' may be precisely the problem, insofar as it may express a contradiction between constitutional commitment and legal and political actuality."[46] Public discussion of the possibility of borrowing, even if the borrowing never actually occurs, may prove to be the catalyst for an eventual constitutional transformation.

In chapter 5, I discuss several doctrinal practices that American takings law might borrow from other jurisdictions that have the potential for contributing to the construction of a more coherent and transparent takings jurisprudence.[47] As I will discuss, some of the proposed borrowings, particularly the use of a proportionality doctrine, are riskier than others, and I am more tentative about whether they would usefully contribute to improving American takings law. However, all of them, including the proportionality doctrine, offer at least the possibility of improving American takings jurisprudence, if only in the sense of making the normative underpinnings of judicial decisions more transparent. They deserve to be studied if for no other reason than to sharpen awareness of our own doctrinal practices by contrasting those practices with the differing doctrinal practices of other countries.

Why Germany? Why South Africa?

The primary countries compared in this book are the United States, Germany, and postapartheid South Africa. I have chosen Germany and South Africa as the main countries to compare with the United States for several reasons. First, the three countries are exemplars of the three generations of written liberal constitutions. The American Constitution is a first-generation, classical liberal constitution. It is an eighteenth-century document, and it protects only civil and political rights. The German Basic Law (1949) is a second-generation (that is, post-1945) constitution. There are two salient aspects of such a constitution. First, although it is a liberal document, it is not classically liberal. It stresses duties as well as rights. Second, to borrow Donald Kommers' terminology, it is a "dignitarian" constitution rather than a "libertarian" constitution like the American Constitution.[48] The South African Constitution (final 1996, interim 1993) is a third-generation constitution, from the most recent wave of democratic constitutions. Like second-generation constitutions, it is not classically liberal. It recognizes duties as well as rights and stresses as its core value human dignity rather than individual liberty. In addition, and unlike second-generation constitutions, it recognizes specifically enumerated economic and social rights as positive constitutional rights.

Another reason for choosing the German Constitution is its influence in the modern world. Of all the world's written constitutions, more than half were written since 1974.[49] Of those, many were influenced by the German Basic Law.[50] In fact, the German Basic Law has become the most influential constitution in the world.

The South African Constitution merits special attention not only because of its recent vintage but also because the property clause was such a divisive issue during the drafting process. Perhaps more than in any other new democracy in the world today, in South Africa the status of property rights is at the very center of the nation's future. Whether and how South Africa will be able to fully transform itself and completely eradicate all vestiges of its apartheid past is substantially a matter of property. So, although relatively little case law interpreting the property clause has developed, the South African debate over inclusion of a property clause may well serve as a case study for future new constitutional democracies.

Finally, although all three countries are constitutional democracies with a private property/free market economic system, their experiences concerning the relationship between a constitutionalized property right and governmental redistribution of wealth are very different from each other. The United States Constitution's takings clause, although it has hardly ended all redistribution of wealth (much to the consternation of some American commentators[51]), is widely thought to have an antiredistributive valence (although, as I will argue, it is not the clause itself that does the antiredistributive work, but background nonconstitutional aspects of our political and legal culture). The German and South African constitutional property clauses have certainly not frozen property's distribution or uses. To the contrary, they have permitted (and in South Africa's case, encouraged) reform redistribution to a considerably greater extent than that seen in the United States. They are exemplars of constitutional provisions that recognize the centrality of private property rights while simultaneously undergirding a very different calculus of individual and community interests from the one that is usually expressed in the United States. With respect to the relationship between constitutional property and redistribution, then, comparing these three experiences tends to demonstrate the relative unimportance of the constitutional provision.

Although most of the book's attention is devoted to the United States, Germany, and South Africa (for the reasons I have just given), the experience of a few other countries that have struggled with the question of a constitutional or entrenched right of property will be examined as well. Canada, which I discuss in chapter 1, is an example. I discuss Canada, which considered but rejected the idea of including a property clause in its Charter of Rights, primarily for two reasons. First, it provides particularly clear evidence in support of my contention that strong and secure property rights depend less on being given constitutional or entrenched status and more on background legal and political traditions and culture. (The United Kingdom, which I have not discussed because it lacks any written constitution or bill of entrenched rights, is another obvious example.[52]) Second, it illustrates the further point that the constitutional right of property may be controversial for reasons that have nothing to do with economic arguments or questions of fairness. In Canada's case, one reason why an entrenched property right was so controversial was because of its impact on Canadian federalism.

Convergence or Difference?

One of the core themes of comparative legal scholarship is convergence and difference. Comparative scholars often take as their main task identifying points of similarity between the systems under study, or differences, or both, reaching an overall judgment about whether convergence or difference best characterizes how the systems relate to each other. My approach in this book is to consider convergence and difference but without providing a bottom-line conclusion. The truth, trite perhaps, but true nevertheless, is that both convergence and difference emerge from my comparative project. As a guide to the remainder of the book, it may be helpful to preview the main points of convergence and then the differences that I have identified.

Points of Convergence

A main point of convergence is the very existence of a constitutional property clause. Several of the world's liberal democracies with written constitutions (or entrenched bills of rights) do not have property clauses, but most do. And the recent historical trend favors inclusion of a provision explicitly protecting property. Although Canada and New Zealand recently (1982 and 1990, respectively) rejected property clauses in their charters of rights, a substantial number of other new (that is, post-1980) constitutions, including, to name only a few, Brazil (1988), Chile (1989), the Czech Republic (1993), Ethiopia (1994), Hungary (1989), Lesotho (1993), Poland (1992), Russia (1993), Rwanda (1991), Uganda (1995), and Zimbabwe (1980),[53] include clauses expressly protecting "property" or "ownership" against uncompensated state expropriations.

A second point of convergence is the structure of property clauses. Most constitutions that protect property do so through a single, unitary clause. (The American Constitution, which has several clauses relating to property, is unusual in this respect.) The core structure of that clause has three parts: *recognition* (institution/right), *expropriation,* and *compensation.* Differences, some quite important, exist in the details of these parts, but these differences should not obscure the fact that there is an overarching similarity to the basic features of all constitutional property clauses.

A third point of convergence is outcome. The overwhelming majority of the world's liberal democracies, even those lacking constitutional protection of property, legally protect private property interests against uncompensated state expropriations. To be sure, there are important differences in such details as which government actions constitute an expropriation[54] and what level of compensation should be provided ("just," "fair," "equitable," or "adequate"?),[55] but the bare fact that a vast majority of democratic nations protect against uncompensated state expropriations of property, not just on paper but in reality, is a datum very much worthy of attention. Compared with the wave of uncompensated nationalization of private interests that characterized global politics forty years ago, the level of stability and security that property rights enjoy today around the world is a remarkable development.

The question that this development prompts is whether the convergence in favor of substantive constitutional protection of private property signifies the hegemony of the political ideology now commonly known as "neoliberalism." It is perhaps tempting to conclude that the considerable degree of agreement about constitutional protection of property is evidence of a gradual convergence toward a single model of liberalism, but I am skeptical that it is. Looking beyond these points of convergence, we see ample evidence of variety and localism among the world's constitutional property practices. Rather than seeing comparative constitutional property law as the "steady march of neoliberal constitutionalism,"[56] I note important differences as well as points of convergence. From my perspective, comparative constitutional property law is a "space[] where difference and similarity [both] reside."[57]

Matters of Difference

Throughout the chapters that follow, I will discuss two levels of difference between the American approach to constitutional protection of property and that of other countries, especially Germany. The first level is doctrinal; the second is theoretical.

As I develop in more detail in chapter 5, three important doctrinal differences exist between American takings law and its counterparts in Germany and elsewhere. First, unlike the jurisprudence developed under the property clause of the German Basic Law, American takings jurisprudence lacks a general, well-developed doctrine of proportionality. There are pockets of such a doctrine in the Supreme Court's takings case law (for example, *Dolan v. City of Tigard*),[58] but no such doctrine applies throughout all of takings law.

Second, American courts, with few exceptions, have not adopted an overtly functional approach to determining when government regulations have "go[ne] too far"[59] and become takings. By "functional approach," I mean a judicial method according to which the court explicitly sets out to identify the core purpose(s) for which the federal constitution protects property and then determines whether the property interest in the case before the court implicates that purpose(s). Exactly such an approach is the method used by the German courts and courts elsewhere in the world. Throughout the book I emphasize the importance of the particular legal system's jurisprudential tendencies. In chapter 5, I specifically argue that the legal system's use of an explicitly purposive approach is one important factor that enhances both the transparency and predictability of its constitutional property law. I suggest that the failure of American courts to use such a functional method of analysis has contributed to the muddled state of American takings law, in contrast with the relatively clear state of constitutional property law in Germany, and I urge that American courts adopt the explicitly purposive approach used by German courts.

The third doctrinal difference is substantive rather than methodological. It is the absence of an explicit, well-developed social-obligation norm in American takings law. Unlike its German counterpart (Article 14 of the Basic Law), the takings clause of the Fifth Amendment is silent about obligations. Textually, it draws no connection between ownership and obligation, and, following this textual lead, the courts have, with few exceptions, likewise been silent regarding obligations that owners owe to the communities of which they are members. One of the strongest differences—perhaps *the* strongest difference between German and American constitutional property law—is American takings jurisprudence's lack of an explicit social-obligation norm. The gains for American law of explicitly recognizing and developing such a norm will be a main theme of chapter 5.[60]

Beyond these doctrinal differences, there are major theoretical differences between American takings law and its German counterpart (and property clauses elsewhere that are modeled on the German clause). The most important of these is the dialectical character of American takings jurisprudence. Although American legal scholars all recognize that American takings law is a "muddle,"[61] few of them recognize the reason for this muddle. A "fundamental tension"[62] in American takings law exists, a tension between two values—wealth, on the one hand, and civic virtue, or "propriety" as I have elsewhere called it, on the other hand.[63] Chapter 2 examines how the tension between these two social visions permeates takings law. This tension is not present in German constitutional property law or its cognates elsewhere. Largely because a social-obligation norm is a formal part of the property clause and an explicit, well-developed aspect of its jurisprudence, German constitutional property law is more normatively coherent and doctrinally stable than American takings law.

Related to this difference is another. In Germany's Basic Law, the South African Constitution, and many other modern constitutions, human dignity has been formally enshrined as the foundational substantive value by which the courts are to develop all other constitutional interests, including property. As we will see in chapter 3, in German constitutional law human dignity is understood as the basis for an objective ordering of values. The Basic Law's fundamental purpose is to instantiate what is considered as the objectively proper, or well-ordered, society, one that is based on human dignity.[64] Property is considered a fundamental constitutional right insofar as it promotes the human dignity value. In contrast, American constitutional law lacks any explicit foundational norm. Certainly, in some areas of constitutional law, free speech law, for example, American courts refer to "foundational norms," but the Constitution lacks a single explicit norm that undergirds the entire Constitution in the way that human dignity does the German Basic Law. The American Constitution does not expressly refer at all to human dignity, a modern norm whose widespread recognition postdates the American Constitution, and it has no other counterpart to human dignity. This difference between the American Constitution and more recent constitutions is yet another factor contributing to the confused state of American takings law.

The Comparative Method of This Book

A word is in order about the comparative method I use in this book. There is no such thing as "the comparative method." I doubt that there ever has been, but even if there has, that "glorious past" of comparative law is over. The practice of comparative law has now fragmented into several competing discursive practices. The methodological wars of comparative law have largely been confined to the realm of private law, with relatively little attention being given to comparative constitutional law. The institutional and cultural differences between private law and constitutional law are great enough that much of what is said about comparative methods in the private setting has no clear applicability to the constitutional setting. I cannot pretend to have worked out anything like a complete theory of comparative constitutional law. Still, I have not written this book with indifference to methodological issues.

My main methodological commitment is, in a word, interpretive. The commitment may also be characterized as realist, for it shares with the American legal realists the conviction that form, though not irrelevant, has far less impact on the eventual effect of legal texts and doctrines than interpretation does. This thesis regarding the central importance of interpretation responds to an assumption that is implicit in some discussions of whether the constitutions of new democracies—and even some older ones—should include a property clause. The assumption, which I refer to as the formalist trap, is that the degree of legal protection that extant property holdings within a society enjoy turns in large measure on the existence or absence of a property clause in that country's constitution. Neither side in the debate over constitutionalizing property has a monopoly on the formalist trap. Both proponents and opponents of constitutional property clauses have been guilty of lapsing into it. They have failed to pay much attention to the relationship between interpretation and formal text in analyzing how much legal protection existing property holdings within any society actually enjoy and the means that legal protection is provided. Most importantly, they have largely failed to address one of the interpretive factors identified below, path dependency. Chapter 1 is a critique of this formalist mistake.

My discussion of the interpretive process focuses on two factors. The first is the society's background legal and political traditions and culture. Adopting a term that has become popular in recent years, I call this factor the *path-dependent* quality of legal interpretation. The second aspect of the interpretive process that is stressed is the legal institutional context within which constitutions and the courts interpreting them operate. Both of these factors will be developed in more detail in subsequent chapters, but a brief explanation of them at this point should clarify my interpretive, legal realist method.

The path-dependency thesis argues that where you end up may depend on where you started out. The actual legal situation of property holdings in a society is strongly affected by the background history, culture, and traditions of that country's legal and political regime. In a society that lacks any legal tradition or culture of strong protection of property rights, a constitutional property clause that was intended to render property rights secure may end up eviscerated through the process of legal interpretation. Conversely, in a society with a strong legal tradition of protecting the extant holdings of property, a property clause that was designed to have politically progressive, or even transformative, results may be effectively neutered by a community of judicial interpreters who were all acculturated in the old regime and whose own legal consciousness has not been transformed. As we will see in chapter 4, this is the single greatest risk now confronting South Africa's constitutional property and socioeconomic clauses. By the same token, a society with a strong legal tradition of secure property rights probably has no need for a constitutional provision expressly protecting property. In such a society, constitutional protection is largely redundant.

My use of the term "background legal and political traditions and culture" is intentionally broad. It includes a country's historical political ideologies and conflicts, its private law system, especially the rules and concepts relating to property, and its political and judicial attitudes toward the ordinary processes of democratic politics and how those processes affect property interests. Historical political ideologies matter because constitutional interpretation always occurs in a historical context, even if the interpreter does not acknowledge that fact. Even—perhaps one should say especially—rejected ideologies of the past exert a strong influence on interpretation of constitutional provisions, including property clauses. As we will see, this is especially true of countries like Germany and South Africa. National socialism and apartheid are political pentimenti, images from the past that remain visible just beneath the surface of the constitutional present that has tried to erase them.

A nation's private law system, especially its property regime, is another important background factor. A basic question confronting interpreters of any constitutional property clause is the role of the private law meaning of property. Is the constitutional meaning of property limited to how private law defines property, or is it independent of the private law meaning? Even if private law does not formally define the constitutional meaning of property, it still exerts an influence on it. The private law meaning of property is a rhetorical trope that runs throughout the entire legal discourse of property.

Closely related to this second aspect of the relevant background traditions and culture is a third: political and judicial attitudes and beliefs about the processes of ordinary politics. Countries have varying experiences with democratic politics, and those experiences create different attitudes toward the use of constitutional rights to correct perceived defects in the country's political legislative processes. Within the relevant community, what are the dominant views and attitudes about the nature of ordinary democratic politics and how the political process affects private property rights? To the extent that widely shared beliefs and attitudes about ordinary majoritarian politics are positive or optimistic, there will be less pressure to use constitutional mechanisms to correct perceived abuses or defects in the legislative process. Conversely, where there is a prevalent anxiety that democracy is prone to systemic process abuses, more pressure exists for courts to use constitutional tools, especially individual rights such as property, to correct perceived power imbalances. The experience with the constitutional property right in the United States is the primary example of the influence of this factor. As we will see, other countries lack our degree of skepticism about the workings of ordinary politics, and, partly as a consequence, they have been less inclined to make property an entrenched right at all or to give the constitutional property clause a robust interpretation.

Closely related to the nation's background political and legal traditions and culture, the institutional context of constitutional provisions strongly influences interpretation. To give just one brief example of what I have in mind by the phrase "institutional context of constitutions and interpreting courts," it is, I believe, extremely dangerous to study German constitutional law on the basis of decisions of the German Constitutional Court (*Bundesverfassungsgericht*) alone. Under the German system, several different courts have overlapping jurisdiction in connection with the property clause. The Constitutional Court is the guardian of the constitutional order, and only it has the authority to declare statutes unconstitutional. Other federal courts, however, have power to interpret the constitution. With respect to the property clause the most important of these courts are the Federal Supreme Court (*Bundesgerichtshof*) and the Federal Administrative Court (*Bundesverwaltungsgericht*). In addition, the Federal Court of Justice in Civil Matters has authority to award the compensation that the constitution requires for "expropriations."

The Constitutional Court's pronouncements about compensation provide an incomplete picture. As we will see in chapter 4, until recently, a certain degree of tension has existed between the Constitutional Court and these high civil courts, especially the Administrative and Supreme Courts, in the area of compensation practices. This is especially important in connection with the question whether Germany recognizes what in American takings law is known as an "inverse condemnation," that is, compensation for excessive regulatory limitations. Studying the operation of the German property clause on the basis of the Constitutional Court's decisions alone, one might quickly answer that nothing resembling the American practice of inverse condemnation awards is possible. However, looking at the practices of the civil and administrative (that is, nonconstitutional) courts, the answer is more complex. A recent decision of the Constitutional Court appears to have resolved that tension, but the way in which the court resolved that tension cannot be understood except in light of decisions of the nonconstitutional courts. Nor can one provide a complete answer to the question whether anything analogous to the American doctrine of inverse condemnation exists in Germany without knowing of the decisions of the high civil and administrative courts as well as of the Constitutional Court. This experience illustrates the need for an understanding of the full institutional context within which constitutional interpretation and related judicial practices occur.

This book then operates at both a positive and a normative level. One of the main positive theses is that beneath the surface convergence around constitutional protection of property throughout most of the world in recent years there are several important areas of difference, both doctrinal and theoretical. The bottom line of constitutional protection of property in Germany may be substantially the same as in the United States, but the means by which the courts get there are different in important ways. What drives constitutional property law in the United States is not the same as what drives it in Germany or South Africa.

Another important positive thesis is that granting constitutional status to property rights does not necessarily imply ending or even significantly inhibiting governmental redistribution of property. This point may seem perfectly obvious to some readers, but others may assume that constitutional protection of property is incompatible with progressive democratic politics. The experiences of Germany and other countries with constitutionalizing property undermine this assumption.

A third positive thesis is that constitutional recognition is neither a necessary nor a sufficient condition for a legal regime of robust property rights. Examples can be found of states with highly secure property rights but no constitutional protection and, conversely, of states whose constitutions formally protect property but whose legal systems in fact treat them lightly. An important critical lesson that grows out of this observation is that the formalist insistence on constitutional recognition of property rights by proponents of the neoliberal agenda is a red herring. Constitutional recognition has little effect in promoting security of property rights where the background political and legal culture lacks internal respect for them.

Perhaps the most important normative thesis, at least to American readers, is that American takings law would be improved, both substantively and methodologically, by borrowing features of constitutional property law that are common in other liberal democracies. The most important of these is an explicit social-obligation norm. In its failure openly to recognize that individual owners owe duties to maintain the common welfare of their communities, the American constitutional property clause lags behind the rest of the world. It is time that we catch up.

CHAPTER ONE

The Formalist Trap: Text and Tradition in the Interpretation of Constitutional Property Clauses

Property occupies an uneasy position in the constellation of the constitutional interests of democratic societies throughout the world. Constitutional political rights such as free speech and freedom of association are relatively (although not universally[1]) uncontroversial, but no such certainty exists about economic rights, notably the right to private property. The lack of anything close to a global consensus about property as a constitutional right has become apparent in recent years as new democracies have written new constitutions and some established democracies have revised existing ones.

To be sure, the constitutions of most democracies throughout the world do contain property clauses, but several advanced democracies with written constitutions or a charter of rights do not. India, whose original postcolonial constitution expressly protected property, entirely expunged a property clause from its constitution after several years' experience.[2] Postapartheid South Africa's constitution contains a property clause, but the decision to include it came only after an extended and heated debate.[3] In Singapore, a country with a strong commitment to free markets, the rights to own property and to receive fair compensation for state expropriations were deliberately omitted from the postindependence constitution.[4] The same is true of New Zealand and Canada, two countries that have no written constitution but do have a written bill of rights that entrenches individual rights. Property was deliberately omitted from New Zealand's Bill of Rights in 1990[5] and from Canada's Charter of Rights in 1982.[6] Underscoring the point, property nowhere appears in Franz Wieacker's "basic inventory" of rights accepted by "most western countries" as of 1989.[7]

Why this hesitation to include property as a constitutional right? From an American perspective, it might seem natural to include property in the scheme of constitutionally protected interests of any nation that is committed to a private property/free market system. Private law in all market-based societies takes private property rights seriously, at least as seriously as is feasible, given the complications that rapidly increasing complexity both in the economies and societies of advanced countries create for their private law regime. But private law can only do so much by way of protecting private property. A property rights advocate might suppose that in countries that respect private property rights constitutional protection would be a logical complement to private law's protection of individual property interests. Why, then, is there any controversy about the inclusion of a clause expressly protecting private property in the constitutions of countries with free market/private property economic systems?

At least part of the answer, as I will argue in this chapter, is that both sides of the debate over property as a constitutional right are victims of what I will call "the formalist trap." In the context of the property clause issue,[8] the formalist trap is the assumption or claim that without constitutional protection, property rights are unlikely to enjoy the degree of security and stability that is necessary for a properly functioning liberal democracy as well as for an efficient free market economy. Stated differently, the claim, which frequently is left implicit in arguments about constitutionalizing property, is that the degree of legal protection that extant property holdings within a society enjoy is strongly affected by the existence or absence of a property clause in that country's constitution. Hence, in a liberal democracy whose written constitution expressly guards against uncompensated state expropriations, extant property holdings are likely, *by virtue of that formal constitutional guarantee,* to enjoy a high degree of security and stability. And, because of the materially higher degree of security of individual holdings, such democracies are likely to enjoy a comparatively greater degree of economic development and more robust citizenship. Conversely, in a democracy that has not made property a constitutional or entrenched right, property holdings are likely to be unstable or insecure. Concomitantly, such a society is less apt to be one that is characterized by a robust civic life.

To be clear about the formalist trap, no one, at least as far as I am aware, asserts that constitutional status is either a necessary or a sufficient condition for stable and secure legal property rights. The claim is weaker than that, but it is still strong. It is usually framed as a probabilistic claim, but occasionally the claim is stated in even bolder terms. Cass Sunstein, for example, in discussing inclusion of a constitutional property clause like the American takings clause in new constitutions, gives an especially clear example of a relatively strong version of the core formalist trap claim. He states, "A provision of this general sort is indispensable on both economic and democratic grounds. Without such a provision, there is not, in fact or in law, a fully functioning system of private property."[9] Elsewhere Sunstein states,

> The right to constitutional protection of private property has a strong democratic justification: If people's holdings are subject to ongoing governmental adjustment, people cannot have the security and independence that the status of citizenship requires . . . The right to private property helps to ensure deliberative democracy itself.[10]

In recent years the formalist trap has been perhaps most conspicuous in a political and legal agenda pursued by major international lending institutions.[11] Commentators have referred to this agenda using various labels, including the "new law and development movement," "globalization theory,"[12] or "rule-of-law orthodoxy." Since my focus is on the constitutional dimension of this agenda, I will primarily use Stephen Gill's term, "the new constitutionalism."[13] The new constitutionalism is, as one of its critics explains, "the political project of attempting to make transnational liberalism, and if possible liberal democratic capitalism, the sole model for future development."[14] It is the neoliberal project spearheaded by large international financial organizations like the World Bank and the International Monetary Fund. As conditions for lending money to new democracies, these institutions have imposed a set of background legal requirements, both in private law as well as on the constitutional law side, that are designed to secure investor property rights by limiting the sovereignty of local majoritarian politics.[15]

The new constitutionalism has older roots. Its direct lineage traces back to the work of political economists like James Buchanan, who argued explicitly and consistently for the necessity of constitutional protection to prevent majoritarian interventions in the market. He states, for example, "Until and unless *constitutional* constraints are placed upon the authority of legislative majorities to intervene in the workings of the economy, there will be no means of forestalling the continuing need for economic 'reform,' defined as the dismantling of prior interventions."[16] Although he does not call for constitutional property clauses by name, that is doubtless what he envisions. Property clauses are ordinarily thought to be the central constitutional device for controlling majoritarian interventions in market economies. The requirements, among the most important of which is a strongly phrased constitutional property clause, constitute a nearly uniform blueprint. The approach is one of standardization, where one size fits all.[17] Little or no account is taken of social, economic, or cultural differences among borrowing nations.

The required or recommended legal institutions and practices have several purposes. Among the most important of these purposes is providing security for the property rights of foreign investors by constitutionally immunizing their holdings from domestic redistributive policies.[18] Both international institutions like the World Bank and individual lender nations from the West consider constitutional provisions protecting property necessary to prevent democratization of property and redistribution of private assets.[19] Absent such property protection, they believe, the foreign investment that is necessary for economic development simply will not occur.[20]

Advocates of strong property rights do not hold a monopoly on the formalist trap. Ironically, the same assumption underlies both of the opposing arguments that repeatedly appear in legal and policy discussions about property's status in the constitutions of liberal democracies. Just as commentators like Professor Sunstein and participants in the neoliberal economic order lapse into the formalist trap in arguing for the need for constitutional protection of property, so also political progressives have fallen victim to the same mistaken assumption. Progressives generally provide two reasons for opposing constitutional protection of property.[21] First, they argue that making property rights a matter of constitutional protection frustrates the realization of a just society. Social justice requires a fair distribution of holdings, and constitutional property clauses make collective adjustments of property holdings much more difficult than they would be if property rights were left subject to majoritarian control. Second, by removing the question of whether the extant distribution of property holdings is fair from the agenda of ordinary democratic politics, the progressives' argument goes, constitutional property clauses create an unacceptable (and ironic) risk that many citizens will lack the material wherewithal to practice democratic citizenship.

In this chapter, I argue that, contrary to both the new constitutionalism's brief for constitutional property clauses and its progressive critics, constitutional protection of property is far from being "indispensable," as Sunstein puts it,[22] for either economic or democratic well-being. No legal text, constitutional or otherwise, has that much effect. What proponents of the new constitutionalism and its critics have both overlooked is the effect of background nonconstitutional legal and political traditions and culture on the status of property rights in new democracies. These background traditions and culture have a path-dependent effect that undermines the case for any standard approach to the questions of whether and how to constitutionalize property. In deciding whether and how to constitutionalize property, policy makers need to pay serious attention to a variety of contextual factors. These include the method of formal constitutional amendment; the relationship between the judiciary and the legislature; the nature of judicial review in the local country and local attitudes toward it; the status of property under local private law traditions and culture;[23] the legal system's jurisprudential tendencies; and, finally, how politicized the general subject of property rights is within the local society. None of these factors will be given any weight if policy makers succumb to the formalist trap.

To be clear about my thesis, I do not say that property clauses are irrelevant or otiose. Text matters, as chapter 3 and 4, discussing the German and South African property clauses, will show. The text of the property clauses of both of those countries' constitutions has made certain interpretations easier, especially with respect to issues relating to the social-obligation aspect of constitutional property. In South Africa, for example, the explicit social welfare commitments of the property clause and cognate provisions of the constitution have made a significant difference in how housing rights cases are handled in the Constitutional Court. Conversely, the absence of specific textual locutions makes particular interpretations more difficult. As I will later discuss, the absence of a textual reference to a social obligation of ownership in the American takings clause has made interpretations like those made by the constitutional courts in Germany and South Africa more difficult, although not impossible, as chapter 5 will discuss.

At the same time and just as important, text alone is not outcome determinative. The formalist thesis ignores or underestimates the importance of the other factor that figures in the interpretive process: background (nonconstitutional) legal and political traditions and culture. Tradition and culture also matter a great deal in the interpretive process. The experiences with interpretation of the constitutional property clauses of both Germany and South Africa demonstrate how traditions and culture have influenced the constitutional courts in those countries. In South Africa, for example, the private law tradition of property threatens to undermine the transformative purpose of the property clause and related provisions of the 1996 constitution.

By the same token, background tradition and culture strongly influence constitutional interpretation, but they do not dictate how a legal community of interpreters will react to a new constitutional provision. The effect of a constitutional property clause may vary over time, as traditions and cultures change. No constitutional provision, including a property clause, is a true precommitment device. Constitutions can be amended not only explicitly, but also implicitly, through the process of interpretation.[24] All that the decision to include a property clause in a constitution signals is the existence of a political consensus in favor of (relatively) strong property rights, *at this moment in time.* It is not a guarantee for the future.

My emphasis on the role of background traditions and culture raises one argument that is sometimes made for inclusion of a constitutional property clause in the new constitution of a nation. When a nation lacks a historical legal culture or tradition of secure property rights, there is special reason for a new constitution to include a constitutional property clause in order to promote the transition to a rights-respecting legal environment. Such a provision, that is, will serve as a catalyst for creating a new legal culture. For example, a constitutional property provision might be a place to start in developing a new legal culture that is committed to those liberal values that are commonly associated these days with the label "rule-of-law order," that is, the values of economic liberalism.

This argument has considerable force. Still, it is worth considering in any given case whether constitutionalizing property is an effective way to begin creating a new legal culture, one that is oriented by economic and political liberalism. Especially in a society with a history of economic injustice, a constitutional property clause may be extremely controversial. A property clause may ultimately be adopted but only at a cost of substantial political capital. In such cases a constitutional property clause can do more harm than good.

It is also possible that a constitutional property clause may serve as a catalyst for legal, political, and social transformation in a progressive direction. Perhaps the best current example is South Africa, where some of the proponents of the new constitution's property clause argued that a carefully constructed property clause, far from having the laissez-faire effects that some opponents claimed, would be a catalyst for land reform, tenure reform, and land restitution.[25] As we will see in chapter 4, the most important question in South African constitutional law today is whether the new property clause will have that effect.

Finally, constitutional provisions have symbolic and expressive value. A transforming society may wish to include a property clause in its new constitution simply for the purpose of expressing particular political or moral values, regardless of uncertainty about the instrumental effect of the clause. At the same time, however, the expressive value of a property clause may be negated or undermined by the government's use of the clause for propaganda purposes. History is filled with stories of dictators who have used formal constitutional rights provisions as propaganda to counter criticisms of their regimes.[26]

My claim does not deny either of these arguments. I argue only that the instrumental effects, both political and economic, that a property clause ultimately has turns at least as much, if not more, on the two interpretive factors I briefly stated in the introduction, namely, the country's background political-legal traditions and culture (that is, the path-dependency argument) and the legal institutional context within which constitutions and the courts interpreting them operate.

I argue that a comparative look at the experiences of other nations with and without constitutional property clauses suggests that what matters is less whether or not a constitutional property clause exists than how it is interpreted.[27] I agree with the South African legal scholar Andre van der Walt, who states, "[T]he problem is not the constitutional entrenchment of property, but the model of constitutional review in terms of which the property clause is interpreted and applied."[28] More concretely, the thesis here is that the crucial factor affecting economic growth and democratic redistribution of wealth is the relevant country's background nonconstitutional legal and political culture (including its history). In a country whose background political-legal culture respects private property rights, constitutional protection of property is not essential for economic development. Conversely, in a country whose background political-legal culture makes individual property holdings highly vulnerable to democratic adjustments, a constitutional property clause will have little effect by way of resisting legislative action.

This chapter begins with a brief description of the two main objections to constitutional property that have been made during the course of debates over constitution making around the world. In the next section I critically evaluate these objections, concluding that while they cannot be dismissed out of hand they are nevertheless overstated. I then discuss the experience of Canada, which ultimately rejected constitutionalizing property. The case of Canada illustrates not only the fears that make the issue of constitutionalizing property so politically contentious but also why, contrary to the neoliberal argument, formal constitutional protection is sometimes not necessary for stable and secure property rights. Despite the absence of a formal text entrenching the right of property, property rights in Canada enjoy a high degree of security and stability primarily because of Canada's background tradition of strong property rights.

Next I examine the case of India, a country that once had but later repudiated a regime of Super Property. India's experience with constitutional property illustrates how interpretation and the institutional setting within which the process of interpretation takes place is what is decisive in determining the effect of a constitutional property clause. In the final section I explain the path-dependent role played by background history and political-legal culture in the interpretation process.

As to both sides of the debate over constitutionalizing property, my view can be summarized by the Scottish verdict "not proven." Although I remain agnostic on the basic question, I unreservedly reject all versions of the formalist trap.

Two Objections to Constitutional Property

In the debates that have occurred around the world over including or retaining a constitutional property clause, two concerns recur. Opponents argue that constitutionalizing property is undemocratic insofar as it removes questions about property, how it is used, and how it is distributed from the realm of ordinary democratic politics. Their second objection is closely related to the first. Granting property constitutional protection, they contend, exacerbates inequality in the distribution of wealth. In this section I will summarize the basic arguments made along these two lines. Throughout the summary I will use the experiences of constitutional property clauses in the United States and India to illustrate the arguments. I choose these two countries because critics of constitutional protection[29] routinely point to them as examples of what is wrong with a regime of constitutional protection of property.[30]

Constitutionalizing Property Is Undemocratic

The first basic concern with property as a constitutional right is that such a right shrinks the scope of democratic deliberation. By that I mean that protecting property rights not just as ordinary legal rights but as an extraordinary right—a constitutional right—exactly means that the right is beyond change, modification, or ending through ordinary political processes. Constitutionalizing property removes many important political issues from public debate and control.

The concern about the relationship between property and democracy is an old one. As C. B. Macpherson observed, "[N]othing has given more trouble in liberal-democratic theory than the liberal property right."[31] The dilemma, as political theorists from Mill to Marx have conceived it, is simply this: government can have democracy, understood as a system of self-management, or it can have protection of property, but not both. Choosing property creates a monopoly of political power by the propertied, denying the very diffusion of power that democracy requires.[32] Some critics, usually those on the extreme left, flatly assert that democracy and private property are totally irreconcilable.[33] Most political progressives, however, believe that reconciliation is possible, but only if property rights are closely circumscribed.

In constitutional democracies, those on the left often believe that the problem of reconciling property rights with democracy requires denying property rights constitutional status.[34] Indeed, probably the most common objection to making the right of property a matter of constitutional protection is that such an action closes the door on the project of reconciling private property with democracy. Property wins; democracy loses.

Critics of constitutional property argue that property as a constitutional right poses core questions about democracy, about how government can and should function in a democracy. Making property a constitutionally protected right means that the core disputes about property, especially how it is distributed and how its use is regulated, are substantially removed from popular control through the normal processes of democratic politics. True, constitutional rights, including those designated as fundamental constitutional rights, are not totally immune from political control. Constitutional rights *can* be regulated, but government is not free to regulate them however it may wish. Constitutionalizing property does not mean that property rights become trumps, to use Ronald Dworkin's term,[35] but it does mean that majoritarian politics does not always get its way. Because of their antidemocratic function and effect, all constitutional rights, but especially property rights, with their direct impact on the use and distribution of wealth throughout society, trigger debates about the role of majorities, elites, interest groups, legislatures, and courts.

The argument from democracy, then, is basically that making property a constitutionally protected right removes property, or more accurately, the entire panoply of issues that are associated with property from the realm of ordinary public discourse and control. Jennifer Nedelsky expresses this concern in terms of property "implicat[ing] the very core issues of politics." Nedelsky explains that those core issues include,

> [W]hat system of property best achieves protection for "just deserts", the fruits of one's labour? What system will provide optimal and secure access to material resources? How should we conceptualize the distinction between public and private? What kinds of power should be allocated to individuals

> or groups, what kinds should be exercised through collective, democratic decision-making? How should the tensions between equality and freedom be resolved?[36]

The result of constitutionalizing property, Nedelsky objects, is that "[this] whole set of basic issues are removed from ongoing public debate and public comprehension."[37]

All of the issues that Nedelsky identifies directly affect the basic structure of society. Property structures society. Property is, quite literally, foundational. All rights confer power over others, but property rights are the ultimate basis of power. This is because, unlike other rights, the right of property is allocative and distributive in function. Its functions include determining how scarce resources are used and who is entitled to exclusive use of resources. Property rights grant to some individuals and simultaneously deny to others access to and control over scarce resources, including resources that are literally essential to human (and nonhuman) life. As Laura Underkuffler has observed, "Any scheme for the super-majoritarian [that is, constitutional] protection of the appropriations by some persons means, correspondingly, the denial of the appropriation of the same goods, resources, and essentials of life by others."[38]

Property rights pose this zero-sum problem even when they are not constitutionally protected. The problem is much more aggravated, however, when property is a constitutional right. Nonconstitutional rights may be altered through the ordinary processes of democratic politics, that is, simple majoritarian decision making. When property rights acquire constitutional status, however, they are immune from such revision. They can be changed only through extraordinary political means, with the result that the whole question of how resources are distributed and used is largely removed from the realm of public deliberation. Put simply, the ability of democratic legislatures or other politically accountable bodies to engage in social engineering for the public good is severely compromised in a legal system where property rights are a matter of constitutional protection.

The notion that constitutional property and democracy are inevitably at loggerheads draws apparent sustenance from the standard account of the American experience with constitutional protection of property interests. The conventional story of *Lochner*[39] equates constitutional property with the substantive due process jurisprudence that was antiredistributive, politically motivated, unprincipled, and undemocratic. The term "Lochner," in fact, is a trope signifying judicial activism protecting the property rights of a few at the expense of the democratic will of majorities. American courts during the *Lochner* era are seen as illegitimately using property as the means to shrink the scope of democracy.

The message that critics of constitutional property draw from the *Lochner* experience is not simply that the constitutional property provision can be deployed for some very dysfunctional politics but, more fundamentally, that any regime of constitutional protection of property inevitably inhibits democracy. The critics equate legislative power with democracy and label judicial use of the constitutional property clause to invalidate legislative actions that limit ownership interests in some more or less direct way as undemocratic. Of course, all constitutional rights enforced through the power of judicial review can be characterized this way, but critics of its constitutionalization view property as especially undemocratic because of its direct effect on the distribution of wealth throughout society. The two—constitutional protection of property, indeed, to some critics, the very existence of the private property as an institution,[40] and democracy—are seen as mutually incompatible. They stand in a zero-sum relationship with each other; the existence of one necessarily precludes the existence of the other.

Adding to these problems in reconciling constitutional property with democracy is the fact that constitutional protection of property requires judicial review.[41] The objection, of course, is familiar: judicial review involves unaccountable judges overturning majority-based decisions of legislatures or politically accountable agencies. "By what license," William Fischel asks, "are courts of law, presided over by people who are at best indirectly accountable to the electorate, to tell duly elected legislators how to conduct their business?"[42] Alexander Bickel famously termed this the "counter-majoritarian problem."[43] He articulated the problem this way:

> [N]othing can finally depreciate the central function that is assigned in democratic theory and practice to the electoral process; nor can it be denied that the policy-making power of representative institutions, born of the electoral process, is the distinguishing characteristic of the system. Judicial review works counter to this characteristic.[44]

In the context of the right to property, this objection to judicial review has been expressed in especially strong terms. Fischel captures the objection succinctly when he states, "[T]he issue is why property needs extra protection [through judicial review] in a world in which property is generally well thought of by a majority of people."[45] In the words of another commentator, "Under a constitutional property right the judiciary would be handed the power to regulate the regulators in the name of a right originally of its own creation, and central to its traditions. That is a worrisome prospect."[46] Since property is the basis of power, the argument goes, judicial review means that courts, not legislatures, ultimately determine the distribution of power in their societies.

Here again, the ghost of *Lochner* looms very large. According to the conventional wisdom,[47] *Lochner* was all about the excesses of judicial power and the undermining of democracy that comes with judicial review. The American Supreme Court was activist to the point of political illegitimacy. The Court misused its authority to frustrate the efforts of political majorities to provide just conditions in a new social order. Through its judicial review power the Court built a wall around the narrow property interests of elites in the marketplace, severely limiting the scope of democratic self-governance.

Constitutionalizing Property Entrenches Wealth Inequality

The second prominent objection to property as a constitutional right is closely related to the first: constitutional protection of property has a fundamentally antiredistributive effect. In societies in which wealth is already unequally distributed, a constitutional property clause entrenches this inequality.[48]

The argument begins with what to many critics of constitutional property is a truism: in market economies property is the primary source of inequality.[49] Like the thesis that property and democracy are mutually incompatible, this premise has a long history. Proudhon's famous answer to the question, "What is property?" namely, "Property is theft,"[50] is but one example. Recently, this argument has reemerged in some new democracies that are trying to overcome histories of gross inequality in the distribution of wealth as well as political oppression. While the argument has not led these emerging democracies to abolish the right to property, it has led in some of them to considerable opposition to constitutionalizing property rights. South Africa, whose experience I will discuss in detail in a later chapter, is the prime example. For present purposes we need only note that in South Africa's constitutional debates a concern was strongly expressed that making property rights a subject of constitutional protection would simply freeze the widely unequal pattern of wealth distribution that apartheid produced.[51] So long as property rights in the form of holdings to land were protected as a constitutional matter, the injustice of apartheid could never be finally eliminated. "The constitutional right to property," Michael Chaskalson argued, "is equated with the constitutional protection of existing distributions of ownership."[52] For Chaskalson and some other South Africans, the implication for a country where that distribution of ownership was egregiously unequal had to be the rejection of any constitutional property right.

American constitutional history seems to critics clearly to support the claim that constitutional property and inequality of the distribution of wealth go hand in hand. Nedelsky, for example, has argued that the most important consequence of property's supreme constitutional rank in the American regime has been to "place[] inequality [that is, of wealth distribution] at the center of American constitutionalism."[53] James Madison, the principal author of the American Constitution, Nedelsky argues, "opposed laws with redistributive consequences."[54] Protecting property from what he perceived to be the depredations of the democratic majorities meant that the distribution of property had to be unequal. The conception of property that Madison and other Framers of the Federal Constitution held was what Frank Michelman has called the "possessive" conception, which Michelman distinguishes from the "distributive" conception.[55] The basis of this possessive conception is, Michelman writes, that it "understand[s] property in its constitutional sense as an antiredistributive principle, opposed to governmental interventions into the extant regime of holdings for the sake of distributive ends."[56] Redistribution is considered to be a political act that requires justification, while property is a natural right that is presumptively just. While this possessive conception of property need not invariably underlie a constitutional property clause, it is highly likely to do so. Chaskalson argues, "Traditional notions of the constitutional right to property," by which he means Michelman's possessive conception, "are very deeply entrenched."[57] A main reason why they are so entrenched is the fact that the American constitution is the template for constitution making throughout the world. In constitution writing as in many other things these days, as America goes, so goes the rest of the world. Thus, many critics believe that the decision to include a property clause in a new constitution almost certainly means replicating the historical American reality of great disparities in the distribution of wealth.

Responses to the Objections

Property, Democracy, and the Madisonian Anxiety

Opposed to the argument against constitutional property because of its antidemocratic effects is a theory of the relationship between property and democracy that has gained wide acceptance among American scholars in recent years.[58] This theory is rooted in a deep skepticism about the actual workings of democracy.

The modern critique of democracy focuses on the problem of factions. The term "faction" is usually attributed to Madison, whose thought highly influenced the Federal Constitution.[59] His discussion in "Federalist No. 10" is now the standard reference for what Mark Kelman calls "democracy bashing."[60] It is not altogether clear what Madison actually *meant* by the term "faction" and what he saw as the core problem with democracy. Many commentators today read Madison as concerned with interest group politics, that is, well-defined and well-organized interest groups exerting their will on legislatures against a disorganized majority.[61] Others believe, probably more correctly, that this reading is anachronistic and that Madison thought the problem, at least at the local level, was with *majorities*, not minority special interest groups.[62] Whoever is right in this dispute, it is clear that Madison linked the problem of factions with property.[63] In "Federalist No. 10," for example, Madison stated that "the most common and durable source of factions has been the various and unequal distribution of property."[64] Political virtue could not be relied upon, Madison argued. "It is vain to say that enlightened statement will be able to adjust these clashing interests, and render them all subservient to the public good."[65] The answer, he insisted in "Federalist No. 51," was institutional: "Ambition must be made to counteract ambition. The interest of the man must be connected with the constitutional rights of the place."[66] A strong right of private property was the key "constitutional right[] of the place."[67] Making property the subject of constitutional protection was, then, Madison's response to his anxiety about factions.

Today, skepticism about democracy comes mostly through public-choice theory and its cousin, the interest group theory of legislation. Whether or not public-choice theory accurately expresses Madison's views about factions, their problem and solution,[68] it is now the leading theoretical foundation for doubts that democracy works and for concomitant calls for constitutionalizing property rights.[69] Public-choice theory, especially the Chicago School version thereof, takes a strikingly dim view of the propensity of democratically elected bodies to reflect majority will.[70] Public-choice theory's account of legislation is one of interest group politics. It holds that, in the words of the noted economist Gary Becker, "[t]he basic assumption is that taxes, subsidies, regulations, and other political instruments are used to raise the welfare of more influential pressure groups."[71] As a positive theory of democratic government, public-choice theory holds that well-organized interest groups corrode and frustrate democracy by hijacking the political process and blocking popular (that is, majoritarian) aims. It is no exaggeration to say that public-choice theory is largely based on the Madisonian anxiety that majorities have a tendency to be taken over by factions and that factions threaten private property rights by pursuing their own narrow and short-term goals at the expense of the interests of others. Scholars influenced by public-choice theory share Madison's belief that the best security measure against factional power is to strengthen property rights by constitutionalizing them.[72]

Despite ostensibly being a strictly positive theory, public-choice theory has provided commentators with clear normative implications. Devotees of public-choice theory and its concomitant, the interest group theory of legislation, have argued that the United States Supreme Court should police legislation to protect citizens against "rent-seeking" depredations, spearheaded by factions.[73] The most important tool in that effort, they have argued,[74] is the takings clause. Judicial interpretation of constitutional property rights as Super Property is, in their estimation, the most effective way to successfully prevent factions from thwarting the proper running of majoritarian democracy.

Interpreted as Super Property, the constitutional right of property is a "precommitment device," that is, a voluntarily self-imposed constraint by which one prevents oneself from engaging in activities that are harmful to oneself but that are otherwise difficult to resist. (The tale of Ulysses lashing himself to the mast of his ship in order to resist the call of the Sirens is the now commonly cited instance of such a precommitment device.[75]) Constitutional provisions like the takings clause are the constitutional precommitment device by which a democratic polity protects itself from succumbing to the temptations of interest group politics by rendering itself incapable of making decisions about how resources are distributed and used solely through normal political processes.[76] Ordinary political bargaining is not enough. Parties with competing visions of how resources should be distributed and used must bargain in the shadow of the Constitution.

It is not only academics whose opinion about the need for more robust constitutional property rights is premised on a dim view of politics. Members of the U.S. Supreme Court, Justice Antonin Scalia in particular, have unambiguously articulated the same sentiment. In the widely discussed case of *Nollan v. California Coastal Commission*,[77] for example, the Court struck down as an unconstitutional taking of private property a regulatory land-use permit requiring that private landowners who wished to build a new and larger house on the beach provide the public lateral access across their beach. Justice Scalia dubbed the exaction scheme "'an out-and-out plan of extortion.'"[78] Doubtless he and some other members of the Court share the same view about many other legislative acts.

William Fischel recently offered a variation on public-choice accounts of the need for constitutional protection of property. The declared objective of Fischel's book, *Regulatory Takings,* is "to seek a viable middle ground between judicial deference to the often unfair regulations that burden property owners and judicial imposition of compensation for every legislative infringement on private rights."[79] Fischel shares the Madisonian anxiety about majoritarian exploitation of property owners, but he seeks a more restrained role for courts than do other public-choice theorists. His basic theme is that "the comparative advantage of constitutional courts in protecting property rights is to intervene when the economic protections of 'exit' and the political protections of 'voice' are attenuated."[80] By that, he basically means that judicial intervention to protect constitutional property rights is warranted when politics does not work, that is, when political insiders exploit powerless outsiders.[81] Fischel argues that in the context of economic regulation, the political process is most likely to malfunction when the asset being regulated is immobile—usually land—and when the individuals harmed by a regulation are nonresidents or residents who are not current owners. The type of regulation where these two conditions usually exist is local land-use restrictions. It is at the level of local governments, "small republics," as Fischel calls them,[82] that constitutional protection of property rights is most needed. James Krier effectively states Fischel's thesis: "The majoritarian politics of small governments generate land use controls that benefit residents while foisting costs on housing consumers who live elsewhere and on builders and owners of undeveloped land (who, even if they are residents, are only a small minority)."[83] The upshot is that judicial activism, via constitutional protection, on behalf of property rights is warranted but only with respect to local government actions.

Although more nuanced than most public-choice analyses of how property rights fare under the workings of ordinary democratic practices, Fischel's theory remains flawed. William Treanor and Daniel Farber point out that developers and property owners, having disproportionately high stakes at risk, exert more rather than less influence in ordinary local politics.[84] Moreover, says Treanor,[85] even if these groups lose at the local level, they can carry their case up to the state level, where Fischel agrees ordinary democracy works well enough that constitutional solicitude is less necessary. James Krier makes the particularly telling point that because state and national governments are more remote from individuals than local government, one would expect that the democratic voice would be more effective at the local level, not the state or national level, as Fischel argues.[86]

None of this is to say that the democracy-based concerns that supporters of Super Property express are without any basis. Democracy obviously is not a perfect system. The challenge is to determine when, as a general matter, its ordinary processes are most apt to fail. Thus far no model of democracy's actual operation, especially in relation to property interests, has gained widespread acceptance.

A Constitutional Property Clause Is Distributively Indeterminate

The second argument against constitutional property, which is based on its supposed antiredistributive effects, is also problematic. Constitutional property clauses, taken by themselves, are distributively neutral. Constitutionalizing property has no necessary effect on a society's distribution of wealth or, more generally, on the relationship between the individual and the community. Within any society, the meaning and the effect of a constitutional property clause is determined by that society's background political traditions and culture. I am not saying that the particular language of a constitutional property clause is irrelevant to decisions about governmentally triggered wealth redistributions. My point rather is that the mere presence of a clause guarding against uncompensated "expropriations" or "takings" of "property" does not commit that country to a policy against governmental redistributions of wealth. Governmental policies of wealth redistribution can and have proceeded despite the presence of constitutional property clauses. Indeed, in some instances, constitutional property clauses have facilitated such policies. For those who favor governmental programs of social justice based on redistribution of wealth, constitutional property clauses, in and of themselves, should not be considered anathema.

This state of affairs should hardly be surprising. How *could* any property clause effectively bar all forms of wealth redistribution while allowing effective public policy? Strictly as a matter of theory, the line between such public policy and redistribution cannot be defined with any degree of clarity. As Judge Richard Posner, no defender of the activist welfare state, has pointed out, "a good deal of compelled redistribution of wealth may be the cheapest method of preserving social peace and so may be cost justified."[87] As examples, Posner cites prolabor union legislation that is designed to forestall labor violence and generous welfare benefits that reduce the risk of violence in urban slums. One could cite many other examples. The point is that any constitutional property clause that was effective in banning all redistributive activity would throw the baby out with the bathwater. It would restrain legislative activity that clearly is in the public interest along with special interest legislation. The general point, then, is that, for better or worse, it is virtually impossible for any constitutional property clause to be drafted in a way that is guaranteed to block all forms of wealth redistribution.

There have, of course, been experiences of strong judicial resistance to redistribution. The *Lochner* era is an obvious example. During that era, American judges did resist, though not uniformly and not with complete success, legislative efforts at wealth redistribution. But does the *Lochner* experience really support the view that the inclusion of property as a constitutional right foreordains the antiredistributive state? The short answer is no. First, as historians have recently shown, governmental redistributive activity did not shut down during the *Lochner* period.[88] The Supreme Court's famous decisions striking down redistributive legislation such as the eight-hour workday have obscured the fact that a great deal of public welfare legislation, legislation that was clearly redistributive, was enacted during that era.[89] Second, and more basically, during the *Lochner* era and in every other instance in which courts resisted government redistribution of wealth, it was not a constitutional property clause in and of itself that compelled the judicial reaction. Rather, it was how the courts chose to use the clause, how they interpreted the clause, that was decisive. They chose to interpret their property clause in a particular way. The clause did not compel their conclusion; the judges could have chosen differently.

Canada: An Example of "Super Property" Rejected

Canada is an example of a liberal constitutional democracy in which the objections to constitutional property have carried the day. Canada considered, but ultimately rejected, including a property clause in its Charter of Rights. Despite that fact, however, and contrary to what the neoliberal argument for constitutional property would predict, property rights enjoy a high degree of legal protection in Canada. Their nonconstitutional status has not made them insecure or unstable. The Canadian story then is an important one in analyzing the case for making property a matter of constitutional protection.

The Canadian rejection of constitutional property is, on the surface of things, surprising. In many relevant respects Canada resembles the United States (leading many Canadians to bear a deep resentment toward Americans, who tend to view Canadians as ersatz Americans). It has a highly democratic political system and a market-based economic system that is based on private property rights. Its legal property system, like ours, is based on the English common law,[90] and its modern property law fundamentally resembles its American counterpart. Finally, Canada's Charter of Rights and Freedoms (1982) sets out a liberal bill of rights that recognizes nearly all of the individual rights recognized in our Bill of Rights. The exception is property. The 1982 Charter does not include a property clause, and thus far no provision of the charter has been interpreted to provide substantive protection for property.[91] In this respect, Canada's constitution is something of an outlier among the liberal constitutions of the world. Relatively few constitutional democracies with written constitutions lack a property clause. (Singapore and, arguably, Japan[92] are examples.) Western written constitutions lacking a property clause are especially rare.

On the surface of things, then, Canada, not the United States, appears to be the exceptional case, the odd one out with respect to legal protection of property. The formalist trap assumptions tell us that we should expect property interests in Canada to be insecure and economic growth to be anemic. Neither of these expectations comes anywhere close to conforming with reality. The reality is that property rights are highly respected and protected in Canada; there is no evidence of the kind of insecurity that the formalist trap assumptions would lead us to expect. Nor would any observer of Canada's economic condition describe it as anemic. While not as wealthy as the United States, Canada is, by any reasonable accounting, a wealthy and economically well-developed nation in comparison with the rest of the world. Canada, then, is an important data point casting doubt on the neoliberal formalist reasoning that insists that formal constitutional protection of property is necessary for secure property rights, which in turn are necessary for economic well-being and, by some accounts,[93] civic well-being as well.

Canada's general experience with property has not been marked by a pervasive anxiety that ordinary politics threatens property rights or by a sharp discord between the rhetoric of property rights and the reality of legal protection. To be sure, there have been occasional expressions of concern about the vulnerability of property rights in the Canadian constitutional regime, lacking as it does a tradition of constitutional protection.[94] But those occasions have been the exception rather than the rule. Canada's political-legal culture on the whole reveals little concern with the possible threat that democratic politics poses for property rights, given the absence of constitutional protection.

Despite the absence of a federal constitutional property clause, the level of legal protection of property against government action in Canada is substantially on a par with that in the United States. Indeed, one Canadian academic goes so far as to say, "[T]here exist in Canada certain measures, constitutional and *quasi*-constitutional in nature, that equal—and in some ways may even surpass—the American regime governing 'takings.'"[95] One must certainly acknowledge that property rights are not on exactly the same footing in Canada as they are in the United States, but the differences in result are a matter of degree, not fundamental. Canadians do not routinely experience uncompensated government expropriations, nor have Canadian state regulations encroached upon private property interests to a significantly greater extent than comparable American regulatory regimes have.[96]

One obvious difference between Canadian and American constitutional law that might be used to explain why property rights are relatively secure in Canada is the absence of the power to expropriate at the federal level. Neither the federal Bill of Rights of 1960 nor the 1982 Charter contains an eminent domain clause or any equivalent. One might argue, then, that there is no need for a federal constitutional property clause because the federal government lacks the requisite power to "take," to borrow an American constitutional term, property.

This explanation, although superficially plausible, is not persuasive for several reasons. First, and most obvious, the federal government has been found to have the power to expropriate under its residual power under section 91 of the Constitution Act of 1982.[97] Second, most of the controversy over constitutional protection of property in the United States involves regulation of property rather than condemnation, and Canada's federal government certainly possesses the power to regulate the use and enjoyment of property.[98] Third, although the federal government lacks the eminent domain power, the provinces do have the power to expropriate property by virtue of their legislative power over property and civil rights,[99] and although they have sometimes exercised that power without payment of compensation to the owner,[100] compensation is usually paid when the expropriation power is exercised.[101]

Several mechanisms give property this protected status without the benefit of an entrenched constitutional property clause. Probably the most important of these are expropriation statutes. There are a number of diverse statutory schemes, most but not all of which are provincial, in Canadian law that protect against uncompensated expropriations of land.[102] All of these follow a common pattern: once the state expropriates land, the owner is granted a right of compensation. Moreover, the statutory right to compensation under these statutes is not limited to formal expropriations. The statutes also apply in cases of regulatory, or de facto, takings.[103] Just how much interference with the traditional incidents of ownership is required to trigger the compensation requirement is difficult to say, largely because there is surprisingly little case law on the question.[104] One court has stated that a de facto taking occurs only when the regulation prevents all reasonable private uses of the land.[105] In cases where the regulation destroyed most of the owner's incidents of ownership, de facto takings are always found.[106] How far short of denial of all or nearly all uses a regulation may go and still require compensation is unclear, making Canada's version of regulatory takings even more like its "muddled" American counterpart.

Another property-protective mechanism is a common law presumption applicable in all Commonwealth nations. Canadian courts,[107] like other Commonwealth courts,[108] follow the House of Lords decision in *Attorney General v. De Keyser's Royal Hotel, Ltd.*[109] that there is a common law presumption in favor of a right to compensation following legislative expropriations. This presumption can be rebutted only by an explicit statutory statement denying a right to compensation.[110] Theoretically, uncompensated expropriations are possible as a matter of both federal and provincial law, but the expropriating legislation must explicitly provide for this, an action that is unlikely to occur, at least in the ordinary case.

The protection afforded by the common law presumption is strengthened by the fact that Canadian case law recognizes the possibility that property regulations can constitute de facto expropriations for purposes of the common law as well as under expropriation statutes. The leading case on the issue is *Manitoba Fisheries Ltd. v. The Queen.*[111] There the Canadian Supreme Court treated what the legislature intended to be a regulation as a de facto deprivation, an expropriation rather than a regulation. The court reached this decision without any reference to the federal 1960 Bill of Rights, suggesting that the common law presumption requiring compensation applies to de facto takings generally. The decision effectively moved Canada toward a degree of legal protection of property that is close to that reached under American takings law.

A third source of strong protection for property is the federal Bill of Rights. Section 1(a) includes an explicit property guarantee as well as a due process clause that is similar to our Fifth Amendment due process clause. Although the Bill of Rights is a normal, unentrenched statute, one that can be amended like any other statute, and applies only to federal legislation, it does have some bite. It provides due process protection for extant property holdings.[112] Some distinguished Canadian scholars have suggested that the due process protection of Section 1(a) might not be limited to procedural guarantees, such as notice and a hearing, but may extend to substantive protection, including compensation, as well.[113] Such an interpretation would greatly extend and deepen the degree of constitutional protection of property in Canada. Currently, the point remains unsettled, largely because there is very little case law on the protection of property under the Bill of Rights.[114]

A fourth source of substantive protection comes from provincial law. While only one province (British Columbia) has a written constitution (and even that one is statutory only),[115] several provinces have bills of (unentrenched) rights that specifically include the right of property.[116] Each province has jurisdiction over "property and civil rights," and this gives each province the power to expropriate property. Although that power can be exercised without payment of compensation, in fact compensation is usually paid, as statutes seldom rebut the common law presumption in favor of compensation. As one Canadian legal scholar has observed, "[A]n exercise of the power of expropriation usually is accompanied by payment of adequate compensation for the property affected."[117] As we will see, the provinces' traditional jurisdiction over protection of property was a main factor leading to the rejection of a proposed property clause in the federal Charter of Rights.[118] These four sources, then, the common law, the due process provision of the federal Bill of Rights (1960), and some provincial bills of rights, place property owners in Canada, in fact, although not formally, in a position that approximates that of their American counterparts.

In view of the relatively high degree of security and stability of property in Canada, the interesting questions are, first, why there was any effort to introduce an entrenched constitutional property right at all and, second, why that effort failed. To answer these questions, we need to delve into some Canadian constitutional history. That history provides a basis for understanding the standard ideology regarding constitutional property, the ideology that prevails among the overwhelming majority of the world's liberal democracies, and how that ideology contrasts with our own.

During the debate leading up to the adoption of the Charter in 1982 and in subsequent years, several proposals were made to include a property clause, but these proposals thus far have been rejected.[119] The debates over a property clause are revealing because they provided an opportunity for the Canadian public openly to discuss the status of property as a constitutional right. These debates give us a glimpse of a more subdued rhetoric of property accompanying a reality of fairly robust property rights.

From the time modern Canada was first established under the Constitution Act of 1867 until 1960, no constitutional provision protected property. The 1960 Canadian Bill of Rights was the first national document of constitutional dimension to guarantee property. Section 1(a) recognizes a right to the "enjoyment of property" and a right not to be deprived of property "without due process of law." This provision resembles the American Constitution's Fifth and Fourteenth Amendments' due process clauses; the Canadian Bill of Rights contains no provision analogous to the Fifth Amendment takings clause. Indeed, Canadian federal constitutional law has never recognized a general power of eminent domain, that is, a general power to expropriate property for public use.[120] The Bill of Rights, moreover, is an unentrenched federal statute, and its property right has been characterized as "a relatively feeble and underemployed right."[121] It applies only to matters within federal jurisdiction, and as a statute, it is subject to future legislative control.

It is the Charter of Rights that creates entrenched constitutional rights. In the period leading up to the Charter's adoption in 1982, there was considerable discussion about whether to include a property clause.[122] This public debate over the role of property and the effect of constitutionalizing property was renewed several years later when, in 1991, the Canadian federal government proposed amending the Charter in several ways, including adding a property clause.[123] In both debates the federal government supported a constitutional property clause. Much of the original impetus for such a provision came from Pierre Trudeau, who, as minister of justice, first proposed a property clause in his 1968 document *A Canadian Charter of Human Rights* and again in 1969 as prime minister.[124] Trudeau renewed his efforts on behalf of a property clause several times thereafter (in 1978, 1980, and 1981), introducing proposed constitutional amendments explicitly protecting "the right of the individual to the enjoyment of property."[125] Some commentators, opposing the renewed effort for a property clause in 1991–92, predictably cited "big business" as the force behind the campaign for including property in the Charter.[126] This quasi-Marxist explanation seems overly simplistic, however (as Marxist explanations commonly are). For one thing, Pierre Trudeau, who introduced the first bill proposing a property clause[127] and who unambiguously supported all subsequent property clause initiatives, was no toady of big business. As prime minister, Trudeau supported a social program that was basically social welfarist, a program that two authors have called "big-L Liberalism."[128] He embraced, at least at times, openly statist policies designed to redistribute wealth to the weaker and poorer segments of society.[129] He basically supported Canada's political culture, which Canadian political commentators have characterized as "democratic-communitarian."[130] More to the point, Trudeau's support for a property clause stemmed from his view that the Charter was the best means of stabilizing Canadian national unity against the dynamic of provincial power that threatened to tear Canada apart.[131] The property clause initiative was essentially an effort to stitch all of Canada's provinces together in economic matters, as part of a broader effort to strengthen national unity.

Historically, the provinces have had primary jurisdiction over property matters,[132] and the growth of the welfare state was a main source of the growth of provincial power after 1945.[133] A property clause in the federal Charter threatened to undercut the provinces' prerogative. It is no coincidence that a principal source of opposition to the property clause proposals came from several key provinces.[134] Trudeau and others hoped that the Charter generally, and the property clause specifically, would provide an entrenched legal basis for staunching the separatist designs of these provinces, especially Quebec.[135] In this respect, Trudeau accorded no preferential treatment to property rights. The idea behind the property rights clause was that the right of property was but one of a number of liberal constitutional rights that, taken together, promoted national unity.[136]

Several major concerns emerged in the course of discussions over whether to create, for the first time in Canadian history, an entrenched constitutional right of property. These concerns led each property clause initiative to fail. One concern was the American *Lochner* era. As Sujit Choudry has aptly observed, "The *Lochner* era and its multilayered legacy loom large in the Canadian constitutional imagination."[137] Opponents of a constitutional property clause pointed to the *Lochner* Court's decisions striking down health and safety legislation like maximum work hours laws as examples of the potential for a constitutional property clause to undermine Canada's status as a social welfare state.[138] Canadian social legislation that opponents cited as being at risk under an entrenched constitutional property right included rent-control legislation, occupational safety and health regulation, marital property distribution statutes, and environmental regulation.[139] Of course, none of these forms of regulation have been successfully attacked under the American takings clause, even during the recent takings renaissance, but that fact was never acknowledged by Canadian critics of a constitutional property right.

A related argument was that the clause would constitutionalize a laissez-faire economy, contrary to the widely shared conviction that the Charter should not entrench any particular economic system or ideology. A lower federal court in *Archibald v. The Queen*,[140] for example, stated, "The *Charter* has never before and still does not protect economic liberty or property rights. A deliberate choice was made to exclude them from the document. No form of economics, laissez-faire or otherwise, is part of the Constitution."[141] Here again, *Lochner* was always cited as historical precedent for the likelihood that a property clause will constitutionally embed some economic theory, specifically, laissez-faire economics.[142] Canadian critics were fond of drawing on Holmes's famous dissent in *Lochner* as establishing a seemingly unanswerable argument against constitutionalizing property (although none of them bothered to point out the irony that it was Holmes who later, in *Pennsylvania Coal v. Mahon,* sharpened the teeth of the takings clause by announcing the regulatory takings doctrine).

No single factor explains why Canada rejected a constitutional property clause. Certainly one factor is what Canadians call "the democratic principle."[143] That principle embodies the idea that the fundamental concern of governmental decision making is realization of the democratic will and community values.[144] The democratic principle resists what one Canadian commentator calls the "proprietarian"[145] idea that "the basic role of government is restricted to the preservation and protection of property."[146] The provinces argued that the democratic principle requires strong restrictions on the use of judicial review to frustrate or overturn legislative action that expresses the democratic will. An entrenched constitutional property clause, in their view, was fundamentally incompatible with this conception of the democratic principle. As Alexander Alvaro has noted, the provinces' strong stand against a property clause "indicates the strength of the fear that, once placed in the hands of a non-elected judiciary, such a clause had the potential to subvert the seeming victory of democracy by proprietarian interests, interests which desired to diminish the scope of the economic power of governments."[147] Conceding that a constitutional property clause would not necessarily have had that effect, the opposing provinces believed that such was the intention of the federal government.[148] Moreover, they pointed to the American experience with *Lochner*-era judicial activism as evidence that the clause's antidemocratic potential might be realized.[149] Taking the democratic principle seriously, they argued, requires a modest role for courts and that, in turn, requires rejection of any regime of Super Property.

At the end of the day, the factor that ultimately explains why Canada rejected an entrenched constitutional property right is Canada's federalism. Most of the provinces opposed a property clause.[150] They did so because they wished to continue their traditional prerogative with regard to regulation of property relations. Different provinces had different reasons for jealously protecting their control of economic regulation. Quebec, for example, was concerned about protecting its own income-security program, while the interest of provinces like Saskatchewan was its power, which it frequently exercised, to institute province-owned crown corporations.[151] A constitutional property clause was thought to threaten all of these diverse province powers.

Buttressing this argument was the fact that several provinces already protected property rights through their own provincial constitutions. Alberta and Saskatchewan, for example, had recently enacted bills of rights that expressly included property clauses. They argued that local constitutions were more effective than a federal constitution in responding to local property concerns. One Alberta government minister, for example, asserted, "It is the responsibility of the Government of Alberta on behalf of the people of Alberta, to ensure that property laws for Albertans are made according to the wishes of Albertans."[152]

What the Canadian example illustrates, and what the neoliberal formalist argument misses then, is the importance of background political and legal culture.[153] Canada's heritage of secure property rights made constitutional protection seem unnecessary, and its version of federalism made it politically unacceptable. From the Canadian perspective, constitutional protection of property was not about economic efficiency or fairness, as neoliberal theory suggests; it was about localism and the important role that localism plays in Canada's background political culture.

How far can one generalize from the Canadian example? Does the fact that property rights in Canada are strong and secure despite their nonentrenched status have any lessons for countries emerging from a political and legal regime in which property rights were not respected or perhaps not even recognized? Or is there some peculiarity to the British Commonwealth legal tradition that makes the Canadian experience not germane to such countries? While it certainly is the case that the Commonwealth countries share with the United Kingdom a strong tradition of property rights that are secure despite the lack of constitutional or entrenched status, they are not unique in this respect. At least some of the new democracies that have emerged from political regimes in which private property rights were either not recognized or drastically reduced have legal and political traditions of strong property rights that existed prior to the imposition of repressive regimes. Several of the countries in formerly communist Eastern Europe are examples. Poland is the clearest case. Unlike other Soviet bloc countries, Poland continued a regime of private ownership of land following the onset of communist rule. Over ninety percent of land in communist Poland was privately owned, although owners did not feel that their rights were secure under communist rule.[154] The strong culture of private property rights in land in Poland is attributable to several factors, some of which, particularly the influence of the Catholic Church, make the Polish experience somewhat special but not unique. In Hungary, for example, the 1959 Civil Code recognized certain limited private property rights in a variety of assets, including land (although the communist government continued to use various tactics to induce farmers to accept collectivization).[155] This formal recognition of property rights was a response to the strong popular cultural support of private property rights in land, or the informal norm of property rights, that existed prior to communist rule and persisted despite attempts to end the regime of property rights. Private ownership of land had been a symbol of rank as well as insurance against economic calamity for many years.[156] The same experience of property rights whose path dependency was based on strong cultural norms was repeated in other Soviet bloc countries as well.[157] The general point, then, is that while the experience of property rights in Commonwealth countries like Canada may be unusual in some respects, it is not unique. The same general phenomenon of the persistence of property rights based on background culture, tradition, and informal norms rather than on constitutional recognition or other methods of formal legal entrenchment can be found in a number of countries outside the British Commonwealth. This finding further supports the general claim here: tradition and culture matter. The new constitutionalism overlooks this fundamental fact in its zeal to standardize American-style constitutional recognition of property rights.

Legislative Supremacy, Wealth Redistribution, and Constitutional Property: The Case of India

The standard rendering of the story of constitutional property in India seemingly supports the argument frequently repeated by opponents of constitutional property that constitutionalizing property has both strongly antidemocratic and antiredistributive effects. With respect to the effect on democracy, the tension between constitutional property and democracy played out in India as a protracted institutional battle between the courts and parliament. As one commentator notes, "It is a well-known story how the legislature carried on the battle against the abusive potentiality of [the] power aspect of property through enacting constitutional amendments and legislations providing for abolition of . . . agrarian intermediaries, wiping out of monopolies, equitable distribution of material resources of production and protection of these economic reforms from constitutional challenges."[158]

The "well-known" story is in fact a highly complex story to which I cannot possibly do justice here.[159] For my limited purposes, it is enough to note that parliament and the courts were engaged in a pitched battle for nearly thirty years (1950–78) over the now defunct property clauses (Articles 19(1) and 31) of the original (1950) Indian Constitution.[160] To simplify the story greatly, the Indian prime minister, Nehru, pushed the two property clauses through the constitutional assembly in the belief that they would apply only to limited government expropriations and not to large-scale social engineering programs. His calculus proved false. The Indian courts persistently held that the property clauses applied to land reform and other economic reform legislation, despite the obvious fact that such reforms were badly needed. As opponents of the constitutional property clause tell the story, the Indian judges baldly wrested power away from a legislature that voiced widely shared democratic preferences for social reforms following decades of colonial rule. Much as English colonial rulers denied an opportunity for the Indian masses to participate in democratic self-governance, the Indian judges arrogated to themselves the authority to deprive the duly elected representatives of India's citizenry the final say over how society would be structured in what was supposed to be a new and democratic polity. Many commentators believe that it was precisely the undemocratic consequences of judicial review that led to the eventual demise of constitutional property in India. So long as India had a system of constitutional protection of property, administered by unaccountable judges, it would never realize its democratic potential. Critics of constitutional property widely regard India's experience as nearly conclusive evidence of the inherently undemocratic character of the constitutional right to property enforced through judicial review.

As the courts struck down one land-reform act after another, the legislature overturned their decisions through constitutional amendments. The courts fired back, deciding variously that any future constitutional amendment restricting fundamental rights, including property, would be held invalid,[161] that the court had the power to determine the adequacy of compensation despite a constitutional amendment declaring adequacy of compensation to be nonjusticiable,[162] and that legislation nationalizing the fourteen largest commercial banks in India was unconstitutional.[163] The entire interaction between the courts and parliament was a battle, not a conversation. "The politicians started reviling the judges for their status-quoist [sic] and over-protective approach toward property rights—a view which was not only shared but openly expressed even by some progressive judges in and out of court."[164]

The denouement of this battle was the Forty-Fourth Amendment (1978).

This amendment deleted Articles 19(1)(f) and 31, the property provisions, from the fundamental rights in part 2 of the constitution.[165] In their place, parliament inserted Article 300A in part 12 of the constitution. Article 300A simply provides that "no person shall be deprived of his property save by authority of law."[166] Included in part 12 rather than part 2 of the constitution, Article 300A made property a constitutional but not a fundamental right. It guarantees only that any deprivation of property will be made by a valid law that is within the legislature's power and that does not violate any fundamental rights or other constitutional restrictions.[167] The upshot, according to the general account of the story, was that democracy, widely seen as the victim of constitutional protection of property, prevailed through the exercise of public will.

For critics of constitutional property, the Indian experience provides even greater support for the view that constitutional protection of property and wealth redistribution, in this instance land reform, are mutually incompatible. Through the thirty-year period during which India's constitution protected property, no meaningful progress was made in redistributing land.[168] Literally every major government action aimed at redistribution was blocked in the name of constitutional protection of property. It was only after the entrenched property right was removed from the constitution that India succeeded in instituting significant redistributive programs.[169]

The stock version of the Indian story is overstated in several respects. One problem with the conventional version is that it overlooks the significant fact that the supreme court's early cases dealing with land-reform legislation were all decided on the basis of the constitutional guarantees of equality and reasonableness rather than on the basis of the right of property. Although the decisions did invalidate aspects of the land-reform legislation before it, the supreme court did not invoke the right of property in order to justify its actions. It was only later, when the constitutional assembly enacted the First Amendment (1951), which ousted judicial review of certain land-reform measures, that the court shifted the basis of its decisions from the right of equality to the right of property.[170]

More important for our purposes is the fact that the Indian Supreme Court did not strike down all of the legislative land-reform measures that came before it. Despite its reputation as reactionary during this period, the Indian Supreme Court upheld several land-reform statutes that were challenged under the constitutional property clause. In fact, the court's activist posture developed only by 1960, ten years after the constitution's adoption.[171] During the first ten years, the court's record demonstrates a fairly sympathetic attitude toward the need for land reform. It struck down only two agrarian reform measures on constitutional grounds.[172] Of the two, the more important was the *Kameshwar* decision, a case that is worth extended discussion because it involved perhaps the single most important land-redistribution reforms in India's postcolonial history.

The *Kameshwar* case involved a challenge to the Bihar Land Reform Act of 1950. That act was an attack on the *zamindari* system. The *zamindars* were Indian "tax farmers," that is, intermediaries who collected revenue on land from cultivators for the crown (and before that, Moghuls).[173] Though strictly speaking the *zamindaris* were not owners, over time they became more and more entrenched and increasingly took on attributes of ownership. By the end of the British rule, these intermediaries represented a powerful vested interest, controlling about forty-three percent of all of India's land.[174] They were the most distinctive aspect of India's land tenure system, a quasifeudal arrangement in which the actual farmers received minimal security as tenants or sharecroppers.[175]

The Bihar Land Reform Act's clear objective was abolition of the *zamindari* system. The Act represented an attempt to fulfill the Congress Party's longstanding promise of justice for the small farmer.[176] Under the Act, the state expropriated virtually all interests and rights of the *zamindars*, with payment of compensation. The problem was with the Act's treatment of the compensation issue, which was the main point of controversy throughout the twenty-year battle between the supreme court and parliament.[177]

Rather than providing for full compensation at market value, the Act stipulated a sliding-scale form of compensation in which the amount paid per acre was in inverse relation to the total extent of the land holding.[178] The reasons for this approach are clear. As one commentator states, "Not only would full and immediate compensation have put an impossible burden on Central and State finances, but also many in India saw the *zamindars* as usurpers of the land, minions of past rulers, and hence entitled to little or no payment."[179]

Whether this method of compensation was constitutionally permissible was hardly clear. During the drafting of Article 31 the decision was made to use the word "compensation" without any modifier like "just" or "equitable,"[180] leaving it unclear whether the intention was to follow the American and Australian practice of requiring full market value compensation. Not only was there uncertainty over the level of compensation that was due, but there was also controversy over whether courts should have the power to review the adequacy of compensation that the legislature set. Especially with respect to abolition of the *zamindaris*, there was a strong sentiment to make the question of adequacy of compensation nonjusticiable.[181] At

Prime Minister Nehru's urging, the legislature added to Article 31, the main property clause, provisions that exempted major land-reform measures like the Bihar Land Reform Act from judicial review under Article 31. The clear purpose of these provisions was to vest ultimate authority regarding social engineering reforms in the legislature rather than the courts.[182] The legislature's plan was frustrated, however, when a court held that the Bihar Act violated the equality clause of Article 19 by discriminating between expropriatory laws passed before and after the constitution's adoption.[183] The legislature responded by enacting the First Amendment to the constitution. This provision freed the legislature from any compensation requirement for certain expressly identified expropriation measures, including the Bihar Act, and explicitly excluded the state acquisition of agricultural "estates" from the protection of Articles 14, 19, and 31 of the constitution.[184]

On appeal, the Indian Supreme Court held that while in general the Bihar Act was saved from judicial review with respect to the compensation requirement, the scope of nonjusticiability was limited to the amount of compensation. The court did go on to strike down some provisions of the Act as a "colorable exercise" of legislative power.[185] That aspect of the court's decision prompted the legislature to enact the Seventh Amendment to the constitution (1956), repudiating the colorable legislation doctrine.[186]

Commentators have tended to be harsh in their judgments about the *Kameshwar* case. Professor van der Walt, for example, has characterized the decision as "reactionary" and states that the decision signaled the court's defiance of the legislature's attempt to exercise authority with respect to land-reform legislation.[187] While there is considerable truth in that assessment, it is important not to exaggerate the reactionary character of the court's decision. As one commentator has noted, the decision "secured the constitutional future of agrarian reform by upholding the validity of art 31B [which ousted judicial review of existing land-reform legislation]."[188] The decision gave the legislature a green light on its existing land-reform projects. Within ten years after Indian independence, the *zamindari* system, probably the most egregiously inequitable aspect of India's colonial land regime,[189] had been completely dismantled.

The second aspect of the *Kameshwar* case that is important for my purposes is that the basis for the court's resistance to the legislature had as much to do with institutional competency and the nature of constitutional amendment in India as it did with land redistribution. The legislature was attempting to establish plenary authority on two matters: first, to effect sweeping social-economic changes and, second, to amend the constitution, including fundamental rights provisions, as it saw fit.[190] The courts, particularly the supreme court, in turn, were concerned with defining the constitutional limits of the legislature's amendment power generally.[191]

Compensation continued to be the focal point over which this struggle for institutional power continued to be fought. The legislature enacted the Constitution (Fourth Amendment) Act (1955), which inserted into the constitution's compensation provision (Article 31(2)) a provision ousting the court of the power to strike down legislation on the basis of inadequate compensation. The court responded to this amendment with a series of decisions aimed at reestablishing its jurisdiction over the compensation question.[192]

The ongoing struggle between the supreme court and the legislature was brought to a head by two decisions from the court, *Golak Nath v. State of Punjab*[193] and *RC Cooper v. Union of India* (the "*Bank Nationalization*" *Case*).[194] In *Golak Nath,* the immediate issue in the case did not involve compensation as such. At issue was the validity of the Seventeenth Amendment with respect to the constitution (1964). This provision extended the operation of the First Amendment by expanding the definition of "estates" to include tenures that the court had previously held to be not within the purview of the First Amendment. The court held that the amendment was invalid. The court declared that the legislature's amending power could not be used to deny or abridge any rights, including but not limited to property, that the constitution guarantees as fundamental. The court recognized that existing amendments could not be undone but declared that any future amendment that purported to repeal or even restrict a fundamental right was invalid. At the same time, the court made it clear that while parliament lacked the constitutional authority to amend the constitution to remove a right from the list of enumerated fundamental rights, if the constitutional assembly wished to do so, the constitution could be so amended by it.

In the *Bank Nationalization Case,* which did involve compensation, the court struck down an act of parliament nationalizing the fourteen largest commercial banks in India. It reasserted its jurisdiction to decide whether compensation practices were "reasonable" by invalidating the act on the ground that the act's principles for determining the amount of compensation related to the value of certain assets only and that the acquisition affected the firms in their entirety. In the court's view, then, those principles were irrelevant and, hence, unreasonable.

The legislature responded to these decisions by enacting the Twenty-Fourth and Twenty-Fifth Amendments. The Twenty-Fourth Amendment was intended to overturn the *Golak Nath* decision, and the Twenty-Fifth

Amendment, aimed at the *Bank Nationalization Case,* effectively tried to remove the compensation issue from judicial review by removing the duty to pay "compensation" from Article 31(2) and replacing it with a duty to pay an "amount." Amazingly, however, when it was given a clear opportunity once again to assert its primacy over legislative power with respect to the power to amend fundamental rights provisions, the court backed down. In the important case of *Kesavananda v. State of Kerala,*[195] the court upheld both amendments. Withdrawing from the position it had taken in *Golak Nath,* it stated that the legislature *did* have the power to amend the fundamental rights provisions of the constitution so long as in doing so it did not abrogate the basic structure of the constitution. The major concession was its acknowledgment that the right of property was not such a basic feature of the constitution. This was a crucial compromise because it effectively permitted the government's program of land redistribution to be fully implemented.[196]

The court's ongoing struggle with the legislature during the period between 1950 and 1973 is as much about the institutional limits of the legislature's competency to amend or abolish fundamental constitutional rights, *whatever they happen to be,* as it was about the redistribution of land. As one commentator has observed, "In the ultimate analysis, the successes and failures of the process of land socialisation in India were not greatly influenced by the constitutional contests between courts and parliament."[197] The fact is that much, if not most of the government's land-redistribution program was implemented, and the failure of the other aspects of the program were due largely to chronic problems of corruption and patronage.[198] The key issue affecting property rights was compensation, and by 1978, the court had conceded that issue to parliament.[199]

In view of that fact, why did parliament in 1978 enact the Forty-Fourth and Forty-Fifth Amendments, deleting Articles 19(1)(f) and 31, the core of the property-rights provisions, from the constitution? What does this action tell us about the role of text, the constitutional property clause itself, in judicial responses to redistributive programs? The short answer, I believe, is not a great deal. Those amendments were largely about politics and political symbolism. The amendment was enacted immediately in the wake of the 1977 elections in which Prime Minister Indira Gandhi's Congress Party was soundly defeated by the Janata Party, which had campaigned on a platform of citizens' rights and abolition of the constitutional property clause.

Some background is necessary to understand the role of politics and political symbolism in the passage of the Forty-Fourth and Forty-Fifth Amendments. Shortly after the *Kesavananda* decision, Gandhi's party fell into strong disfavor with the public, and Gandhi personally encountered serious problems, including a conviction by a court of corrupt electoral practices.[200] Her response to these problems was to announce, on June 26, 1975, a state of emergency. During the emergency, parliament (or what remained of it after she detained many members of her own party) retroactively repealed the legislation on which her conviction was based and also enacted a constitutional amendment (Amendment Thirty-Nine) that removed from the supreme court the jurisdiction over alleged electoral offenses committed by the prime minister. The supreme court, although upholding the legislation on the basis of which Gandhi was convicted, held that the Thirty-Ninth Amendment violated the basic structure of the constitution by impairing free elections.[201] Gandhi's government reacted to this decision by circulating proposals to introduce a new constitution, one that abrogated the power of judicial review.[202] These proposals were not pursued, however.

Finally, in 1977, some nineteen months after it was first announced, the emergency was lifted. Shortly thereafter, elections were held, and Gandhi was defeated by a populist coalition that thereafter made good on its campaign promise by passing the Forty-Fourth and Forty-Fifth Amendments. The winning Janata Party had used the property clauses, especially Article 31, as one the main symbols of its campaign. Capitalizing on Prime Minister Gandhi's precipitous decline in popularity, especially in the wake of the emergency, the Janata Party campaigned on a platform of returning power to the people, and the demotion of the constitutional right of property was one of the main planks in that platform.

The decision to use the constitutional right of property as a campaign mainstay was by no means arbitrary. Land reform and redistribution was a crucial, perhaps *the* crucial political issue since India first gained independence, and the constitutional property clauses *were* relevant throughout the struggle between the supreme court and the legislature. Article 31, the compensation provision, in particular was, as one scholar has put it, "an important arena of constitutional politics."[203] It was, therefore, an obvious political symbol around which to organize a populist campaign and thereafter through which to gain political legitimacy by successfully pursuing its demise.

Property, then, or more specifically, the text of property clauses, certainly is relevant to understanding the Indian experience with constitutional property. But the controversy over text is best understood within a deeper context, the context of a fundamental institutional struggle between two branches of government. Constitutional property was "the focal point of the struggle for hegemony between the [Supreme] Court and Parliament."[204] The property clause, as an Indian legal scholar has observed, "merely served as a peg on which have hung the vital questions of limits of State power and the role of the Court."[205] The intersection of institutional conflict and land redistribution created the "perfect storm" in Indian constitutional law and politics from 1950 until 1978.

Was the constitutional property clause (especially Article 31) essential to judicial efforts to attack redistributive legislation in India? Of course, one cannot answer such a counterfactual question with any certainty, but it is at least plausible to speculate that the supreme court might have reached the same result, at least in some of its cases, on the basis of other provisions of the constitution. Its early decisions in land-reform cases were decided on the basis of the right of equality, and in the absence of a property clause the court might have used the equality provision as a tool to resist what it considered to be ultra vires actions by the legislature in the realm of property redistribution. Moreover, it is possible that some of the tenure reforms might have been judicially frustrated on the basis of the private law tradition that India inherited from Britain, including that tradition's understanding of property rights. As chapter 4 will discuss, this is precisely what has happened in a number of lower court cases in postapartheid South Africa.

All of this is possible, but speculative. The important point, however, is that while text matters, so too do tradition and background political culture. The core weakness of the formalist thesis is its failure to acknowledge the role of tradition and culture. In this respect, the Indian experience does indeed provide a valuable lesson for questioning the formalist thesis.

The Key Is Interpretation

Is it possible to keep property constantly open to continual redetermination through the processes of normal democratic politics despite the existence of a constitutional clause protecting property? I think it is. The decision to have a constitutional property clause is one step; interpreting that clause is a different step. Whether questions about property, especially how it is used and how it is distributed, remain open to democratic determination depends less on the decision whether to have a constitutional property clause and more on the separate step of its interpretation. Constitutionalizing property can lead to insulation of private property holdings from the public realm of politics, but that is not an inevitable consequence. It all depends on how courts interpret the clause.

"Guarantee-Oriented" Interpretation vs. "Limitation-Oriented" Interpretation

In explaining why interpretation is the key to the effect that a constitutional property clause has, Andre van der Walt draws a useful distinction between what he calls a "*guarantee*-oriented" view of a property clause and a "*limitation*-oriented" view. The distinction is this: a guarantee-oriented interpretation is based on the assumption that the role of any constitutional property clause is to create a minimalist role for government by maintaining a radical divide between the public and private spheres, while a limitation-oriented interpretation, as van der Walt defines it, "emphasizes the fact that property is intrinsically created by and therefore open to further democratic redefinition and regulation . . ."[206] Under this conception of a limitation-oriented interpretation, a property clause protects private holdings against arbitrary or discriminatory deprivations by the state, but it leaves holdings open to periodic readjustments made by the state through normal democratic processes so long as those adjustments are nonarbitrary and nondiscriminatory. A guarantee-oriented approach to interpretation is what critics of constitutional property clauses have in mind when they assert that the necessary effect of making property a matter of constitutional protection is instantiation of laissez-faire or the minimalist night watchman state. "Lochnerism," as that term is usually understood, is the result of a guarantee-oriented approach. A limitation-oriented approach avoids Lochnerism because it does not presuppose that a categorical separation of the private and public realms is a necessary presupposition of any constitutional property clause. Rather, such an approach presupposes that the private and public realms are inextricably intertwined in the context of property insofar as the public realm creates the very realm of private property. No categorical separation between public and private being possible (or desirable), the limitation-minded interpreter says, constitutional protection of property is a matter of constant adjustments between individual and social interests.

It is important to clarify what the limitation approach, at least the version that I propose, is *not*. It is not such a loose standard of judicial review that it renders all property holdings open to de facto evisceration through the exercise of a virtually unlimited power of the state to "regulate" as it sees fit. Stated in terms of American doctrine, it is not a matter of reading the doctrine of regulatory takings out of existence. The limitation approach proposed here does not naively assume that all government regulation of property is the product of fair-minded and well-functioning democratic politics. Nor does it assume, with equal naiveté, that constitutional property law is an effective tool for realizing a vision of distributive justice.[207] The point instead is to avoid an approach that is based on the Madisonian anxiety, that is, one that interprets the property clause in a way that assumes at the outset that the government measure in question is the product of some pathology in the democratic process. A balanced approach is one that steers between the two extremes of the Madisonian anxiety and the progressive call for eviscerating the property clause in the interest of distributive justice. Thus, it rejects both a progressive no-compensation approach, which risks harming the poor and other underrepresented classes as much as it harms the wealthy,[208] and a conservative approach, which insists on monetary compensation for all government regulations of property unless the burdens of the regulations are completely and immediately offset by the same regulation's benefits.[209] As I will discuss in chapter 3, such a middle-course limitation approach is well illustrated by the German Constitutional Court in interpreting the German Basic Law's property clause.

Limitation-Oriented Interpretation Is Purposive

Perhaps the most important aspect of a limitation-oriented interpretation of a property clause is the fact that it is purposive in character. By the term "purposive," I mean that the court openly and systemically inquires what substantive value underlies the decision to make property a constitutionally protected right. An interpretation is purposive when the interpreter openly and systemically asks what is the core purpose (or core purposes) that can most plausibly be attributed to a constitutional property clause. Within liberal theory, there are, of course, competing views about the core goal of making property a constitutional right. Securing individual autonomy is obviously one candidate, but others exist as well. Indeed, one might plausibly conclude that a purposive theory of constitutional property that is most compatible with liberalism is one that is pluralist, recognizing multiple purposes inhering in the constitutional protection of property.[210] The important feature for a limitation-oriented approach to interpreting constitutional property clauses is that the interpreter openly and systemically analyzes the core social objectives that underlie the decision to protect property constitutionally. As I discuss more fully in subsequent chapters, the constitutional courts of Germany and South Africa have engaged in exactly this sort of purposive reasoning.

The Role of Background Legal and Political Traditions

The factor that most strongly bears on how a constitutional property clause affects both political readjustments through democratic processes and wealth redistribution is the clause's nonconstitutional context, particularly its background political and legal traditions and culture. In particular, three aspects of the nonconstitutional political-legal background are important: the society's private law system, its historical political ideologies, and its dominant social beliefs about the operation of ordinary democratic politics.

The first factor in the political-legal background is the country's private law system, especially its rules and concepts relating to property. A crucial question for the meaning of any constitutional property clause is whether the constitutional concept of property is intended to follow the traditional private law meaning of property or to have a separate constitutional meaning of property?[211] Even if the constitutional concept of property is formally uncoupled from the traditional private law concept, the latter will continue to influence to former. The constitution's concept may have its own life, but that life begins in the private law concept. The private law meaning of property invariably anchors the constitutional meaning. Regardless of how much weight judges say they have placed on property's private law meaning, private law influences how they understand the constitution's reference to "property." Anyone who ignores the private law of property in the process of interpreting judicial interpretations of constitutional property clauses will have an incomplete picture. More than one "view of the cathedral"[212] is required in painting property's constitutional portrait.

The second aspect of a society's background political traditions and culture are the political ideologies that have shaped the societies' political debates, particularly as those debates pertain to property. In Germany and South Africa, for example, those ideologies include political ideas that have now been officially repudiated. Despite such repudiation, ideologies that once formed the core of a society's political system can never be entirely erased. National socialism and the racist ideology that supported the apartheid regime continue to exert their influence on legal thought in Germany and South Africa, respectively, through a negative valence. They represent what Andre van der Walt calls "historical hangover[s]."[213] The constitutions of both countries are explicit negations of those ideologies, but precisely because of their negations every term in those constitutions has to be interpreted in light of the negations.

The third relevant factor is the dominant social understanding of and attitude about how ordinary democratic politics work. Discussions about the effect of constitutionalizing property on democratic practices often overlook or underestimate the importance of background political traditions and culture in liberal democracies. Democracies come in many different stripes. Some have written constitutions; others do not. Courts in some democratic regimes exercise a strong power of judicial review, while in others they are much weaker. These differences result from the distinct political history and political traditions of each democracy. So there is no a priori reason to believe that democracies all share the same basic view about how well their ordinary democratic politics works. For instance, one country's political tradition may be based on what I have been calling the Madisonian anxiety, that is, a concern with factions, while another democracy lacks any tradition of such a concern.

The differences among countries' traditions regarding the operation of ordinary democratic politics compel neither the structure and content of a constitution nor the presence or absence of any particular constitutional provision. That being said, it is also the case that countries with different understandings of democracy may and frequently do contain the same or similar constitutional terms. Moreover, the background traditions and beliefs about democracy affect not only the existence of certain provisions, but also how those terms are characteristically interpreted. The best way to understand a democratic country's interpretation of its constitutional property clause is as an expression of its dominant outlook on the functioning of ordinary political processes.

As we will see in later chapters, Germany and South Africa are examples of nations whose background political traditions vest considerable trust in their legislative and regulatory systems and, therefore, whose property clauses operate with a substantial degree of deference toward ordinary political processes.[214] Their experiences contrast with that in the United States, which has a political tradition of suspicion toward ordinary democratic politics, exhibited by a strongly active judiciary whose longstanding practice has been to police legislative and regulatory acts for an undemocratic taint. The judicial activism of the *Lochner* era reflected a skeptical attitude toward the legislative process. As I indicated earlier, the Supreme Court of that era regarded the processes of ordinary legislative politics as being highly vulnerable to undemocratic, nonmajoritarian manipulation by well-organized interest groups. During a later period of judicial activism, the Warren Court had a different concern with democracy. Its concern was that majoritarian excesses might undermine the proper functioning of democratic politics.[215] These two eras represent an ongoing American preoccupation with the fact that ordinary political processes are constantly prone to abuses and that strong constitutional rights, vigorously enforced by courts, are the necessary cure for democracy's diseases.

Constitution makers need to understand that property clauses do not all have the same valence. Any analysis of the effects of such clauses must pay close attention to exogenous local factors, what I have called background traditions and cultures. Any analysis that neglects these factors is the sheerest form of empty formalism. The ultimate lesson of this chapter is to abandon formalism once and for all.

CHAPTER TWO

The Aborted Revolution in American Takings Law

American constitutional property law is all too commonly misunderstood, especially by non-Americans. Many commentators, even some Americans, have characterized the U.S. Constitution, as deployed by the Supreme Court, as idolatrously committed to the protection of private property rights against all but the most necessary governmental restrictions. The less well-informed of these commentators point to the aggressive use of the substantive due process and contract clause doctrines during the infamous *Lochner* era. They seem to suppose that the doctrinal practices of the *Lochner* era continue to this day. The more informed commentators recognize that *Lochner* and its progeny are a thing of the past and that even during the heyday of "laissez-faire jurisprudence," the Supreme Court's decisions fell far short of instantiating Richard Epstein's night watchman state. Nevertheless, they point to what they consider a revolution in American takings law, transforming the Fifth Amendment's just-compensation clause into a tool for aggressively policing the actions of the regulatory state that violate the sanctity of private property rights.

The primary purpose of this chapter is to demonstrate why this understanding of current American takings law is wrong. While the Supreme Court has somewhat strengthened the just compensation clause as a device for protecting property rights,[1] its recent takings cases fall far short of reviving the *Lochner* era's politically reactionary jurisprudence. The revolution in takings law that many commentators had pronounced has not occurred. Or if it began in the Supreme Court's 1987 term, it has since been aborted. It is time to pronounce the takings clause dead as a tool for conservative judges to end the expansion of the regulatory state.

Another purpose of this chapter is to make the point that American takings law recognizes a norm of social obligation as inherent in ownership.

Anticipating a lengthier discussion in chapter 5, I indicate where extant takings doctrine is implicitly based on such a notion. Chapter 5 argues that the social-obligation norm should be made explicit in takings jurisprudence. Once it is recognized that American takings law does implicitly recognize a social-obligation norm, then it becomes clear that U.S. case law is not as far out of alignment with its counterparts in other liberal democracies, including Germany and South Africa, as is commonly assumed.

This chapter will first briefly sketch the basic structure of analysis under the takings clause. It will then describe the Supreme Court's modern takings jurisprudence prior to 1987. That year was thought by many observers to be a watershed in the effort of conservative proponents of property rights to transform the takings clause into the central constitutional device for instantiating Richard Epstein's vision of the minimalist state. I will review the 1987 decisions that inaugurated the takings revolution and then describe and analyze the Court's succeeding takings decisions that aborted the revolution.

For American readers, much of this material will be familiar territory. Even American readers, however, may find that some of the discussion, especially that concerning more recent Supreme Court cases, provides fresh perspectives, either in an interpretive or a normative sense. For non-American readers the discussion will make no attempt to provide anything like a comprehensive study of American takings law. That would require far more space than is available here and is not necessary for the limited purposes of this chapter.[2] Still, readers who know a little but not a great deal about American takings law will hopefully find this chapter useful. It provides a perspective that likely differs from that which they have had of American takings law. For both sets of readers, my aim is primarily interpretive, not normative, although normative judgments will occasionally enter the discussion.

The Basic Structure of the Takings Clause

The takings clause of the Fifth Amendment of the U.S. Constitution is terse. It simply provides, "nor shall private property be taken for public use, without just compensation." The implication is that the state, by virtue of its power of eminent domain,[3] may expropriate private property. It may do so, however, only under two conditions: first, the expropriation must be for "public use"; second, the expropriation must be done only under payment of "just compensation." These requirements will be examined before turning to the questions that have occupied most of the Supreme Court's attention, namely, whether the affected interest is "private property" and, second, whether there has been a "taking."

The Public-Use Requirement

Until recently, relatively little attention was paid to the restriction that the state expropriate ("condemn" is the preferred American term) private property only for "public use." The lack of sustained attention to the question of which uses are *public* uses is a bit surprising, for the limits of the public-use requirement have not been clear, either historically or even today. Historically, the conventional wisdom states that there have been two opposing views about the meaning of "public use": (1) the so-called broad view, according to which a use is public if it provides any benefit or advantage to the public; and (2) the so-called narrow view, which holds that a use is public only if it is the public that is given the right actually to use the condemned property.[4] The two views competed for attention, with each holding sway during different periods. Even today, at the state level, jurisdictions disagree over the meaning and effect of the public-use requirement.

In the Supreme Court's modern takings jurisprudence, the meaning of public use was relatively clear, at least until quite recently. Describing the scene as of just a few years ago, Professor Thomas Merrill accurately stated, "[M]ost observers today think the public use limitation is a dead letter."[5] The Court's approach has been highly deferential to legislative judgments about what uses satisfy the public-use requirement.[6] This deferential approach dates to the seminal case of *Berman v. Parker*,[7] where the Court upheld a redevelopment plan that was designed to eliminate slum housing from a section of the District of Columbia. The Court summarized its attitude this way: "[T]he legislature, not the judiciary, is the main guardian of the public needs to be served by social legislation."[8]

The Supreme Court's decision in *Hawaii Housing Authority v. Midkiff*[9] illustrates the approach it consistently took after *Berman v. Parker*. In *Midkiff*, the Court unanimously upheld a Hawaii statute authorizing tenants in developments of five acres or more to condemn their landlord's interest and acquire a fee simple estate.[10] It specifically concluded that the statute satisfied the public-use requirement, reasoning that the statute was aimed at "[r]egulating oligopoly and the evils associated with it."[11] The test that the Court used provides little, if any, basis for invalidating condemnations on public-use grounds. "[W]here the exercise of the eminent domain power is rationally related to a conceivable public purpose," Justice O'Connor stated, "the Court has never held a compensated taking to be proscribed by the

Public Use Clause."[12] This rational-relationship test makes the public-use inquiry a matter of ends, not means. That is, the test focuses on the intended end use of the condemned property. It does not focus on the question of legitimate means, that is, whether it is appropriate for the state to condemn the property rather than acquire it through a market transaction. Moreover, the Court's formulation of the ends-focused test in *Midkiff* is so broad that the limit on the state's eminent domain power is really the same as that used for the (theoretically) far weaker police power, a power whose exercise triggers no compensation requirement. As Merrill states, "[I]f public use is truly coterminous with the police power, a state could freely choose between compensation and noncompensation any time its actions served a 'public use.'"[13] At a minimum, the upshot of the deferential ends-focused approach is that nearly all compensated expropriations of private property will be permitted because there will almost always be some public purpose that can be found as the justification for the exercise of eminent domain.

The United States Supreme Court recently reaffirmed this deferential approach, albeit by a closely divided vote. In *Kelo v. City of New London,*[14] the question was whether condemnation of privately owned land for purposes of urban economic development satisfies the public-use requirement. The city of New London, Connecticut, like many northeastern cities, has experienced serious economic decline in recent years. In an effort to reverse this trend, the city condemned several parcels of land incident to a comprehensive redevelopment plan. The redevelopment plan included new upscale housing, shops, and recreational facilities. The condemned land was a residential area that was economically depressed but not blighted. The area was adjacent to land recently purchased by a large pharmaceutical company, Pfizer, for the purpose of building a new major research facility. While the plan did not involve transferring any of the condemned land to Pfizer, it plainly contemplated that the company would benefit from it. Pfizer's decision to relocate was contingent on the city redeveloping the targeted area; indeed, Pfizer participated in some aspects of the redevelopment plan.

The question in the case was whether the condemnation with the intention of turning ownership of the land over to private parties for the purpose of urban development that would create new jobs and increase tax revenues violated the public-use provision of the federal takings clause. The Court held that it did not. In reaching that decision, the Court reiterated the deferential approach it had taken in *Midkiff* and refused to adopt a bright-line rule that would totally preclude exercise of eminent domain for economic development purposes. Justice Stevens, in his majority opinion, stated that the city's "determination that the [condemned] area was sufficiently distressed to justify a program of economic rejuvenation is entitled to our deference."[15] Moreover, he stated, "Just as we decline to second-guess the City's considered judgments about the efficacy of its development plan, we also decline to second-guess the City's determinations as to what lands it needs to acquire in order to effectuate the project."[16] Responding to Justice O'Connor's argument in her dissenting opinion that "nearly all real property is susceptible to condemnation on the Court's theory,"[17] Justice Stevens stated that "an unusual exercise of government power would certainly raise a suspicion that a private purpose was afoot . . ."[18]

The strong reaction against the use of eminent domain for the purpose of economic development is understandable. The individual right of property is not simply an economic right. Maximizing aggregate wealth is one, but only one, purpose served by property rights. Individual property rights are also about self-expression, self-governance, belonging, and civic participation. A proper theory of constitutional protection of property should therefore be concerned about possible abuse of government power when cities condemn land, especially residential land, to enable projects whose benefits redound substantially to private entities. Monetary compensation, even when it satisfies the constitutional requirement of being "just," is not always enough to make the dispossessed landowner whole.

One interesting and sensitive approach that has been suggested would have the Supreme Court inquire into a number of factors that carry little, if any weight, under its current approach of broad deference. In a widely cited article,[19] Professor Thomas Merrill argues that even if the legislature's objective in exercising its eminent domain power is legitimate, the means it has selected may not be. If the government wants land so that a business and technology park can be developed, fine and good, but is condemnation rather than a consensual sale a legitimate means of acquiring the land? Looking at the public-use requirement from this choice-of-means perspective, Merrill identifies several factors to which courts should look in assessing whether the proposed act of condemnation is legitimate. Is a consensual purchase of the targeted parcel feasible? Is an alternative site whose acquisition can be made consensually available? Or, if no such site exists, is there an alternative site that will less severely impact individual landowners? Will acquisition of the land in question involve unusually high subjective losses to the landowners? This factor will be especially important in cases like *Kelo,* where the condemned land is a residential neighborhood. Will the owner's subjective losses, losses that are not compensated under the standard compensation rule discussed below, be unusually high? Would the surplus generated by the forced sale go to only one or a few identified individuals or firms, creating a high potential for "secondary rent seeking"? Where the exercise of eminent domain involves a retransfer to another private party, done for the putative purpose of community economic development, there is a high risk that the government action involves rent-seeking behavior by the benefited transferee-owner. Under these circumstances judicial deference is not warranted because the government action is not a genuine expression of the vox populi but rather the product of an abuse of democratic government by a powerful individual or small number of individuals.[20] As I discuss in chapter 5, these factors could be incorporated within a proportionality analysis of the exercise of eminent domain. Such an approach would steer a middle course between a highly deferential approach that is premised on a naively benign view of government and a strict scrutiny approach, which is animated by the Madisonian anxiety about the abuses of property rights in majoritarian politics.

"Just Compensation"

The meaning of "just compensation" is seemingly well settled in the Supreme Court's case law.[21] The Court has consistently held that "just" compensation does not necessarily mean full compensation. Judge Richard Posner explains what was, at least until recently,[22] the settled meaning of "just compensation," stating,

> [J]ust compensation has been held to be satisfied by payment of market value . . . Compensation in the constitutional sense is therefore not full compensation, for market value is not the value that every owner of property attaches to his property but merely the value that the marginal owner attaches to *his* property.[23]

The reason usually given for not measuring compensation by the owner's personal value is that there are insuperable "practical difficulties" in doing so.[24] Commentators have proposed alternative methods of dealing with these problems,[25] but the Court has consistently adhered to the fair market value standard.

The Constitution does not define the meaning of "just compensation." In theory, then, courts could develop compensation practices that depart from the conventional practice. They could conceivably award less than full fair market value in certain circumstances. They might use compensation as a means of dealing with problematic exercises of eminent domain, as commentators have recently suggested.[26] It is even possible that they could award some measure of compensation in cases where they have not found a taking, as commentators have also suggested.[27] Such compensation practices would move American constitutional property law further in line with its counterparts in Germany and South Africa. I discuss these possible borrowings in chapter 5.

Has "Property" Been "Taken"?

We come then to the fundamental questions: has the state "taken" some "property" of the complaining owner? In the modern regulatory state, the questions of what counts as "property" and especially what government actions count as "takings" become most embarrassingly difficult and most politically charged in the context of government actions that nominally are mere regulations, that is, exercises of the police power, for which there is no compensation requirement. So, the American law of takings today has become virtually synonymous with what are called "regulatory takings."

WHAT COUNTS AS "PROPERTY"? Not all economic interests are protected under the takings clause. The Supreme Court has expressly held that no compensation is due for governmental actions that affect interests that are not "private property."[28] The requirement that an interest be property, however, is seldom a problem. The overwhelming majority of governmental actions that are likely to implicate the takings clause, including both overt exercises of the eminent domain power and regulatory measures, involve interests that clearly satisfy the "property" requirement, usually standard estates or lesser interests in land. Certainly all interests that are classified as property under the private law rules of property, real and personal, satisfy the constitutional requirement. Thus, easements, leases, mineral rights, and security interests have been considered to be property under the takings clause.[29] On the other hand, the Court has held that such economic interests as future Social Security benefits and heads of water are not property for takings purposes.[30]

On what basis has the Court determined whether an interest counts as property for takings purposes? Unfortunately, the Court has been less than clear about this. A few important points, however, are clear. The Court has unambiguously stated that the Constitution does not itself create property interests. "Rather," the Court has said, "[property interests] are created and their dimensions are defined by existing rules or understandings that stem from an independent source such as state law—rules or understandings that secure certain benefits and that support claims of entitlement to those benefits."[31] This passage tells us that for takings purposes property is identified and its dimension determined by looking to positive law, especially state law.

As Professors David Dana and Thomas Merrill have pointed out,[32] an important ambiguity lurks in the above statement. It might mean, they point out, that state law both supplies the definition of property and determines whether, in a given case, property has been created. Alternatively, the Court might have meant that federal constitutional law defines property and that state law is the source to which courts should look to determine whether property has been created, applying the constitutional definition.[33] The Court has never clarified which meaning it intended, although the decisions in several of its cases are inconsistent with the first meaning.[34]

Assuming that federal constitutional law, not state law, defines property, the problem is that the Court has never attempted to provide such a definition. Still, some aspects of such a definition are clear from the Court's decisions. Property certainly includes all discrete assets, that is, "things."[35] This is the ordinary person's conception of property, or what Bruce Ackerman called "Layman's Things,"[36] and it would be passing strange if the Court did not mean to include in the federal constitutional definition what most people understand the term "property" to include. Implicitly if not explicitly, American courts, like the German Constitutional Court, have rejected the definition of property as wealth. This is implicit, for example, in the conventional assumption that general tax laws are not challengeable as takings.[37]

Beyond discrete assets,[38] other features of the constitutional definition of property are less clear. The Court has approvingly referred to the "bundles of rights" conception of ownership on more than one occasion.[39] Among the twigs in that bundle, the Court has repeatedly stressed the importance of the right to exclude[40] and has described the rights of inheritance and devising property as "part of the Anglo-American legal system since feudal times."[41] On the other hand, it has held that a statute that in effect abrogated the right to commercially exploit a particular set of assets (eagle parts and artifacts made from eagle parts) did not constitute a taking of property.[42] The Court's endorsement of the bundles of rights conception might appear to open the door to an approach that defines constitutional property as every single incident of property, an approach now commonly called "conceptual severance."[43] I take up the question of conceptual severance later in this chapter.

WHAT IS A "TAKING"?: THE PROBLEM OF REGULATORY TAKINGS We come now to the last, and most difficult, question—what governmental actions affecting property constitute a "taking" of property? What has made this question so difficult for the Court is the fact that it has not confined the meaning of "takings" to formal expropriations, although such actions certainly do constitute takings. The Court has recognized that some government actions, although formally only regulations of property, nevertheless are substantively tantamount to expropriations. This is known as a "regulatory taking," and it is the type of government action that has most occupied the Court's attention for several decades.

Pennsylvania Coal Co. v. Mahon[44] was, by most accounts,[45] the case that first created the regulatory taking doctrine. In that case, Justice Holmes stated that a purported exercise of the police power, which normally triggers no compensation requirement, becomes a taking, requiring compensation, when it "goes too far."[46] As of 1986, the Court had not made much progress in specifying the parameters of regulatory takings since the *Mahon* case, but it had made *some* headway.

In determining whether a regulation has "gone too far," the Court has regularly focused on three factors, which it summarized in the seminal 1978 case of *Penn Central Transportation Co. v. City of New York.*[47] These factors are (1) the character of the governmental action; (2) the extent to which the action interferes with what the Court calls "distinct investment-backed expectations"; and (3) the degree of diminution in value.[48] Joseph Singer has succinctly summarized the gist of the first factor. "The 'character of the government action,'" Singer writes, "concerns the issue of whether the regulation is more closely analogous to a physical invasion or seizure of a core property right or to a general regulatory program affecting numerous parcels and designed to protect the public from harm by adjusting the benefits and burdens of economic life to promote the common good."[49] There was some indication in the Court's *Penn Central* opinion that the harmful character of the conduct that the regulation proscribes was no longer important, or at least less important.[50] As we will see, however, that turned out to be a false signal.

The "distinct investment-backed expectations" factor derives from Frank Michelman's justly famous article, "Property, Utility, and Fairness."[51] The idea is essentially one of protecting the owner's reliance interest. A taking is more likely to be found where the regulation interferes with an investment that the owner has already made, relying on some preexisting regulatory arrangement rather than some future investment opportunity. This factor did not appear in the Supreme Court's analysis prior to *Penn Central,* but since then it has played a prominent role.[52]

The third factor is the degree to which the regulation causes a diminution in the value of the owner's relevant property interest. Two problems have plagued this test from the time when the Court first introduced it in *Pennsylvania Coal Co. v. Mahon.* First, what is the relevant interest, the denominator of the fraction? Second, how much diminution is too much?[53] Until recently, however, neither of these problems has had much practical significance. Between 1922 and 1991, the Supreme Court had never found a taking on the basis of diminution in value.[54] As we see shortly, however, these questions have bedeviled the Supreme Court in its recent takings cases.

Fortunately, one apparent complication in the Supreme Court's definition of a regulatory taking has now been clarified. In 1980, the Court seemed to have added another test for determining when a regulation constitutes a taking. In *Agins v. City of Tiburon,*[55] the Court announced that a regulatory taking occurs when either the challenged land-use regulation "denies an owner economically viable use of his land" or it fails to "substantially advance legitimate state interests."[56] While the first factor, as we have seen, had played a major role in current takings analysis, the second factor had not.[57] The appearance of that language, couched in the disjunctive along with the reference to economically viable use, seemed to suggest that a regulation could be struck down under the takings clause of the Fifth Amendment of the U.S. Constitution on the sole ground that it failed to "substantially advance" a legitimate government objective, that is, solely because of a nonexistent or inadequate means-end fit. Perhaps because the test seemed unprecedented in the Court's previous takings jurisprudence, few takings claims were based on the "substantially advance[s]" factor alone until recent years, when such claims began to be made in litigation brought or supported by property-rights advocacy organizations. However, in 2005, the Supreme Court summarily and unambiguously ended any possibility that it might strike down a regulation as a taking on the basis of the *Agins* "substantially advance[s]"language.

In *Lingle v. Chevron U.S.A. Inc.,*[58] the Court clarified the law of regulatory takings by stating that the substantially advances test applied to challenges brought under the due process clause but not under the takings clause. The case involved a challenge to a Hawaii statute capping the maximum rent that oil companies could collect from dealers who leased company-owned service stations. The reason for the statutory cap was high retail gasoline prices that resulted from a highly concentrated market for oil products in Hawaii. Chevron argued that the cap constituted a regulatory taking because the regulation did not substantially advance the state's asserted interest in controlling consumer gasoline prices. The district court agreed, striking down the statute on this basis alone,[59] and the Ninth Circuit affirmed.[60] The Supreme Court unanimously reversed, holding that the substantially advances formula is not a "stand-alone regulatory takings test that is wholly independent of *Penn Central* or any other test."[61] Rather, the Court said, the *Agins* substantially advances formula "prescribes an inquiry in the nature of a due process, not a takings, test, and [therefore] it has no proper place in our takings jurisprudence."[62] The basic reason is that the due process clause focuses simply on the existence of a means-end fit, for which the substantially advances test is appropriate, while the takings clause is concerned with the magnitude and character of the burden and the manner in which that burden is distributed among property owners. Those concerns are addressed by the multiple regulatory takings factors identified in *Penn Central* and other cases, not by the substantially advances test.[63]

Two points need to be made about the implications of *Lingle*. The first is that it may lead to fewer challenges to government regulations being made under the takings clause of the Federal Constitution. Some commentators have suggested that property-rights claimants will now begin to turn to the due process and equal protection clauses and pay less attention to the takings clause, at least in federal court.[64] The second important aspect of *Lingle* is the fact that the Court unanimously reaffirmed its previous takings decisions and did so in a way that clarified the typology of regulatory takings and the tests that apply to the various types of regulatory takings. The next section summarizes that classificatory scheme.

Methodology: Balancing and Two Categorical Rules

As of 1986, the Supreme Court's method of analyzing takings cases was fairly well settled, if not coherent. A brief overview of the scene will set the stage for later developments that many thought ushered in a new age of property-rights activism.

The dominant methodology was balancing. While the Court did develop two bright-line categorical rules that it applied in unusual circumstances, it nearly always analyzed takings claims by engaging what Justice Brennan candidly acknowledged to be "essentially ad hoc, factual inquiries."[65] The conventional wisdom among commentators is that the Court's balancing method has produced a body of takings case law that is a "crazy-quilt pattern,"[66] "a welter of confusing and apparently incompatible results,"[67] and, more simply, "chaos."[68]

While more than a few commentators attacked the Court's pre-1987 takings analysis for its excessive informality,[69] the Court's balancing method did not entirely lack formality. The Court has generally structured its analysis on the basis of several factors, most of which derived from Justice Holmes's opinion in *Pennsylvania Coal Co. v. Mahon*. The case is worth a closer look.

At issue was a state statute, the Kohler Act, which prohibited the mining of coal in such a way as to cause subsidence of houses located on the surface of the land under which the coal was located. The Pennsylvania Coal Company had deeded the land but expressly reserved the right to mine the coal, a right that under state law constituted a separate estate. The company challenged the Kohler Act as an uncompensated taking of the pillars of coal that the company had to leave intact in order to avoid subsidence of the surface. The Court agreed that the statute did effect a taking. Writing for the majority, Justice Holmes said that in determining whether a regulation, otherwise permissible under the police power, has gone "too far" for takings clause purposes depends on the particular facts of the case. He identified several relevant factors: (1) the diminution in value caused by the regulation; (2) whether the regulation served to avoid a harm to the general public; (3) whether the regulation provided an "average reciprocity of advantage" among all affected property owners; and (4) whether the regulation effectively destroyed discrete property and/or contract rights. Assessing those factors under the instant facts, Justice Holmes said that the degree of diminution in value was "great" because the regulation effectively destroyed the commercial value of the coal needed to remain in place to prevent subsidence.[70] Second, Holmes said, the regulation sought to avoid damage to a single private home rather than abating a harm to the general public.[71] Third, the statute failed to secure an "average reciprocity of advantage," according to Holmes, because it gave a benefit to the surface owners while placing a burden on the owners of the subsurface coal. Finally, the Kohler Act, in Holmes's view, effectively destroyed the company's contract and property rights. Specifically, it destroyed "what is recognized in Pennsylvania as an estate in land—a very valuable estate—and what is declared by the Court below to be a contract."[72] There was general consensus on the Court about the relevance of all of these factors. When the Court later reaffirmed its commitment to a multifactor balancing approach in the *Penn Central* case, it revised the factors somewhat. It retained the diminution-in-value factor, but added others. The other three factors mentioned in *Pennsylvania Coal Co. v. Mahon* were either ignored or assigned a lesser role. In their place, *Penn Central* added two new factors, the character of the governmental action and "distinct investment-backed expectations."

The Court applied those three factors to a challenge to the New York City

Landmark Commission's refusal to permit development of the air space above the famous Penn Central Terminal. The Commission had previously designated the terminal as a historical landmark because of the building's remarkable Beaux Arts design. The owner wished to erect a multistory commercial building atop the existing terminal, and the Commission disapproved two submitted plans. The owner challenged these decisions as unconstitutional takings of its private property.

The Court upheld the Commission's actions. It first concluded that there was no substantial diminution in value because the owner was still able to earn a reasonable return on its investment. Moreover, said the Court, the development denial did not eliminate all of the owner's possible uses of its preexisting rights in the airspace above the terminal. The owner has been granted transferable development rights (TDRs) in the airspace, and it could uses those rights to develop the airspace above other buildings that it owned in the vicinity. The Court said, "While these rights may well not have constituted 'just compensation' if a 'taking' had occurred, the rights nevertheless undoubtedly mitigate whatever financial burdens the law has imposed on [the owner] and, for that reason, are to be taken into account in considering the impact of the regulation."[73] The Court concluded next that the Commission's action did not interfere with any investment-backed expectation of the owner because the company had not yet actually invested any money in the development project. Turning to the third factor, the Court said that the denial of the development permit did not involve any physical invasion by the government of the owner's airspace. Rather, the Court said, the effect of the action was similar to that of a routine zoning decision.

Putting *Pennsylvania Coal Co. v. Mahon* and *Penn Central* together, at least six factors are involved in the Court's balancing analysis. To summarize them, they are, briefly, (1) diminution in value; (2) reciprocity of advantage; (3) prevention of a public harm; (4) destruction of an existing and discrete property interest; (5) character of the government action (that is, physically invasive or not); and (6) interference with investment-backed expectations. While all of these six factors are potentially relevant, it is impossible to predict how much weight any one of them will carry in a given case. The Court has made it clear that it will weigh each factor on the basis of the specific facts of each case.

Prior to 1987, the Court departed from its usual balancing approach in just two situations. The two categories of regulations that triggered per se rules were regulations that involved *permanent physical occupations* and those that were *nuisance-abatement measures*. According to the first rule, a per se taking occurs when the regulation authorizes the state or someone acting with its authority physically and permanently to occupy the owner's property (regardless of how slight the occupation, how trivial the effect, or how compelling the need for the state's action). In *Loretto v. Teleprompter Manhattan CATV Corp.*,[74] the Court held that such actions are always takings. The Court, speaking through Justice Marshall, stated that its rule was quite narrow, and, until recently, it has been. The occupation must be direct, and it must be permanent. This is why in *PruneYard Shopping Center v. Robins*,[75] the Court had earlier (and unanimously) held that there was no taking when a state law required shopping center owners to permit members of the public to enter shopping centers for the purpose of distributing leaflets. The state-authorized occupation, although direct and physical, was only temporary. The upshot was that the category of per se physical takings was quite narrow, occupying a very small corner of regulatory takings law.

The other per se category concerns regulations designed to abate public harms, or "noxious uses." Government actions of this sort are never takings, the theory being that the range of legally protectable behavior that ownership confers on individuals does not include the power to harm the public.[76] When the state acts to prevent such unauthorized property uses, therefore, it does not take any property right because the owner's bundle of rights did not include the proscribed use in the first place.

The noxious-use doctrine has attracted its share of critics. Several commentators have pointed out that many regulations characterized as harm abating can just as easily be viewed as public benefit conferring, in which case the per se rule does not apply.[77] Professor Michelman illustrates the problem with an example of a regulation forbidding erection of billboards along highways. Michelman asks,

> Shall we construe this regulation as one which prevents the "harms" of roadside blight and distraction, or as one securing the "benefits" of safety and amenity? Shall we say that it prevents the highway abutter from inflicting injury on passing motorists, or that it enhances the value of the public's highway facility?[78]

Michelman points out that the nub of the problem is that to distinguish between harm-preventing regulations and those that confer benefits on the public, we need "a benchmark of 'neutral' conduct which enables us to say where refusal to confer benefits (not reversible without compensation) slips over into readiness to inflict harms (reversible without compensation)."[79]

The Supreme Court, as we will see, has been equivocal about the noxious-use doctrine in recent years. In *Keystone Bituminous Coal Association v. DeBen-*

edictis,[80] the Court appeared to approve the doctrine, but in *Lucas v. South Carolina Coastal Council*,[81] Justice Scalia, writing for the Court, expressly pointed out the dilemma and reduced the doctrine to being "simply the progenitor of our more contemporary statements that 'land-use regulation does not effect a taking if it "substantially advance[s] legitimate state interests.'"[82] The doctrine's status is now unclear.

Apart from this critique, the harm-abatement doctrine is important for a quite different reason. As I will elaborate in chapter 5, the doctrine is an indication that American takings law implicitly includes a social-obligation norm. In effect, it defines the parameters of the public dimension of private ownership. Disagreement about the breadth of that dimension inevitably occurs, but the important point is that the doctrine implicitly acknowledges that there is a public dimension of private ownership. Stated differently, the doctrine's core premise is that private owners owe responsibilities to society to protect and promote its well-being. It is an implicit acknowledgment of the fact that, as Laura Underkuffler puts it, "[p]roperty rights are, *by nature*, social rights."[83] This fact is made explicit in a number of other national constitutions, notably those of Germany and South Africa, but it is not in the American Constitution. There is no social-obligation clause as such. Yet, even without doctrinal glosses such as the noxious-use doctrine, the takings clause indirectly acknowledges the existence of a social dimension of private ownership. The power of the state to expropriate property for public uses is premised on the necessity of subordinating private will to public well-being. The police power, the basis of regulation of how property is used, possessed, and transferred, is premised on the same assumption. Likewise, the state's power to restrict private owners from using their property entirely as they wish, without paying compensation, is best explained by the notion that owners inherently owe society certain obligations. Certain takings doctrines and decisions that otherwise appear inscrutable become intelligible when viewed through the lens of an implicit social-obligation norm. We will return to this topic in chapter 5, where I will argue that considerable clarity would be added to the American takings doctrine if courts explicitly recognized and systemically developed the social-obligation norm.

1987—The Beginning of a Takings Revolution?

Beginning with the Supreme Court's 1987 term, it appeared to many commentators that the picture was beginning to change. Three major doctrinal developments in the Supreme Court's post-1987 takings jurisprudence warrant special attention. These are (1) the rise of what is now known in the takings literature as "conceptual severance"; (2) the broadening of the physical-occupation factor; and (3) the emergence of a new per se rule in *Lucas v. South Carolina Coastal Council.*

The Rise of "Conceptual Severance"

American lawyers conceive of property as a bundle of rights. Although several scholars have provided powerful critiques of that metaphor,[84] the Supreme Court has frequently invoked it in determining whether a regulation has "taken" "property."[85] The bundle-of-rights metaphor is intended to express the idea that property is "a malleable, divisible, disaggregable, functional set of rights among people."[86] The rights usually associated with ownership are the rights to exclude, use, possess, and transfer property, but there is no consensus on exactly what rights comprise the bundle, whether any or all of them are essential to ownership, or even whether some hierarchy of importance exists among them.

The insight that originally animated the bundle-of-rights metaphor is the view of ownership as a complex set of legal relationships among individuals. The scholars who popularized the metaphor, the legal realists, intended to replace the simple physicalist image of ownership as a relationship between an individual and an object, the picture that they associated with Blackstone's discussion of property,[87] with a relational and nonphysicalist way of understanding property.[88]

The bundle-of-rights conception of ownership supplies the foundation for a technique that has become the primary theoretical device for an aggressive, indeed activist, interpretation of the takings clause. The technique is now commonly referred to, both in academic discussions and in Supreme Court opinions,[89] as conceptual severance. "Conceptual severance," a term first coined by Margaret Jane Radin,[90] refers to the idea that each incident or set of incidents of ownership in the bundle of rights itself constitutes a fully protectable property interest. If accepted, this idea obviously would enormously broaden the reach of the takings clause. Conceivably, *every* regulation that does not fit into a properly defined nuisance exception could be viewed as a taking under this theory.[91]

Earlier decisions of the Supreme Court had pretty clearly rejected the technique of conceptual severance.[92] The 1987 term cases sent some very mixed, if not contradictory, signals about the Court's attitude toward conceptual severance. On the one hand, *Keystone Bituminous Coal Association v. DeBenedictis*[93] pretty clearly rejected conceptual severance. Quoting from its earlier decision in *Andrus v. Allard,* the Court stated, "[W]here an owner possesses a full bundle of property rights, the destruction of one strand of the bundle is not a taking because the aggregate must be viewed in its entirety."[94] On the other hand, two other decisions from the same term indicated that the Court was indeed prepared to apply the conceptual severance technique. In *Hodel v. Irving,*[95] the Court struck down a federal statute that provided that upon the death of the owner of an excessively fractionated undivided ownership share in tribal Indian lands allotted to individuals, the interest shall not pass either to the deceased owner's devisees or heirs but instead shall escheat to the tribe whose land it originally was.[96] Characterizing the statute as a total restriction on the power to control the disposition of property at death, the Court ruled that it constituted an uncompensated, and therefore unconstitutional, taking of property. The right to pass on property at death, the Court said, is among "the most essential sticks in the bundle of rights that are commonly characterized as property."[97]

The other case in which the Court employed the conceptual severance technique is *First English Evangelical Lutheran Church v. County of Los Angeles.*[98] There the Court held that a landowner was entitled to damages in an inverse condemnation action when an ordinance temporarily deprived the owner of all economically viable use. The ordinance, while not stating any durational limit, was rescinded after it was judicially declared to constitute an unconstitutional taking. The rescission, the Court held, did not deprive the owner of its right to recover damages for the period of time when the ordinance was in effect. Temporary takings, Justice Rehnquist reasoned, have the same status as permanent ones because for the period in question it *is* permanent.[99] This is *temporal,* or durational, as distinguished from *functional* conceptual severance. The bundle of rights is sliced into temporal shares, each of which is a whole "thing." As Frank Michelman has pointed out, this "establishe[s] a major new beachhead in takings jurisprudence for conceptual severance."[100] It does not take a great deal of effort to imagine the same technique—dividing each interest into discrete segmented ownership interests that are formally undivided—being used to extend the functional version of conceptual severance much more broadly than the Court did in *Hodel v. Irving,* in effect repudiating its disavowal of conceptual severance in both *Penn Central* and in a case decided in the same term as *First English,* that is, *Keystone Bituminous Coal Association v. DeBenedictis.*[101] The Court has not yet taken that step, and perhaps it will not do so. It could fairly easily distinguish *First English* from the more typical situation by relying on an interpretation that Michelman has offered. According to Michelman,[102] what was crucial to the decision in *First English* was the fact that the ordinance, as enacted, had an indefinite duration and, therefore, *would* have effected a total taking without any offer of compensation. "Such behavior on the part of government," Michelman states, "is (by hypothesis) unconstitutional and lawless."[103]

So what can we conclude about the status of conceptual severance as of the end of the 1987 term? As Michelman emphasized, the majority in *First English* included Justice Brennan, the author of three opinions explicitly rejecting conceptual severance—the majority opinions in *Penn Central* and *Andrus v. Allard* and a concurring opinion in *Hodel v. Irving* affirming the continued vitality of *Andrus*. The majority also included Justices White, Blackmun, and Marshall, all of whom had joined Brennan in *Penn Central* and *Andrus*. None of those four justices is on the present Court, and at least some of their replacements—Justice Thomas leaps most quickly to mind, but perhaps Chief Justice Roberts as well—may well be more favorably disposed to extending the reach of conceptual severance. At least two members of the Court now can probably be counted as firm conceptual severance supporters: Justices Scalia and Thomas. Chief Justice Roberts may well also adopt the Scalia-Thomas view, and perhaps Justice O'Connor's replacement will as well. That leaves us just one short of a conceptual severance majority. Still, even if a majority of the Court were to accept conceptual severance in some contexts, it seems unlikely that it would be willing to do so across the board. Only Justices Scalia and Thomas have shown any signs of willingness to apply conceptual severance across the board. An across-the-board use of conceptual severance would constitute a dramatic change in takings law, both methodologically and substantively, and a majority of even a newly constituted Court seems unlikely to make a change of that magnitude.

The Broadened Physical-Occupation Factor: The Nollan-Dolan *Doctrine*

The second major post-1987 development concerns the physical-occupation factor. Since 1987, the Supreme Court has sent several signals indicating that it may be prepared to expand somewhat the physical-occupation category of regulatory takings. The most important of these signals is the development of the *Nollan-Dolan* doctrine.

The doctrine concerns a practice that has been quite common in cities throughout the country in recent years—exactions. Exactions are concessions that cities extract from landowners who wish to change the use of their land in some way and are required to obtain the city's permission to do so. The typical scenario involves an application for a development permit that the city conditions on the landowner agreeing to dedicate a portion of her land to some public use. The ostensible purpose of the exaction is to minimize the negative externalities of the proposed development.[104] Clearly, however, their increased popularity reflects the fact that few cities today can afford to pay for public dedications of private land.

In *Nollan v. California Coastal Commission*,[105] the Court for the first time imposed a requirement that there be an "essential nexus" between the purpose of an exaction and the purpose that would be served by denying the requested development permit. Then, just a few years later, the Court in *Dolan v. City of Tigard*[106] added to this doctrine the further requirement that a "rough proportionality" exist between the exaction and the expected impact of the proposed development. The city has the burden of proving that this proportionality exists.

The two requirements have cast doubt on the viability of exactions generally. Commentators have suggested that the doctrine will be means for constitutionalizing a wide variety of disputes between local governments and landowners concerning land development[107] and severely limiting the flexibility of local governments to regulate land use in the public interest.

All of this may yet come to pass, but there are reasons to think that the reach of the new doctrine is more limited. Both cases involved exactions that authorized the public to enter private land over which the owners had previously had an unlimited right to exclude. In *Nollan*, the California Coastal Commission required the owners of beachfront property to permit the public to laterally cross their private stretch of beach, located between two state parks. The requirement in effect exacted a public easement of way, an action that if done directly clearly would have required compensation. In *Dolan*, the city conditioned a permit to expand the owner's store and parking lot on dedicating a portion of the land to the city for the purposes of creating a pedestrian and bicycle path and a flood-control greenway. As in *Nollan*, the exaction would have had the effect of restricting the owner's power to exclude the public from her land. Both decisions then reflect, as Frank Michelman stated with respect to *Nollan*, "the talismanic force of 'permanent physical occupation' in takings adjudication."[108] To date, there has been no indication that the Court would apply the same heightened scrutiny where the government condition does not interfere with the landowner's right to exclude.[109]

Further evidence that the Court seems unprepared to launch a massive expansion of the physical-occupation category, subject to a rigid per se rule, is its decision in *Yee v. City of Escondido*.[110] That case involved a mobile home rent-control ordinance. California state law restricts the ability of owners of mobile home parks to order, while a rental agreement is still in effect, the removal of a mobile home upon its sale. The combined effect of that law with a local rent-control ordinance, the park owner argued, was to constitute a taking by physical occupation. The Supreme Court disagreed, emphasizing that there was "no compelled physical occupation" here.[111] It is, the Court stated, the "element of required acquiescence [that] is at the heart of the concept of occupation."[112] The exactions involved in *Nollan* and *Dolan* were both of the type that could easily be viewed as "required acquiescence" of just that sort, but many other municipal exactions cannot. It seems unlikely then that the *Nollan-Dolan* doctrine will put an end to that practice.

Another Categorical Rule (Sort of): **Lucas** *and Total Economic Deprivations*

The final development is the one that has received the greatest public attention. It may also be the one that has the least practical effect. It is the appearance of another categorical rule, the "total economic deprivation" rules, first announced by the Supreme Court in *Lucas v. South Carolina Coastal Council.*

At issue in *Lucas* was the constitutional validity of a South Carolina statute, the Beachfront Management Act. The statute prohibited the construction of any permanently inhabitable structure on certain stretches on the beachfront land on South Carolina's fragile barrier islands. Two years before the statute's enactment, a real estate developer, David Lucas, paid close to $1 million for two beachfront lots, on which he had planned to build permanent residences for sale to others. The statute foiled his plans, and he sued, claiming a taking. The trial court found that the statute made Lucas's lots valueless, a finding that many commentators have challenged as extremely unlikely. The state supreme court held that despite this effect there was no taking because the statute's purpose was "to prevent serious public harm," invoking the "noxious-use" line of decisions.[113] The United States Supreme Court reversed.

In an opinion written by Justice Scalia, the Court announced that "when the owner of real property has been called upon to sacrifice *all* economically beneficial uses in the name of the common good, that is, to leave his property economically idle, he has suffered a taking."[114] In this passage Justice Scalia created what most commentators consider to be a new categorical rule, the rule that a land-use regulation whose effect is a complete deprivation of all economic value constitutes a per se taking. As soon as Scalia announced this categorical rule, however, he carved out an exception to it. "Where the State seeks to sustain regulation that deprives land of all economically beneficial use, we think it may resist compensation only if the logically antecedent inquiry into the nature of the owner's estate shows that the proscribed use interests were not part of his title to begin with."[115] In other words, the state, to avoid a compensation obligation, must locate some land-use prohibition existing in the historical common law of nuisance and link that prohibition with the use proscribed by the challenged regulation.

There are many problems with Justice Scalia's analysis, as several commentators have effectively pointed out.[116] The point to be emphasized here is that *Lucas*'s categorical rule may not amount to all that much if it is confined to the highly unusual circumstance of a judicial finding of fact that the regulation deprived the owner of *all* economically viable use and if the Court does not broaden that circumstance through a more extensive use of the conceptual severance technique. The real significance of *Lucas* may be less its practical effect than the signal it sends regarding the current Court's desire to remold takings law along more formal lines. The Rehnquist Court seemed to be signaling that it was increasingly impatient with the open-ended balancing approach of *Penn Central. Lucas* and *Dolan* appeared to indicate, then, that the Court was finally responding to calls from commentators for "a good dose of formalization."[117]

The End of the Takings Revolution: The Post-1987 Cases

If the Rehnquist Court was signaling a new push toward greater formality in takings law, the effort did not last long. Within just a few years after *Lucas*, the Court was issuing takings opinions that had none of the swaggering pro-property-rights activism of Justice Scalia's majority opinion in that case. A full retreat was on.

What Is "Private Property"? What Defines It? Phillips v. Washington Legal Foundation *and* Palazzolo v. Rhode Island

Analytically, it would seem that the issue that needs first to be resolved in any takings case is whether the interest asserted for protection constitutes property. That issue implicates the problem of determining the source of "private property" for constitutional purposes.

As previously discussed, the Supreme Court has devoted comparatively little attention to these questions. As Laura Underkuffler has pointed out, "[F]inding any coherent, underlying analysis or understanding of constitutionally cognizable property in the Supreme Court's takings cases is a difficult task. In fact, in the mountains of Supreme Court takings jurisprudence in recent years, comparatively little attention has been devoted to this first, threshold question."[118] Nearly all of the litigated takings cases involved land,[119] and here the affected interests, with few exceptions, are the sort that for private law purposes are clearly recognized as property, such as a fee interest or an easement. At the same time, the Court has held that prospective interests such as future customers are not constitutional property.[120]

Some aspects of the problems of the meaning and source of constitutional property were resolved in a series of recent Supreme Court cases. Of these cases, *Phillips v. Washington Legal Foundation*[121] and *Palazzolo v. Rhode Island*[122] are especially important.[123]

Phillips involved a constitutional challenge to so-called IOLTAs, Interest on Lawyer Trust Accounts. IOLTAs are the exclusive creation of state law. Nearly all states have rules requiring lawyers who hold small amounts of funds for clients to deposit such amounts in bank trust accounts. IOLTA programs require that where the costs of tracing and distributing the small amounts of interest derived from these interest-paying trust accounts exceed the amount of interest that the client funds can earn, the lawyer must deposit the funds in special IOLTA accounts. The interest is then paid to nonprofit IOLTA organizations that distribute the funds to programs that provide legal services for the poor. Not all lawyer-held client funds are deposited in IOLTA accounts, only those that are small enough that, given administrative costs, they would not generate net interest for the client.[124]

The question before the Court was "whether interest earned on client trust funds held by lawyers in IOLTA accounts [is] a property interest of the client or lawyer" for purposes of the takings clause.[125] The client clearly owned the money that produced the interest (that is, the principal), but a third party, not the client, was the only one entitled to benefit from the interest. Did the client nevertheless have a constitutionally recognizable property interest in that item? Applying the common law maxim that "interest follows the principal," the Court held that the interest income belonged to the client. The Court remanded the case for a determination whether the regulation requiring that the interest income be paid to a charity constituted a taking of that property. (The Court later addressed the taking question in *Brown v. Washington Legal Foundation*,[126] which we will discuss shortly.)

The lynchpin of the decision was the Court's observation that constitutional property is identified by sources outside the Constitution. Chief Justice Rehnquist stated, "Because the Constitution protects rather than creates property interests, the existence of a property interest is determined by reference to 'existing rules or understandings that stem from an independent source such as state law.' "[127] This is the positivist approach that we previously discussed.[128] Under it, constitutional property is dependent upon independent sources, such as (but not limited to)[129] state law.

As was previously discussed, the approach is ambiguous. It could mean that we look to nonconstitutional law both for the definition of constitutional property and to see whether such private property has been created ("pure positivism"). Or it could mean that the definition of property for constitutional purposes is a matter of constitutional law itself (that is, that the courts must develop a constitutional meaning of property) but that whether such property has been created is a matter of nonconstitutional law. The Court in *Phillips* did not clearly indicate its views regarding these two versions of positivism, but it seems unlikely that the Court meant to endorse pure positivism. A purely positivist approach to resolving the issue in *Phillips* would seem to say that since the independent nonconstitutional law in effect at the time the deposit was made clearly indicates that the client would receive no income interest off the deposit, the client should have no property in the income. The fact that the Court found that the client did have a constitutional interest implies that independent nonconstitutional law does not entirely control the definitional issue.

Further evidence that the Court rejects a purely positivist approach to defining constitutional property was provided in its subsequent decision in *Palazzolo v. Rhode Island.* In *Palazzolo,* the Court faced the question of whether a landowner who purchased the land after the challenged land-use restriction took effect has no protection under the takings clause.[130] The challenged action was the Rhode Island Coastal Resources Management Council's application of a state wetlands regulation, rejecting a proposed development of a waterfront parcel of land. At the time the Council rejected the proposal, the land was owned by a corporation whose sole shareholder was Palazzolo. Subsequently, title to the parcel passed to Palazzolo individually, and he filed an inverse condemnation action, claiming that the Council's decision was a taking. The Rhode Island courts rejected his claim on multiple grounds, including the theory that Palazzolo "had no right to challenge regulations predating 1978, when he succeeded to legal ownership of the property."[131] The U.S. Supreme Court disagreed, concluding that no categorical exception from takings protection exists under such circumstances.

The decision is important for purposes of the definitional problem because the Court rejected a strictly positivist approach to defining constitutional property. The Court framed the argument that it was rejecting this way: "[B]y prospective legislation the State can shape and define property rights and reasonable investment-backed expectations, and subsequent owners cannot claim any injury from lost value . . . [T]hey purchased or took title with notice of the limitation."[132] Justice Kennedy pithily responded to this positivist argument by stating, "The State may not put so potent a Hobbesian stick into the Lockean bundle."[133] The Court's rejection of this argument indicates that the existence of a constitutional property interest does not depend solely on positive state law, for if it did, then constitutional claims would rise and fall, expand and contract with changes in state law. The decision suggests, then, that positive nonconstitutional law is not the source, or at least not the exclusive source, of property for takings clause purposes. Constitutional property may exist where nonconstitutional law says it does not.

The implications of these cases for the takings revolution thesis, like the cases themselves, are unclear. On one level, they do seem to strengthen the takings clause insofar as they indicate that the range of constitutional property may be broader than positive law alone would define. On the other hand, the Court did not say that the definition of constitutional property is entirely a matter of constitutional law. To the contrary, in *Phillips*, the Court made it clear that constitutional law does *not* create property, even for constitutional purposes. Positive law then must provide some limitation on the range of interests that the Court is prepared to call constitutional property. Moreover, even under the most capacious definition of constitutional property, one that is entirely untethered to positive law, the takings clause cannot be an agent of an antiredistributive "revolution" unless the Court is prepared to adopt an equally capacious conception of a "taking." That question—and more—were before the Court in a more recent takings clause decision, to which we turn next.

Taking without Compensation Due? **Brown v. Legal Foundation of Washington**

Brown[134] arose out of a factual background similar to that in *Phillips*, namely, IOLTA accounts. This time it was the state of Washington's program that was challenged, but the program was otherwise identical to that involved in *Phillips*. The Supreme Court granted certiorari to address the questions it left open in *Phillips*, namely, whether state IOLTA programs effect a "taking" of property and, if so, what amount of compensation is due to the client whose funds are deposited in the account.

In a subtle opinion, the Court stated that the requirement that the client funds must be deposited in IOLTA accounts did not itself effect a taking. That requirement, the Court said, "is merely a transfer of principal and therefore does not effect a confiscation of any interest."[135] However, the later transfer of earned interest to the legal services foundation was another matter. The Court said that, on the basis of the conclusion reached in *Phillips* that this interest is the client's "property," this transfer "seems more akin to the occupation of a small amount of rooftop space in *Loretto* [*v. Teleprompter Manhattan CATV Corp.*]."[136] Hence, the Court "assumed" that the transfer of the interest to the foundation was a "taking" of property. However, this did not end the matter, for two more requirements exist under the takings clause, the public-use and just-compensation requirements. The Court had no difficulty finding that the taking was for public use.[137] The real question was what did just compensation require.

The Court held that no compensation was due. The crucial steps toward reaching this holding were the Court's conclusions that just compensation[138] is not due for nonpecuniary consequences of the taking and is measured by the property owner's net loss rather than the government's gain. Thus, although in *Phillips* the Court had concluded that, despite the fact that the item of property had no economically realizable value to its owner, "possession, control, and disposition are . . . valuable rights that inhere in property,"[139] in *Brown*, the Court said that only pecuniary losses, not the nonpecuniary factors identified in *Phillips*, were compensable. Moreover, because only net losses to the owner were compensable, no compensation was due wherever, as here, the transaction costs exceed the gross value of what was earned.

The Court's focus on the net loss as the measure of compensation is odd. The overwhelming case law adopts a fair market value standard: the owner is entitled to an amount that a willing buyer would pay a willing seller of the property.[140] The Court's analysis of what the owner lost lends itself to an interpretation that it is adopting a different standard, an "indemnification" standard that in some cases could yield greater compensation than the fair market value standard and in other cases less.[141] It seems unlikely, however, that the Court meant to signal wholesale abandonment of the fair market value standard. Its discussion of the measure of compensation, and certainly its conclusion that no compensation was due following a taking, are probably best read as narrowly limited to this unusual set of facts.

On balance, the decision does not seem to have major significance for takings jurisprudence. The facts were highly unusual, and the "taking but no compensation" conclusion is unlikely to be replicated in other cases, especially cases involving land-use or environmental restrictions. Perhaps the most significant aspect of the case was the Court's capacious approach to defining public use. Were the Court to apply the same approach, finding that a transfer to private owners constitutes a public use if the state could have imposed a tax for the same purpose, more broadly, the public-use condition on the state's taking power would be substantially empty of any real content. However, since the IOLTA program was not challenged on the basis of the public-use requirement, Justice Stevens's discussion of the issue appears to be dictum only. As one commentator has noted, "Given the context in which the discussion is presented, it seems likely that this leg of the case will have no growing power."[142] Still, the case is significant as part of a broader trend in the Court's recent takings jurisprudence. Observing that *Tahoe-Sierra Preservation Council, Inc. v. Tahoe Regional Planning Agency,* which we will discuss next, appeared to signal a shift away from a revival of the takings clause as a major restriction on the regulatory state, another commentator has observed, "The *Brown* decision, by handing takings claimants yet another defeat, seems to confirm this shift. After years of controversy, is it possible that the regulatory takings agenda has reached the limits of its ambition?"[143] My answer is yes.

Repudiating Temporal Conceptual Severance: Tahoe-Sierra

Some questions about both the status of conceptual severance and the prospect of more categorical takings rules were answered in the Court's decision in *Tahoe-Sierra Preservation Council, Inc. v. Tahoe Regional Planning Agency.*[144] Other questions were not answered.

THE FACTS The question before the Court in *Tahoe-Sierra* was whether a temporary, thirty-two-month[145] moratorium on development of land in the Lake Tahoe basin constituted a taking of property per se, requiring compensation under the just compensation clause of the United States Constitution. The Court held that it did not. It is important to note that the Court did *not* hold that there was no taking as a result of the planning agency's actions. The only decision was that temporary development moratoria do not constitute per se takings under the *Lucas* doctrine. The Court expressly left open the possibility that such moratoria might yet constitute takings under the *Penn Central* balancing approach.[146]

The building moratoria were an integral part of the TRPA's[147] effort to prevent continued degradation of Lake Tahoe. Lake Tahoe is unique and uniquely beautiful. President Clinton referred to it as "a national treasure."[148] Mark Twain described it as "surely the fairest picture the whole world affords."[149] It is renowned for its exceptional clarity, which Twain characterized as "not *merely* transparent, but dazzling, brilliantly so."[150] Lake Tahoe's clarity is due to the absence of algae, which clouds the visibility of most lakes, and the absence of algae is due, in turn, to the lake's lack of nitrogen and phosphorus, nutrients of algae. In recent years, however, Lake Tahoe had been losing its pristine clarity and its characteristic cobalt blue color as the result of development around it. The enormous growth in development since the 1960s, the district court found, had caused "increased nutrient loading of the lake largely because of the increase in impervious coverage of land in the Basin resulting from that development."[151] The district court went on to explain the problem:

> Impervious coverage—such as asphalt, concrete, buildings, and even packed dirt—prevents precipitation from being absorbed by the soil. Instead, the water is gathered and concentrated by such coverage. Larger amounts of water flowing off a driveway or a roof have more erosive force than scattered raindrops falling over a dispersed area—especially one covered with indigenous vegetation, which softens the impact of the raindrops themselves.[152]

The district court predicted that "unless the process is stopped, the lake will lose its clarity and its trademark blue color, becoming green and opaque for eternity."[153]

Responding to this problem, the Tahoe Regional Planning Agency (TRPA), created by the states of California and Nevada in 1969, enacted two development moratoria. The first, adopted in 1981, provided that it would remain in effect until adoption of a permanent plan in 1983, as required by the 1980 Tahoe Regional Planning Compact. When the TRPA determined that it would not be able to meet the deadline,[154] it adopted the second moratorium in 1983. The two moratoria prohibited construction of any new residences on sensitive lands in the Tahoe basin for a total of thirty-two months.[155]

Shortly after the 1984 plan was adopted, the petitioners filed actions against the TRPA. The petitioners included the Tahoe Sierra Preservation Council, a nonprofit corporation representing over 2,000 owners of improved and unimproved land in the Tahoe basin and additional owners of vacant lots located in areas covered by the moratoria. These individual owners had purchased their lots prior to the effective date of the 1980 compact, with the intent of constructing single-family homes as vacation or retirement residences. When they purchased their lots, they did so with the understanding that construction was permissible so long as "they complied with all reasonable requirements for building."[156] Following extensive litigation, the district court held that the two moratoria constituted categorical takings under the *Lucas* doctrine because the restrictions denied the owners "all economically viable use of their land." [157] The district court ordered the TRPA to pay petitioners damages for the thirty-two-month period. The court of appeals reversed the district court's finding regarding the existence of a categorical taking and further held that no taking occurred under the *Penn Central* balancing test. The Supreme Court granted the appeal on the narrow question of whether the mere enactment of the temporary moratoria constituted a taking per se.

THE COURT'S DECISION The Court held that the temporary development moratoria did not constitute per se takings. The Court first disposed of the contention that *First English* supposed the rule proposed by the petitioners. It concluded that *First English* was not relevant. That case had held that once a taking is found to have occurred, the government must pay compensation for the period of time between when the regulation first effected a taking and when the government rescinded the regulation. *First English*, the Court said, spoke only to the remedial question of whether compensation must be paid for a temporary taking. It did not address the "logically prior question" [158] of whether a taking had occurred, the very question at issue in *Tahoe-Sierra*.

Turning then to the petitioners' argument that the case fell within *Lucas*'s categorical taking rule, the Court [159] concluded that it did not. *Lucas*'s categorical rule, the Court said, applies "when a regulation deprives an owner of '*all* economically beneficial uses' of his land." [160] The regulation must result in "permanent 'obliteration of the value'" of the owner's estate. [161] The question, of course, is what is the relevant unit of temporal measurement, and the answer to that question turned on the Court's reaction to the petitioners' "conceptual severance" argument. The petitioners argued that the Court should sever the thirty-two-month period of the moratoria's duration from the remainder of the owners' fee simple estate and then determine whether the value of that limited unit had been totally obliterated. The Court rejected the argument, stating, "Petitioners' 'conceptual severance' argument is unavailing because it ignores *Penn Central*'s admonition that in regulatory takings cases we must focus on 'the parcel as a whole' . . . We have consistently rejected such an approach to the 'denominator' question." [162] The owners had argued that the moratoria should be analogized to condemned leaseholds. Under the Court's prior case law, condemnations of leaseholds required compensation. [163] The Court distinguished those cases on the ground that they involved physical appropriations in which the owners were deprived of their right to exclude, whereas the moratoria did not do so.

Turning to the question of whether it should carve out a new categorical rule, the Court provided several arguments against doing so. First, the Court said that "[a] rule that required compensation for every delay in the use of property would render routine government processes prohibitively expensive or encourage hasty decisionmaking."[164] Second, development moratoria like those involved in this case are, the Court said, "an essential tool of successful development."[165] Closely related to this consideration, the Court emphasized the importance of protecting the decisional process for planning agencies and stated that a per se rule would jeopardize that process. It might force planners to rush through the process or abandon it altogether. Moreover, perverse incentives would result from holding that owners must wait for "a takings claim to ripen so that planners can make well-reasoned decisions while, at the same time, holding that those planners must compensate landowners for the delay."[166] This is especially true, the Court said, in cases of regional planning rather than permits for a single parcel. "Since a categorical rule tied to the length of deliberations would likely create added pressure on decisionmakers to reach a quick resolution of land-use questions, it would only serve to disadvantage those landowners and interest groups who are not as organized or familiar with the planning process."[167] There is less likelihood of a "singling-out" problem in the context of a regional development moratorium. Related to this, there is a "reciprocity of advantage" with such a restriction because "it protects the interests of all affected landowners against immediate construction that might be inconsistent with the provisions of the plan that is ultimately adopted." Indeed, the Court said, it is quite possible that real estate values will increase during this moratorium because of the assurance that Lake Tahoe will remain in pristine condition. Finally, the Court emphasized that it was not holding that the regulations in this case did not effect a taking. It expressly left open the possibility that such a taking might be found under the *Penn Central* multifactored balancing approach, under which the length of the moratorium is certainly one factor taken into consideration. The point decided was only that *Penn Central*'s approach applied, not *Lucas*'s categorical rule.

WHAT WAS CLEARLY RESOLVED IN *TAHOE-SIERRA?* What was clearly resolved by *Tahoe-Sierra,* and what remains murky? Perhaps the clearest message is that conceptual severance cannot be used temporally. That message is important because it blocks one avenue for expanding the reach of *Lucas*'s per se rule. *Lucas* does not apply to land-use regulations that temporarily halt all development. The holding in *Tahoe-Sierra* was narrow in one sense but important in another. Conservative property-rights activists had hoped to use the case to expand *Lucas*'s reach, however slightly. Their defeat was important for symbolic reasons even if the practical effect of the decision is not great. The likelihood is that property-rights proponents will have to fight their fight within the analytical framework of balancing.[168] Their favored tool of categorical, per se rules is unlikely to be available.[169]

THE PRESENT STATUS OF CONCEPTUAL SEVERANCE Still, it is important to recognize that the future of conceptual severance after *Tahoe-Sierra* remains murky. While the Court unambiguously repudiated that argument in the context of temporal slices of ownership, the door remains open for other possible uses of the theory. In addition to temporal conceptual severance, there are at least two other forms of the theory, spatial and functional conceptual severance.[170] Spatial conceptual severance involves physical division of assets, particularly land. What is the relevant parcel for purposes of determining the degree of the regulation's impact? The question is certainly relevant to *Penn Central*'s diminution-in-value factor (what is the relevant denominator?), but it is crucial to *Lucas*'s total-wipeout rule. Professors Dana and Merrill provide a useful illustration of the problem. They ask,

> [I]f a landowner buys two adjoining lots with separate deeds in a single closing, and one lot is wetland and one upland, is the relevant property interest for Takings Clause purposes the two lots together or is it the wetland lot alone, assuming it becomes subject to development restrictions? And does the answer to that question change if the wetland and upland were held subject to a single deed?[171]

As they point out, the lower court case law is "not instructive" and the Supreme Court's decisions provide no answer.[172] *Tahoe-Sierra* certainly is not very helpful in answering such questions. The Court stated that the analysis must focus on the impact of the regulation on the "parcel as a whole," but it neglected to provide any guidance on how the relevant parcel should be determined.[173]

The second version of conceptual severance is functional. Here the idea is that each right in the owner's bundle of rights itself may be treated as a discrete property interest. So a regulation that prohibits the right of the owner of an artifact made from eagle feathers from selling that artifact is a total taking of the owner's right to sell.[174] This is precisely the argument made by Professor Richard Epstein in his book, *Takings.* As Professor Epstein is well aware, the effect of functional conceptual severance, if broadly implemented, would be enormous. Ownership can be split into virtually an infinite number of sticks, and nearly all regulations can therefore be characterized as completely wiping out some discrete property interest. The result would be that nearly any government regulation that changes the extant distribution of wealth would trigger the takings clause.[175]

The Supreme Court's signals regarding functional conceptual severance have been mixed.[176] On the one hand, in *Andrus v. Allard,* the Court unambiguously rejected the attempt to sever the right of commercial exploitation from the remainder of the bundle. "[W]here an owner possesses a full 'bundle' of property rights," Justice Brennan wrote, "the destruction of one 'strand' of the bundle is not a taking, because the aggregat[ion] must be viewed in its entirety."[177] On the other hand, as we have seen, just eight years after *Andrus,* the Court held that complete abrogation of the right of descent and devise was a taking. In *Hodel v. Irving,*[178] the Court said that the right of descent and devise is "one of the most essential sticks in the bundle of rights."[179] Still, the Court did *not* say that the right of descent and devise is *itself* property. Nor did the Court hold that the total abrogation of that stick was a taking per se, for the Court applied the *Penn Central* balancing test to determine whether there was a taking. Further complicating the picture, the Court has frequently singled out the right to exclude as one of the most essential, if not *the* most essential stick in the bundle of rights.[180] And as we have seen, a regulation that effects a permanent physical occupation triggers a categorical taking rule under *Loretto v. Teleprompter Manhattan CATV Corp.* Complicating the picture even more, the Court in *Phillips v. Washington Legal Foundation,* as we saw earlier, has held that interest is a discrete item of property, separate from the principal that produced it. As one commentator has frankly stated, "The *Phillips* decision acquiesced in an egregious form of conceptual severance."[181]

The picture concerning functional conceptual severance then is muddy. It appears, however, that even assuming that the newest members of the Supreme Court were to accept the functional conceptual severance argument, a majority of the Court still appears to be resisting the argument, although even that majority does seem willing to engage in a weak form of it for purposes of engaging in its balancing method. Some twigs in the bundle of rights are weightier than others, and where the twig is one that the Court regards as especially important, that factor is more likely to lead the Court to hold that a taking has occurred.

TOTAL WIPEOUT—OF WHAT? Another important question that remains unclear after *Tahoe-Sierra* concerns the meaning of "total wipeout" in *Lucas*'s categorical rule. *Lucas* held that whenever a regulation effected a total economic wipeout, a taking occurred per se. But as various commentators have noted,[182] in *Lucas*, the Court ignored the very fact that the landowners' lots, even with the prohibition against construction of any permanent buildings, retained some value. What did the Court mean, then, when it said that the lots were valueless? Professors Dana and Merrill perceptively point out that there are two possible interpretations of the *Lucas* total-wipeout rule. The first is that it refers to market value. A total wipeout occurs when the governmental action deprives the land (or relevant interest therein) of all its market value. The second focuses on possession or use, rather than value. A total wipeout occurs when the governmental action prohibits the owner from all development of the land in question.[183] *Tahoe-Sierra* unfortunately did not unambiguously resolve the question. In its discussion of *Lucas*, the Court appeared to have adopted the first construction. In *Lucas*, the Court took as given the trial court's finding of fact that the owner's lots had been rendered "'valueless'" by the regulation,[184] but, as Dana and Merrill point out, given the narrow issue involved in *Tahoe-Sierra*, much of the Court's language regarding *Lucas* could be considered dicta.[185]

The three dissenting Justices made it very clear that in their view, *Lucas*'s total-wipeout standard refers to *use*, not value. Specifically, it refers, in their view, to the owner's ability to develop the affected land. A ban on development of land, even if the land retains some market value, the Court said, is the equivalent of physical appropriation of the land and triggers the *Lucas* per se taking rule.

The upshot is that *Tahoe-Sierra* has left the door open for a broad reading of *Lucas*. Given the importance of the question, it seems likely that property-rights advocates will continue to push the issue. Still, combined with *Palazzolo*, *Tahoe-Sierra* does leave one with the impression that a majority of the Court, even the newly constituted Court, is not inclined to expand either the number of per se taking rules or the breadth of such existing rules.

So, after all of the hyped discussion about a takings revolution, the constitutional property landscape is largely where it was after *Penn Central*. With two narrow exceptions, balancing remains the method of choice, and using that method, the Court is unlikely to strike down any but the most extreme property-regulating government action.

Can we say, then, that a "revolution" in American takings jurisprudence has occurred? Hardly. Or at least the most we can say is that the revolution, if indeed it began in 1987, was aborted by the Court's post-*Lucas* cases.

Methodologically, the Court's analysis has changed very little since the *Penn Central* balancing approach was announced in 1978. The one new categorical takings rule, the "total takings" doctrine, has not been applied in any case since *Lucas,* and efforts to add more categorical rules have been repudiated. Substantively, the takings clause still provides relatively little restriction on the power of state and local governments to regulate property. Only in the area of exactions has the law of takings significantly affected the relationship between local governments and private landowners. Other forms of land regulation that property-rights activists had hoped would fall to takings challenges, such as rent control and wetlands regulations, have successfully resisted constitutional challenge.

More broadly, the expansion of the regulatory state continues to be a one-way ratchet. It now seems clear that the takings clause will not be the constitutional tool that property-rights advocates had hoped it would become, one that ushers in a new *Lochner* age. Battles over property rights will continue to be fought in the courts, but the locus of the property-rights activists' energies will increasingly shift from the courts to the legislatures. Whether their efforts will yield more dividends in that arena is anyone's guess, but based upon the limited results of the property-rights legislation that has already emerged in recent years,[186] it seems unlikely that a major shift in the power of the regulatory state over land and other resources will occur.

CHAPTER THREE

Constitutionalizing the Social Obligation of Ownership: The German Example

> Freedom and social justice go together. Social peace is the prerequisite for a nation's inner strength. Without that inner strength it has no strength internationally. Our constitution upholds the concept of ownership as the basis of a free economic order. But at the same time it postulates the social obligation inherent in ownership. That is what our constitution, the Basic Law of the Federal Republic of Germany, prescribes. And this has been the approach of all Governments of the Federal Republic of Germany.[1]

Private ownership of property inherently has limits. No one denies that the owner of a gun is not entitled to use it by shooting someone on a whim. Private law acknowledges the fact that ownership is inherently limited and has developed a body of rules that define, however imperfectly, the scope and contents of the limits of private ownership. Constitutional law also acknowledges that property as a constitutional right, assuming that it is recognized, is limited. But constitutions differ in the way that they acknowledge this fact of property's inherent limits and the basis of these limits.

This chapter examines the property clause of the German Constitution, or more accurately, the Basic Law (*Grundgesetz*). My specific focus is on the social-obligation (*Sozialbindung*) clause provision of the property clause. This provision expressly requires the legislature to define the limits on the individual owner's autonomy interest through the lens of a general norm of social obligation.[2]

My interest is both in the substantive meaning of the social-obligation norm, as the German courts have interpreted it, and how the explicit constitutional social-obligation norm has influenced the way in which courts reason about the basis for limiting the constitutional right of property. Substantively, while the German and American limits on the constitutional property right are basically the same, there are significant differences, particularly in the areas of environmental regulation and housing. These differences can be attributed to the social-obligation norm. Rhetorically and analytically, the differences are quite significant. To mention only one difference, the German courts have not developed any rules that are the equivalent of per se categorical takings rules. Their opinions are more transparent concerning the competing interests at stake and the normative reasons for the decision, particularly when the social-obligation norm is immediately implicated. Finally, the courts have developed an openly purposive, or functional, approach to analyzing the constitutional property right, one that effectively creates a hierarchy of types of property for purposes of constitutional protection. The result is a body of constitutional property jurisprudence that is both analytically and normatively more coherent than American takings law and a better model for constitutional property adjudication than the experience of the U.S. Supreme Court.

Another reason for my focus on the German social-obligation norm is that it illustrates the role of background legal traditions and cultures in constitution making and constitutional interpretation. The Basic Law did not create the social-obligation norm out of whole cloth. That norm existed as part of Germany's background legal tradition and culture for decades prior to its recognition in the property provision. Even as a strictly textual matter, explicit recognition of a social obligation in Germany's current constitutional property law was new. The social-obligation provision was deliberately drawn from a very similar provision in the constitution of the Weimar Republic. Even then, there was no sheer constitutionalization of the norm. As I will show, the roots of the norm lie not in constitutional law, formally understood, but in the country's background legal and political traditions prior to the era of National Socialism.

A third reason for explaining German practices in constitutional property law concerns compensation practices. Certain German courts have ordered the payment of compensation in cases of regulatory excess that result in "unusual sacrifice" (*Sonderopfer*) on their theory of "equalization rights" (*Ausgleichsanspruch*). These payments are not considered compensation for expropriations as such but instead as a device that ameliorates the problem of the burdens of otherwise legitimate property regulation being disproportionately distributed. It is a via media between the two extremes of total compensation (that is, full fair market value) and no compensation whatsoever. Moreover, German courts accept the possibility that some amount less than full fair market value can be paid as compensation where that is necessary to maintain an equitable balance between the interests of owners and the public interest. This practice further reflects the social dimension of the constitutional property right in Germany. As I will discuss in chapter 5, something like both of these practices might be used to deal with the similar problems of property regulation and expropriation in the United States.

Comparing the German and American Constitutional Property Clauses: Surface Similarities and Deeper Differences

On the surface of things, the German and American approaches to constitutional protection of property appear very much alike. Both recognize the legitimacy of private property, and both explicitly protect property against uncompensated expropriations. Both affirm that while the state may legitimately act in ways that may impair the property owner's interest, the state's power so to act is restricted to actions that serve the public interest. Finally, both expressly give the constitutionally injured property owner a right to fair or just compensation.

Textual Differences

Below the surface, however, the resemblances end. Important differences, both textual and interpretive, set the two approaches to constitutional protection of property apart. Textually, the German Constitution has a single property clause. Article 14 of the *Grundgesetz* is the sole textual provision explicitly treating the relationship between the state and the individual concerning property.[3] This unified textual handling of property contrasts with the American Constitution. The federal Constitution mentions property in two different provisions, the due process clause of the Fourteenth Amendment and the just compensation (or takings) clause of the Fifth Amendment. This divided treatment of property has created a host of problems. To pick just one, there is considerable uncertainty about the meaning of property under the two provisions and the interrelationship between those meanings.[4]

Second, Article 14 recognizes the institution of private property (literally, *Eigentum*[5]). Its first sentence provides, "Ownership and inheritance are guaranteed." The Federal Constitutional Court (*Bundesverfassungsgericht*) has interpreted this sentence as guaranteeing the existence of private ownership as an institution.[6] Given the fact that the United States is probably the most property-focused nation on Earth, it seems more than a little curious that the American Constitution nowhere expressly guarantees the institution of private ownership of property.

Related to this difference is a third textual difference. Article 14 is stated affirmatively rather than in negative terms. It does not simply say, as the due process and takings clauses do, that property shall not be deprived or taken except under certain conditions. Rather, it states, "Ownership and inheritance are guaranteed."

The final and most important textual difference between the German and American constitutional property clauses is the social-obligation (*Sozialbindung*) clause, Article 14(2). This provision explicitly indicates that in the German constitutional scheme, a social obligation is inherent in ownership: property must serve the needs and interests of the political community as well as those of the individual owner. There is no textual counterpart to this provision in either of the two property clauses of the American Constitution. The main purpose of this chapter is to examine what effects, substantive and methodological, the social-obligation norm has had on what we can loosely call German takings law. Before turning to the German Constitution's social-obligation norm, however, I need to address one other apparent difference, one that leads us to see some deeper differences that have important normative implications for American takings law.

An Apparent Paradox

In comparing German and American constitutional property law, some American commentators have emphasized the difference between how the courts of the two countries have characterized the relative position of property in the constitutional hierarchy of individual rights. Professor David Currie, for example, has observed that "property rights are by no means relegated to an inferior position in Germany, as they have been in the United States."[7] The basis for this view is the fact that the German Constitutional Court has consistently and expressly characterized the right to private ownership of property as "an elementary basic right,"[8] roughly corresponding to the American notion of certain rights as "fundamental."

As Currie's statement suggests, while the right of property is characterized as a fundamental constitutional right in Germany, in the United States it does not enjoy that designation. As all American law students are taught, the right of property has not been treated as a fundamental right since 1937. In that year, the Supreme Court effectively ended the doctrine of economic due process with its decision in *West Coast Hotel Co. v. Parrish*.[9] Since that decision the Court has not struck down any economic regulation on due process grounds.[10] Property rights have become, as some commentators put it, a "poor relation" to liberty interests for substantive due process purposes.[11] Courts treat certain liberty interests and rights like the rights to vote, procreate, and travel, as "fundamental," vigorously protected against all governmental encroachments save those undertaken for "compelling" reasons. Under modern due process jurisprudence, on the other hand, property interests succumb to any governmental encroachment that passes a weak "rationality" standard. No modern Supreme Court decision has characterized the right of property as "fundamental" for substantive due process purposes.[12] And while property rights arguably have gained greater protection under the takings clause in recent years, their level of protection under that provision is nowhere close to equaling that of certain civil liberties under the Fourteenth Amendment's equal protection clause. Constitutionally speaking, in the United States, property is a "second-rate" right.

Here, then, is the paradox: property is accorded a higher status under the Basic Law of Germany, a social welfare state, than it is under the Constitution of the United States, a country considered by many to be the most property-conscious country in the world. There is no dearth of calls for changing this situation by elevating the constitutional right of property to the ranks of fundamental rights in the United States, as it is in Germany. Scholars like Professor Richard Epstein have argued that, properly understood, the Constitution provides no basis for relegating property to an inferior position in a lexical ordering of constitutional rights. "Under the proper analysis," Professor Epstein contends, "all rights are, as it were, fundamental."[13] Chief Justice Rehnquist has expressed a similar view, stating in one case, "We see no reason why the Takings Clause of the Fifth Amendment, as much a part of the Bill of Rights as the First Amendment or the Fourth Amendment, should be relegated to the status of a poor relation in these comparable circumstances."[14]

How can we explain this apparent paradox of property's different stature within the hierarchy of constitutional rights under the United States Constitution compared with the German Basic Law? It is tempting to answer that the German Constitutional Court has done what the American Supreme Court has refused to do in recent history and what conservative scholars like Professor Epstein have urged it to do, that is, it has recognized the status of property as a fundamental personal right, equal in rank and stature to the personal liberties of speech, religion, and the rest, and as a primary legal tool in the effort to resist redistributive governmental measures. Following this temptation, however, would yield a seriously distorted view of German constitutional property law. While German constitutional law does treat property as a fundamental right, the idea of property as a "fundamental right" has a quite different meaning under the German Basic Law.

There is indeed an asymmetry between the German and American constitutional treatments of property, but not that identified by the commentators. The problem stems from the way the question is framed. Rather than asking whether or not property is a fundamental right *tout court* under either the German or the American constitutions, the inquiry should focus on two closely related matters. First, assuming that the interest involved qualifies as "property" within the meaning of their constitutional texts, do German or American courts, in assessing the degree of protection that property rights warrant under their constitutions, explicitly discuss the primary purpose or function that they attribute to property rights as a general matter? Stated more simply, is their analysis of the constitutional status of property purposive? Second, do German or American courts focus on the values and functions that the particular interest immediately involved implicates? In other words, is their approach contextual? The answers to both questions reveal core methodological differences between the German and American approaches to the status of property as a constitutional right. The German Constitutional Court has adopted an approach that is both *purposive* and *contextual,* while the American Supreme Court has not.

The first question recognizes that the institution of property has multiple potential purposes and that the level of constitutional protection accorded to property, indeed, the basic question whether constitutionally to protect property at all, depends on what purpose(s) the legal system involved has historically assigned to property. Property rights are epiphenomenal. They are not ends in themselves but rather an instrument designed to instantiate and serve deeper substantive values, such as wealth maximization, personal privacy, and individual self-realization. In this sense property rights are never "fundamental." Only the substantive interests they serve can be.

The second question recognizes that in the realm of property, contingency accompanies multiplicity. Just as there are multiple potential purposes that the general institution of property may serve, so there are different functions associated with different types of particular property interests. One type of property interest may primarily protect economic goals like wealth maximization while another type may primarily protect personal privacy. Whether, how, and why property interests are constitutionally protected frequently depends on the type of interest involved. Neither constitutional texts nor judicial opinions typically draw such distinctions openly, but often the only way to make sense of some individual judicial decision or group of decisions is to pay attention to the sort of interest that is immediately at stake. More to the point, the level of constitutional protection that courts grant to property both does and should depend on the interest involved and the core purpose the court associates with that type of property interest.

These two questions illuminate a further difference between German and American constitutional property law, one that is substantive rather than methodological. While American courts generally do not recognize (at least not openly) the functional differences just drawn, the German Constitutional Court sharply and explicitly does. German constitutional law does not treat all property interests alike. The German court has created a hierarchy of types of property interests, granting strong protection to some and relatively weaker protection to others, depending upon the social functions they serve. Property interests whose function is primarily or even exclusively economic, that is, private wealth-creating property interests, receive minimal protection under German constitutional law. Such interests are viewed as not immediately implicating the fundamental values of human dignity and self-realization. Other interests, those that immediately implicate the owner's dignity and self-realization interests and her opportunity to practice self-governance receive strong protection. So, for example, the interest of a landlord who does not personally reside on the premises is given lesser weight than that of her tenant, whose opportunity to remain in possession is considered essential to dignity and self-governance values. By contrast, under the American Constitution, land held for the sole purpose of market speculation is as apt, perhaps more apt, to receive strong protection as is a tenant's interest in remaining in her home.[15]

Here, then, is the solution to the paradox. It is misleading simply to say that in the United States property is treated as an inferior right, while in Germany it is a fundamental right. In practice, the German Constitutional Court has not treated property in a highly deferential way across the board. The court strongly protects a particular property interest only to the extent that the interest immediately serves other, primary constitutional values, in particular, human dignity and self-governance.

Examining the German approach to constitutional protection of property provides a basis for critiquing and rethinking existing American constitutional property doctrine. To know whether we should characterize a right as fundamental, we need to know just *why* we value that right. We need further to consider whether the interest immediately involved implicates the values that the constitutional right of property is intended ultimately to serve. Finally, we need to evaluate the asserted interest in light of a norm of the social obligation of ownership. The German experience provides guidance for each of these questions.

Some Background of the German Basic Law

The "Constant Tension": Rechtsstaat *and* Sozialstaat

The great German legal historian Franz Wieacker wrote, "There is . . . a constant tension between the value-systems of the social state and those of the state under the rule of law, and constitutional lawyers rightly never tire of discussing the relationship between them."[16] Wieacker was right on all counts. This single sentence encapsulates the entire background necessary to understanding not only the property clause in the German Basic Law but all of German constitutionalism. The tension between two ideals, the *Rechtsstaat* (commonly translated as the "rule-of-law state"[17]) and the *Sozialstaat* (something like "social welfare" state), is the leitmotif of German constitutional law, including constitutional protection of property. The literature on this tension is enormous, but no one can possibly discuss any aspect of the German Basic Law without addressing it.

It is entirely clear both that the framers of the 1949 German Basic Law intended to establish both a *Rechtsstaat* and a *Sozialstaat*[18] and that they were all too aware of the tension between the two principles. Their operating premise, however, was that the two ideals could be integrated and be made mutually reinforcing. Before discussing their view about how the two could be integrated, the tension needs to be explained.

Articles 20 and 28 of the German Basic Law indicate that the Federal Republic is grounded in two quite different norms, the *Rechtsstaat* and the *Sozialstaat.*[19] Article 20 specifies a series of core principles that identify the defining features of the German state. These features are protected even against constitutional amendment.[20] Article 20(1) states that the Federal Republic of Germany is "a democratic and social federal state." It goes on to provide that the legislature is bound by the constitutional state and that the other branches of government are bound by "law and justice" (*Gesetz und Recht*). While it does not expressly mention the principle of the *Rechtsstaat,* the generally accepted view is that Article 20 implicitly adopts that principle.[21] Articles 20 and 28 are perhaps more explicit regarding the *Sozialstaat* principle, requiring the definition of the Federal Republic of Germany as a social federation (*sozialer Bundesstaat*)[22] and the creation of a legal regime that is consistent with "the principles of a republican, democratic, and social legal state [*sozialer Rechtsstaat*]."[23]

The term *Rechtsstaat* is frequently translated as a state subject to "rule of law,"[24] but this is a misleading translation.[25] A better translation might be "constitutional state."[26] One commentator has defined the *Rechtsstaat* as including the following features: rejection of absolute power, guarantee and protection of personal and political freedom, separation of powers, supremacy of the constitution, including judicial review, and limitation and judicial control of governmental authority.[27] Other aspects of the *Rechtsstaat* idea also need to be emphasized. One core component was a categorical division between the private realm, regulated by private law, and the public realm, the domain of public law.[28] The *Rechtsstaat* idea also stresses legal predictability, protection of trust and legitimate expectations, and a general principle of proportionality (*Verhältnismäßigkeit*), which we will consider in more detail subsequently.[29] Understood formally, as the traditional nineteenth-century conception of the principle held,[30] the *Rechtsstaat* has a thoroughly liberal, indeed libertarian tilt. It emphasizes the preeminence of individual liberty. Its operation was largely negative—disciplining state authority from interfering with the private interests of state subjects, that is, the individual.[31]

If the *Rechtsstaat* principle reflects traditional liberal values, the *Sozialstaat* principle reflects an effort to counterbalance the socioeconomic injustices that can follow from classical liberalism.[32] While the Federal Constitutional Court has not definitively explained the content of the *Sozialstaat* principle, the basic substantive idea underlying the *Sozialstaat* is that the government has a responsibility to provide for the basic needs of all its citizens. The *Sozialstaat* principle is understood to provide a legitimate doctrinal basis for limiting a number of individual rights, including the right of property.[33]

The immediate force behind recognition of the principle in 1949 appears to have been the socialist values of the Social Democratic Party.[34] However, the roots of the principle extend much further back in German history. Wieacker's account of the disintegration of the hegemony of individualistic private law after the First World War famously traces the rise of what Otto von Gierke called "social law."[35] Aspects of the *Sozialstaat* ideal can even be traced back to the Lutheran notion that the relationship between the prince and his people is one of mutual obligation. The people owe allegiance to the prince, but the prince in turn is obligated to provide for the welfare of his people.[36] This idea is a theme that recurs throughout German constitutional history. It is evident, for example, in the remarkable *Allgemeines Landrecht der Preußischen Staaten*, the comprehensive code for the Prussian States, completed in 1786.[37] While it would be anachronistic to say that the Prussian Code created anything like the modern welfare state, it certainly reflected a continuing commitment to the idea of the state's responsibility to secure the people's basic needs.[38]

A more modern version of the *Sozialstaat* dates to the social welfarist reforms adopted in Prussia between 1830 and 1840. As one scholar has put it, the significance of these legislative measures is the fact that "in an age dominated by the Liberalism of the Manchester School, the state intervened for the first time in the public sector and thus created a precedent for the future."

The social legislation of the Bismarck era and, later, the Weimar Republic greatly deepened and extended the reach of the state's intervention. Today, the concept of the *Sozialstaat* embraces not only the responsibility to provide a social "safety net," as that term is understood in the United States, but further, to redistribute wealth. The notion that the public's welfare depends upon assuring that no one lives in poverty and avoiding gross inequalities in the social distribution of wealth, while heretical in most American circles, is relatively uncontroversial in Germany today.[39] As one German legal scholar put it, it is "well-established knowledge" that "the social situation of the people improves, if and so far as everybody shares the results of what has been produced by society."[40]

Wieacker's claim that a tension exists between the *Rechtsstaat* and *Sozialstaat* ideals is entirely warranted. While it would be too much to say that they constitute an antinomy, the two ideals clearly have different trajectories. The vision underlying the *Rechtsstaat* is basically a liberal vision in which the state's role in the economy is limited strictly to that of facilitating the ability of free and autonomous legal actors to pursue their subjective interests. The *Sozialstaat* ideal, on the other hand, has much in common with socialism. Like socialism, it looks to the state to satisfy the demands of substantive, that is, socioeconomic, justice that the liberal state cannot meet and indeed creates.

Reconciling the Rechtsstaat *and* Sozialstaat

If the existence of the tension between the two ideals is well-known in the legal literature, the intellectual bases for their attempted reconciliation within the context of the Basic Law are less fully understood by legal audiences. To be sure, the relationship between the *Rechtsstaat* and the *Sozialstaat* continues to be hotly debated.[41] Right-wing scholars insist that the Basic Law constitutionalizes an individualistic social vision and a strong free market economic vision, while leftists argue that it constitutionally mandates a strongly redistributive state.[42]

THE "MATERIAL" *RECHTSSTAAT* One important ground for accommodating the *Rechtsstaat* and *Sozialstaat* concepts within the Basic Law is the distinction that had been drawn by the time of the Basic Law's drafting between the "formal" and "material" aspects of the *Rechtsstaat* idea. The formal aspect of the *Rechtsstaat* includes the familiar rule-of-law notions of separation of powers, independence of the judiciary, and administration on the basis of legality.[43] The material dimension of the principle is the innovative notion that facilitates a reconciliation with the *Sozialstaat.* This aspect envisions the Basic Law as committing the state to a set of fundamental ("higher") norms by which all state action must be evaluated. As one member of the Federal Constitutional Court explains,

> The logic of thinking about values and justice demands that the constitution conceived along the lines of the material *Rechtsstaat* should lay claim to an absolute validity extending to all spheres of social life . . . It no longer guarantees liberty unconditionally by way of formal legal demarcation; it does so only *within* the fundamental system of values embodied in the constitution.[44]

In other words, the *Rechtsstaat* is the source of a normative commitment of the Basic Law, one that obligates the legislature to act according to the demands of substantive, not merely formal, justice.[45] The basic thrust of the content of these demands is supplied, in turn, by the *Sozialstaat* principle.

"ORDOLIBERALISM" Another basis for reconciling the *Rechtsstaat* and *Sozialstaat* ideals came from the set of ideas sometimes referred to as "ordoliberalism." Ordoliberalism, a term that apparently first appeared in 1950,[46] refers to the revised version of liberalism that is associated with the so-called Freiburg School of German intellectuals in the immediate postwar period. These thinkers, who included economists like Walter Eucken and Alfred Müller-Armack and lawyers like Franz Böhm and Hans Gross-Doerth, used the failing of the Weimar Republic as well as of the Third Reich to identify the failings of classical liberalism, in the fields of both economics and law.

Ordoliberalism today is sometimes described in a way that makes it sound as though it were synonymous with "neoliberalism" or even libertarianism.[47] That is a misleading view. While ordoliberals were clearly committed to a competitive market economy, strongly opposing a command economy, and to property rights rather than state ownership, and in this sense certainly were "liberals," ordoliberals repudiated the libertarian vision of the laissez-faire minimalist state. To borrow a useful terminology, ordo members were "end-state" liberals rather than "process" liberals.[48] That is, they "presuppose[d] some ethical postulates—some ultimate aims which characterise a 'good society'."[49] As David Gerber explains, "Against the backdrop of chaos, devastation and amassed power, the ordoliberals set out to create a tolerant and humane society that would protect human dignity and personal freedom."[50] Aspects of the ordoliberal program had a decidedly progressive (in our sense of the term) cast, and it is these aspects on which I wish to focus. The point is not that ordoliberalism was a leftist program. That obviously cannot be maintained. Rather the point is to see how certain elements of ordoliberal thinking facilitated the effort to accommodate both the *Rechtsstaat* and *Sozialstaat* ideal within the Basic Law. In particular, these aspects of ordoliberalism, with its dual focus on free economic activity and controlling the behavior of economic agents in order to maintain the morally proper social order, are immediately evident in the Basic Law's property clause.

It was the work of the post–World War II ordoliberals that gave rise to the doctrine of the "social market economy."[51] Indeed, ordoliberalism and the social market economy doctrine are often used synonymously.[52] Ordoliberalism rejected efficiency as the sole or even the main objective of the liberal market economy. Rather, the proper economic order was the proper *social* order, one that "soften[ed] social strife, class differences and alienation of work."[53] As Alexander Rüstow stated,[54]

> The social market economy must be the servant of humanity and of trans-economic values. All social, ethical, cultural and human values are more important than the economy, yet the economy must prepare the ground for their fullest development. For this reason the economy must not take on forms which are incompatible with these trans-economic values.

Ordoliberals drew upon Christian ethics as well as socialism in an effort to accommodate social protection within a competitive market economy.[55] "Social security and social justice are the greatest concerns of our time," Eucken wrote in 1952.[56]

The means by which Ordoliberals sought to achieve this integration was through law, specifically the constitution. Even more specifically, it was their idea of the "economic constitution" that was the key to realizing their vision of the proper social and economic order.[57] Ordoliberals believed that the properly ordered society, one in which a market economy, individual freedom, and social and economic justice existed together in harmony, could develop only if the market was integrated within the law, specifically the constitution, rather than, as classical liberalism insisted, being categorically separated from politics and law. Classical liberalism's approach, ordoliberals thought, failed because it did not recognize that government is the only threat to individual liberty. Ordoliberals did not understand economic liberty merely in terms of free exchange between autonomous agents. Rather, it involved action within a given framework, one based on a set of ethics.[58] From this point of view, private institutions, especially large economic institutions, posed just as serious a threat to all forms of freedom as did the state, ordoliberals believed.[59] The idea of the economic constitution reflected their view that economic choices were not exogenous but resulted from legal and political decisions. Constitutions created not only a political but an economic framework as well.

The economic constitution was based on the notion of *Ordnungspolitik* (order-based policy).[60] The term resists translation, but the basic idea is that the constitution establishes the basic normative framework for the desired economic order and governmental actions must be directed toward implementing the ideals of that normative framework. This does not mean that the community's constitution serves as a complete economic as well as political blueprint, but that it creates a general framework for the state's responsibility within the economic realm. More concretely, the idea of *Ordnungspolitik,* as the ordoliberals conceived of it, reflected a social and political vision in which economic freedom imposed duties. Ordoliberals believed that, as one author explains, "Economic activity is an integrated part of . . . citizenship and so entails rights and duties."[61] The normative framework reflected in the constitution could be implemented in a market economy, one based on individual freedom of property and contract, only if all members of the political community acted in the interest of the principles they had chosen in their constitution. One implication of this view was that a strong state was required to prevent power from negating meaningful individual freedom and to prevent strong economic institutions from dominating both the market and society. The experience with a weak state in the Weimar Republic convinced the ordoliberals that a strong state had to protect the economy. At the same time, they relied on the legal process to monitor and discipline the state, just as the state protected the economy.

While the primary impact of ordoliberalism in post–World War II Germany was in the economic sphere, it also influenced the shaping of the new political constitution, the 1949 Basic Law. Here its influence was somewhat less direct but still highly significant. Ordoliberal ideas were widely disseminated through various channels, including Germany's leading newspaper.[62] Many political leaders, including some who participated in framing the new Basic Law, were committed to ordoliberal ideas. Most of these were members of the Christian Democratic Party (CDU), the main representative of the middle class, two of whose members, Konrad Adenauer and Ludwig Erhard, were the first two chancellors of the new republic. The CDU adopted the social welfare economy as an integral part of its program.[63]

The effect of the social market economy idea and of ordoliberalism's ideas generally on the Basic Law was to ameliorate the tension between the *Rechtsstaat* and *Sozialstaat.* By stressing socioeconomic justice as necessary for the realization of personal freedom and by redefining liberalism as requiring the integration of the public and private spheres, contrary to the classical conception of the rule of law, ordoliberalism helped undermine the possibility that the *Rechtsstaat* guarantee of the Basic Law would be read as requiring the establishment of a classical liberal state. Its views were more compatible with the "material" rather than the "formal" conception of the *Rechtsstaat* principle insofar as both emphasized the notion that the properly functioning social and economic order required the basic conditions of social justice, particularly the economic well-being of all members of the community. This shared social vision was not only compatible with the *Sozialstaat* idea but virtually required its recognition.

The harmonization of the *Rechtsstaat* and *Sozialstaat* principles had obvious implications for the Basic Law's right of property. It provided the footing for the ideas that private property inherently involved not just rights but duties as well and that the duty dimension of private property needed to be stressed every bit as much as the right dimension. This was the germ of the social-obligation norm in the Basic Law's property clause.[64]

THE *SOCIALSTAAT*, HUMAN DIGNITY, AND THE "IMAGE OF MAN" The final piece of constitutional background necessary to a complete understanding of the property clause's social-obligation provision is the most basic commitment in the entire German Basic Law—the commitment to the principle of human dignity (*Menschenwürde*).[65] It is no coincidence that the first article of the Basic Law is the provision that "[t]he dignity of man is inviolable. It is to be respected and safeguarded with the full authority of the State."[66] All other provisions of the Basic Law, including the property clause, must be interpreted in light of the commitment to human dignity.[67] While there is some disagreement about whether the Basic Law created a hierarchy of rights,[68] no one doubts that the right to human dignity is the bedrock of all other constitutional rights.[69] As the bedrock principle of the Basic Law, Article 1 is absolutely entrenched; the Basic Law expressly prohibits any repeal or amendment of it.[70]

Moreover, the Federal Constitutional Court has unambiguously stated that human dignity is the supreme value in the objective value system of the Basic Law.[71]

From an American perspective, the human dignity principle might appear to be in some tension with the *Sozialstaat* principle. To American ears, "human dignity" strongly resonates of the individualist outlook associated with classical liberalism, making the constitutional right negative rather than positive in character. In this sense, the interventionist character of the *Sozialstaat* seemingly contradicts the commitment to individual human dignity.

From the German perspective, however, this is a false trade-off.[72] The conception of human dignity that Article 1 embraces is not one based solely on classical liberalism. Individual human dignity exists in a social and economic context. It cannot be fully and meaningfully protected without attending to the concrete conditions in which individuals live. "[I]t is social conditions that determine the extent to which the individual is truly able to safeguard his own human dignity."[73]

The social aspect of the human dignity norm is evident in the German concept of the "image of man," that is, the nature of the human personality. This concept, which is central to the Federal Constitutional Court's dignitarian jurisprudence, defines the human personality as community centered. Thus, the court early and explicitly stated that "[t]he image of man in the Basic Law is not that of an isolated, sovereign individual; rather, the Basic Law has decided in favor of a relationship between individual and community in the sense of a person's dependence on and commitment to the community, without infringing upon a person's individual value."[74] Ernst Benda, the distinguished and influential former president (chief justice) of the Federal Constitutional Court's First Senate,[75] has noted that the Basic Law rejects the "individualistic conception of man derived from classical liberalism as well as the collectivist view."[76] Perhaps the most accurate description of this conception of the self is to say that it combines the Kantian injunction against treating people as means rather than ends[77] with a strongly communitarian ontology.[78]

SELF-DEVELOPMENT AS THE "FUNDAMENTAL PURPOSE" OF THE CONSTITUTIONAL PROPERTY RIGHT This "image of man" concept strongly influences German constitutional property jurisprudence. In deciding whether an interest is included or excluded from constitutional property,

German courts focus openly and heavily on what they refer to as the "fundamental purpose" of the constitutional right of property. The question that they always ask is whether constitutional protection of the interest would serve the fundamental purpose. That purpose is self-development. The fundamental value to be served by property as a constitutional right is securing in material terms a zone of personal independence that is necessary for proper self-development and responsible citizenship.[79] Property enables the individual to take responsibility for her own life and to participate in the development and functioning of the proper social order.

Perhaps the clearest exposition of this idea of self-development as the fundamental purpose of property was in the famous 1968 *Hamburg Flood Control Case.*[80] The case involved a challenge to a 1964 statute enacted by the city-state of Hamburg that converted all grassland that the state classified as "dikeland" into public property. The statute terminated private ownership of such lands, but it did require that owners be compensated. Several owners of dikeland claimed that the statute violated their fundamental right to property under Article 14.

The basis of this claim illustrates one major difference between the American and German approaches to constitutionally protecting property. Under the American constitution, assuming that the amount of compensation was adequate (and there was no allegation in the case that it was not), there simply would be no basis for a constitutional challenge at all. The purpose of the governmental measure was to build an effective system of dikes in the wake of the devastating floods that hit Hamburg in 1962—certainly public enough to satisfy our weak "public use" requirement.[81] Under our takings clause, once the publicness of the governmental encroachment and the sufficiency of monetary compensation have been satisfied, there is no basis for constitutionally challenging the measure.

German constitutional jurisprudence does not treat property as a market commodity but as a civil, and one may say *civic,* right. The court in the *Hamburg Flood Control Case* made it clear that the core purpose of property as a basic constitutional right is not economic but personal and moral. It stated,

> To hold that property is an elementary constitutional right must be seen in the close context of protection of personal liberty. Within the general system of constitutional rights, its function is to secure its holder a sphere of liberty in the economic field *and thereby enable him to lead a self-governing life.*[82]

The last phrase signals the animating idea behind the constitutional role of property under the German Basic Law—self-governance. Property is a necessary condition for autonomous individuals to experience control over their own lives. Without property, they lack the material means necessary for a full and healthy development of their personality. The court made the connection between property and personhood explicit in its opinion. It stated, "[T]he property guarantee under Article 14 I 2 must be seen in relationship to the personhood of the owner—that is, to the realm of freedom within which persons engage in self-defining, responsible activity."[83]

This conception of the core function of property in some respects echoes what some recent American scholars, most notably Margaret Jane Radin and C. Edwin Baker, drawing on Hegel, have called the "personhood function."[84] As Radin explains, the premise of this understanding is that "to achieve proper self-development—to be a person—an individual needs some control over resources in the external environment."[85] The purpose of legal property rights, then, is to secure the requisite degree of control—self-determination—as a necessary means of facilitating self-development. The theory is most closely associated with Hegel, but Hegel and his followers were by no means the first or the only political philosophers to explain and justify property rights on the basis (and to the extent of) the proper development of the self.[86] Rousseau, for example, developed a comparable theory of property that stressed the importance of property to the proper and full development of the personality.[87] For Rousseau, private ownership was morally justifiable only to the extent that it fulfilled that function.

As the Federal Constitutional Court's opinion makes clear, the German idea of the constitutional property right shares with the self-developmental tradition a conception of liberty that differs from the classical Anglo-American understanding of that term. Borrowing the distinction made famous by Isaiah Berlin,[88] one can say that German constitutional law, like the Hegelian theory of property and the self, understands liberty in its positive as well as a negative sense, that is, freedom *to* rather than freedom *from*.[89] It may be more accurate to describe the German constitutional conception of liberty, in its relation to property, as blending the positive and negative dimensions. The individual owner's freedom from external interference with his property is valued just because it is a precondition for him to act in a way that is necessary to realization of the self. Put differently, property and liberty are connected with each other, not solely through a politics of fear of the state, but through a politics of enabling self-governance. The point of protecting individual ownership is not to create a zone of security from a powerful and threatening state but to make it possible for individuals to realize their own human potential.

The Basic Structure of Article 14

The Dual Guarantees

Unlike the constitutional property clauses of many other countries,[90] Article 14 is stated as a positive guarantee: "Property and the right of inheritance are guaranteed."[91] The guarantee is not absolute, of course; no constitution can absolutely guarantee the right of property. Even if it were possible to do so, the remaining provisions of Article 14, the social-obligation clause (Article 14(2)) and the expropriation clause (Article 14(3)), make it clear that this was not the intent. Moreover, as we have seen, Article 14's guarantee has to be read against the background of the Basic Law's overriding commitment to the protection of human dignity.

The Federal Constitutional Court has repeatedly explained that the property guarantee must be understood in terms of its "fundamental purpose," which itself is directly shaped by the commitment to human dignity. That fundamental purpose of the constitutional property right, as formulated by the court, is to secure for the right holder an area of personal liberty in the "patrimonial" world that enables the individual to take responsibility for the full development of the self as a member of the polity.[92] The purpose, in other words, is not to protect property, rather it is to protect the individual's liberty. Liberty, in turn, is not a goal in itself. Liberty is valued as a necessary condition for enabling the individual to participate in the development of the proper social, legal, and political order.[93] It is the ability and opportunity to participate in the creation and maintenance of that order that is the ultimate purpose of constitutional property. Every aspect of Article 14, including the level of compensation, is analyzed in light of this fundamental purpose.

The positive aspect of Article 14's guarantee is not intended to create claim rights against the state for provision of resources.[94] It does not even guarantee that individuals will be able to acquire property on their own. In this sense the individual guarantee operates in substantially the same fashion as the American negative constitutional property right under the Fifth Amendment. Article 14 really creates two guarantees, a positive guarantee, which applies to the *institution* of private property (*Institutionsgarantie*), and a negative guarantee, which applies to the *individual* right (*Bestandsgarantie*). The negative, individual guarantee is more closely associated with the negative provisions of Article 14, sections 2 (the social-obligation clause) and 3 (the expropriation clause),[95] while the positive, institutional guarantee is tied to the positive statement in Article 14(1).

This dual-guarantee approach is important because it underscores the fact that the constitutional right of property in Germany has neither a libertarian nor a utilitarian (that is, social wealth-maximizing) aim. Rather its aim is moral and civic. The individual guarantee enables individuals to live and develop as autonomous moral agents who are capable of taking responsibility for their own lives. The institutional guarantee ensures the existence of a basic component of the proper social and political order. It does so by preventing the state from abolishing the institution of private ownership of property or eliminating entire categories of property, like land, water, or other natural resources, from the sphere of private ownership.[96] In this way it facilitates the individual guarantee's purpose by protecting the sphere of personal autonomy that is a prerequisite for the citizen's participation in creating and maintaining the proper social order.

Compensation

Article 14's fundamentally social objective is indicated by its treatment of the compensation requirement. Its only direction regarding the level of compensation that must be paid in cases of property expropriation is the following sentence in Article 14(3): "Compensation shall reflect an equitable balance between the public interest and the interests of those affected." The courts have interpreted that language to mean that full fair market value need not always be paid. How much compensation is required in terms of the injunction to maintain an equitable balance between the public interest and the interests of affected owners has to be judged with the basic purpose of the constitutional right of property and the principle of proportionality in mind. In practice this means that the expropriating legislation should specify a framework within which the amount of compensation can be determined under the facts of the specific case.[97] Certainly the property's fair market value and the owner's financial loss are relevant factors, but their weight is judged according to the immediate circumstances and the public interest that is involved in the expropriation.[98] In the typical case, the balance is struck by paying full market value to the owner.[99] But in some cases, less than market value has been held to be a constitutionally valid level of compensation. In the famous *Hamburg Flood Control* (*Deichordnung*) *Case*, for example, the Federal Constitutional Court held that the extraordinary public interest in controlling the land joining the dikes in Hamburg justified payment of less than full market value.

Regulation and Limitation of Property

No constitution's guarantee of property immunizes it, either as an institution or a right, from all state regulatory control. The German Basic Law, like all constitutional property clauses, explicitly gives the legislature the power to expropriate private property so long as it is done in the proper manner and with payment of compensation.[100] Apart from the power of expropriation, legislatures and administrative agencies always have *some* power to regulate property in *some* fashion without compensating the affected owner. The hard question is how a court will go about determining whether the legislature has exceeded the scope of its legitimate power to regulate property without paying compensation.

THE UNCERTAIN STATUS OF INVERSE CONDEMNATION AND THE INSTITUTIONAL TENSION BETWEEN THE CONSTITUTIONAL AND CIVIL COURTS OVER COMPENSATION PRACTICES A highly important preliminary point concerns the effect of finding that a regulation is excessive, that is, exceeds its proper scope. A property regulation may be considered excessive under German constitutional law for either of two reasons: first, because there is no proper statutory authorization for it; or second, because it distributes the burdens of the regulation in such a way that one or a few individuals carry disproportionately heavier burdens than other owners who are similarly situated. The latter problem has been especially problematic doctrinally since it falls within the gray area between mere regulation and expropriation. It is tantamount to what in American takings law is called "regulatory takings." The question is whether the remedy available to the court is limited to declaring the regulation invalid. May the court award money damages to the property owner in this situation?

In the United States today, in cases of regulatory takings the court is not limited to declaring the regulation invalid. Money damages may be awarded where the taking occurs as the result of regulatory takings as well as in cases of direct expropriations. Actions for damages for regulatory takings are known as "inverse condemnation" proceedings.[101] American state courts have permitted such proceedings for many years, and now the U.S. Supreme Court has recognized this remedy as well.[102]

The doctrinal situation is far less clear in German law. What is clear is that in Germany, as in the United States and other jurisdictions with constitutional property clauses, when the government takes property through a direct expropriation or condemnation, as it is called in the United States, it must pay compensation. However, since 1981, the German Constitutional

Court has held that, according to the terms of Article 14, expropriatory compensation may be awarded only in cases of actual statutory or administrative expropriations, that is, legislative or administrative actions that satisfy the terms of Article 14(3). In cases of property regulations that do not meet the requirements of Articles 14(1) or 14(2), that is, in cases of what American constitutional lawyers would call "regulatory takings," the court's power is restricted to declaring the regulation unconstitutional and void. It may not treat the regulation as a de facto expropriation and then order payment of money.[103] The proper route, the German court said, is for the aggrieved owners to attack the validity of the regulation in the administrative courts rather than to seek expropriatory compensation. The court's position was that Article 14(3) imposes clear and strict requirements for any legislative or administrative action to constitute an expropriation, for which compensation must be awarded. The most important of the requirements, which is not met in cases of regulations, is the so-called linking clause (*Junktim-Klausel*) in Article 14(3)(ii), which provides that an expropriation shall be legitimate only if it is authorized by a law that provides for the nature and extent of compensation. Regulations do not satisfy this requirement; hence, the court has said, expropriatory compensation cannot be awarded on their authority.

The court's position was intended to stop a practice in which the civil (nonconstitutional) courts have engaged since 1952.[104] In particular, the civil and administrative courts[105] in 1952 began to apply the doctrine of an "unusual sacrifice" (*Sonderopfer*)[106] in a way that very much resembles inverse condemnation. The unusual-sacrifice doctrine had previously been applied in cases of formal, or explicit, expropriation. The civil and administrative courts went further and applied it in cases where there was no expropriation within the meaning of Article 14(3), drawing on an analogy between actual expropriations and two sorts of regulatory actions. The two regulatory situations to which they extended the unusual-sacrifice doctrine were, first, where a regulation attacked in civil court was not properly authorized and therefore unlawful and, second, where the challenged regulation was properly authorized but considered a disproportionate exercise of the state's power to regulate property.[107] In both instances the civil courts awarded compensation to the owners who were forced to make the excessive sacrifice, despite the fact that there was no formal expropriation for which compensation would be justified under Article 14(3). For these courts, the analogy to such an expropriation was enough.

The theory the courts used was that of an "equalization right" (*Ausgleichsanspruch*).[108] Equalization commonly takes a nonmonetary form. A widely cited example comes from an earlier decision of the Federal Court of Justice, which concerned the problem of excessive noise resulting from a project changing a quiet residential street into a major thoroughfare.[109] The court held that the administrative authorities have several options, including installing noise-reducing barriers such as walls. If such measures are inadequate or not feasible, the developer should rely on the affected owners to insulate their properties by double-glazing their windows or the like and provide them with the necessary funds to do so. As a last resort, the developer should ameliorate the harmful effect of the project by providing appropriate compensation for damage to or loss of use of the property.

The courts rationalized equalization in terms of private law doctrine. Under German tort law, a landowner who is forced to sacrifice some property interest in order to serve some higher social interest is considered a victim who is entitled to compensation. Under this theory, the equalization award is considered comparable to compensation for tort-like injuries rather than constitutional compensation for formal expropriation. Applying this theory to the public law context then, equalization, in these courts' view, is not compensation for an expropriation as such, for there has been no such expropriation. Rather, the equalization benefit, which again is usually nonmonetary in form, is intended to ameliorate the disproportionately burdensome effect of some public property scheme. Normally, if a property regulation or scheme violates the principle of proportionality the result is that the property regulation is held unconstitutional.[110] Equalization can sometimes prevent the regulation from being held unconstitutional by mitigating the degree of disproportionate effects. With respect to the doctrine of unusual sacrifice, the ramification of these nonconstitutional court decisions is that the doctrine applies in the courts (primarily the administrative courts) as a means of determining that a particular regulatory limitation on property would be disproportionate but for the cushioning effect of a state-conferred equalization benefit.[111]

In the famous 1981 *Naßauskiesung* decision,[112] the Federal Constitutional Court addressed the equalization practice, but it did so in less than clear terms. What the court did make clear was that under Article 14 monetary compensation can be awarded only in cases of actual expropriation, that is, for legislative or administrative actions that meet the terms of Article 14(3). Specifically, this means that compensation may be awarded only "pursuant to a law which determines the nature and extent of compensation." The practice of providing compensation, *as such,* to the affected owner in order to ameliorate the problem of unusual sacrifice, the court said, is inconsistent with this requirement. The court was uncomfortable with the practice of providing equalization measures, as some tension existed, at least from the court's perspective, between that practice and the *Junktim Klausel* requirement for expropriations. But the court did not unambiguously foreclose the possible use of equalization measures that were not intended to be compensation for expropriation. The court was equally murky about whether such noncompensatory equalization measures required statutory authorization.

The nonconstitutional courts persisted in their practice of providing for equalization. In post-*Naßauskiesung* cases,[113] courts provided equalization in cases where the regulation was lawfully authorized but excessive, that is, imposed an "unusual sacrifice."[114] These decisions created some degree of tension between the Federal Constitutional Court and the high nonconstitutional courts, especially the Federal Court of Justice and the Federal Administrative Court.

The institutional and doctrinal tension between these courts over the equalization practice appears to have been resolved by the 1999 decision of the Federal Constitutional Court in the *Denkmalschutz* case (*Monument Protection Case*).[115] It is worth pausing on that case because it clarifies the practice and validity of the equalization practice.

The case involved a challenge to the constitutionality of the Monument Protection Act of the state (*Land*) of Rhineland-Palatinate. The claimant was the owner of a villa built during the *Grunderzeit,* a period during the late nineteenth century known for the grandeur of its buildings. The villa was subject to protection under the Act and could not be demolished without the state's permission. The owner wished to demolish the villa because its upkeep had become prohibitively expensive and the owner was not permitted to use it as an apartment building or for any nonresidential purpose. The owner had been unable to find any buyer, and the villa had remained empty since 1981. His application to demolish it was denied under the Act, despite the fact that the building had no market value for the owner and in fact it was costing the owner a substantial amount of money just to continue owning it. The basis for the denial was the fact that under the Act the regulatory agency should only consider the public interest in reviewing an application for demolition and not the owner's interest.

The Federal Constitutional Court found that the use restriction under the Act was a *regulation* and not an *expropriation* under Article 14.[116] If it had been found to be an expropriation, then under Article 14(3), the owner would have been entitled to compensation, but not if it were found to be a regulation. The basis for testing the validity of the Act being viewed as a regulation was Article 14(1), and the only remedy for a regulation that violated

Article 14(1) was a ruling holding the statute invalid. The argument had been made that the statute should be treated as an expropriation because it produced an extremely harsh effect on the owner, but the court squarely rejected that theory, just as it had previously rejected it in the *Naßauskiesung* case. Regulatory intention, not impact, the court plainly said, was the basis for determining whether the restriction was a regulation or an expropriation. Even when the impact is so severe that nothing remains of the content of ownership of the property—circumstances that made the factual setting of the case very similar to that in the American *Lucas* case—the use restriction is still not treated as a compensable expropriation where the legislature, as here, did not intend to remove the asset from the owner. The upshot of this approach is to create a categorical dichotomy between regulations and expropriation, eliminating any overlap or middle ground between them.[117]

Having determined that the Act should be treated as a regulation, the court held that the Act violated Article 14(1) and was therefore invalid. The decisive factor appears to have been the fact that no meaningful possibilities remained for using the building. Under such a heavy burden, the court indicated, the relationship can no longer be considered to be ownership. This suggests that the Federal Constitutional Court is prepared in certain circumstances to treat the intensity of impact as determinative.[118]

That did not end the matter, however. The court went on to consider whether the problem with the regulation's excessive impact on the owner might be remedied not through compensation for an expropriation but through some form of equalization. The court said that where the degree of disproportionality is not intense, the matter should not wind up in court but should be managed administratively by way of some nonmonetary form of equalization, such as noise abatement devices, for which provision was already made. More important, the court indicated that the legislature should anticipate and leave room in the regulatory measure for the possible need for equalization. Presumably, this means including a clause (*salvatorische Entschädigungsklausen*) in the regulatory statute allowing the relevant agency in its discretion to make equalization in the appropriate fashion. The importance of this aspect of the case is that it seems to indicate that in instances where the unusual sacrifice was totally unforeseen and no provision was made in the regulation for equalization, the regulatory action is unconstitutional as a result of its disproportionate effects and cannot be salvaged by equalization that really does not fit within the regulatory scheme in question. This aspect of the case clearly ties equalization to the *Junktim Klausel* requirement, about which the court had expressed concern in the *Naßaus-*

kiesung case, and it sets a stricter test for equalization than the civil and administrative courts had used. Legislatures subsequently have taken this suggestion seriously, routinely adding such clauses to much land-use regulation, especially in the areas of historical and cultural heritage protection.[119]

Where does this leave us, then, with regard to the question about the availability of inverse condemnation in Germany? Unfortunately, there is no simple answer. The shortest possible answer is that the *theory* of the American doctrine of inverse condemnation has been rejected by both constitutional and nonconstitutional courts. Both courts agree that if there has been no formal expropriation in terms of Article 14(3), a challenged regulation may not treated as though it were an expropriation, with compensation being available to the affected owner who challenges such the offending regulation. That is clearly not possible under German law.

It is also clear that equalization is not the functional equivalent of the compensation payment that is made by American courts in inverse condemnation cases. Equalization and inverse condemnation differ in several important respects. Most important, in inverse condemnation proceedings, money (and only money, unlike equalization) is awarded as full compensation for a de facto expropriation, rather than, as equalization provides, as protection against or mitigation for the negative effects of a property regulation. Another important difference is that in inverse condemnation cases courts award money damages without legislative authorization. The court in effect tells the legislature or the administrative agency that promulgated the challenged measure that it was wrong to treat the measure as a mere regulation. The measure, the court says, in fact is an expropriation (a "taking," in American parlance). That is not at all the implication of equalization. The regulation remains a regulation, one that would have been unconstitutional but for equalization. Moreover, the *effect* of equalization is similar to the effect of compensation in inverse condemnation. In both cases, the result is to sustain the validity of the property regulation. Were no equalization payment made, under German law the regulation would be unconstitutional according to Article 14(1) and (2), using the metric of the proportionality principle. Similarly, were compensation not paid in inverse condemnation cases, the regulation would be struck down.

The point is not that equalization means that there is something like inverse condemnation in German law. There is not. The point rather is that the simple statement that inverse condemnation is not available in German law ignores a degree of complexity in German constitutional practice that must be taken into account in order to provide a "thick description"[120] of German constitutional property jurisprudence.

LIMITATIONAL VERSUS DEFINITIONAL APPROACH In general, courts have tended to follow either of two methods for analyzing exercises of the state's power to regulate property rights without compensation that are challenged on the grounds that they are constitutionally excessive. One is what has been called a *definitional* approach, and the other, a *limitational* (or "justification," as it has also been called[121]) approach.[122] The basic difference is this: under the definitional approach the focus is on whether the specific entitlement asserted is or is not "property" for constitutional purposes and whether or not the challenged restriction is or is not a "taking." Definitions, rather than straightforward judgments about whether the action is a constitutionally justified limitation on property, do most of the work. Under the limitational approach, rather than focusing heavily on such questions as "Is this interest property?" and "Is the government's action a taking?" the court focuses on whether the limitation that the state has imposed on the property interest is constitutionally justified. Usually this analysis is implemented through a multistep proportionality principle, which somewhat resembles a balancing approach. American takings jurisprudence is an example, par excellence, of the definitional approach.[123] Germany is an example of the limitational approach.

In most jurisdictions that follow the limitational approach the basis for that analytical method is an expressly stated general limitation clause in the constitution. Germany is an exception. The Basic Law contains no general limitations clause. Two express provisions of the Basic Law do provide general restrictions on constitutionally valid limitations of all fundamental rights, including property, but these provisions have not been very influential in the court's reasoning.[124] Article 19(1) specifies formal requirements for restrictions on such rights,[125] while Article 19(2) provides an outer restriction on the legislature's constitutional authority to limit any fundamental right. It states, "In no case may the essential content of a basic right be encroached upon."[126] As David Currie has pointed out,[127] however, this provision has had little effect in the Federal Constitutional Court's decisions, primarily because the proportionality principle, which because of its importance I will discuss separately,[128] does most of the analytical work in evaluating the constitutional validity of restrictions of fundamental rights, including property.

Three other sources provide the real bases for the German court's limitational approach to defining the state's power to regulate the individual right of property. These are, first, the specific constitutional provision stating the right in question (in this case, Article 14); second, the *Rechtsstaat* idea, via the proportionality principle; and third, the purposive approach, which the court takes in analyzing questions about the scope of all fundamental rights, including property.[129] All three of these sources will be discussed in more detail later,[130] but some comments on how the property clause itself invites, if not requires, a limitational rather than a definitional approach are in order at this point.

Article 14(1)(ii) states that "the contents and limits [of property] are determined by law [that is, the legislature]."[131] This provision does not mean that the legislature has free rein to decide what the "contents and limits" of ownership are. The institutional and individual guarantees of property assure that this is not the case. Article 19(2) enjoins the legislature against encroaching upon the "essence" of the property right. It is the Federal Constitutional Court's task to determine what that essence is and whether the legislature has exceeded its legitimate authority to define the contents and limits of property in a particular case.

At least as important as the contents and limits clause, if not more so, is the social-obligation norm of Article 14(2), which provides a direct source for the limits of the constitutional property right. It states, "Property entails obligations. Its use should also serve the public weal." As I will discuss in more detail later,[132] this provision serves as a kind of general overlay on the individual guarantee of property rights in Article 14(1). Article 14(1) always has to be read together with Article 14(2). The aim, the court has said, is to strike an equitable balance between individual liberty, understood in terms of the fundamental purpose of making property a matter of constitutional protection, and the common welfare.[133]

With respect to the institutional guarantee of property, the court has largely analyzed the scope of the legislature's regulatory power on the basis of the fundamental purpose of the property guarantee. For example, the court has held that the legislature may remove a whole category of property from the sphere of private rights altogether where the social value and the purpose of the type of property are sufficiently great to justify removing that category from private control.[134] The institutional guarantee of property does not mean that resources that were once within the sphere of private control must remain there. Where it becomes apparent that allowing a resource to remain within private control, including the power to transfer by market exchange or otherwise, seriously jeopardizes the community's well-being, the legislature does not violate the Basic Law's institutional guarantee of property by removing that category of property from the private realm altogether. Here, once again, the fundamental purpose of the property right, as the court has defined it, works in close tandem with the social-obligation norm of Article 14(2) to establish a broad power of the legislature to define the limits of the constitutional right of property.

What Counts as "Property"?

The Basic Law does not define "property" (*Eigentum*). This leaves the question, what range of interests are protected under Article 14? The fact that the Federal Constitutional Court uses a limitational rather than a definitional approach to determining the constitutional validity of state regulations of property does not mean that it can entirely avoid the question of what counts as property for constitutional purposes. The definitional question still must be addressed occasionally. The usual occasion for raising it is when the asserted interest is not a traditional property interest.

PROPERTY DEFINED ACCORDING TO ITS "FUNDAMENTAL PURPOSE"

Unlike the American Supreme Court, the German Constitutional Court has been clear about the legal sources that it uses and does not use to define what interests count as property for constitutional purposes.[135] One source that the German court does not use, or at least on which it places little weight, is the text of the constitution itself. Rather than purporting to base its decisions on direct textual interpretation, the court has stated that it relies on the "fundamental purpose" of property as a constitutional right and on the substantive values that animate the Basic Law as a whole. As we have seen,[136] that purpose is securing a sphere of personal liberty necessary for the individual to take responsibility for her own life and to participate in the development and functioning of the proper social order. In deciding whether an interest is included in or excluded from constitutional property, the question is whether constitutional protection of the interest would serve this fundamental purpose. Is the interest one that will facilitate the purpose of enabling the individual's self-development, both as an autonomous moral agent and as a participating member of the community?

CONSTITUTIONAL PROPERTY IS NOT DEPENDENT ON PRIVATE LAW

The Federal Constitutional Court has rejected a second possible source of property under the Basic Law. The constitutional conception of property is not dependent upon the private law concept, as defined by the German Civil Code (*Bürgerliches Gesetzbuch,* or BGB).[137] The court has unambiguously rejected a historical-positivist approach to defining constitutional property. The court's decision to decouple the public and private law meanings of property is based on the fact that the right guaranteed by Article 14 *is* a constitutional, not a private law, right.[138] The purposes of property as a constitutional right are not identical to those underlying traditional private law, and it is the constitution's values that control what can be property under Article 14. Whether any given interest is or is not a constitutionally protected interest has to be determined from the constitution as a whole and the fundamental value that the constitutional property right is intended to serve rather than being controlled by the private law meaning.[139]

This approach avoids temporally freezing the meaning of constitutional property to any particular historical moment, permitting Article 14's protection over time to embrace new sorts of interests, unprecedented in the historic private law of property. The result has been a constitutional concept of property that is considerably broader than the private law meaning provided in the BGB.[140] Of course, all "ordinary" interests, that is, private law property interests, are included in the constitutional meaning. But the established private law meaning serves only as a point of departure for the constitutional meaning of property.

The court's rejection of a historical-positivist basis for defining constitutional property has been controversial. One case illustrating the controversy of the court's more expansive reading is the so-called *Landlord-Tenant Case.*[141] What was at issue in the case was the validity of a landlord's exercise of her statutorily authorized power to cancel a lease. German statutory law gives tenants a wide measure of protection against eviction and rent increases, but it does allow landlords to evict under some circumstances. One such circumstance was involved here, namely, the landlord's intention to use the premises for her own benefit. The landlord, who was in poor health, lived in an apartment one floor below the tenant's apartment and wanted to have her son live in the tenant's apartment so that he could take care of her. The court denied the owner's application for cancellation and eviction, reasoning that the owner could not prove that eviction, which under existing rent-control law could only be justified by her need to use the premises for her own purposes, was really necessary. The landlord's son lived in an apartment in a house next door to his mother's, so the level of necessity for eviction was not great.

The controversial aspect of the case was the preliminary question whether the tenant had a property (ownership) interest protected under Article 14. The tenant claimed that he did under Article 14(2), the social-obligation provision, and that granting the eviction order infringed on that right. The court concluded that the tenant did indeed have a property interest but not under Article 14(2), which, the court said, only provides the legislature with a standard with which to define the contents and limits of property and does not create subjective rights. The tenant's property interest instead rests, the court said, in Article 14(1), just as the landlord's ownership interest does. Both the landlord and the tenant, then, have property interests in terms of Article 14, although they have different forms of property interests. The court premised its decision that the tenant does have a constitutionally recognizable property interest on the central function of the constitutional property right, namely, to secure for individuals an area of freedom in the material sphere within which they can take responsibility for developing and controlling their own lives. The home, the court said, is critical to this purpose, and in this sense the tenant's lease interest fulfills the interest that tangible property serves for others. Rent-control laws are one way in which the state protects the tenant's interest, and this protection is enforceable against everyone, including the landlord. Rent-control legislation strikes an equitable balance between the interests of the tenant and those of the landlord with due regard for the proportionality principle.

The conclusion that the tenant had a constitutionally protected property interest under any part of Article 14 has drawn strong criticism.[142] While traditional private law doctrine certainly recognizes the tenant's interest as a subjective right that is legislatively protectable in various ways, critics of the decision have argued that it does not fall within the Civil Code's (BGB's) definition of ownership. Section 903 of the BGB defines ownership as including the unlimited right to dispose of the asset and to exclude the rest of the world from its use.[143] These critics have reasoned that, contrary to the court's reasoning, the tenant has only a right of use and occupancy, not an unlimited right of disposal. The effect of the decision, they object, is that the court has now functionally split ownership between landlord and tenant in flagrant disregard for the civil law's traditional unitary conception of ownership, which rejects anything like the Anglo-American "bundle-of-rights" conception of ownership.[144]

The objection perhaps is understandable but ultimately without merit. Although the court attempted to reconcile its conclusion with the BGB's definition of ownership, its analysis was primarily based on functional considerations. The court reasoned that the tenant's occupancy right is "property" for constitutional purposes because it serves the same purpose as the traditional property owner's interest does, that is, it secures a sphere of personal autonomy in which the individual takes responsibility for her own life as a member of the community.[145] The family home, including a rented apartment, is so important to fulfilling this objective that it can be described as being at the core of human existence. For this reason, while the landlord's interest certainly is property, so also is the tenant's. The effect is to recognize two simultaneously existing ownership interests, seemingly in contradiction to the civil law idea of ownership.

By departing from the civil law's traditional unitary conception of ownership, the case rejects what Andre van der Walt has called "private law fundamentalism." [146] It eliminates any basis for claiming that the constitutional meaning of property is the same as that of private law or that private law controls the scope and meaning of property for constitutional purposes.

Does the case open the door for adoption of the bundle-of-rights conception of ownership in Germany, at least for constitutional purposes? This seems highly unlikely. The constitutional meaning of ownership (or property), while not tied to the traditional private law meaning, nevertheless seems likely to remain unitary in the sense that it is more than just the sum of its parts. Conceptually, it would be difficult to interpret Article 14, taking all of its sections together as a whole, as it is understood, in a way that permits the disaggregated bundle-of-rights conception. Rather than being read as being predicated on some version of the bundle-of-rights conception, the *Landlord-Tenant Case* is better read as simply saying that the tenant had a constitutional property interest that is different from the landlord's private law ownership interest. Read that way, the decision does not attempt to split the traditional ownership atom.[147]

PROPERTY AS THINGS, NOT WEALTH The Federal Constitutional Court has interpreted the statement in Article 14(1) that "[p]roperty [is] guaranteed" to mean that the property clause does not protect wealth as such. What Article 14 protects are discrete, concrete assets, not wealth or value.[148] As the court stated in one case, "The function of Article 14 is not primarily to prevent the taking of property without compensation—although in this respect it offers greater protection than Article 153 of the Weimar Constitution [149]—but rather *to secure existing property in the hands of its owner.*" [150] To paraphrase Justice Holmes's famous quip in *Lochner v. New York,* [151] the German Basic Law does not adopt Judge Richard Posner's legal economics. The German Constitutional Court rejects an interpretation of the property clause that views economic efficiency as the primary purpose for constitutionally protecting property interests. This view reflects, once again, the crucial role that is played by the court's definition of the substantive purpose of the constitutional protection of property. The primary purpose for protecting property as a fundamental right under the German constitution is rather to secure the material conditions necessary for each person's self-development.

The public interest requirement of Article 14(3) implements this interpretation of the guarantee of Article 14(1). It provides that "[e]xpropriation shall only be permissible in the public interest."[152] The requirement that expropriations may be made only if a public necessity exists underscores the fact that property and wealth are not always interchangeable under the Basic Law. An expropriation is not constitutionally valid merely because the legislature paid the owner adequate compensation.[153]

"THE NEW PROPERTY" UNDER ARTICLE 14 Perhaps the clearest difference between the private law and constitutional definitions of property is the inclusion of at least some government entitlements (*öffentlich-rechtliche Rechtspositionen*) in the realm of constitutionally protected interests. No line of decisions better illustrates the relationship between the fundamental constitutional values and constitutional protection of property than cases dealing with the status of social benefits as constitutional property.

In general, German constitutional law does recognize some but not all forms of public or social benefit interests, or what Charles Reich called "the New Property,"[154] as property for constitutional purposes. Examples of protectable interests include pension expectancies (*Rentenanwartschaften*), that is, claims to payments from a statutory pension scheme;[155] medical insurance;[156] and unemployment insurance.[157]

Public social benefit interests are constitutionally protected only if they serve the basic purpose of the property guarantee, namely, to protect the sphere of personal autonomy that enables the individual to constitute and organize her life in the material realm. Specifically, three requirements must be met.[158] First, the interest must be one that is aimed at securing the individual's existence or subsistence (*Existenzsicherung*). Second, it must have vested in the beneficiary and be her own in a meaningful sense. Purely discretionary state payments are not protected by Article 14.[159] Third, the beneficiary must have acquired the right, at least in part, as a result of her own personal and substantial contributions (*Eigenleistung*). This requirement may be met not only by premiums paid directly by the beneficiary herself but also by premiums paid on her behalf by third parties, including her employer.[160] The degree of the personal contributions is not fixed. The court has stated, "For premiums that [like those in the instant case] are produced throughout the year at varying levels because of changing legislation, a complete examination will be required for fixing the degree of the personal contribution."[161]

The *Eigenleistung* requirement effectively excludes from constitutional protection those public law entitlements that are based solely on the state's duty to provide welfare maintenance. One example is social security benefits that are strictly transfer payments by the state, that is, "pure" welfare benefits. These do not qualify as constitutional property for purposes of Article 14. Other examples of excluded interests are housing subsidies[162] and family allowances.[163] The personal contribution (*Eigenleistung*) requirement is not satisfied by the fact that the claimant has paid taxes, which indirectly fund the program in question. The contributions must have been made directly to the program itself. To hold otherwise would effectively eviscerate the requirement, for few claimants will have paid nothing to the state through taxes or other contributions to the public fisc.

A well-known 1985 decision of the Federal Constitutional Court illustrates the interaction among these three requirements. The issue in the case was whether Article 14 covered the interest of beneficiaries of a federal program providing medical benefits for the elderly.[164] More specifically, the question was whether later statutory amendments that introduced additional requirements for receiving the benefits violated Article 14. The court held that they did not.

The threshold question was whether such benefits counted as property under Article 14. The court concluded that the interests of some but not all of the claimants were property for Article 14 purposes. Referring to the *Existenzsicherung* requirement, the court said, "The feature that constitutes the basis for protecting as property a legal entitlement to social security is that it should serve the subsistence-level security of the person entitled."[165] The court provided the following rule of thumb for determining whether this requirement is met: "Legal protection for social insurance interests is possible only in the event that their termination or reduction would vitally affect the freedom-assurance function of the constitutional guarantee of ownership."[166] The court noted that many entitlement claims in social insurance law clearly do not involve any consequences for the claimant's personal subsistence. Claims of that sort do not merit the constitutional guarantee of property ownership. At the same time, however, it is not necessary that the claimant be destitute or poor. Protected pensioners include white-collar employees (*Angestellten*) as much as they do blue-collar workers (*Arbeiter*). The court expressly observed that in German society "the great majority of citizens . . . expect their subsistence-level security to come more from employment-based programs than from their own personal resources."[167] Medical insurance claims, for example, qualify as property if they promote the well-being of a majority of the population and if the benefits have been paid as an essential service over a long period of time.

While this line of thinking obviously does reflect the strong influence of

Germany's status (explicitly recognized in its Basic Law) as a social welfare state, it is *not* a version of state socialism. While the state and its benefits play a large role in Germany, so too does private property. The German economy is, it bears remembering, predominately a market economy. The court's point in the *Eigenleistung* case is that the core constitutional function of property is to provide the material security that is necessary for both human dignity and civic self-governance. In the German scheme, that function is served by both private wealth and certain public benefits.

The problem in the case was not the *Existenzsicherung* requirement but the other two requirements. The vesting requirement was problematic because under the program payments are partly in the state's discretion. The court said that this fact alone did not disqualify the interest from being considered property for Article 14 purposes. The third requirement, that of personal contribution (*Eigenleistung*), was more problematic. The difficulty was the fact that the claimants, as pensioners, no longer made payments to the program, so that the benefits were now state supported. The mere fact that the benefits were supported in part by state funds did not mean that the personal contribution requirement was not met, although the legislature's power to determine the contents and limits of the rights in question increases when the proportion of the state subsidy is higher. The court stated that the question whether the right to the benefits in programs of this sort was based, at least to a noninsignificant extent, on the claimant's own contributions has to be answered on the basis of the specific facts involved. The court specified several factors to be taken into account in making that determination. Among these are the level of both the claimant's own contributions and those by third parties (for example, employers) on the claimant's behalf and whether the contributions have changed considerably over time. Applying all of these factors together, the court concluded that the interests of some of the claimants did constitute property. That conclusion did not mean, however, that the amendment violated Article 14. The court found that the statute in question was a justifiable regulatory provision that did not undermine the constitutional property interests in an unconstitutional way.

The upshot of these requirements is that while German constitutional law does extend protection to some forms of state-originating benefits, it by no means embraces all of Charles Reich's "new property" theory. The scope of what can be property under the Basic Law is broad, but it is not unlimited. What Reich called for in his famous 1964 *Yale Law Journal*[168] article was full constitutional protection for all forms of what he termed government "largesse." This concept included everything from welfare benefits to federal

Social Security to taxicab medallions. Reich drew no distinction between those forms of government-provided wealth to which the recipient had personally contributed and those that were pure state transfer payments intended for the recipient or for members of the recipient's family, such as Aid to Families with Dependent Children. German constitutional law, like its American counterpart, clearly excludes the latter from substantive protection.

Nevertheless, there is a significant difference between the treatment of public benefit interests under German and American constitutional property law. While both largely agree on the meaning of "property" in this context, German law extends substantive, not merely procedural, protection to those interests that are protected.[169] American constitutional law limits protection of state-derived interests to the procedural requirements of notice and a hearing. No American case has come remotely close to suggesting that the takings clause of the Fifth Amendment applies to such interests. German constitutional protection, while limited with respect to the scope of the public-derived interests that are covered, is, by contrast, substantive. In this respect at least, German constitutional law embraces the "new property" theory to a greater extent than does American constitutional law.

More fundamentally, the Federal Constitutional Court's refusal to embrace all new property interests indicates that there are important limits on the implications of the *Sozialstaat* idea for constitutional property rights. In this sense, the court's restrictions on the range of protectable new property interests illustrate one of the basic claims of this book, that interpretation matters. The *Sozialstaat* commitment did not provide the basis for treating all social welfare benefits as constitutional property. The significance of the provision turns on interpretation, which is shaped to a substantial degree by background traditions and culture. The relevant deep background to understanding the court's position on which social benefits are constitutional property and which are not is the tension between the *Sozialstaat* and *Rechtsstaat* ideals that has characterized the Basic Law since its inception.

Defining the Social Obligation of Property

The defining feature of German constitutional property law is its social-obligation norm. There is no counterpart in the American Constitution to the two short sentences in Article 14(2): "Property entails obligations. Its use should also serve the public weal." As we have already seen, the presence of those sentences strongly influences both the outcomes and the reasoning of cases challenging the constitutional validity of government measures regulating various aspects of property. The section directly examines the German social-obligation norm. My main focus is on how the courts, especially the Federal Constitutional Court, have implemented that norm and used it as a tool for realizing the progressive vision of making social responsibility "a constitutive component of the conception of ownership."[170]

An Overview

The full text of the social-obligation clause in Article 14 provides little or no guidance regarding its substantive content. The Anglo-American lawyer might be tempted to construe it to state little or nothing more than the familiar common law idea that private ownership of property is not absolute in the sense that the owner may do literally anything he wishes with his property. As every law student in the common law world learns, property rights are not absolute. There is always implicit in the legal concept of private property the obligation not to use your thing so as to interfere with another's legal interests. *Sic utere tuo ut alienum non laedes* ("Use your land so as not to injure another's."), the common law's apothegm states. So construed, the social-obligation term would provide little substantive basis for distinguishing the German and American approaches.

But this not at all how the social-obligation norm has operated in German constitutional property law. To the contrary, as David Currie has stated, "[T]he social duties of property in Germany . . . justify limitations that go far beyond the simple case of preventing affirmative harm to others."[171] As Currie goes on to point out,

> Renters may be protected from unusual or sudden rent increases as well as against eviction and the diversion of rental property to other uses. Farm and forest lands may be protected against sales that appear detrimental to the interests of agriculture or forestry. For the well-being of the wine industry, the legislature may forbid the growing of grapes on unsuitable soil. To promote recreation it may establish associations to administer private fishing rights and distribute the profits to their former owners.[172]

The constitutional duty of private owners to serve the well-being of the community, in short, is powerful and pervasive.

The social-obligation clause does not itself create subjective property rights.[173] That is, it does not provide the basis for positive claim rights for individual citizens to assert against the state.[174] Instead, like the *Sozialstaat* principle,[175] it is understood to impose a duty on the legislature and administrative agencies actively to advance community well-being.[176] Acting under this duty, the legislature imposes negative limitations on what private owners may do with their property. At the same time, the individual owner is understood as being under an immanent positive duty to use her property so that it serves the public weal.[177] An earlier draft of Article 14(2) better captures the intended substance of the current version: "Ownership entails a social obligation. Its use shall find its limits in the living necessities of all citizens and in the public order essential to society."[178]

The idea that property entails social obligations derives, most immediately, from the 1919 Weimar Constitution.[179] More fundamentally, it is an elaboration and application of the *Sozialstaat* principle, which standing alone does not invalidate governmental action or inaction.[180] As David Currie has observed, "The Sozialstaat provisions . . . reflect the growing conviction . . . that it was not enough for the state to protect citizens from one another and to protect the individual from the state; the state should also be required affirmatively to promote the public weal."[181] Ernst Benda, a former and influential member of the Federal Constitutional Court, has expressed the same view, stating, "[T]he common good does not just happen[;] the state has to work actively for it . . . [T]he *Sozialstaatklausel* [social state clause] entitles and obliges the state to become more active."[182] Indeed, the *Sozialstaat* principle has probably had its greatest effect in justifying governmental redistributive actions, such as welfare legislation, and environmental regulations against objections that such state measures unduly interfere with individual property rights.[183]

The Proportionality Principle

The social-obligation norm requires that the legislature establish and the courts maintain an equitable balance between the owner's individual liberty interests and the well-being of the community. The central doctrinal tool that courts use to strike that balance is the proportionality principle (*Verhältnismäßigkeit*),[184] to which we have already been introduced. As one commentator succinctly explains, "The function of the proportionality principle . . . is to ensure that the regulation starts with but also ends with the public interest, and that it respects and protects both the public interest and the individual interests equally."[185]

The proportionality principle is nowhere expressly mentioned in the Basic Law. Nevertheless, it is a fundamental and pervasive aspect of German constitutional jurisprudence. The current conventional wisdom is that it is derived from the *Rechtsstaat* principle,[186] although neither the Federal Constitutional Court nor commentators have been successful in explaining exactly how the two are linked.[187] The basic idea behind the modern proportionality principle in fact has a long history predating the 1949 Basic Law, dating at least to a set of lectures delivered in 1792 by Carl Gottlieb Svarez, the principal drafter of the influential codification of Prussian law (*Allgemeines Landrecht der Preußischen Staaten*).[188]

In its German version,[189] the modern proportionality principle has three requirements.[190] For a limitation of a fundamental right to be valid, it must (1) be suitable (*geeignet*) for attaining its (legitimate) purpose; (2) be necessary (*erforderlich*) for that purpose; and (3) not be excessive (*unzumutbar*) in relation to the benefits to be achieved from the limitation's purpose.[191]

The first requirement is a matter of instrumental fit. The legislative limitation must have some rational connection to the intended aim of the limitation. A height requirement on beachfront houses has little, if any, functional relationship with promoting public access to the beach and probably would not satisfy this requirement. The second requirement, necessity, means that among the available measures by which the intended goal might be achieved, the legislature must adopt the measure that least restricts the fundamental right.[192] However, this requirement is not simply a clone of the American fixed "strict scrutiny" test. Varying levels of scrutiny apply according to the degree and seriousness of the infringement of the right.[193] The third requirement, sometimes referred to as proportionality in the narrow sense (*Angemessenheit*),[194] asks whether the harm caused to the rights holder is disproportionate to the stated objective. It is closely related to the second requirement insofar as both focus on regulatory excess, unlike the first requirement, which is a matter of instrumental connection.[195]

Proportionality review applies only where the court has first determined that the state's action in fact conflicts with the right in question. In this respect it is the last stage of the inquiry into the validity of the governmental restriction. In many cases the courts do not even reach the stage of proportionality review because analysis of the scope of the right indicates that the government action did not violate it.

Although obviously similar to judicial balancing, proportionality review is not considered to be identical with it. One crucial difference was mentioned earlier.[196] Unlike American-style balancing, which blends together the questions of the right's scope and the justification of the regulation, proportionality review applies if and only if the governmental action is found to have encroached within the scope of the right. In many cases, this precondition does not exist and the court does not look at the factors involved in proportionality analysis. German law does include a balancing-of-interests theory, but that theory, although it overlaps somewhat with the proportionality principle, differs from it. The balancing-of-interests theory (*Güterabwägung*) applies in cases when different constitutional rights conflict.[197] In applying the balancing theory, the courts in effect engage in a ranking of the constitutional rights.[198] This ranking involves an assessment of the relative importance of the respective rights and the intensity of the infringement of those rights. This latter aspect of the inquiry is the main similarity with proportionality analysis.

The primary American objection to judicial balancing has been that it is little more than the exercise of political judgment.[199] It would be an understatement to say that German constitutionalists are aware of that risk. Proportionality review, after all, is based on the very idea that it is a means of implementing the *Rechtsstaat* ideal. Proportionality is not intended to provide the courts with an opportunity to review the wisdom of the legislative act but rather to check to make sure that the legislature has not exceeded its institutional competence. It implements the prohibition against regulatory excess (*Übermaßverbot*) while giving the legislature wide berth in regulating property for the purpose of defining and enforcing the property owner's social responsibilities.[200]

A key practice that the courts have developed to perform this checking function is the so-called scaling function (*Abstufung der Sozialpflichtigkeit*). The court scales, or grades, the social-obligation norm's limitation on property according to its relation to the individual owner. As one observer explains,

> [T]he closer the specific property right is involved in providing security for the personal liberty of its holder, the narrower the restrictions which prevent the legislature from interfering with that right; and the further a specific property right is removed from the sphere within which the personal liberty of its holder is preserved, the easier it becomes for the legislature to regulate the limits of that right.[201]

As part of this analysis, the court inquires whether and to what extent other persons are dependent on the use of the owner's property. The greater the degree of dependency, the greater the social function and, consequently, the greater the degree of legislative freedom to define the individual owner's zone of autonomy more narrowly.

This scaling analysis is functionally dynamic in the sense that the courts consider social and economic changes that have affected the purposes that particular resources serve over time. An influential treatise on German constitutional law aptly captures this focus on the functional change of property and its relevance to constitutional protection:

> As a basis for the individual existence and individual conduct of life as well as a principle of social order the individual ownership of property has lost its importance. Modern life is based only to a limited extent on the individual power of disposition as the basis for individual existence, with respect, for example, to the peasant farm or the family enterprise. The basis for individual existence is usually no longer private property as determined by private law, but the produce of one's own work and participation in the benefits of the welfare state.[202]

The relevance of functional changes of property to constitutional protection is illustrated by the *Small Garden Plot Case* (*Kleingartenentscheidung*).[203] In that case the court struck down a federal statute that severely limited the right of landowners to terminate garden leases. The historical background of the statute and changes in social conditions are crucial to understanding the decision. At one time in German history it was common for large landowners, particularly on the outskirts of cities, to lease to people who owned little or no land small plots for the purpose of small gardens. These garden plots were an important method of feeding the German public. As the dominant means of agricultural production shifted to large-scale commercial productions, these individual garden plots lost their original social purpose and indeed became something of an anachronism. The individual landowners in the case wanted to change the use of their land from agricultural purposes to commercial development because the amount of annual rent from the leasehold had become insubstantial. They applied for a permit to terminate the garden lease on their land, but the regulatory agency refused to grant the permit because the federal statute did not recognize this sort of change of circumstances as a permissible basis for terminating leases. The court held that the statute was unconstitutional because the magnitude of the restriction on the owner's freedom of use was disproportionate to the public purpose to be served. While the original function of these garden allotments was to provide a source of food in times of social emergency, the purpose had by modern times become no more than to be a source of recreation, a social function that the court regarded as decidedly less weighty than its original purpose. Comparing the weakness of the new function with the severity of the restriction on the owners' use, the court had little difficulty in concluding that the statute was unconstitutional.

From an American perspective, perhaps the most striking application of the scaling approach is the very important *Codetermination Case* (*Mitbestimmungsentscheidung*).[204] That case involved a challenge to the constitutional validity of the Federal Codetermination Act of 1976, an extremely important piece of legislation regulating the relationship between labor and management in German industries. The Act mandates worker representation on the boards of directors of large firms, defined as firms with 2,000 or more employees. It further requires that the firm's legal representatives as well as its primary labor director be selected by the supervisory board according to specified procedures and that the board's chair and vice chair be elected by a two-thirds majority.

The ostensible purpose of the Act was to extend and strengthen worker participation in the governance of business enterprises, a practice that has a long history in German labor-management relations. But anyone who has read James Buchanan and Gordon Tullock's famous book, *The Calculus of Consent*,[205] may be tempted to react skeptically to that explanation. A public-choice analysis of the Act would simply see it as a clear instance of rent-seeking legislation, supported by an obviously well-organized and intensely political interest group. That may indeed have been the real basis for the Act, but the German Constitutional Court did not think so. Squarely addressing the public-choice reading (although not calling it by that term), the court stated that the Codetermination Act,

> does not merely serve a pure group interest. Rather, the cooperation and integration aimed at by institutional co-participation . . . have general importance in social policy; co-participation has especially been regarded as calculated to secure the market economy politically . . . [I]t is intended to serve the welfare of the public. It cannot be regarded as unsuitable or not necessary to achieve this purpose . . .[206]

The plaintiffs, which included a large number of business firms and employers' associations, attacked the Act as a gross interference with their property rights. They argued that the Act violated the constitutional property rights of the shareholders and the firms themselves under Article 14 of the Basic Law as well as other constitutional guarantees.[207] Rejecting this claim, the Federal Constitutional Court concluded that the Act was merely an exercise of the legislature's power under Article 14(1) to define the "contents and limits" of property. It did not violate the injunction of Article 19(2) that "the essence of a basic right [not] be encroached upon." The court stated that while the Act admittedly reduced the powers of shareholders as members of the supervising board, the restriction "keeps within the bounds of a constitutionally permissible social binding."[208] Article 14(2) makes clear, the court pointed out, that "use and disposal do not remain merely within the sphere of the [individual] owner, but affect interests of other persons entitled to rights who are dependent on the use of the [particular] property object."[209] Both shareholders and employees had constitutionally recognized property interests, but the relative strength of those interests and, hence, the effect of the social obligation on them differed significantly.[210] As the Federal Constitutional Court stated, "[T]he legislator's area of discretion in the case of social relation and in the case of social function of property is thus relatively wide in view of its social [obligation]; it becomes narrower if these conditions are not present or are present only to a limited extent."[211] Illustrating how this sliding scale approach works in evaluating particular sorts of property, the court treated investment property as having a very strong social function with respect to employees, but with respect to shareholders its social role is limited. It has relatively less immediate impact on the personal security of shareholders than it does on the autonomy and self-development interests of employees. The court said that shareholding's

> social relation shows itself in the mere fact that, as a general rule, it consists in the mutual participation with others in a company which is the owner of the means of production. Above all, in order to use the share property, the collaboration of the workers is always needed[.][212]

Consequently, the magnitude of owners' social obligation under Article 14(2) was greater because of the social impact and contemporary purpose of their investment property.

Since the text of Article 14 speaks only of "property" and seemingly does not distinguish among various sorts of property, the Federal Constitutional Court in fact has drawn just such qualitative distinctions. The *Codetermination* and *Small Garden* cases, read together, allow one to say that the court distinguishes among different categories of property, creating a kind of hierarchy among types of resources. The sliding scale approach to evaluating the magnitude of the social obligation and the social function of property is the basis for this ordering of property. This is the primary means by which the court has cabined the social obligation, which otherwise would seem to be the proverbial unruly horse. Greater legislative power is recognized over socially important assets like corporate stock than over small garden plots used for leisure.

Purposive Analysis of Constitutional Property

The scaling approach illustrates another aspect of the Federal Constitutional Court's implementation of the social-obligation norm. As the discussion of the *Small Garden* and *Codetermination* cases indicated, the court explicitly relies on a purposive approach to analyzing the implications of the social-obligation norm for the immediate case. The court openly examines and identifies the central value intended to be served by making property a constitutional right and then asks to what extent, if at all, that value is at stake under the circumstances of the case. This requires that the court analyze the nature of the asserted property interest in terms of its type and function.

Nowhere is the way in which the purposive approach affects the court's measure of the scope of the social obligation more evident than in cases involving environmental regulations. Time and time again, the court has said that natural resources, including land, water, and air, are of paramount importance to society.[213] This is especially true of land and water because of their limited supply. Land and water are treated as categories of property that warrant, indeed require, a stricter measure of social control and government regulation. No case illustrates this highly solicitous approach to government regulations aimed at protecting these natural resources than the *Naßauskiesung* case,[214] possibly the most famous and widely discussed[215] decision of the Federal Constitutional Court concerning constitutional protection of property. The case[216] is worth some extended discussion because it reveals a great deal about how the crucial role that purposive analysis of property interests plays in defining the scope of the social obligation.

The litigation concerned the constitutional validity of the 1976 amendments to the Federal Water Resources Act (*Wasserhaushaltgesetz*), first enacted in 1957. The most important of these amendments was a provision requiring that anyone wishing to make virtually any use of surface or groundwater obtain a permit. That amendment represented an extension of the Act's basic premise, which was that "the attainment of a sensible and useful distribution of the surface water and groundwater, in quantity and quality, for the whole Federal Republic . . . [can be achieved only] if the free disposition by private owners is restricted and if the interest of the public weal is the starting point for all action."[217] Under the Act, the owner of the surface has no entitlement to such a use permit; indeed, the permit must be denied wherever the proposed use threatens the "public weal."

The plaintiff, who owned and operated a gravel pit, applied for a permit to use the water beneath his land. He had previously taken groundwater for the purpose of extracting gravel for decades, but the city denied him permission to continue to do so because his quarry operation threatened the city's water wells. He sued for damages, claiming that the permit denial was an uncompensated expropriation of his property, unconstitutional under Article 14 of the Basic Law.

The Federal Court of Justice (*Bundesgerichtshof*), the highest civil court in Germany, held that the permit denial indeed violated the plaintiff's constitutional property right and that the amendment to the Water Resources Act was unconstitutional under Article 14(1).[218] Relying on a provision of the Civil Code (BGB),[219] the court held that the right to dispose of the groundwater found on the premises is a right inherent in ownership of the land and that the Act therefore violated a right inherent in the constitutional right of property.

Under German law, only the Federal Constitutional Court has the authority to declare statutes unconstitutional, so the Federal Court of Justice was required to submit the case to the Federal Constitutional Court. The latter court held[220] that the Water Resources Act was constitutional and that the permit denial was not an expropriation of the plaintiff's constitutionally protected property. The Act did not expropriate or intrude upon an existing constitutional entitlement to use groundwater but only established the content and limits of whatever rights to use groundwater may inhere in the rights of a landowner. The Act, in other words, did not take away the claimant's preexisting constitutional right to use groundwater; rather it only determined that the landowner's rights did not include the right to use groundwater. The real question then was whether, by removing an entire category of property, namely, groundwater, from the sphere of private ownership, the legislature had exceeded the limits of its legislative power. Stated differently, did the right to use groundwater fall within the scope of the social obligation so that the legislature was justified in removing it from private control and subjecting it entirely to pubic control. The court answered that it was.

In the course of a long and extraordinarily complicated opinion, the court squarely rejected an economic, or wealth-maximizing, conception of property. The court said, "From the constitutional guarantee of property the owner cannot derive a right to be permitted to make use of precisely that which promises the greatest possible economic advantage."[221] The court acknowledged that the institutional guarantee of property in Article 14(1) prohibits the legislature from undermining the basic existence of the right that is embedded in the private law of property in a way that removes or substantially impairs the guaranteed zone of freedom under Article 14.[222] The legislature does not violate the institutional guarantee of property, however, when the security and defense of resources that are vital to the paramount common welfare of the public are placed under the authority of the public rather than the private legal order.[223] Water is such a resource.

To explain why water is too important to be left completely to the market, or private ordering, to allocate, the court relied on two factors, history and social purpose. Historically, the court pointed out, German private law has separated property rights concerning land and water. This separation was constitutionally authorized at least since the time of the German constitution of 1871, the court noted.

The court gave more extended consideration to the functional role of water in society. As part of its reasoning that the water law falls within the "contents and limits" (*Inhalt und Schranken*) of ownership of land, a matter over which the legislature has complete regulatory authority,[224] the court emphasized that social changes occurring in this century have made certain adjustments in the legal regulation of water necessary.[225] Water has always been a vital resource to society, the court pointed out, but it has become even more so in modern German society.[226] The processes of growing industrialization, urbanization, and construction have increased the scarcity and social importance of water. "Water is one of the most important bases of all of human, animal, and plant life. [Today] it is used not only for drinking and personal use, but also as a factor of industrial production. Because of these simultaneous yet diverse demands, it was previously established as a matter of constitutional law that an orderly water management scheme was vital for the population as well as for the overall economy."[227]

At this point, one wants to say, yes, water is essential to life, but so are many other resources. Would the court be prepared to hold that the Basic Law does not recognize private property rights in all other natural resources that are necessary for life? Indeed, what about land, which clearly is also essential to the existence of animals and plants? Are we to surmise that private ownership of land is somehow being put in jeopardy? That hardly seems likely. The point is that it begs the question simply to declare that because certain resources are essential to human existence, the constitutional status of property rights in those resources must somehow be different from property rights in other resources.

The most obvious respect in which subterranean water differs from land, of course, is water's "fugitive," or ambient character. While land is necessarily immobile, underground water is not. The Federal Constitutional Court alluded to this factor is discussing the functional significance of water. The court pointed out that, as a human resource, water is now vital both for the purposes of drinking and industry and the increase in these social uses has brought the two more and more in conflict with each other. This is especially true in the case of groundwater, the court noted. In that context there is an inevitable conflict between commercial uses such as excavation of subsurface resources and the community interest in protecting both the supply and quality of subterranean water. The constitutional status of water must be determined by taking into account the need to reconcile these conflicting social interests. The first priority must be to preserve the quality of drinking water. Industrial uses of groundwater, such as the discharge of chemicals into it, simply cannot be left to the discretion of each owner of parcels of land. Why? Why not rely on the market, predicated on private property rights, to achieve an efficient allocation of groundwater?

The court's answer here was a bit murky, but its reasoning echoes points that some American property scholars have made concerning the limits of the market as a means of allocating rights in surface water. These scholars have pointed out that, left as a commons, groundwater involves major problems with externalities, or spillover effects.[228] Self-interest is not a reliable means of protecting resources whose uses, especially given the resource's fugitive character, have substantial external effects. As Professor Freyfogle has stated, "In the case of water, . . . many external harms affect ecosystems and future generations, or are otherwise uncertain in scope and infeasible to calculate or trace."[229] Flowing water, Freyfogle points out, is "communally embedded," both in a social and an ecological sense. The ecological community includes "soils, plants, animals, microorganisms, nutrient flows, and hydrological cycles."[230] These two communities are themselves so interdependent that a threat to one is a threat to the other.[231] Under these circumstances, any individual use of water profoundly affects the entire community and directly implicates the common weal.

The major legal question, the Federal Constitutional Court stated, is whether shifting water regulation from the private to the public realm can be constitutionally justified. The argument had been made that individual rights in groundwater are constitutionally inseparable from ownership of the surface. Rejecting this argument, the court stated that federal regulation of groundwater use would not effectively empty landownership of all its content (*"Substanzentleerung des Grundeigentums"*[232]). Landownership would not become completely subordinated to the social obligation. Merely subjecting the owner's right to use groundwater to regulatory approval does not remove the entire use interest from the bundle of rights. Even if it did, there would be no constitutional violation because the right to use groundwater is not a twig that is essential to private ownership of the land. Ownership of land is valuable primarily with respect to use of the surface, not subterranean, water, the court said. Even with respect to the surface, the constitution permits regulation of various uses. "The constitutionally guaranteed right to property does not permit the owner to make use of just that use having the greatest economic value."[233]

The second basis the court gave for the constitutional validity of the Federal Water Law did not involve the constitutional property right itself but the principle of equality. Article 3 of the constitution secures a principle of equality (*das Gleichbehandlungsgebot*), which the court has repeatedly stated informs the meaning of other constitutional values, including property. The plaintiff had argued that the Federal Water Law arbitrarily burdened him in violation of his Article 3 equality right because his quarry was located close to groundwater while other quarry owners were not affected. The court had little difficulty dismissing that objection, pointing out that the regulation affected all similarly situated quarry owners equally. Similarly, the regulation did not violate the constitutional principle of proportionality. There appeared to be no less intrusive means of regulating the gravel extraction process while still achieving the obviously legitimate goal of protecting the purity of subsurface water. The effect on the owner was indeed drastic, but this was not the determinative factor. It was an incidental by-product of the regulatory means selected. A suitable instrumental fit existed, the court found, between means and ends. The means chosen were necessary to achieve the regulatory objective, and there was no singling out of a particular owner to bear a disproportionate share of the burden necessary to attain the benefits the legislature legitimately sought.

The final significant aspect of the case concerns the recurrent problem of legal transitions.[234] The Federal Water Law denied the plaintiff a legal right that he once had and had exercised. He had been quarrying gravel since 1936, and under the law existing at that time, the right of property clearly protected the right to use groundwater. The court directly confronted the familiar dilemma: stability versus dynamism. On the side of stability, the court stated,

> It would be incompatible with the content of the Constitution if the government were authorized suddenly and without any transitional period to block the continued exercise of property rights that had required substantial capital investment. Such a law . . . would upset confidence in the stability of the legal order, without which responsible structuring and planning of life would be impossible in the area of property ownership.

The court was equally frank about the need to avoid freezing the distribution of property rights extant at any given time:

> The constitutional guarantee of ownership exercised by the plaintiff does not imply that a property interest, once recognized, would have to be preserved in perpetuity or that it could be taken away only by way of expropriation [that is, with compensation]. [This court] has repeatedly ruled that the legislature is not faced with the alternative of either preserving old legal positions or taking them away in exchange for compensation every time an area of law is to be regulated anew.[235]

The Constitution resolves this dilemma, the court said, by permitting the legislature to "restructure individual legal positions by issuing an appropriate and reasonable transition rule whenever the public interest merits precedence over some justified expectation, based on continuity of practice, in the continuance of a vested right."[236] The statute followed this constitutionally sanctioned path by providing a grace period of five years, during which owners could continue to use groundwater without a permit. Since the Act did not take effect until thirty-one months after its enactment, the claimant effectively had almost eight years of continued use. Moreover, owners could get an extension if they had filed for a permit. The upshot of these provisions in the instant case, the court noted, was that the plaintiff was able to continue his gravel operations for some seventeen years after the statute's enactment. Under these circumstances, the statute's transition provisions were reasonable by sufficiently accommodating the plaintiff's economic interest.

Three points need to be made about the *Naßauskiesung* case. First, the case makes clear that the German Constitutional Court, like its American counterpart,[237] has rejected what in American takings literature has become known as "conceptual severance." Conceptual severance, a term first coined by Professor Margaret Jane Radin,[238] means that every incident of ownership, every twig in the bundle of rights, is itself ownership. The implication of conceptual severance, of course, would be vastly to strengthen the bite of the takings clause because virtually every regulation affecting private ownership of any resource would become a taking of ownership itself. The United States Supreme Court's reaction to conceptual severance has been somewhat ambiguous,[239] but the German Constitutional Court clearly rejected it, at least with respect to the relationship between land and subsurface resources. In fact, none of the court's decisions under its constitutional property clause provides any plausible basis for supposing that the court is prepared to entertain such an approach.[240]

The second point concerns the court's statement in the *Naßauskiesung* case that the constitutional right to property does not guarantee the right to exploit the resource for its highest economic value. This statement indicates that German constitutional protection of property is not rooted either in notions of wealth maximization or libertarianism. Eliminating those two possible theoretical bases of constitutional protection of property has important implications for how a wide variety of contemporary American takings disputes would be resolved under German law. Wetlands regulations are an obvious example. Landowners (especially farmers) whose parcels include regulated wetlands have been very vocal in recent years about their supposed constitutional right to capture the full potential market value of the affected land. Using the takings clause, they have challenged wetlands regulations precisely on the ground that they deprive the owner of the ability to put the land to its highest economic use. Whether or not German courts might find another basis for striking down wetlands regulations, they clearly would reject the basic premise of the attack on American wetlands regulations.

The third respect in which American property lawyers can learn from the *Naßauskiesung* case concerns the approach that the German court took to determining that the property interest in question was what Carol Rose has called "inherently public property."[241] The court focused on both the social necessity of the resource and the degree of social interdependence associated with the resource in the conditions of contemporary society. What the court implicitly said was the following. Any use of flowing water by any single person or group of persons affects both the social and ecological communities in multiple ways, and it is unrealistic to suppose that any given owner will take all of these external effects into account. Indeed, precisely because of the intensity of the social and ecological interdependence that characterizes flowing water, no owner can possibly take all or even most of the external effects of a given use into account when making choices among possible uses.[242] The consequences of any given use by an individual are both wildly unpredictable and profoundly felt by the entire community. Under such circumstances of intense interdependency, the boundary between *meum* and *tuum* is both meaningless and dangerously misleading.[243] A resource whose use so profoundly affects the interdependent social and natural communities is inherently public and can only be regulated by public norms as expressions of the common will. Under this view, the German

Federal Water Law at issue in the *Naßauskiesung* case is not redistributive. It does not take an asset from A and give it to B. Rather, the statute is premised on the understanding that groundwater, for constitutional purposes at least, is now and always has been both A's and B's. It is not the property of the state but property that is "inherently public."[244]

Following the Federal Constitutional Court's decision, the case went back to the Federal Court of Justice. That court awarded the plaintiff compensation.[245] It did so on the theory that, although the basic principle of protection of property emerges from constitutional principles, the particulars of protection have to be determined on the basis of nonconstitutional law (*einfaches Recht*). The relevant nonconstitutional basis for state liability in this case, said the court, was the principle of individual sacrifice (*Aufopferungsgedanke*). Where the governmental action sacrifices an individual for the benefit of the general public, the state is liable to compensate the individual in an action that is similar to but not explicitly falling under the term "expropriation," as used in Article 14(3).[246]

The *Naßauskiesung* case illustrates how the Federal Constitutional Court relies on a purposive form of reasoning to determine the scope of the social obligation of ownership. Where the property interest in question serves a purpose that implicates a strong need and simultaneously does not strongly implicate the personal function of the owner's self-governance, the court regards the interest as falling within the scope of the social obligation. Conversely, where the court perceives that the interest immediately involved in the case primarily serves this personal function, it is less apt to find that the social obligation is triggered.

The German constitutional property clause's social-obligation and compensation provisions have been a highly workable tool for mediating the property clause's dual normative commitment to individual liberty and social welfare. Together they express the social vision that "land ownership is a source of special responsibility toward the landowner's community," and they illustrate how constitutional property law can develop in ways that "promot[e] the virtue of social responsibility."[247] At the same time, they assiduously protect the constitutional commitment to individual liberty. In the German context, however, liberty is not a matter of preference satisfaction. Rather, at its core is the ontological idea of living a life of self-realization as a member of a community. The German courts have recognized that some forms of property are more important than others in maintaining liberty in this sense, and their purposive method of analyzing constitutional property claims has enabled them to distinguish among different sorts of property according to their relationship to the deeper value of self-realization. Similarly, the community's interest, recognized and protected through both the social-obligation provision and the compensation clause, is more intense in some contexts than in others. As the *Naßauskiesung* case makes clear, environmental well-being is an area in which the individual landowner's social obligation is especially important. The *Flood Control* (*Deichordnung*) *Case* makes clear that the public interest sometimes warrants, indeed requires, that less than full fair market value be paid to the affected owner.

For American lawyers, perhaps the most important point is that the German courts have rejected any sort of categorical approach to determining when legal regulation of property has "gone too far." They have not only openly acknowledged that property necessarily involves a basic tension between the individual and society, but have also recognized that addressing that tension requires an interpretive approach that is explicitly purposive and contextual. The contextual and purposive approach that the German Constitutional Court has developed has enabled the court to use the social-obligation norm as an effective vehicle for expressing the twin messages that property rights, like all other constitutional rights, inherently implicate the basic tension and that no categorical rule can possibly dissolve that tension.

CHAPTER FOUR

From Social Obligation to Social Transformation? South Africa's Experience with Constitutional Property

If the German Basic Law broke new ground in modern constitutional property law by expressly invoking a social-obligation norm, the 1996 South African Constitution planted the seeds for a vast crop to be grown in the social-obligation soil. The property clause extends, at least on paper, the idea of a social-obligation norm by including an explicit commitment to land reform and social justice.[1] Equally striking, if not more so, are other provisions that create an array of positive socioeconomic rights.[2] The result is a constitution that has been called "the most admirable constitution in the history of the world."[3] Even if that assessment is considered excessive, there is no question that the South African Constitution is a truly remarkable document, one that is unprecedented and that unambiguously seeks to be transformative in nature. Its overriding goal is effecting the fundamental transformation of a society that has suffered profound political and economic injustices not only during the apartheid regime that was formally created in 1948 but also during the years of de facto apartheid before that.[4] The very fact that the South African Constitution aims at being one of the primary engines of a fundamental social transformation in its society makes it historically unparalleled and worthy of serious attention by constitutional scholars around the world.

In the context of South Africa today, "social transformation" includes land reform and restitution. The eventual outcome of the country's attempt to realize its verbal commitment to creating "an open and democratic society based on human dignity, equality and freedom"[5] depends heavily on its ability radically to transform its land regime, not only as a legal system but as a social reality. This is so in a country where landlessness and homelessness are the norm among nonwhites, where literally millions of blacks live in the desperate poverty of "informal" housing settlements (that is, squatter settlements),[6] and where many blacks did not enjoy secure land tenure rights until recently.[7] Without access to land, and where land restitution has been slow, South Africa's black majority will find no solace in the noble sentiments expressed in the new political and legal rhetoric, including that of the constitution.

While the South African Constitution aspires to effect a fundamental transformation in South African society, based in substantial part on a new regime of property, it is too soon to say whether it will produce genuinely transformative results. It will be a number of years before we know what kind of society emerges in the new democracy. The proof of whether the constitution's transformative potential has been realized will be how courts interpret and implement its most ambitious provisions, particularly those concerning property and the related socioeconomic rights. To date, the South African Constitutional Court has referred to section 25 of the final constitution in a very small number of decisions.[8] There are a handful of lower-court decisions interpreting section 25[9] and one important decision of the Constitutional Court interpreting the interim constitution's property clause, section 28.[10]

My aim in this chapter is not to provide an exhaustive study of the property and socioeconomic rights provisions of the constitution but to shed some light on the principal threats to their potential to fulfill the constitution's express promise to transform South African society. Chief among these threats is the country's background legal culture, more specifically, its private law juristic tradition, which is based largely on Roman-Dutch law.

South Africa provides an example, par excellence, of one of the central arguments of this book: that background legal traditions and cultures play a central role in the development of the normative pull of any constitutional property clause. The normative trajectory that will eventually emerge as courts interpret South Africa's new constitutional property clause is still unclear. One point that is clear, however, is that the property clause's eventual normative trajectory will depend to a very substantial extent on which of two discursive frameworks currently available in South African law prevails as the dominant discourse in all aspects of the South African legal system, including (or perhaps one should say especially) its constitutional jurisprudence.

One discursive framework is that of traditional South African private law, particularly its historic Roman-Dutch common law.[11] This is the discourse of private law as a science that is objective and neutral, of legal conceptualism and abstraction, of adaptability and scientific certainty, of gradual incremental legal change. It is also the discourse of classical liberal discourse of an inviolable private realm, within which the individual rights bearer is immunized from the depredations of the state. One of the gravest of these depredations is encroachment upon private property rights.

The other discursive framework is that of the new constitution as the preeminent and pervasive source of normative guidance. Substantively, this is the discourse of social transformation and social justice. The constitution's discourse, at least as reflected in the formal text, elevates social transformation and social justice over all other values. Within such a framework, there would appear to be no room for talk about property rights as trumps. Methodologically, the new discourse, as indicated by the Constitutional Court's opinions thus far, is the discourse of purposive reasoning, contextuality, and contingency. Here again, there is seemingly no room for the private law–based tradition's conceptualist reasoning, scientific pretense to neutrality or objectivity, or categorical rules.

Which of these two discursive frameworks dominates constitutional jurisprudence, especially in the realm of constitutional property, is the real question. Indeed, it is no exaggeration to say that *the* central issue in South African constitutional, including constitutional property, law today is the relationship between constitutional law and private law.[12] Will South Africa's traditional private law *mentalité* dominate judicial interpretation of the new constitution, particularly as it relates to the nominally private sphere? If it does so, then the South African Constitution's attempt to achieve radical social transformation will fall short.

As background before discussing the question of the relationship between private and constitutional law in South Africa, this chapter begins with an overview of the Bill of Rights of the 1996 constitution. It then turns to a brief historical summary. The focus then turns to section 25, the property clause itself, examining it both from doctrinal and cultural perspectives. Along the way, several points of comparison are made with other constitutional experiences, particularly as they concern matters that bear on the idea of a social-obligation dimension of the constitutional right of property.

Overview of the South African Constitution's Bill of Rights

The final (1996) South African Constitution[13] is an ongoing attempt to transform society. Not surprisingly, it departs from the American Constitution, a classical liberal document, but perhaps somewhat more surprising, it also departs from modern twentieth-century constitutions like the German Basic Law. Karl Klare captures the difference in observing that "[t]he South African Constitution intends a not fully defined but nonetheless unmistakable departure from liberalism . . . toward an 'empowered' model of democracy."[14] The break from extant models of constitutions was viewed as a necessary part of the more fundamental break from the apartheid past. As the late Justice Mahomed stated in *State v. Makwanyane*,[15] one of the leading early Constitutional Court cases interpreting the new constitution, "The South African Constitution is different: it . . . represents a decisive break from, and a ringing rejection of, that part of the past which is racist, authoritarian, insular, and repressive and a vigorous identification of and commitment to a democratic, universalistic, caring and aspirationally egalitarian ethos, expressly articulated in the Constitution."[16]

The remarkable, and remarkably novel, character of the 1996 constitution is apparent from even the most casual glance. The Preamble begins in striking fashion:

> We, the people of South Africa,
> Recognize the injustices of our past;
> Honour those who suffered for justice and freedom in our land;
> Respect those who have worked to build and develop our country; and
> Believe that South Africa belongs to all who live in it, united in our diversity.

It goes on the declare that the constitution is adopted in order to "[h]eal the divisions of the past and establish a society based on democratic values, social justice and fundamental human rights . . ." Section 1 states that the Republic of South Africa is founded on the values of "[h]uman dignity, the achievement of equality and the advancement of human rights and freedoms."

Chapter 2 is the constitution's Bill of Rights. Two provisions require special attention at the outset of this brief review of the Bill of Rights. The first is section 7. As we will see later, subsection 2 has become an extremely important provision in recent cases.[17] It requires the state to "respect, protect, promote and fulfill the rights in the bill of Rights." The constitution imposes an affirmative obligation on the courts to ensure that the individual rights specified in chapter 2 are fulfilled. Not surprisingly, this provision has provoked considerable discussion and litigation over the question of just how the courts are to enforce chapter 2's socioeconomic rights. We will discuss this question in greater detail later. For now, it bears mention that the words "respect," "protect," "promote," and "fulfill" are understood to impose quite different obligations on the state. While the duty to "respect," for example, is understood to mean that the state must refrain from enacting any action that directly or indirectly interferes with people's enjoyment of their socioeconomic rights, the duty to "promote" imposes, at least in some circumstances, an affirmative duty to undertake actions aimed at informing citizens of their rights and the available means for enforcing those rights.[18] The duty to fulfill similarly means that the state must take certain positive steps to enable people to have their constitutional socioeconomic rights implemented.[19]

Section 7(3) articulates the overarching normative premise for the Bill of Rights. It declares, "This Bill of Rights is the cornerstone of democracy in South Africa. It . . . affirms the democratic values of human dignity, equality and freedom." It goes on to state that the rights enumerated in chapter 2 are subject to the limitations provided in section 36, the general limitations provision, "or elsewhere in the Bill."

Section 8 is the second preliminary provision requiring special attention. Subsection (1) states that the Bill of Rights "applies to all law, and binds the legislature, the executive, the judiciary and all organs of state." Section 8(3) importantly states that when applying a provision of the Bill of Rights to a person, "a court (a) in order to give effect to a right in the Bill, must apply, or if necessary develop, the common law to the extent that legislation does not give effect to that right; and (b) may develop rules of the common law to limit the right, provided that the limitation is in accordance with section 36(1)."

At the core of the Bill of Rights is its collection of positive socioeconomic rights. The list of substantive rights included in South Africa's Bill of Rights is striking by American standards. Even as progressive a constitution as the German Basic Law does not include many of the rights expressly included. In addition to comparatively familiar constitutional rights like equality (section 9), human dignity (section 10), privacy (section 14), religion (section 15), expression (section 16), and association (section 18), the Bill of Rights includes a number of positive socioeconomic rights that are absent from most other constitutions.

The constitution's socioeconomic rights provisions can be classified into three main categories. The first includes those rights as to which the constitution explicitly requires the state to "take reasonable legislative and other measures, within its available resources, to achieve the progressive realization of . . ."[20] These include the rights of all persons to have access to housing (section 26), health care services (section 27(a)), sufficient food and water (section 27(b)), and social security (section 27(c)). The second category entrenches several protective guarantees for children, including basic nutrition, shelter, basic health care services and social services (section 28), and a right to education (section 29). These rights are, at least textually, unqualified by budget constraints or references to "progressive realization," "reasonable accommodation," or the like. The third category includes rights that are expressed as a prohibition against the state (and perhaps private parties[21]) but that are not classical negative rights. Section 26(3) provides that "[n]o one may be evicted from their home, or have their home demolished, without an order of court made after considering all the relevant circumstances." Section 27(3) declares that "[n]o one may be refused emergency medical treatment."

The section 26 right to housing is worth pausing on, for it has figured in a number of recent controversies, notably the landmark *Grootboom* litigation.[22] It states that "(1) Everyone has the right to have access to adequate housing." This right is then immediately qualified: "(2) The state shall take reasonable legislative and other measures, *within its available resources,* to achieve the progressive realization of this right." Finally, section 26(3) is an antieviction provision that has been especially important, given both South Africa's apartheid history of evictions and its present experience with land invasions. It states, "No one may be evicted from their home, or have their home demolished, without an order of court made after considering all the relevant circumstances. No legislation may permit arbitrary evictions."

One of the objections that had been raised to including socioeconomic rights in the constitution was that such rights are nonjusticiable. In the important *First Certification Case,*[23] the court rejected this objection, holding that socioeconomic rights "are, at least to some extent, justiciable."[24] The court acknowledged that such rights "almost invariably" will involve budgetary complications, but it stated that such complications do not impose a bar to their justiciability. "At a minimum," said the court, "socioeconomic rights can be negatively protected from improper invasion."[25] The implication of this statement is that fiscal complications created by the constitution's socioeconomic rights are not themselves a reason for judicial abstention, but they may influence the standard of review in individual cases.[26]

Section 39 is a provision concerning how provisions of the Bill of Rights are to be interpreted. It begins with an injunction that has frequently appeared in the cases: "(1) When interpreting the Bill of Rights, a court . . . (a) must promote the values that underlie an open and democratic society based on human dignity, equality and freedom . . ." It requires courts to consider international law and, remarkably, permits them to consider foreign law.[27] Section 39 goes on to require that courts, when interpreting legislation and when developing the common law, "must promote the spirit, purport and objects of the Bill of Rights."[28] As we will see later, this last instruction has loomed large in the ongoing debate concerning the relationship between the constitution and South African common law (Roman-Dutch law).[29]

The final provision to note at this point is the important general limitation provision, section 36. It states, in relevant part,

> (1) The rights in the Bill of Rights may be limited only in terms of law of general application to the extent that the limitation is reasonable and justifiable in an open and democratic society based on human dignity, equality and freedom, taking into account all relevant factors, including—
>
> a. the nature of the right;
> b. the importance of the purpose of the limitation;
> c. the nature and extent of the limitation;
> d. the relation between the limitation and its purpose; and
> e. less restrictive means to achieve the purpose.

In addition to this general limitation provision, some individual rights provisions contain specific limitations.

Like Germany, South Africa has a Constitutional Court that is the ultimate interpreter of the constitution.[30] Its jurisdiction is limited to constitutional matters.[31] Besides the Constitutional Court there is a Supreme Court of Appeal, which is the highest appellate court in nonconstitutional matters.[32] Below it are several high courts, which have constitutional and nonconstitutional jurisdiction.[33] At the bottom of the judicial hierarchy are magistrates courts, which lack jurisdiction to decide on the constitutionality of legislation or conduct of the president.[34]

The Historical Background of the Property Clause

During the debates that led up to the adoption of the interim constitution in 1993, an extraordinary amount of attention was focused on the property question. Indeed, the property clause question was perhaps the single most controversial issue during those debates.[35] These debates will be discussed subsequently, but for present purposes it is enough to say that opponents feared that constitutionalizing property would mean freezing the existing gross maldistribution of resources, especially land, that resulted from decades of apartheid.[36] If a constitutional property clause did not entirely freeze the extant distribution, opponents argued, at a minimum it would significantly frustrate the cause of land reform, which they regarded as the bedrock of any true social transformation in the new South Africa.[37]

The pre-1993 debate about a property clause in the Bill of Rights was less about whether to include one than about its exact formulation. That there would be a property clause in the new constitution was virtually a foregone conclusion.[38] Even the staunchest opponents conceded as much, directing their energies instead on its content.[39] The real parameters of the debate then were whether the property clause would be the traditionally liberal sort or one with a thick social-obligation dimension.[40]

The eventual property clause's strong formulation was the product of stratagems, compromise, and mistake on the part of its drafters. It was promulgated against a background of academic and popular mistrust as well as general knowledge of fellow Commonwealth countries that had decided against including a property clause in their own constitutions, or that even, in the case of India, had removed an extant clause. It is remarkable that a right to property, however qualified, was included at all, given the extreme resistance to such a clause in South African society. Consider, for instance, the view of a group of academics from the Western Cape:

> We think that there should be no property clause in a South African Bill of Rights . . . [E]nshrining property rights in the Constitution will finally render legitimate the unjust distribution of land which is the result of the process of dispossession commenced by colonization and continued under apartheid.[41]

Mixed in with this opposition to the property clause was a certain sense of fear: fear that entrenching privilege would so impede the necessary social and economic reforms facing the country that a severe crisis—based on popular dissatisfaction and frustration— would ensue, one that would ultimately cast the credibility of the Bill of Rights into doubt and the constitutional government into danger.[42] This danger was perhaps not so farfetched when one considers the South African situation: not only was eighty-five percent of the land held by the white minority, but ninety-five percent of the productive capacity as well.[43]

The original proposals of the ruling National Party (NP) and the African National Congress (ANC) for what eventually became the property clause of the interim constitution staked out diametrically opposed positions. Bent on ensuring that the extant property holdings of white owners would be safe from the foreseeable redistributive incursions of a democratic government,[44] the NP proposed, under the title of "private ownership," a clause that mimicked classical liberal constitutional property clauses.[45] Conveniently ignoring the effect of colonial conquest and exclusionary racial legislation on land distribution patterns in South Africa,[46] the NP justified a high degree of protection for property rights by claiming that "the prospect of acquiring property is the principal incentive to hard work, thrift, responsibility and the development of the individual's full potential."[47]

The ANC's proposed property clause sought to temper the individual's right to the incidences of ownership by a strong and explicit social obligation.[48] Above all, the clause reiterated that the property rights of individuals are limited by the public interest in ensuring subsistence for all.[49] The ANC perceived these two parts, operating together, as the basis for state intervention to promote land restitution and rural restructuring[50]—which the South African Law Commission reproachfully viewed as a back door approach to nationalization without compensation.[51] From the NP's perspective, most damning was the failure to assure either market value or cash payment to compensate for an expropriation, leaving open, for instance, the possibility of payment in long-term government bonds for a substantially below-market amount.[52]

Ideology was by no means the only factor shaping the property clause of the interim constitution. ANC-aligned negotiators recognized that some sort of property clause must be included in the interim Bill of Rights because property rights were a "bottom line" for the government, without which the transition could not proceed.[53] Seeking a compromise between the NP's emphasis on protecting extant title and the ANC's commitment to land restitution for victims of apartheid, the Technical Committee added a subclause ensuring that private property holdings would not be completely insulated from redistributive initiatives.[54] While the clause represented a second-best solution for the land lobby, the NP quickly reacted to ensure that any future policies of restitution would be subordinate to the property rights of white farmers, and not the other way around. In doing so, however, the NP more than compensated for the ANC's earlier strategic mistake through the misstep of its principal negotiator on the Ad Hoc Committee.[55] The negotiator was preoccupied by the fear that the South African Constitutional Court would interpret the property clause as covering only land, and not "shares, jewellery [sic], coins, money, etc.," which ought to, in her opinion, be provided for in the Bill of Rights as well. As an extension of this concern, she further argued that land restoration was distinct from property rights and should be treated elsewhere in the interim constitution.[56] Based on this stance, the government mistakenly and obsessively concluded that the best way to protect white farmers was indeed the constitutional separation of property rights and land restoration.[57] While holding firm on this issue—eventually, the call for land restoration fell under the equality clause, and not the property clause, of the interim constitution and its substantive treatment was deeply buried elsewhere[58]—the government significantly conceded on other issues relating to property,[59] if only as a result of clever manipulation on the part of the ANC and at the bitter end of the multiparty negotiating process as a whole.[60]

The NP's most important concession was that market value would not dictate the compensation to be paid for government expropriations of land. For the ANC, this meant that in all practicality the property clause would not obstruct land restoration, regardless whether it were worded to be subordinate to property as in the government's proposed clause.[61] Reflecting the government's concession while at the same time seeming to present a compromise, the Technical Committee prepared a revision stating that the amount of compensation was to be judicially determined on the basis of "all relevant factors, including the use to which the property is being put, the history of its acquisition, its *market value* [italics added for emphasis], the value of the owner's investment in it and the interests of those affected."[62] Curiously, however, one ANC negotiator strongly feared that listing even these factors would lead to a judicial setting of compensation at a level higher even than market value.[63] As a result, more than two months later the Technical Committee withdrew the list of factors from its progress report, which was then sent to the Ad Hoc Committee with the NP's minister of justice, Kobie Coetsee, in attendance.[64] Coetsee, of course not sharing the ANC's fear but perhaps not grasping the big picture, insisted that "market value" was to find a place in the compensation requirement, even if it were to be only one of a list of factors. And so the list of factors guiding compensation made it back into what became section 28(3) of the interim constitution[65]—this at the property-protective government's own insistence! While debate was still whirling over wording such as "rights in property" and "expropriation of rights in property," the ANC and the NP held their final bilateral meeting to finalize the Bill of Rights.[66] In the meeting of October 25–26, 1993, agreement was reached upon section 28.

The debate over the property right was hardly ended by the adoption of section 28. In negotiations over the final constitution, property continued to be the center of contention. Indeed, it was one of the last three issues to be decided by the Constitutional Assembly.[67] To the very end, property was the straw that threatened to break the camel's back.[68]

When formal negotiations over the property clause question began in 1995, there were three options on the table. One was the Pan-African Congress's continuing opposition to any property clause at all. The second was a clause closely resembling section 28. The third option proved to be the basis for final agreement. It was the NP's proposed compromise. The NP agreed to drop section 28's positive guarantee of the right of property in exchange for a prohibition, lacking in section 28 (at least not expressly), against arbitrary deprivations and a requirement that deprivations be made only by laws of "general application."[69] The compromise was nearly scuttled over the fundamental question of land reform.[70] The proponents of land reform insisted on various add-ons intended to assure that the basic right itself did not block the way for tenure reform, restitution, and the like. After considerable wrangling, these demands were eventually accommodated in the form of subsections (4)–(8).

Still, the matters of both the basic right itself and the institution of property remained unresolved. In the end the negotiators could only agree on the provisions regarding deprivations and expropriations. Nothing was said positively about either the institution or the right. As one member of parliament who participated in the negotiations has observed, "The fact that the right itself was rendered silent and assumed is the measure of the difficulty of the negotiations—it simply could not be resolved, and was safest silent."[71]

The ultimate version of the property clause obviously was the product of a series of compromises. It was also the product of sheer exhaustion. Neither side, those favoring a strong entrenched property right and those opposing anything that threatened fundamental land reform, was happy with the final product, but, pragmatically acceding to the twin realities that *some* kind of property clause was inevitable and that *some* room for land reform had to be created, both sides apparently could agree that they had run out of time and energy. Any unresolved issues—and there were many—would have to be left up to the Constitutional Court's eventual resolution.

The Structure of the Property Clause

This section provides an overview of section 25, the property clause of the final constitution, together with section 36, the constitution's general limitation provision. I will focus particular attention on the case of *First National Bank of SA Ltd. v. Commissioner, South African Revenue Service* (the "*FNB Case*").[72] The South African Constitutional Court in that case, while leaving many questions unanswered, set out the basic parameters of how it will analyze claims under the property clause in the future. The analytical framework that emerged from that case is one that focuses on the fundamental question, which is whether the challenged governmental act struck an appropriate balance between private property rights and the public interest. The case was examined through the analytical lens of an arbitrariness test.

While the court set out a multistage mode of analysis, the real work is done at one stage, the stage at which it asks whether the state-induced deprivation of property was arbitrary. The result was to create what Theunis Roux has termed an "arbitrariness vortex."[73]

Before turning to the *FNB* analysis, some preliminary aspects of South Africa's constitutional property right need mentioning. First, the property clause, section 25, guarantees property as an individual right but not as an institution.[74] This is an important point of similarity between section 25 and the American takings clause and a point of difference with the German constitutional property clause.[75]

It is possible, of course, that an institutional guarantee could be read into section 25, but that seems both unlikely and unwise. It is unlikely because section 25(1), unlike its counterpart under the interim constitution, is stated in negative rather than positive terms. A positive formulation like section 28 of the interim constitution can more easily be interpreted as implicitly including an institutional as well as an individual guarantee.[76] The positive guarantee of section 28(1) was similar to Article 14 of the German Basic Law, which contains an express institutional guarantee. Section 25(1), by contrast, reads like the American takings clause, which has not been interpreted to provide an institutional guarantee.

It would be unwise to read an institutional commitment into section 25(1), at least if the institutional guarantee is the sort provided under the German Basic Law. The effect of the Basic Law's institutional guarantee is to restrict the state's power to remove particular categories of resources, say, mineral rights or navigable water, entirely from the realm of private ownership in the absence of an overriding state interest in doing so. In a nation committed to social transformation, including through the redistribution of property rights, such a restriction might well turn out to be counterproductive. Fulfilling the constitution's promise "to bring about equitable access to all South Africa's natural resources" might require that certain categories of resources be withdrawn from the private sphere and maintained exclusively in the public domain.[77] One simply cannot foresee what future circumstances will require with respect to that promise.

A second preliminary point concerns the relationship between section 25 and socioeconomic rights provisions elsewhere in the Bill of Rights. As we will discuss, section 25 and these socioeconomic rights provisions are closely related, both in the way the court analyzes claims under them and substantively. The basic substantive relationship is that, just as the land-reform provisions of section 25 make evident the fact that the constitutional property right is nothing like a classical liberal property right, so also do the constitution's socioeconomic rights provisions. They plainly contemplate that the state may, indeed must, engage in a significant measure of wealth redistribution, state actions that would be in no small amount of tension with a classical liberal constitutional right of property. The property clause, read *in pari materia* with the socioeconomic rights provisions, underscores the intended transformative character of the South African Constitution.

The third preliminary point follows closely on the heels of the second. Although it does not refer to a social-obligation norm as Article 14 of the German Basic Law does, section 25 *is* a social-obligation-type constitutional property clause. Indeed, it instantiates a social-obligation norm more completely than Article 14 does, for it does not leave to judicial construction many of the difficult questions regarding the scope of the social-obligation norm. The land-reform provisions of section 25 leave no doubt that private property rights are subject to the social needs for land redistribution, tenure reform, and restitution of land rights, the so-called three pillars of South African land reform.[78] Moreover, the socioeconomic rights provisions also make clear that the interests of private owners coexist with constitutional entitlements of nonowners to have basic needs such as housing and medical care satisfied. Viewing these provisions together with the property clause itself, section 25 emerges as a social-obligation-type property clause par excellence.

FNB *and the Constitutional Court's Decision Tree Analysis under Section 25*

The *FNB* case involved a commercial property of the sort that bore no relation to social transformation. What was at stake was a conflict between the government's need to enforce payment of tax debts and a lender's interest in securing repayment of its loan. A bank had reserved ownership in several motor vehicles as security for its loan to finance their lease or purchase by an importer. The importer owed a large amount of money to the South African Revenue Service (SARS) for unpaid customs and duties. To secure payment of this debt, SARS imposed a statutory lien on all moveable property, including the motor vehicles owned by the bank, which was found on the importer's premises. The tax debt was unrelated to the vehicles in question, but the vehicles were subject to the state's lien simply by virtue of being physically present on the tax debtor's business premises and therefore falling within the broad scope of the lien. The question was whether the statute that authorized the state's detention and sale of the vehicles constituted an unconstitutional interference with the property of the bank as the unrelated and innocent owner.

The lower court held that the statute did not violate section 25 because it established a lien or tax rather than an expropriation. The basis for this conclusion was the court's view that one effect of the statute was to make third-party owners of assets subject to a statutory lien coprincipal debtors along with the customs debtor. Legislation creating mechanisms for enforcing debts owed to the state are generally understood in South Africa not to raise any constitutional issue,[79] and as a result the court's reading of the enforcement statute seemed to eliminate any basis for a constitutional objection.

The Constitutional Court rejected the lower court's characterization of the issue. In the Constitutional Court's view,[80] the question was not whether the statute made the third-party a codebtor with the original debtor but whether the statute improperly interfered with any property interest of the affected third party. In addressing that question, the court set out a formulaic six-step mode of analysis.[81] In any constitutional property challenge under section 25, the court said, the following questions must be addressed in the following order:[82]

(a) Does that which is taken away from [the party affected by the statute] by the operation of [the statute] amount to "property" for purpose of s 25?
(b) [If yes,] Has there been a deprivation of such property by the [state agency]?
(c) If there has, is such deprivation consistent with the provisions of s 25(1)?
(d) If not, is such deprivation justified under s 36 of the Constitution [i.e., the general limitations clause]?
(e) If it is, does it amount to expropriation for purpose of s 25(2)?
(f) If so, does the deprivation comply with the requirements of s 25(2)(a) and (b)?
(g) If not, is the expropriation justified under s 36?

As we will see, however, and as Roux has argued, there is less here than meets the eye. In fact, the bulk of the analytical work is done at stage 3, more specifically, that part of stage 3 where the court asks whether the challenged statute effects an *arbitrary* deprivation of property.

IS THE AFFECTED INTEREST "PROPERTY"? The threshold question is whether the government action affected a property interest within the meaning of section 25(1). The court in *FNB* declined to give a comprehensive definition of property for section 25 purposes, purporting to limit its holding to tangible moveable assets, which along with land, the court said, is "at the heart of our constitutional concept of property."[83] However, it is highly unlikely that the court will confine the scope of constitutional property to these two obvious categories in the future. Indeed, it seems likely that the court will seldom decide a section 25 case at this first stage but will instead treat the affected interest, whatever it is, as property so that it can move on to the next stage.

Several signs point in the direction of a broad scope of constitutional property. First, in the first *Certification Case* the court had rejected the assertion that the draft of the constitution was deficient because it failed explicitly to recognize intellectual property and mineral rights, and this signaled the possibility that such rights count as "property."[84] The court's duty in that case was simply to assure that the proposed constitution complied with universally recognized norms. Mineral and intellectual property are not universally recognized human rights, so there is no need to specify them explicitly. Moreover, while it is uncommon for constitutional property clauses to spell out the particular types of property rights that are included within the clause, intellectual property and mineral rights are typically understood as included in constitutional property clauses.

Second, the court cited with approval Andre van der Walt's argument in favor of a "dynamic, typically public-law" conception of constitutional property.[85] Third, as Roux points out, one of the reasons the court gave for extending section 25 protection to juristic persons, namely, that intangible forms of property play an important role in the country's economic and democratic growth, applies equally to the protection of a wide variety of forms of property.[86] The most likely course for the court to take will be to assume that the affected interest is constitutional property and move on to the arbitrariness inquiry.

The question of what counts as property for constitutional purposes will be especially problematic for South African courts in the context of the so-called new property. On the one hand, *FNB* suggests that the court might take an approach that is based on or at least is consistent with a conception of property that is both nonphysicalist and purposive. Such an approach conceives of property in increasingly abstract terms, facilitating a shift away from property as land or property as things to a conception that accommodates a wide variety of interests that serve particular political, social, and moral functions, especially personal security and self-development. Such an approach would closely resemble the one followed by German courts under the property clause of the German Basic Law.[87] It would also bring the South African courts in line with the approach to constitutional property that is increasingly predominant throughout the world. On the other hand, traditional understandings of property in South African private law may be a countercurrent to this more expansive approach. Roman-Dutch law has traditionally conceived of property in narrow, physicalist terms, taking land as the emblem of what property is. This conception is based on the conceptual pandectist theory of property that still prevails in the minds of South African lawyers.[88] It is possible, but highly unlikely, that this traditional South African private law conception would be capable of embracing contingent state-conferred benefits as "property."

The question came up in a lower-court case under the property clause of the interim constitution.[89] In dictum, the court stated that "the meaning of 'property' in section 28 of the [interim] Constitution may well be sufficiently wide to encompass a State housing subsidy."[90] The Constitutional Court might be prepared to follow this view under the final constitution, although this result is by no means certain. While the Constitutional Court is reluctant to grant such benefits substantive rather than procedural protection for fear of locking the state into a particular pattern of distributing benefits, the conclusion that government entitlements are constitutional property would do no more than move the inquiry one step along the court's decision tree. The court's real scrutiny would come, again, at the arbitrariness stage, at which the court might well conclude that while the government action constitutes a deprivation of a constitutional property interest, the deprivation is nonarbitrary. The conclusion that government entitlements are constitutional property would have the salutary result of granting such interests procedural protection even if they are not substantively protected through compensation.[91]

The tension between an expansive, nonphysicalist conception of property and the narrow, traditional private law meaning clouds another aspect of the meaning of constitutional property. Were the Constitutional Court to adopt a capacious definition of property for section 25 purposes, it is possible that the court would accept some version of the "conceptual severance" theory. As we have previously discussed,[92] that theory supposes that every incident of ownership is itself property, with the consequence that virtually every governmental undertaking that affects a privately owned asset in some way is one that affects "property." The court's analysis in *FNB* raises the possibility that it will adopt just this view. As we will see, one question in its analysis of the arbitrariness issue is whether a challenged deprivation "embrace[s] all the incidents of ownership" or "only some of the incidents of ownership and those incidents only partially."[93] Since the arbitrariness inquiry occurs only after the court has already determined that the affected interest is "property," this language suggests that the court is not prepared to end a section 25 challenge at stage 1 simply because the government action affects only some of the possible incidents of ownership.

On the other hand, conceptual severance would constitute a radical departure from the private law meaning of property. Indeed, the whole idea of ownership as a bundle of rights, which is the theoretical premise for the conceptual severance theory in the United States, is itself unlikely to be acceptable to the traditional Roman-Dutch lawyer.[94]

It is not entirely clear how much rides on whether or not the court accepts the conceptual severance theory. Opponents of a constitutional property right feared that conceptual severance would effectively end any possibility of transformative land reform or other government actions aimed at ameliorating the gross inequality of property distribution in postapartheid South Africa. There is some basis for this fear, even under Roux's interpretation of the *FNB* decision tree. If the court accepts conceptual severance, then it would be possible to accept the Epsteinian view that every twig in the bundle of rights, in and of itself, constitutes ownership. Then at step three of Roux's decision tree there is a greater likelihood of a judicial finding of arbitrariness precisely because the entire twig has been destroyed. If all of the incidents of that twig have been destroyed by the regulation, then the regulation appears to have a far more arbitrary effect.

On the other hand, if the court were to adopt the conceptual severance theory, it might stop short of Professor Epstein's theory that every possible twig in the bundle of rights constitutes ownership in and of itself. Here South Africa's background traditional private law conception of property might come into play and place limits on just how far the bundle-splitting theory might extend. The right to exclude, for example, might be considered essential to ownership, but not the right of commercial exploitation. Such a qualified use of the conceptual severance idea would mean that in many, and perhaps most, cases, the real work is still done at the arbitrariness stage. It seems highly unlikely that a law affecting only one or a few of the incidents of ownership would be considered to constitute an "arbitrary" deprivation. The upshot is that conceptual severance probably has less significance in South African constitutional law than it does in American takings law.

HAS THERE BEEN A STATE-INDUCED "DEPRIVATION"? Assuming that the court finds that the affected interest is property for section 25 purposes, the next question is whether the state's action has caused a "deprivation" of that interest. The court in *FNB* declined to provide a comprehensive definition of what constitutes a "deprivation," short of saying that "[d]ispossessing an owner of all rights, use and benefit to and of corporeal movable goods, is a prime example of deprivation in both its grammatical and contextual sense."[95] The court did observe that in a sense any law that interferes with the "use, enjoyment or exploitation" of property "involves some deprivation in respect of the person having title or right to or in the property concerned."[96] This suggests that the court is unlikely in the future to devote much attention to whether a state interference with property is or is not a deprivation. Even if the state act interferes with only one or two twigs in the bundle of rights, the court is likely to treat it as a deprivation and attach significance to the limited degree of interference at the stage of inquiring into the deprivation's arbitrariness.[97]

The court's ready willingness to find that a deprivation has occurred whenever a statute interferes with a twig in the bundle of rights was underscored by its subsequent decision in *Mkontwana v. Nelson Mandela Metropolitan Municipality.*[98] That case involved a challenge to a statute that in effect prevented an owner of land from transferring her property unless utility charges due to a municipality were paid, even if the charges were for consumption by someone other than the owner.[99] The court held that the statute did constitute a deprivation of the owner's property under section 25(1) of the constitution. It stated that "at the very least, substantial interference or limitation that goes beyond the normal restrictions on property use or enjoyment found in an open and democratic society would amount to deprivation."[100] Applying that standard, the court said that the decisive feature of the statute was the fact that the statute imposed a "substantive obstacle to alienation." "The right to alienate property," the court observed, "is an important incident of its use and enjoyment."[101]

While the court in *FNB* did not provide a comprehensive definition of deprivation, it did clarify the relationship between the deprivation and expropriation requirements. It stated that expropriations are a subset of deprivations,[102] with the result that any law that provides for an expropriation of property must first satisfy the requirements of section 25(1). If these requirements are met, the law must then be tested under the requirements of section 25(2). The effect of this view is to make the distinction between deprivations and expropriations somewhat less important because the question whether the law is a valid expropriation will come up only if the court determines that the law either meets the section 25(1) requirements or, if not, is a valid limitation under section 36. If it does not, as it did not in the case itself, "that is the end of the matter," as the court put it.[103] The point is important because, as van der Walt notes,[104] this is likely to be the outcome in most cases. A law that passes muster at the section 25(1) stage is unlikely to fail at the expropriation stage, and, conversely, a law that would fail the section 25(2) expropriation requirement will likely fail at the earlier section 25(1) stage.[105]

IS THE DEPRIVATION "ARBITRARY"? Prior to *FNB*, South African commentators had argued over the best way of interpreting the requirement that a deprivation of property not be "arbitrary" within the meaning of section 25(1). Some commentators had argued that the requirement of nonarbitrariness should be interpreted to be the same as a rationality review.[106] Another view was that, even if it is rational in the sense that it has some plausible means-end relationship, a deprivation must satisfy the section 36 proportionality requirement.[107] The court in *FNB* rejected both of these approaches. First, it rejected a thin, "mere rationality" approach, stating that the term "arbitrary" in section 25(1) "refers to a broader concept and a more controlling principle that is more demanding than the enquiry into mere rationality."[108] It also rejected a view that would conflate the section 25(1) and section 36 stages of scrutiny, stating that nonarbitrariness is not as intrusive a concept as the proportionality requirement of section 36. The court instead steered a position between the two extremes, adopting an approach that clearly involves a degree of substantive review that pushes first-stage, section 25(1) analysis in the direction of second-stage, section 36 proportionality analysis.

The court articulated a multistep test for determining whether a law amounts to an arbitrary deprivation of property. It is worth setting out the test in full. "[D]eprivation of property," said the court, "is 'arbitrary' as meant by s 25 when the 'law' referred to in s 25(1) does not provide sufficient reason for the particular deprivation in question or is procedurally unfair."[109] The court stated that insufficient reason is to be determined as follows:

(a) It is to be determined by evaluating the relationship between means employed, namely the deprivation in question and ends sought to be achieved, namely the purpose of the law in question.
(b) A complexity of relationships has to be considered.
(c) In evaluating the deprivation in question, regard must be had to the relationship between the purpose of the deprivation and the person whose property is affected.
(d) In addition, regard must be had to the relationship between the purpose of the deprivation and the nature of the property as well as the extent of the deprivation in respect of such property.

(e) Generally speaking, when the property in question is ownership of land or a corporeal movable, a more compelling purpose will have to be established in order for the depriving law to constitute sufficient reason for the deprivation than in the case when the property is something different and the property right something less extensive. This judgment is not concerned at all with incorporeal property.

(f) Generally speaking, when the deprivation in question embraces all the incidents of ownership, the purpose for the deprivation will have to be more compelling than when the deprivation embraces only some incidents of ownership and those incidents only partially.

(g) Depending on such interplay between variable means and ends, the nature of the property in question and the extent of its deprivation, there may be circumstances when sufficient reason is established by, in effect, no more than a mere rational relationship between means and ends; in others this might only be established by a proportionality evaluation closer to that required by s 36(1) of the Constitution.

(h) Whether there is sufficient reason to warrant the deprivation is a matter to be decided on all the relevant facts of each particular case, always bearing in mind that the enquiry is concerned with "arbitrary" in relation to the deprivation of property under s 25.[110]

On the facts of *FNB*, the court held that the statute failed the test. Where, as here, the statutory means involved total deprivation of the owner's property, there must be a close nexus among three factors: (1) the owner and the transaction giving rise to the debt, (2) the property taken and the debt, and (3) the owner and the debtor.[111] In this case the court said that there was no nexus.

Although the court's test has the superficial appearance of formality, upon closer inspection, it resembles in some ways the United States Supreme Court's multifactor balancing approach to regulatory takings cases. Clearly, there is considerable room for judicial discretion. Roux rightly observes that "[a]ll that can be said with any certainty is that the level of scrutiny will vacillate between two fixed poles: rationality review at the lower end of the scale, and something just short of a review for proportionality at the other."[112] Where the law deprives the owner of land or movables of all or most of the twigs in the bundle of rights, judicial review will be intense. On the other hand, where only a few of the incidents of ownership are affected and the regulatory purpose is highly important, the level of scrutiny will be weak.[113]

SECTION 36 LIMITATION ANALYSIS. PART 1: DEPRIVATIONS Assuming that the court finds that the challenged government measure amounts to an arbitrary deprivation of property under section 25(1), the infringement may still be justified under section 36, the general limitation provision. That, at least, is the theory. The practice is likely to be different. Certainly if the measure is held to be arbitrary because it is procedurally unfair or provides insufficient reason for the property deprivation, it will not meet the requirement of section 36(1) that it be "reasonable and justifiable in an open and democratic society based on human dignity, equality and freedom."[114] After *FNB*, the real question, as we have already discussed, is whether it is realistic to suppose that a court might uphold under section 36 a law that it has held to be an arbitrary deprivation under section 25(1).

There was considerable uncertainty before the *FNB* decision about the relationship between sections 25(1) and 36, and *FNB* has not clarified the situation. The court assumed, without deciding, that section 36 does apply when an infringement fails the section 25(1) test.[115] Applying section 36, the court held that the infringement could not be justified because there was no relationship between the owner and either the asset or the debt in question. The owner was an entirely innocent third party who completely lost all rights in his automobiles. This result was "grossly disproportional" to the state's benefit of collecting the debt.

The case tends to confirm the view that sections 36 and 25(1) are redundant.[116] The court's section 36 analysis focused on exactly the same factors as its section 25 test. This "telescoping" effect creates potential problems for the next stage of analysis, that is, whether the infringement amounts to an expropriation under section 25(2).

DOES THE DEPRIVATION CONSTITUTE AN EXPROPRIATION? AN IRRELEVANT QUESTION Under the *FNB* decision tree, if the court determines (as it did not in *FNB*) that an arbitrary deprivation is justified under section 36, the next question is whether the offending act constitutes an "expropriation" within the meaning of section 25(2). According to that provision, the state may expropriate property only under three conditions: first, through a law of general application; second, through a law that was enacted in pursuit of a "public purpose" or otherwise is in the "public interest"; and third, if the law provides for payment of constitutionally acceptable compensation. After *FNB*, inquiry into these factors is unlikely to occur, at least not if the court takes *FNB* into account.[117] The court's analysis in that case effectively mooted the distinction between deprivation and expropriation. By treating expropriations as a species of deprivation, thereby requiring that even overt acts of expropriation go through section 25(1) analysis, the court made it unnecessary in most cases for expropriation analysis under section 25(2). A law that substantially deprives an owner of her use or enjoyment of the property without compensation will almost certainly be struck down as arbitrary under section 25(1) and unjustified under section 36. Similarly, an expropriation for which compensation is provided but which is not for a public purpose or in the public interest is hardly likely to be viewed as nonarbitrary or justified.

This telescoping will be problematic in cases where the desired remedy is not to have the statute struck down but to retain the law with the court ordering more compensation or a different form of compensation. South African commentators have taken the court to task on this outcome, arguing that in cases of explicit expropriations the court should adjust its *FNB* analysis by allowing attention to focus directly on relevant issues regarding public use or compensation.[118]

The characterization in *FNB* of expropriations as a subset of deprivations represents a departure from the analysis of expropriations in the earlier *Harksen* case. In that case, the court had treated deprivations and expropriations as categorically distinct from each other. Expropriations, the *Harksen* court said, involve a permanent acquisition by the state of some asset (usually an immovable).[119] State actions in which the state did not actually acquire the asset or did so only temporarily are not expropriations but deprivations. *FNB* appears to abandon this view in favor of one that defines the two forms of state infringement as substantially overlapping rather than as mutually exclusive. It is entirely possible, however, that the court will refine its understanding of the relationship between expropriations and deprivations in the future in a way that leaves permanent physical acquisitions as a separate category, subject to section 25(2).

Less certain are the prospects that the court will recognize the intermediate category of government actions. These actions, known in American law as "inverse condemnations" and in South Africa as "constructive expropriations," find little room for recognition under either the *Harksen* or *FNB* approaches.[120] Following *Harksen*, there was some indication in lower-court case law that a constructive expropriation doctrine might be recognized,[121] but *FNB* makes that less likely. The fact that all deprivations, which, per *FNB*, include all expropriations, must first either pass muster under section 25(1), that is, not constitute an arbitrary deprivation, or be justified under section 36 makes it highly unlikely that a law that imposes a disproportionate burden on the petitioner but which would otherwise be unobjectionable if adequate compensation were paid will reach the section 25(2) stage of scrutiny. Such a law will very likely be deemed an arbitrary (and unjustified) deprivation.[122]

This would be an unfortunate consequence. Transformative land reform in South Africa may involve situations in which the state wishes to enact an otherwise desirable land-reform law that is not an overt expropriation but whose effects make it tantamount to an expropriation. In terms of facilitating social and economic transformation, the desirable approach to take in this situation would be not to strike down the law as an arbitrary deprivation but to keep it in effect with payment of some form of compensation. Such an approach will require adjustment in the mode of analysis laid out in *FNB*.

DOES THE EXPROPRIATION PASS MUSTER UNDER SECTIONS 25(2) AND (3)? Assuming that an infringement is found to constitute an expropriation, to be valid it must satisfy the requirements of sections 25(2) and 25(3). Basically, this means that the infringement must meet the public purpose/public interest requirement and provide for adequate compensation. The *FNB* analysis makes it extremely unlikely that either of these requirements will ever be addressed.[123] An expropriating law that is not for a public purpose or in the public interest will be struck down under section 25(1) as an arbitrary deprivation.

Putting this problem aside for the moment, an important question is whether the state may legitimately exercise its expropriation power to transfer property, especially land, from one private party to another with no acquisition itself. If section 25(2) were construed to forbid that, South Africa's goal of transformative land reform would be virtually impossible to achieve. A fundamental aspect of its land-reform program is direct redistribution of land from one private party to another. Fortunately, section 25(4)(a) eliminates any doubt about the constitutional legitimacy of this program, for it expressly states that "the public interest includes the nation's commitment to land reform . . ."

The compensation requirement is a trickier matter. While the American Constitution requires payment of fair market value, this may not always be the case under the South African Constitution. Section 25(3) identifies several relevant factors, including the extent of state involvement, the use to which the property will be put, and the history of the state's acquisition, signaling that something less than market value may be paid. Lower courts have seen fit to do just that.[124] An important and unresolved question is whether the reference in section 25(3) to striking an equitable balance between the public interest and the interests of the private owner justifies awarding materially less than full market value in cases where transformation of land rights is not involved. Arguably, the public interest factor should weigh differently in different contexts, leading to different compensation practices in land-reform cases than in cases where the government's expropriation is for a more prosaic end.[125] It remains to be seen how the Constitutional Court will use the public interest factor.[126]

The Relationship between Socioeconomic Rights and Property Rights

One of the most novel features of section 25 is its specification of positive rights[127] as part of the constitutional treatment of property. Unlike the American Constitution, which treats the property right as strictly negative in function, subsections 5–8 of section 25 specify certain socioeconomic rights as part of the overall constitutional scheme of property. Those provisions make the transformative purpose of the South African Constitution abundantly clear by undertaking such remarkable measures as imposing an obligation on the state to "enable citizens to gain access to land on an equitable basis" and granting restitution and other forms of redress for persons who were dispossessed of land as a result of apartheid. Such measures go far beyond anything found in most other constitutional property provisions, including those, like Germany's, that explicitly recognize the social obligations of ownership.

The land rights provisions of section 25 are part of a broader network of socioeconomic rights provisions included in the 1996 constitution.[128] Among these is section 26, the constitution's main provision concerning housing. One of the most pressing problems under the constitution today is defining the interrelationship between sections 25 and 26. The constitution envisions the property clause as interdependent with the socioeconomic rights provisions, especially the housing clause.[129] But what is the proper balance between the need to provide decent housing and the obligation to protect property rights? The two most important decisions dealing with that question are the famous case of *Government of the Republic of South Africa v. Grootboom*[130] and a more recent case, *Port Elizabeth Municipality v. Various Occupiers*.[131] Both cases grow out of a common problem—eviction of squatters from informal housing settlements. Some background about that problem is necessary to understand the two cases.

Land Invasions, Squatter Settlements, and Evictions: South Africa's Housing Crisis

One of the most shocking sights in South Africa today is the ubiquitous presence of appallingly poor housing settlements throughout the country. These settlements, some of which are created following illegal invasions of either public or private land,[132] differ in size, but all of them are inhabited by desperately poor (and mostly black) South Africans living in desperate conditions. Land invasions have a long history in South Africa. In the *Port Elizabeth Municipality* case the Constitutional Court stressed that this history and the way in which the South African government historically has reacted to land invasions directly informs the relationship between the property right and the right to housing under the constitution.[133]

Residential segregation on the basis of race was the defining component of the apartheid policy.[134] Blacks, who comprised the substantial majority of the South African population, were evicted from land that was designated for whites only and were removed to so-called reserves, which by 1936 made up only thirteen percent of South Africa's total land area.[135] These reserves were located in rural areas, leaving urban land available for settlement by whites and other minorities. Blacks were legally permitted to reside in urban areas only as migrant workers, and their movement into towns was regulated by a strict system of permits. Nevertheless, even before the apartheid era, urbanization occurred on a large scale, as poor blacks moved to urban areas in search of greater opportunities. Economic development counteracted the government policy of keeping blacks out of urban areas.[136] As Justice Albie Sachs has explained, "In South Africa this process of movement to urban areas took place in the context of colonial domination, segregation, apartheid and the migrant labour system, and consequently took on an enduring racist character."[137] Government efforts to stop black migration into towns and cities failed, as blacks invaded undeveloped public or private parcels of land. This migration established a pattern of land invasions that accelerated during the apartheid era, as economic incentives for blacks to leave the so-called homelands increased.[138] The result was the proliferation of informal housing settlements in which people often lived in the crudest sort of shacks with few or no basic services.

During the apartheid era, the government's reaction to these land invasions and informal settlements was simple, harsh, and swift. It criminalized squatting, and it authorized local governments to evict squatters through a criminal process. Under the Prevention of Illegal Squatting Act, the government's eviction power depended solely on showing that the occupants' possession was unlawful.[139] The length of time the occupiers had lived there, the total lack of alternative places to live, and all other considerations were irrelevant. In addition to immediate expulsion, illegal occupiers were liable for criminal prosecution.

With the end of the apartheid regime in 1993, land invasions by poor blacks and the creation of informal and unauthorized housing settlements continued apace. The years of apartheid policies had created an acute housing shortage for blacks in many parts of the country. In response to the land rights provisions of section 25 and specifically to the direct command of section 26(2) to the state to "take reasonable legislative . . . measures, . . . to achieve the progressive realization of [the right to have access to adequate housing]," local governments enacted housing programs aimed at meeting housing needs, but the combination of the high demand for adequate low-cost housing and constrained government budgets left many desperately poor people with no alternative to the informal housing settlements. The failure of the housing programs to meet the acute and growing housing needs was the backdrop for the *Grootboom* case.

Grootboom

In *Grootboom,* a group of nine hundred people (510 of whom were children) living in an informal and unlawful housing settlement were evicted from their homes. Originally they resided in an informal settlement called Wallacedene, whose living conditions the court described as "intolerable."[140] They had applied for government low-income housing and had been on a waiting list for as long as seven years. Faced with the prospect of remaining in Wallacedene for many years, they unlawfully invaded a parcel of privately owned land that had been earmarked for subsidized low-income housing construction. The owner obtained an eviction order, but the occupants remained beyond the date for final vacation. They stated that they had nowhere else to go, as their former dwellings in Wallacedene were now inhabited by someone else. On a cold, rainy, and windy winter day, they were forcibly evicted. As the court stated, this was done prematurely and inhumanely, "reminiscent of apartheid-style evictions." Their homes were bulldozed, and their possessions were destroyed. Many inhabitants were not present and were not able to salvage their personal belongings.

The occupants initially took temporary shelter under plastic sheeting on a sports field in Wallacedene. When the fierce Cape winter rains began several days later, their attorney wrote to the municipality, describing the intolerable conditions and demanding that the municipality meet its constitutional obligation to provide them adequate shelter. Not satisfied with the municipality's response, the occupants filed an application for relief with the Cape of Good Hope High Court. The Cape High Court ordered the municipality to provide those claimants who were children and their parents with basic shelter immediately and irrespective of available resources. The court based its decision on section 28(1) of the constitution. That provision, in relevant part, provides: "Every child has the right . . . to basic . . . shelter . . ." The court reasoned that this obligation existed independently of and in addition to the state's obligation under the housing rights provision, section 26, which obligates the state to take reasonable legislative measures to provide everyone with adequate housing. On appeal, the Constitutional Court rejected the Cape High Court's decision. It held that section 28 was not violated but that the municipality's housing program did violate section 26 insofar as it "fail[ed] to recognise that the State must provide for relief for those in desperate need." [141]

At the outset there are several important points to note about these two provisions of the constitution. The first is that section 26 imposes both negative and positive duties on the state. More strikingly, perhaps, section 26 also imposes duties on private parties in addition to the government. The court in *Grootboom* stated that subsection 1 imposes "at the very least, a negative obligation placed upon the State and *all other entities and persons* to desist from preventing or impairing the right of access to adequate housing." [142] Moreover, under subsection 3, there is a constitutional duty on landlords not to evict tenants or other occupants without judicial permission. Such a duty exists in other countries, such as the United States, as a matter of private law but not as a constitutional obligation.

The largest question concerning section 26 is whether it imposes a "minimum core obligation," that is, a duty to "ensure the satisfaction of, at the very least, [a] minimum essential level" of housing.[143] The court in *Grootboom* rejected this suggestion on the grounds that it would be difficult to determine in the abstract what the content of that obligation would be. "[T]he needs in the context of housing," the court said, "are diverse: there are those who need land; others who need land and houses; yet others who need financial assistance." [144] The court rejected a minimum core obligation in favor of a reasonableness standard: "whether the measures taken by the State to realise the right afforded by s 26 are reasonable." [145] The key difference between the two is that under reasonableness review, individuals do not have a right to claim specific goods and services from the state. Their right is limited to demanding that the government adopt a reasonable program.[146]

With respect to section 28, the question was whether children have a direct entitlement to state-provided shelter. The text of section 28 seemingly said that they do. Unlike section 26, section 28 does not describe its rights as rights of "access to." Nor are the rights qualified by the kind of qualification that appears in section 26(2), which provides that the state "must take reasonable legislative and other measures" toward realization of the right. Section 28(1)(c) simply states, "Every child has the right . . . to basic . . . shelter . . ." Period.

Apparently not. The court stated that section 28(1)(c) must be read in conjunction with section 28(1)(b), which provides that every child has the right to family care or parental care. Reading the two together, the court concluded that section 28(1)(c) "does not create any primary State obligation to provide shelter on demand to parents and their children if children are being cared for by their parents or families."[147] The state's constitutional duty to children under the care of their parents or families, the court said, was limited to "provid[ing] the legal and administrative infrastructure necessary to ensure" compliance with section 28 and to comply with the various socioeconomic protections covered by provisions other than section 28.[148] The upshot in the immediate case was that, since the children were being cared for by their parents, "there was no obligation upon the State to provide shelter for [them]."[149]

What seemed to have bothered the court was what it termed the "anomalous result"[150] that would have followed from a literal interpretation of section 28. The anomaly was that people with children would have had a direct right to housing under section 28 while those without children, including the old and disabled, would have had none. It seems odd to regard such a result as anomalous. As Cass Sunstein has pointed out, it "might seem to make sense to say that children should have a particular priority here . . . and hence that adults with children would have a preferred position."[151]

Perhaps the most revealing statement in the opinion concerned the practical matter of establishing priorities. The court stated, "The carefully constructed constitutional scheme for progressive realization of socioeconomic rights would make little sense if it could be trumped in every case by the rights of children to get shelter from the State on demand."[152] The court's evident concern was that parents and family might use their child's section 28 right to "trump even reasonable priority-setting," as Sunstein puts it.[153] The court did not wish to engage in second-guessing reasonable policy choices made by the legislature. Providing decent housing for all South Africans is an incredibly complex task that inevitably involves choices among competing social needs. In the court's view, so long as the government was addressing those needs in a reasonable manner, the constitutional duties of the state under both sections 28 and 26 were satisfied.

The basic question, then, was whether the legislature's housing program was reasonable under the circumstances of the case. The court held that it was not. The government's housing program fell short of the injunction of section 26(2) by failing to make provision for the immediate needs of those in desperate circumstances:

> The nationwide housing program falls short of obligations imposed upon national government to the extent that it fails to recognize that the State must provide for relief for those in desperate need. They are not to be ignored in the interests of an overall program focussed [sic] on medium and long-term objectives.[154]

In other words, the constitution requires not only a long-term program to deal with the problem of inadequate shelter but also a short-term program to help those who have no shelter available at all.

The most important aspect of *Grootboom* is the court's evident reluctance to interpret the constitution's socioeconomic provisions in a way that invites individual claims against the state for direct material assistance.[155] The court rejected the argument that section 26 imposes a minimum core obligation on the state, holding instead that all that the provision entitles a claimant to is that the state must adopt a reasonable program of housing. This interpretation significantly limits the impact of the section 26 right to housing, a point that many commentators have critically noted.[156]

The Relationship between Housing Rights and Property Rights: **Port Elizabeth Municipality v. Various Occupants**

At issue in *Port Elizabeth Municipality* was not the validity of a housing program but the validity of an eviction under a postapartheid-era statute regulating the eviction process. Government evictions from informal housing settlements continued after the end of the apartheid policy, but the government policy toward the problems of landlessness, informal settlements, and evictions was fundamentally different. Nothing better expresses the radical change in policy than section 26(3) of the 1996 constitution. It states, "No one may be evicted from their home, or have their home demolished, without an order of court made after considering all the relevant circumstances. No legislation may permit arbitrary evictions."

In response to this injunction, the Prevention of Illegal Eviction from and Unlawful Occupation of Land Act of 1998 (PIE) was enacted to regulate the process of eviction from informal settlements. The statute basically inverted the old apartheid approach toward evictions. It decriminalized squatting and made the eviction process subject to a number of requirements intentionally designed to end the abuses of the old system. The priority between public and private law values was reversed. The old common law remedies were now made subject to both procedural and substantive requirements, and "the overall objective of facilitating the displacement and relocation of poor and landless black people for ideological purposes was replaced by acknowledgment of the necessitous quest for homes of victims of past racist policies."[157]

The most controversial aspect of PIE is that it significantly changes the landowner's right to evict under the traditional South African common law.[158] Under that law, in order to evict, the owner merely had to prove that she was the owner of the property and that the defendant was in possession of it without her permission.[159] Under PIE, the standard for determining whether an eviction order can be issued is whether eviction would be "just and equitable."[160] As the Constitutional Court stated in the case, PIE "has to be understood, and its governing concepts of justice and equity have to be applied, within a defined and carefully calibrated constitutional matrix,"[161] taking all of the relevant circumstances into account.

In *Port Elizabeth Municipality,* a group of sixty-eight people, including twenty-three children, were evicted from shacks they had constructed on privately owned undeveloped land. The occupants had lived in their shacks for periods ranging from two to eight years. They told the municipality that they were willing to vacate if they received reasonable notice and if suitable alternative land was made available to them. They were told to move to a place called Walmer, but they rejected this offer on the ground that Walmer was crime ridden and overcrowded. The municipality contended that it had embarked on a reasonable housing program and that if alternative land were made available to these occupants, they would in effect have been given preferential treatment, contrary to the housing program. The Cape High Court held that the occupants were unlawfully occupying the land and ordered them evicted. The Supreme Court of Appeal reversed, holding that the occupiers were not seeking preferential treatment, only that land be identified where they could put up their shacks. The court stressed that existence of a suitable alternative was especially important in this case because of the length of time they had occupied the land. On appeal by the municipality, the Constitutional Court affirmed, holding that under the circumstances of the case eviction would be neither just nor equitable, as both the statute and the constitution require.

The court began its analysis by noting that much of the case turns on "establishing an appropriate constitutional relationship between section 25, dealing with property rights, and section 26, concerned with housing rights."[162] Under the constitution, the court reasoned, land rights, housing rights, and the right not to be arbitrarily evicted are closely intertwined. "The stronger the right to land, the greater the prospect of a secure home."[163] The court identified three "salient features" of the constitution's "interrelationship between land hunger, homelessness and respect for property rights."[164] First, the land rights of the dispossessed are generally not self-enforcing. While the constitution strongly sanctions land rights, it does not sanction arbitrary seizures, either by the state or by individuals. Section 26(3) is defensive rather than affirmative; it prevents landowners from sending in the bulldozers merely on the basis of their ownership. Second, eviction of people living in informal settlements is permissible even if it results in loss of a home. Finally, section 26(3) is nonprescriptive, requiring that courts must take all relevant factors into account:

> The judicial function in these circumstances is not to establish a hierarchical arrangement between the different interests involved, privileging in an abstract and mechanical way the rights of ownership over the right not to be dispossessed of a home, or vice versa. Rather it is to balance out and reconcile the opposed claims in as just a manner as possible taking into account all of the interests involved and the specific factors relevant in each particular case.[165]

According to section 6 of PIE, in order for a municipality to be in a position of seeking an eviction order[166] it must establish that the occupation is unlawful and that the structures are unauthorized, unhealthy, or unsafe. Those factors, however, are only necessary predicates for municipal eviction. The court has discretion whether to order the eviction on the basis of whether it is just and equitable to do so in light of all relevant circumstances, including three specifically identified factors: the manner in which the occupation was effected, the occupation's duration, and the availability of alternative housing or land.[167] PIE, the court emphasized, has to be understood in light of the historical background of evictions during the apartheid era. It envisions that eviction is not a matter of enforcing technical property rights under the old common law. Rather it is a matter of finding a way of reconciling the "diametrically opposing" interests of both the landowner and the occupiers in a manner that is just and equitable to the two sides. Finding such a solution, the court said, requires that the court go beyond its normal functions and "engage in active judicial management according to equitable principles in an ongoing, stressful and law-governed social process."[168] Identifying a concrete way of fulfilling this managerial role, the court suggested that face-to-face mediation should replace "arms-length combat" wherever possible. "[A]bsent special circumstances it would not ordinarily be just and equitable to order eviction if proper discussions, and where appropriate, mediation, have not been attempted."[169]

In the instant case, the court identified several reasons why it would not be just or equitable to order eviction. One was the failure of the municipal officials to make a real attempt at listening to the problems of this group of occupiers. Another was the lengthy period of time during which the occupants lived on the land in question. Third, neither the municipality nor the owner had demonstrated any need to evict from the land in order to put it to some productive use. Finally, the group is relatively small in size and genuinely in need.

Justice Albie Sachs's opinion for the court is remarkable in many respects. It is extraordinarily clear in its analysis of the relationship between sections 25 and 26 and their relationship, in turn, to PIE. Justice Sachs provides a virtual roadmap for lawyers litigating a section 6 eviction case, especially in the context of informal housing settlements. For example, his observation that "[a] court will . . . be far more cautious in evicting well-settled families with strong local ties, than persons who have recently moved on to land and erected their shelters there" illustrates how he concretely explains how each factor that is part of the balancing process is to be weighted.

The opinion's discussion of the judicial function in eviction cases is also remarkable. It is sensitive to the interests of all of the affected parties, explicitly rejecting any notion that the owner's interest is privileged over that of the occupant or vice versa. Moreover, Sachs's suggestion that mediation first be used as an alternative to the more confrontational dispute resolution method, litigation, is both imaginative and sensitive to the personal stakes in eviction cases. The approach, although open to possible criticisms,[170] is compatible with the spirit of South Africa's Truth and Reconciliation Commission and to the indigenous South African ideology of *ubuntu* ("humanity toward others"), an ideology that is foundational in the new South Africa.[171]

Perhaps the most significant aspect of his opinion was his analysis of precisely how section 26 of the constitution and PIE are transformational.

Sachs explains that the historical background of section 26 and PIE must inform judicial analysis in eviction cases. He explicitly repudiates the view that the common law's approach to evictions was in fact politically neutral, a view that we will discuss in the next part of this chapter. Sachs states, for example, "The principles of ownership in the Roman-Dutch law . . . gave legitimation in an apparently neutral and impartial way to the consequences of manifestly racist and partial laws and policies."[172] The statement is highly significant, for it unambiguously indicates that the eviction process, especially in the context of informal housing settlements, is no longer governed by the old common law rules, concepts, or values. As Sachs succinctly explains, "In sum, the Constitution imposes new obligations on the courts concerning rights relating to property not previously recognized by the common law. It counterposes to the normal ownership rights of possession, use and occupation, *a new and equally relevant right not arbitrarily to be deprived of a home.*"[173]

Taken together, *Grootboom* and *Port Elizabeth Municipality* create a unique approach to defining the constitutional dimension of the social obligation of ownership. This approach has three defining characteristics. First, as *Grootboom* makes clear, the state is under positive duties in relation to both the section 25 property right and to socioeconomic rights. These duties exist in tension with the more conventional negative duties that section 25 also imposes on the state, and the Constitutional Court has directly faced this tension, particularly in the context of the pressing need to address the country's urgent housing problem. The South African Constitution makes clear, to a far greater extent than does the German Basic Law, just what the social obligation is and how it relates to the basic property right.

Second, the social obligation defined by the socioeconomic rights provisions is limited in a highly important way. The state's obligation is neither absolute nor unqualified. Rather, it has three components: (1) to undertake reasonable legislative and other measures and (2) to achieve progressive realization of the socioeconomic rights (3) within the range of available resources. An important consequence of this definition of the social obligation is that individuals do not have a constitutional entitlement to demand direct provision of services or benefits from the state.

Third, the social obligation, as the court has thus far defined it through the socioeconomic rights provisions, has primarily been imposed upon the state. This is especially true with respect to positive obligations, which have been the basis for claims in most of the court's socioeconomic rights cases.[174] Whether the socioeconomic rights provisions create causes of action in litigation solely involving private parties has been a highly controversial topic, one that remains still largely unsettled. The possibility that those provisions will be given "horizontal effect," as it is called, will be discussed in the next part. The prospects for the South African Constitution's promise of social transformation to be fully realized depends in large measure on the extent to which the constitution and its values replace private law and private law values, especially in litigation in which the state is not a party. In the context of South Africa's need to eradicate all traces of its apartheid past, the social obligation of ownership must be placed on all of society, not merely on the state.

Beyond Social Obligation to Social Transformation? The Relationship between Traditional South African Private Law and the New Constitutional Law

Both before and after South Africa's first democratic elections on April 27, 1994, one of the biggest uncertainties about the new constitution was what effect the constitution would have in the future on South Africa's traditional private law regime.[175] The Constitutional Court has issued no definite pronouncements, and South African lawyers, both academics and practitioners, remain deeply divided over this matter. While some commentators argue that South Africa's traditional common law system is sufficiently flexible to accommodate if not actually advance social transformation in South Africa,[176] other lawyers strongly dispute this and insist that genuine social transformation in the newly democratic South Africa will come only if the historical primacy of private law over public law in South Africa is abandoned.[177] True social transformation, they urge, depends upon the new constitution's norms and principles guiding all aspects of the entire legal system and upon traditional private law being subordinated to the constitution. The core normative message of this chapter is that the latter group of commentators is absolutely correct. The possibility of genuine social transformation in South Africa will be fundamentally undermined if South Africa's background legal culture, its tradition of the conceptualist and naive positivist Roman-Dutch private law jurisprudence, is not overtly subordinated to the basic values of the constitution, especially in relation to rights in land.

A Brief Summary of Traditional South African Private Law Methodology, Especially in Relation to Property Rights

To understand both why there is such a marked contrast between the traditional South African civil law discursive methodology and that of the new constitution and why that contrast looms so large for the future development of constitutional property law in South Africa, a brief survey of South Africa's civil law method is necessary. My aim here is to be suggestive, not exhaustive. All legal systems, of course, are complex, but South Africa's mixed private law system is especially so. I can hardly do it justice in a few paragraphs, but I do hope to capture its distinctive characteristics.

Traditional South African civil law methodology is strikingly conceptualist. Based substantially on the work of the Dutch conceptualist legal theorists Hugo Grotius (1583–1605) and Johannes Voet (1647–1713),[178] it analyzes legal questions on the basis of a system of dichotomous legal concepts that is supposed to exhaustively define the entire universe of legal relations. In broad outline Grotius, Voet, and the other founders of this methodology[179] set out to define a system of rights that would serve as the foundation for a scientific legal method, one that would provide objective solutions to legal problems. This system of rights took the form of a hierarchy of private law rights, consisting of a number of conceptual dichotomies. For our purposes the most important of these dichotomies is that between "property rights" and "possession." Grotius and Voet defined "property rights" as including "real rights," which they divided further between "ownership" and "limited real right." The key category was ownership. Ownership is the most important and valuable property right. All other private rights, real and personal, are measured in relation to how far short of ownership they fall. All private law rights are defined in terms of a relationship between a person and an object, and ownership is the ultimate in such relationships. It is not a relative right but is instead absolutely enforceable. Its core characteristic is the right to exclude. By giving its holder the right to exclude the rest of the world, ownership created an inviolable private sphere, a negative space with which the privileged individual reigned supreme. The owner, by virtue of her right to exclude the rest of the world, prevailed not only over other individuals bearing lesser private rights but also over the public sphere, meaning that she was insulated from all but the most limited and unavoidable state actions.

Even this very brief summary of the traditional Roman-Dutch legal method is enough to make clear the strong similarity between it and the classical liberal legal methodology practiced by Anglo-American lawyers in the late nineteenth and early twentieth century. Both rely on abstract legal concepts to do the substantive work of making what are in fact policy choices. Both claim that private law, as properly practiced, is a science and, as such, is objective and politically neutral. Both draw a strict categorical separation between the private sphere, regulated by a strictly individual-intent-facilitating private law, and the public realm, which is the province of public law. And both place private law and its legal relations at the epicenter of the legal system, leaving public law with its collective values at the margins of the properly designed legal universe. In American jurisprudence, classical liberal private law was effectively debunked by the full-scale critique of the legal realists, but in South Africa, its counterpart, traditional Roman-Dutch law, is still very much alive.

"Tradition on Trial"[180]*: An Example of the Privatist Approach to Modern South African Property Relations*

One of the claimed strengths of the traditional South African private law method is its ostensible flexibility and adaptability. Supporters of maintaining a pure private law, supreme within its own realm and not subordinate to the constitution, repeatedly push this aspect of traditional South African private law in debates over the private-public law relationship. Their argument is that if "colonized" by constitutional law,[181] private law will lose its distinctive flexibility and so not be allowed to fulfill its potential to contribute to South Africa's democratic transformation.[182] They totally (and sometimes vehemently) reject any suggestion that traditional South African private law, particularly meaning South African common law, in any way contributed to maintaining the apartheid system. The historical experience of courts applying the common law under the apartheid system, they contend, shows that legislation, not the common law, was the legal basis for apartheid. Moreover, the legislation that introduced and then entrenched apartheid was foreign to both the letter and spirit of traditional Roman-Dutch law. "[T]he apartheid era," one commentator has written,[183] "cannot be attributed to Roman-Dutch law—the blame must be placed squarely on the shoulders of the ruling minority who introduced the system of apartheid by legislation, and they were primarily enabled to this end by the doctrine of parliamentary sovereignty which derives from English constitutional law." Politics, in other words, along with public law was to blame for introducing and maintaining the shameful apartheid regime. The Roman-Dutch system did not itself serve that regime. The change in South Africa's political system and accompanying public law apparatus, the argument goes, does not warrant abolition or any major change in the country's private law system. Indeed, defenders say, purified of foreign apartheid legislative elements, traditional Roman-Dutch law is well suited to adapt to a truly democratic South Africa.[184]

One way to test this claim of traditional private law's ability to contribute to political and social transformation is by examining postapartheid cases in which the traditional private law method has been used in recent disputes. The best cases to use to test this claim are those in which the continuing effects of the apartheid system were front and center in the context of attempted land reform, the single most important challenge facing the attempt to transform South African property law.[185] A good example is a series of controversial cases involving attempted common law evictions of squatters and others allegedly in unlawful possession of land. These cases pose questions both about the relationship between new constitutional and statutory rights and traditional common law rights and the character of the traditional common law rights themselves in the postapartheid environment.

As we have seen, through the new constitution and a number of recent statutes, the legislature has attempted to remedy some of the injustices that were perpetrated through apartheid legislation that dispossessed, sometimes violently, nonwhite persons or left their positions as land occupants highly insecure. Legal questions have been raised about the effect of these constitutional and statutory provisions on common law ownership rights as owners, who nearly always are white, have attempted to evict persons, who nearly always are nonwhite, whose possession of land is allegedly illegal. Two types of defendants have been involved in eviction cases: first, persons who invade vacant land and then occupy structures in so-called informal settlements and, second, occupiers of formal housing under normal lease agreements who hold over after the end of their lease. The terms of the constitution's protective provisions and those of statutory law differ in their details with respect to the two categories of defendants so the specific legal issues differ somewhat in the cases. To pick one example, however, there has been uncertainty over the question whether common law eviction is restricted by the constitution's eviction principle. Stated differently, what is the impact of the constitution's eviction principle on common law eviction of unlawful occupiers where the eviction is not restricted by one of the postapartheid land reform statutes?[186] Some courts have held that the constitutional eviction principle does not affect common law eviction under such circumstances. An example is *Betta Eiendomme (Pty) Ltd. v. Ekple-Epoh.*[187] In that case the Witwatersrand High Court held that the constitutional provision, section 26(3), does not apply under such circumstances. Section 26(3), in relevant part, provides, "No one may be evicted from their home . . . without an order of court made after considering all the relevant circumstances." The constitution does not specify what the relevant circumstances are, but guidance is provided by other constitutional provisions[188] and by land-reform laws that do detail some of the factors to be taken into account in determining conflicting property rights. For example, some reform statutes provide that courts must take into account the position of children, elderly persons, and households headed by women.[189] Under the court's approach, no such considerations are relevant because section 26(3) simply does not apply here.[190] Nor indeed, said the court, does the constitution's injunction to promote the values that underlie the constitution or the spirit, purport, and objects of the Bill of Rights.[191] In the absence of any relevant constitutional or statutory alteration of the ordinary landlord-tenant relationship, the traditional norms of the common (Roman-Dutch) law apply, and under those norms the mere facts that the plaintiff was the *owner* and the defendant was improperly in *possession* are enough to justify granting the petition for eviction.

Two aspects of the case are important: first, the court's analysis of the relationship between the constitution and the common law and, second, the court's method of analyzing the case through the lens of the traditional common law. With respect to the constitutional/common law relationship, the court's analysis of section 26(3) was quite obviously crabbed. The court stated that the provision was aimed only at protecting lawful owners and occupiers against a replay of the kinds of forced removals that occurred under apartheid. The court said,

> The specific formulations and the words in the total setting make it a "never again" provision. It had in mind the District Six (Cape Town) and Sophiatown (Johannesburg) type of interferences where people had what was truly and by all standards "their home" but found that it was taken from them by ejectment or by demolition by or under legislation which affected *inter alia* ownership, possession or occupation. That object does not cover cases of ordinary trespass, whether in the form of squatting or holding over or otherwise.[192]

Section 26(3), in other words, does not apply in "normal" landlord-tenant situations where the tenant's right of occupancy has lapsed for some reason. That is hardly clear from the provision itself, however. The very history of unjust evictions under apartheid that the court mentions, indeed the centrality of unjust evictions to the apartheid system, provides good grounds for doubting the court's interpretation, either as a matter of the drafters' intentions or as a matter of policy. Moreover, even if one assumes that section 26(3) did not directly apply, it hardly follows, as the court seemed to think it did, that section 26(3) is altogether irrelevant to the case. Given the history and effects of evictions under apartheid, the court surely could have found it reasonable to conclude that the constitutional provision, its fundamental purpose if not its letter, should guide the court's interpretation of the common law.

But it did not. What the court did do was to use the language of private law to analyze and resolve a dispute that obviously had public implications. In the context of modern South Africa, no dispute about evictions of black occupants, even technically unlawful occupants, can be meaningfully said to be a strictly private property dispute. Yet that is precisely how the court approached the case. Pushing aside public law injunctions provided in the constitution and land-tenure reform statutes, it began and ended with a baseline set by traditional common law norms. Its analysis of the common law can fairly be characterized as formalistic and conceptualistic. It is an example of what Dennis Davis has pungently labeled "Rip van Winkel jurisprudence."[193]

The court began with the premise that the common law right of ownership is not affected by the constitution. It then simply asserted that ownership "carries within it the right to possession,"[194] providing no substantial reasons for this conclusion or discussion of the immediate context within which it was addressing the meaning of the operative concepts, "ownership" and "possession." The mere facts that the plaintiff is the "owner" and the defendant is an "illegal occupier" (an unexplained conclusion), the court said, render it "right and proper" that the owner be granted an eviction order "against someone who has no business interfering with the possession."[195]

Beyond the court's abstract conceptualism, another aspect of its common law analysis is equally important. The court plainly assumed that the common law furnishes the baseline for measuring the neutral and legitimate distribution of legal rights. The effect is to create a strong presumption favoring the extant pattern of land holdings, placing on anyone who seeks to depart from that pattern a very heavy burden of proving that a departure is required either by virtue of the constitution or statutory law. The court's treatment of the relationship between the constitution and the common law indicates just how heavy that burden of proof is.

It seems difficult, then, to square the court's style of reasoning and its result with the broad claim by admirers of traditional South African common law that Roman-Dutch law's adaptability enables it to advance the goal of social transformation in the new South Africa. Even with express constitutional pronouncements committing the nation and its legal system to land reform, the courts have exhibited a clear tendency to find ways to keep the historic common law in a position of supremacy and to interpret the norms of that system through a traditional discursive framework that undermines social transformation and entrenches the extant distribution of land holdings.

The Intersection of Private and Constitutional Law: The "Horizontality" Debate

In both the United States and Germany, the social obligation that property owners *constitutionally* owe to their fellow citizens, to the extent that they owe such an obligation, exists, if at all, only indirectly. While owners are under a private law duty not to use their property in ways that harm others, the property clauses of the American and German constitutions are conventionally understood as not directly imposing obligations on private owners either affirmatively to act in some way that will benefit the community or to refrain from acting in some socially harmful way.

The shorthand expression for this view is that constitutional rights provisions in these two countries do not have a direct "horizontal effect." The idea of a horizontal effect is that constitutional rights provisions impose duties on private actors as well as on the government. As Stephen Gardbaum puts it, "The horizontal position expressly rejects a public-private distinction in constitutional law . . ."[196]

The conventional wisdom is that, owing to the state-action doctrine, the individual rights provisions of the American Constitution have strictly vertical effect.[197] Under the state-action doctrine, there must be some sort of government action in order for provisions of the Bill of Rights to apply. Private actors are not bound by the constitution. With respect to the constitutional property right this means that the obligation that is owed under the constitution is the state's. The state is obligated to refrain from acting in ways that unduly interfere with the freedom of owners to use or enjoy their property as they wish. Private law, not constitutional law, imposes whatever obligations owners owe directly to individuals. Stated differently, the American Constitution does not ordinarily furnish private individuals with a direct constitutional complaint against private owners whose property uses injure others in some way.[198]

Under the German Constitution, the matter is more complicated. German constitutional theory accepts in principle the idea that private law is not immune from the constitution,[199] but this does not mean that direct horizontality applies. Fundamental rights do not have *direct* horizontal effect (*unmittelbare Drittwirkung*), but they do have *indirect* horizontal effect (*mittelbare Drittwirkung*).[200] The distinction has been explained this way:

> [Under] [d]irect application . . . [i]t would . . . be possible to found a cause of action on specific fundamental [constitutional] rights without recourse to legislation or the common law. Where the fundamental rights in the Bill of Rights apply indirectly, they do not found a cause of action, but function instead as higher values which provide guidelines for the interpretation and application of existing legal rules, which in turn determine the procedures followed and remedies awarded.[201]

Stated somewhat differently, under direct horizontality, individuals as well as government actors are bound by constitutional rights, whereas under indirect horizontality, the constitutional rights provisions apply to private law even if they do not create causes of action for individuals in private litigation.[202] Because private law rules are subject to Article 14, the German constitutional property provision, the question of the horizontal effect has never arisen in Germany in connection with Article 14.

In South Africa the horizontality question is still not entirely settled. The Constitutional Court rejected direct horizontal application of the Bill of Rights provisions of the interim constitution in the famous *DuPlessis v. DeKlerk* decision.[203] The final (1996) constitution, however, contains quite different language that bears immediately on the question of horizontality. In particular, section 8 provides,

> (1) The Bill of Rights applies to all law, and binds the legislatures, the executive, the judiciary and all organs of state.
> (2) A provision of the Bill of Rights binds a natural or juristic person if, and to the extent that, it is applicable, taking into account the nature of the right and the nature of any duty imposed by the right.
> (3) When applying a provision of the Bill of Rights to a natural or juristic person in terms of subsection (2), a court
> a. in order to give effect to a right in the bill, must apply, or if necessary develop, the common law to the extent that legislation does not give effect to that right . . .[204]

This provision made it clear that some version of the horizontality doctrine would be recognized. The question was what form of horizontal application would the court approve.

The first stab at answering that question came in *Carmichele v. Minister of Safety and Security.*[205] Although that case involved tort rather than property law, it is worth some attention here because it indicates the Constitutional Court's current approach to the relationship between constitutional and private law under the 1996 constitution.

In *Carmichele,* the plaintiff alleged that the local police and prosecutor were negligent when they failed to protect her from a convicted sex offender who had assaulted her after he had been released on bail. The Supreme Court of Appeal, South Africa's highest court after the Constitutional Court, held that the defendants owed the plaintiff no duty under Roman-Dutch common law because there was no sufficiently close relationship between them. Before the Constitutional Court the plaintiff argued that the Roman-Dutch common law of delict should have been developed to create an affirmative duty on the state to protect her, on the basis of the equality, human dignity, privacy, and personal freedom and security guarantees of the constitution. The Constitutional Court agreed, ruling that the lower courts failed to meet their obligation under section 39(2) of the constitution to develop the common law in conformity with the constitution. "[W]here the common law as it stands," the court said, "is deficient in promoting the section 39(2) objectives, the courts are under a general obligation to develop it appropriately."[206] In an important passage the court said,

> Our Constitution is not merely a formal document regulating public power. It also embodies, like the German Constitution, an objective, normative value system. As was stated by the German Federal Constitutional Court:
>
>> "The jurisprudence of the Federal Constitutional Court is consistently to the effect that the basic right norms contain not only defensive subjective rights for the individual but embody at the same time an objective value system which, as a fundamental constitutional value for all areas of the law, acts as a guiding principle and stimulus for the legislature, executive and judiciary."
>
> The same is true of our Constitution. The influence of the fundamental constitutional values on the common law is mandated by section 39(2) of the Constitution. It is within the matrix of this objective normative value system that the common law must be developed.[207]

In one sense the court in *Carmichele* stamped its imprimatur on so-called indirect horizontal application. The court agreed that the constitution's fundamental values must inform the common law. It is possible to read *Carmichele* another way, however.

Another Discourse: The State Duty to Protect Constitutional Values

In a sense, the court sidestepped the entire horizontality issue. It did so by introducing another discourse regarding the relationship between constitutional law and values and private law, the German discourse of a state duty to protect constitutional principles.[208] According to this theory, fundamental constitutional rights are conceived as principles that "work[] through mediating law/policy rather than as swords [or] shields . . ."[209] The constitution is not the only law that performs this mediating function. Private law also mediates conflicts between competing claims of entitlement in order to realize the constitution's scheme of values.

The excerpt from the court's opinion in *Carmichele* quoted above can be read, then, as rethinking the question about the relationship between constitutional and the common (and private) law. Rather than asking whether the common law is subject to the constitution, the court focused on a different question, one that Gardbaum has usefully formulated this way: "Do the constitutional duties placed on government include positive ones to prohibit or penalize certain actions by private individuals that touch on constitutional values?"[210] From this perspective the debate over direct-versus-indirect horizontal application is not the point, at least not the only point. The additional and complementary consideration is that the state is under a positive duty to protect and promote constitutional values. The net effect of the protective duty theory complements that of the doctrine of horizontal application, for quite possibly the state's actions in fulfillment of its protective duties will affect private actors.[211] Certainly, in many cases, it will be necessary to change private law or the common law, as *Carmichele* illustrates. The basis for changing the common law then may be either the state's duty to protect fundamental rights or horizontal effect or both. Finding that a gap exists between the common law and the fundamental rights of the constitution, the court in *Carmichele* was under a constitutional duty to change the common law in order to fulfill the relevant constitutional value.[212]

While the court approvingly discussed the German constitutional doctrine of the constitution as an objective value system, it did not explicitly discuss the German duty to protect doctrine. Consequently, the nature of the shift away from the sole focus on the horizontality doctrine after *Carmichele* is not entirely clear.[213] A more recent decision from the Supreme

Court of Appeal, however, indicates the possibility that the discourse of a protective duty will supplement, if not replace, the discourse of horizontality, although the Constitutional Court's subsequent analysis of the case has created doubt about the future of the duty to protect discourse.

A Protective Duty Applied to Property?: Modderklip East Squatters v. Modderklip Boerdery (Pty) Ltd.

In the widely noticed case of *Modderklip East Squatters v. Modderklip Boerdery (Pty) Ltd.,*[214] the problem of evictions of occupants from an informal housing settlement was yet again at issue. This context is the crucible for working out the constitutionally appropriate relationship between the constitutional rights provisions and the norms of the common law. As we have previously seen, lower courts in South Africa have tended to find that the traditional Roman-Dutch concept of ownership is unaffected by the constitution and accordingly have held that eviction is proper solely on the basis of showing that the plaintiff was the owner of the occupied land and that the occupants were there without legal authority. The Supreme Court of Appeal's analysis in *Modderklip* signaled an important theoretical development, but the importance of that development was later thrown into doubt by the Constitutional Court's subsequent handling of the case.

In *Modderklip,* some four hundred residents of an informal settlement in Johannesburg moved onto adjacent land that they mistakenly thought was owned by the city. In fact, the land was privately owned by Modderklip Farm. Within six months, the new settlements included 18,000 people living in 4,000 shacks. The owner sought to evict the occupants, relying on PIE. The lower court granted an eviction order, but the occupants failed to vacate. Meanwhile the Modder East settlement had grown to 40,000 inhabitants.[215] An eviction writ was issued, and the sheriff was ordered to execute it. She insisted on a large sum of money[216] to cover the estimated cost of employing a private firm to carry out the eviction and demolition of the shacks. The owner was unable or unwilling to pay the sum, especially since it exceeded the estimated value of the land. Modderklip then filed trespassing charges against the occupants, some of whom were found guilty. The sheriff, however, failed to take any action, treating the matter as a civil dispute. Modderklip then sought assistance from various public bodies. The president referred the matter to the Department of Land Affairs, which referred the matter to the Department of Housing, which did not respond. In the meantime, the sheriff had increased the sum required for eviction. Understandably frustrated, the owner once again went to court and obtained a declaratory order forcing all of the relevant government officials (including the National Police Commissioner) to take all necessary steps to remove the unlawful occupants (the enforcement order).

The case before the Supreme Court of Appeal was a combined application from the state for appeal from the initial eviction order and from the enforcement order. The court denied leave to appeal the eviction order but granted the appeal from the enforcement order in part. The court issued a different enforcement order.

At first blush the case appears to be solely a matter of private law, enforcement of a simple eviction order. Indeed that is exactly how the state and the police initially treated the case. The Supreme Court of Appeal took a different view of the situation, however. It observed that this attitude "does not reflect an adequate appreciation of the wider social and political responsibilities [that the Constitutional Court in *Grootboom*] identified in respect of persons such as the present occupiers."[217] The case in fact posed an apparent conflict between two constitutional duties of the state: its duty to protect Modderklip's ownership rights under section 25 and its duty to provide access to adequate housing under section 26. The court's resolution of this apparent conflict was premised on its assumption that the state was under a constitutional duty to break the impasse by removing the main obstacle to enforcement of the eviction order, namely, the lack of available alternative land for the occupants. The court treated the state's failure in this regard as simultaneously a breach of the occupants' section 26 housing right and Modderklip's section 25 property right.[218] The hard question, one that the court handled rather summarily, was why the state was under a constitutional duty to provide the occupants of Modder East with alternative housing.[219] Putting that aside, the important aspect of the case was the basis for the court's conclusion that the state had violated both its duty to protect Modderklip's section 25 property right and the occupants' section 26 housing right. The basis for that conclusion was section 7(2) of the constitution, which provides that the state is under a duty to "respect, protect, promote and fulfill the rights in the Bill of Rights." In the court's view, by failing to provide the occupants with alternative housing in accordance with section 26, the state failed to protect the owner's section 25 property right, as section 7(2) requires. The court stated,

> [I]n a material respect the state failed in its constitutional duty to protect the rights of Modderklip: it did not provide the occupiers with land which would

> have enabled Modderklip (had it been able) to enforce the eviction order. Instead, it allowed the burden of the occupiers need for land to fall on an individual . . .[220]

Failure to protect one right, in other words, meant failure to protect another right.

By premising the breach of the state's duties to both the owner and the occupants on the section 7(2) duty to protect, the court avoided the whole debate over horizontality. The protective-duty theory has yet to be fully developed by South African courts, but cases cited by the Supreme Court of Appeal provide some guidance. The court cited cases from the European Court on Human Rights, the Inter-American Court of Human Rights, and the African Commission.[221] The theory adopted in those cases is that the constitutional duty to protect and promote fundamental rights, derived from a constitutional provision placing such a duty on the state, places a general duty on states to protect their citizens from all infringements of their fundamental rights, even when those rights are threatened by the actions of other individuals rather than the state. The Supreme Court of Appeal's opinion in *Modderklip* indicated that this protective duty means that the state must do more than merely adding new laws or creating legal procedures to protect the constitutional rights of owners and the housing rights of occupants. The state had already created a new eviction process through PIE, and it had set in motion a program for providing adequate housing for all citizens. These existing procedures and programs, however, were not adequate to protect the constitutional property and housing rights involved in the case. The owner was not able to get his eviction order executed, and the unlawful occupants were not presented with an alternative source of adequate housing. A new approach was required, one that was not provided by either existing common law or statutory law. Specifically, the needed approach must assure that when the owner's property right is effectively protected by removing the occupants from its land, the occupants' housing right is in turn protected. Presumably that means that the state must somehow find alternative housing for the occupants. Exactly what that will entail remains unclear from the case.

On appeal, the Constitutional Court affirmed the relief ordered by the Supreme Court of Appeal, but it did so on a different theory. The court found that it was unnecessary to decide whether section 25 has any horizontal application and whether Modderklip's section 25 rights and the occupiers' section 26 rights had been violated. Instead, the court decided the case on the basis of section 1's rule-of-law provision and the access-to-court guarantee of section 34.[222] The court said that "[i]t is obvious that only one party, the state, holds the key to the solution of Modderklip's problem." The only question, continued the court, was whether the state was under any constitutional obligation to help resolve that problem. The court's answer was that sections 1 and 34 created such an obligation:

> [T]he state . . . is . . . obliged to take reasonable steps, where possible, to ensure that large-scale disruptions in the social fabric do not occur in the wake of the execution of court orders, thus undermining the rule of law. The precise nature of the state's obligation in any particular case and in respect of any particular right will depend on what is reasonable, regard being had to the nature of the right or interest that is at risk as well as on the circumstances of each case.[223]

The court refused to decide whether it could order the state to expropriate land under such circumstances.[224] It held instead that the award of compensation granted by the Supreme Court of Appeal was appropriate. When the dust settles, what will be clear is that until and unless the state provided alternative land, the occupants will be entitled to remain on Modderklip's land.

The fact that the Constitutional Court decided the case under a different theory than that used by the Supreme Court of Appeal should not obscure the importance of the court's endorsement of the appellate court's remedy. This remedy represents a significant change from traditional private law. No existing common law or statutory norm provided for such a remedy. It enables the transformative aim of the constitution to be fulfilled by assuring that desperately poor persons are not left homeless once again. In the long run the state will be compelled, as a practical matter, to acquire either new land or, more likely, the land currently occupied. In the meantime, the owner's constitutional property right under section 25 is protected, albeit through a liability rule rather than a property rule, that is, through the remedy of damages rather eviction, which would restore its possession of the occupied land. This remedy may not satisfy all of the relevant parties. The state may or may not provide the occupiers with alternative land, and even if it does, it may or may not provide that land quickly. In the meantime, the owner will be forced to maintain its relationship with an enormous contingent of occupiers, a relationship that Modderklip probably would rather not continue. Doubtless Modderklip would prefer to have its land back rather than just getting compensation, relieving it of the necessity of dealing with the equivalent of a small city's population as well as permitting it to use the land for possibly different (and possibly more remunerative) purposes. But money is better than nothing, and given the serious possibility that evicting the occupiers would have been found to constitute a violation of their section 26 rights, it seems that the owner's preferred remedy—eviction—would not have been granted by the courts, including the Constitutional Court. In such circumstances, where no remedy will satisfy anyone, the award of money damages is both creative and just. It further illustrates the capacity and willingness of the South African courts to depart from private law tradition in some situations even while they adhere to that tradition in other respects.

Conclusion

Widely adopted, the protective duty theory has the potential to make South Africa's constitutional property law become genuinely transformative. At a minimum, courts would no longer be able to fall back on the mode of traditional private law reasoning illustrated in the *Betta Eiendomme* case. A court would simply not be able to assume, as the court did there, that the common law right of ownership is unaffected by the Bill of Rights. The right of ownership would have to be viewed through the lens of the values expressed not only by the property clause, but also by the socioeconomic rights provisions. So viewed, the ownership right would not confer immunity on the private individual but nest the individual owner in a network of relationships that involve mutual obligations between and among the owner and all other persons significantly affected by her ownership. The precise parameters of the owner's obligations to these other members of the community (and theirs to the owner) could not be predefined but would instead require specification of how the multiple relevant constitutional values are weighted under the circumstances. Among the constitutional values to be weighted are, on the one hand, the owner's personal security and self-development and, on the other hand, the basic survival needs of members of the community who are homeless. Those needs include shelter, personal security, and human dignity. The court would evaluate these competing needs in light of the constitution's overarching commitment to social transformation. It would be acutely sensitive to the immanence of the constitution's objective values throughout not only the entire legal system but the entirety of South African society. All forms of law, public and private alike, share the common purpose of facilitating the concrete realization of those values.

The future of the protective duty theory in South Africa's constitutional jurisprudence is unclear. So also is the outcome of the tension between the transformative constitutional discourse of property and the discourse of tradition and private law. South Africa's experiment with the constitution, especially constitutional property, as an engine for fundamental social transformation remains ongoing.

CHAPTER FIVE

Lessons for American Takings Jurisprudence

One of the conventional arguments given for studying comparative law is legal borrowing.[1] While that is certainly not the only reason for this or any other comparative study, a comparative approach to constitutional property law does disclose some potential borrowings for American takings law. In this chapter, I consider four possible doctrinal innovations in takings jurisprudence that this comparative study indicates as especially worth considering. These are a proportionality doctrine, a purposive mode of judicial analysis, a social-obligation norm, and compensation practices. All four of these doctrines or techniques are used in other legal systems in which property rights are strongly protected, so they are all basically congenial with the fundamental commitment of the Fifth Amendment's takings clause. All four have the potential to go a long way toward addressing the takings "muddle."[2] Yet all four are almost entirely absent from the agenda of issues that dominate American takings law scholarship. This chapter will sketch their operation in other legal systems and will indicate how they might be deployed in American takings law. Implemented together, they would significantly contribute to a body of takings jurisprudence that is both more analytically coherent and more normatively defensible. Specifically, they would remedy the twin defects of American takings law that I identified in the introduction: its opaque reasoning and its lack of an expressly recognized and well-developed norm of the social obligation of ownership.

Proportionality

In the United States the proportionality norm is not entirely unknown, but its use is limited. Its most notable use in recent years was in *City of Boerne v. Flores*.[3] In that case, the United States Supreme Court used proportionality as a means of testing the constitutionality of the Religious Freedom Restoration Act. The issue was whether Congress had validly exercised its Section 5 powers under the Fourteenth Amendment. The Court said that Congress's exercise of its remedial power under Section 5 must be proportional to the constitutional harm sought to be remedied.[4] Use of the proportionality requirement evoked criticism from commentators, who argued that the test was unprincipled and unprecedented.[5] This criticism is not surprising since, as Vicki Jackson has pointed out, "U.S. constitutional law does not ordinarily and explicitly resort to the idea of proportionality as a measure of constitutionality . . ."[6]

The only other context in which the U.S. Supreme Court has used a proportionality test is a limited area of takings law. In *Dolan v. City of Tigard,*[7] the Court held that for a local land-use planning agency to sustain a public land-use dedication that it requires of a private owner in exchange for issuing a development permit, the agency must show that a "rough proportionality" exists between the proposed development's impact and the public dedication sought.[8] The test focuses on the value of the public harm caused by the proposed development and, on the other side, the value of what the owner loses as a result of the dedication.[9] The Court has expressly limited its proportionality requirement to these so-called land-use exactions and has not made it a general requirement for all land-use regulations.[10] In general then proportionality is an unknown concept to American constitutional law.

The situation is very different elsewhere in the world. Proportionality is a widely used legal test throughout the world.[11] It is used in many areas of public law, including administrative and constitutional law.[12] However, proportionality does not have a single, fixed meaning either in all countries or across all fields of public law in the same country. In some countries, such as Canada, for example, different versions of the proportionality requirement are used in different aspects of constitutional law. A different version of the proportionality test is used in federalism cases than is used in individual rights cases.[13]

Among the areas of constitutional law in which the proportionality principle has been used is constitutional protection of property. Proportionality review is a common aspect of constitutional property law in many countries, including countries that have no conventional type of constitutional property clause. It applies, for example, in Canada[14] and Australia.[15] The same is true in Germany, where the German Constitutional Court applies the proportionality principle to limitations on property, although the Basic Law does not expressly call for it.[16] As we saw in chapter 3, the German courts apply basically the same three-part analysis as the Canadian courts do. The proportionality principle is also used, as we have seen, by the South African courts in constitutional property cases,[17] and their mode of analysis largely tracks that of the Canadian and German cases,[18] which the South African courts have followed.[19]

The Mechanics of Proportionality

As commonly applied in individual rights cases in Canada and elsewhere, the proportionality principle is the second of a two-part approach. The first part requires that the court find that the statute or regulation violates some particular constitutional or entrenched right.[20] If no such violation has occurred, the inquiry stops there. Assuming, however, that the court finds that the statute has violated the right, the statute will nevertheless be sustained if the legislative means are proportional to the ends. To establish proportionality, three requirements must be met. First, the means must be rationally connected to achievement of a legitimate state objective. Second, they must impair the affected right as little as possible. Third, the legislative measure must be generally proportional to the ends to be achieved.[21]

The upshot of this three-pronged proportionality test, in Canada and elsewhere, has not been what one might expect, judging from the surface meaning of the principle. On the basis of the language of the principle alone, the principle seems to require a high degree of stringency. The second requirement in particular, requiring that the legislative means must impact the protected rights as little as possible, could potentially make the proportionality principle a basis for a very rigorous form of judicial review. To the American listener, the second requirement sounds like the highly demanding "least restrictive alternative" standard that is used in some areas of American constitutional law. But at least in Canada, it has not been applied in the way that the original articulation of the test in the Canadian case of *Regina v. Oakes* seemingly indicates. Rather than requiring that the selected method be the one that minimally impairs the protected right, the second requirement has been used, as Vicki Jackson notes, as "a more fluid, sliding-scale standard measuring the nature of the intrusion on the protected right against the importance of the objective."[22] In all of the jurisdictions where it has been adopted, the proportionality principle has functioned, as Jackson puts it, "as a more flexible analysis of whether the degree of impairment of protected rights is justifiable, considering the importance of the right, the degree of intrusion, and the nature of the asserted governmental interest."[23]

The Characteristics of Proportionality

Discussing the Canadian experience, Jackson has identified four salient characteristics of judicial proportionality analysis: contextuality, transparency of the relevant factors and reasons, breadth in the competing considerations, and overt normativity.[24] Contextuality means that the court focuses its attention on the immediate circumstances of the challenged provision. Proportionality analysis, as it is practiced in Canada, rejects the formalist, categorical approach taken by the U.S. Supreme Court in some areas of constitutional law, including aspects of takings law. In a case involving a challenge to hate-speech regulation, for example, the court closely examined empirical material concerning the problem of hate crimes in Canada to determine the magnitude of the problem.[25]

The second factor is transparency. The Canadian court is quite explicit and candid in its discussion of the conflicting considerations involved in the case. Discussing one major case in which the Court used proportionality analysis, Jackson states, "[T]he Canadian Justices identified the baseline constitutional values and empirical judgments that divide them, providing differing assessments of the weight to be given to the competing values and of the likely effects of enforcing the particular law."[26] The effect of this approach has been to make the Canadian decisions, and the real reasons for the decisions, more accessible, although not necessarily more predictable, to the public.

The third factor is closely related to transparency. The Canadian court considers a wide range of competing factors, interests, and approaches involved in the regulation. The Court has explicitly taken into consideration and openly assessed all relevant considerations, including possible social consequences of the regulated behavior and the governmental restriction. Further, it has taken international and comparative materials into account, contrary to the American practice.

Finally, proportionality analysis is, as Jackson puts it, "frankly normative" in character.[27] This is perhaps the major difference between the Canadian Supreme Court's approach and that of the U.S. Supreme Court. The Canadian Supreme Court has explicitly acknowledged the normative character of its reasoning when it assesses the relative weight it assigns to the right being restricted as well as its judgment about the importance of the governmental interest.[28] Members of the Court have openly addressed their differences over the amount of weight they assign to the constitutional values at stake. Moreover, the court takes moral and political considerations into account as well as more strictly legal factors.

Proportionality = Balancing?

Does the proportionality principle amount to balancing? Is it just another term for the method of balancing with which American lawyers are highly familiar? Putting aside for the moment whether proportionality as another form of balancing would be a good or bad thing for American takings law,[29] it is certainly possible that proportionality, in the hands of American courts, might morph into balancing. The similarity between the two is obvious, and some commentators have treated proportionality testing as a matter of balancing.[30] Both reject the formalism of a strictly categorical approach. However, from both an analytical and experiential perspective, proportionality is different from balancing. Analytically, the two are distinct, although proportionality analysis clearly involves aspects of balancing. The most apparent analytical difference is that while the American balancing approach begins and ends with weighting factors, under the three-prong approach used in Canada and Germany, the balancing of benefits and burdens comes, if at all, only at the end of the inquiry, after the court has analyzed the purpose of the restriction and the restriction's necessity.[31] One purpose of this structured approach, in fact, is to minimize the amount of balancing involved in the process. As South African legal scholar Henk Botha puts it, the aim is "not to banish the balancing metaphor from constitutional adjudication, but to find an alternative to a crude model of weighting and ranking interests."[32]

German constitutional law draws a theoretical distinction between balancing (*Güterabwägung*) and proportionality (*Verhältnismäßigkeit*). Balancing is a matter of an abstract weighting or ranking of fundamental rights. Proportionality, on the other hand, is seen as a matter of legislative competence. The court uses the proportionality test to determine whether the legislature overstepped its competence to determine the content and scope of the property guarantee.[33] Of course, the point of both bases of judicial review is the same, namely, to determine whether the legislative limitation on the property right is excessive. Moreover, this theoretical difference at times is just that—theoretical. The actual processes of balancing and proportionality review substantially overlap and often yield the same result.[34]

In the United States, balancing is basically a form of cost-benefit analysis, in which multiple factors are weighed in the abstract rather than in a contextualized fashion. Proportionality analysis, on the other hand, is a form of contextualized practical judgment. Like balancing, the court takes multiple factors into account, but it evaluates the relative weight to be given to each factor in the immediate context of the problem before the court. The proportionality test places context at the front and center of legal analysis. Moreover, proportionality analysis is less formless and more structured than balancing. As the three-prong analysis used in Canada, Germany, and elsewhere makes clear, it explicitly unpacks different questions and requires the court to focus on each separately. Balancing involves a more amorphous process of tossing all relevant factors into a single calculus.

Experience provides another reason to resist reducing the proportionality test to balancing. The experience of the U.S. Supreme Court with balancing in some areas of constitutional law, especially freedom of speech under the First Amendment, has been that a balancing approach tends to translate into blanket deference to the legislature. This was most obvious in Justice Frankfurter's analysis in the infamous and now repudiated case of *Dennis v. United States*,[35] and it is the reason why many progressive American constitutional lawyers reject balancing in dealing with fundamental constitutional rights.[36] Proportionality analysis in Canada, Germany, and South Africa has not translated into blanket deference to the legislature. This is largely due to the contextual nature of the court's analysis. It evaluates interests differently in each case on the basis of the immediate considerations involved.

The contextuality and transparency of proportionality analysis distinguishes it from balancing practice in another way. In American judicial practice, balancing tends to amount to a form of cost-benefit analysis, with a pretense of scientific rigor that makes the outcome appear objective.[37] Courts that have engaged in balancing commonly are less than candid, hiding the real bases for their decisions. This contrasts strongly with the Canadian experience with proportionality. The courts using proportionality analysis have made no such pretense of objectivity, certainly not of science, and their opinions have laid open the factors animating their decisions.

Would a Proportionality Principle Make Any Difference in Takings Law?

Would it matter if American courts applied a general proportionality principle in takings jurisprudence? Would there be any practical effect of this doctrinal borrowing? Were American courts to use the proportionality principle in the way the Canadian courts have, at a minimum there would be a difference in judicial opinions. As I have already indicated, Canadian opinions in which the proportionality test is used are highly transparent, something that no one would say about the U.S. Supreme Court's takings opinions. If American courts applied a general proportionality principle in takings jurisprudence, the courts would more frankly disclose what considerations were the driving force in their decisions and they would more directly acknowledge competing considerations and the reasons why those considerations did not carry the day. The courts' reasoning would also be more contextual. Because the Supreme Court's dominant method in takings cases is ad hoc balancing, there is necessarily some degree of contextuality in its opinions. But even in those cases where the Court has frankly engaged in ad hoc balancing, the Court has not focused in a sustained way on matters like the nature and function of the property interest immediately before it or even the public interest involved in the challenged restriction. Its discussion of these matters, which constitute the core of proportionality analysis, is typically vague and short.

Consider the majority opinion in *Penn Central Transportation Co. v. City of New York*,[38] the locus classicus of modern balancing in takings law. In that case, the Court upheld the action of the New York City Landmark Preservation Commission denying the owners of the famous Grand Central Terminal building the legal right to construct a tower in the air-space above the building. The Court's opinion is characterized by a degree of contextuality and transparency but only a limited degree. The Court provided a considerable amount of information about the contextual background of the case, but when it turned to analysis its discussion turned formulaic. As I discussed in chapter 2,[39] the Court specified three factors involved in its "essentially ad hoc factual inquir[y]": the economic impact of the regulation on the affected owner, interference with "distinct investment-backed expectations" of the owner, and the character of the governmental action.[40] Marching through each of these factors, the Court devoted most of its attention to rejecting the owner's arguments and distinguishing cases. The most context-specific aspect of the opinion concerned the severity of the economic impact of the regulatory decision on Grand Central's owner, Penn Central Transportation Corporation. The Court did not discuss how the landmark designation of Grand Central fit into the Commission's overall regulatory plan or what specific injury to the public welfare would occur were the proposed development to go ahead. What specific values did the landmark designation serve? Were they strictly aesthetic in character, or was there another dimension to the public interest?

The failure to address questions like these also limited the degree of transparency of the Court's opinion. By transparency, I mean clarity and candor regarding the immediate factors that led the Court to reach its decision and the reasons why the Court weighted those factors more heavily. One wonders, for example, whether the Court was influenced by the fact that the property interest involved was strictly commercial in character.

Would the case have been decided differently if the affected property had been the owner's personal residence? A more functional approach to analyzing the property interest, another possible borrowing from other jurisdictions that I will discuss shortly,[41] would have prompted the Court to be more candid about all of the relevant factors at work in its thinking. Another doctrinal borrowing that will be discussed later, an explicit social-obligation norm, would also have greatly added to the opinion's transparency. To what extent did the Court regard owners of special properties, buildings whose specialness was well-known even before any governmental stamp of approval like the Landmark Commission's designation, as inherently owing duties to the public to preserve the integrity of buildings such as Grand Central Terminal? Reading the Court's opinion, one has the sense that such a notion played a role in the Court's thinking, but nothing of the sort was acknowledged.

Along with transparency, predictability also suffered from the Court's approach. Critics of "ad hocery"[42] often make this charge against the Supreme Court's current balancing approach in takings cases. But the Court's experience with balancing seems to point exactly to the opposite conclusion. There is a great deal of predictability of outcome under the balancing approach. Constitutional challenges to property regulations rarely win. In the vast majority of takings cases where the extant balancing approach applies, the outcome is nearly always in favor of the government. It is only in those pockets of takings law where the Court has fashioned some sort of formal, categorical rule that it has been more apt to strike down land-use regulations and other forms of property rights limitations. Ironically, it is just the effort to develop a more categorical approach to takings case that has exacerbated the "muddle" of Supreme Court takings law. Cases like *Lucas v. South Carolina Coastal Council*[43] have made takings jurisprudence less predictable rather than more because the Court's newly minted categorical rule of finding per se that a taking has occurred where the regulation results in total economic deprivation undercuts itself with a nuisance exception. That exception restricts predictability in *Lucas*-type cases not because it is a standard rather than a rule but because it establishes a formal benchmark—what counts as a "nuisance" under historical local state law—that will be troublesome to identify. The general point is not that standards better promote predictability than rules do, but that a context-specific form of analysis, encouraged by the proportionality principle, does not necessarily result in unpredictability. As Vicki Jackson aptly observes, "Much of the answer to the question whether 'proportionality' analyses will be too unpredictable will lie in the 'doing.'"[44]

An open, and important, question is what effect, if any, the proportionality principle would have on the Court's use of categorical rules. Would adoption of the proportionality test as a general part of takings law prevent the Court from developing any categorical rules, rules like the *Lucas* "total economic deprivation" rule or the *Loretto* "permanent physical occupation" rule? Putting aside the question whether such rules are desirable, the answer is, again, not necessarily. Proportionality analysis might lead to development of formal rules. One could imagine the Court relying on contextual judgment about a wide variety of factors, including the owner's privacy interest and less restrictive alternative forms of regulation to justify a *Loretto*-like rule that applies only in the context of cases like *Loretto,* where the affected property interest is the owner's personal residence. While it seems unlikely that proportionality analysis would commonly produce formally realizable rules, it is not out of the question.

Substantively, there is no guarantee that the proportionality principle in takings cases would significantly add clarity to American takings doctrine. Again, to paraphrase Jackson, the answer will lie in the doing. One uncertainty is whether American courts would adopt the full structure of proportionality analysis, especially the distinction between the proportionality test and the analytically prior question whether the regulatory limitation violates the plaintiff's constitutional property right. Proportionality should be analyzed only if the court has determined that the regulation has encroached upon the proper constitutional boundaries of the affected property interest. If American courts adhered to this structure, as they should, that would add special weight to how the court analyzes the property interest.

At that point the other doctrinal borrowings that I propose in this chapter, a functional mode of analyzing the property interest, recognition of a social-obligation norm, and changes in compensation practices, would become especially important. The effect of those three innovations, especially the social-obligation norm, might well be to make proportionality review unnecessary in many cases. The social-obligation norm would take considerable weight off the proportionality principle by narrowing the scope of the property right at stake in some cases. In cases like *Penn Central,* for example, the court might conclude that the regulation did not encroach upon the affected property right because the social obligation associated with ownership of a historically unique building like Grand Central Terminal was sufficiently broad that the scope of the owner's constitutionally cognizable property interest was well within the parameters of the Landmark Commission's action. Conversely, rejection of a social-obligation norm and broadening the scope of constitutional property rights would place greater weight on the proportionality principle. Proportionality analysis would then become the locus of the political war that is the background of takings jurisprudence today. At that point the substantive effect of the proportionality principle on takings law will depend on how the courts interpret the principle. If proportionality analysis morphs into balancing, then no change will occur, and takings challenges will continue usually to fail. On the other hand, if as I will discuss later,[45] the courts interpret the proportionality requirement to apply a version of "strict scrutiny" to takings law generally, then the takings clause will become a far more powerful check on regulation than it currently is. Takings jurisprudence would move substantially in the direction that Richard Epstein outlined in his famous book *Takings.*[46] If the version of proportionality analysis that is practiced in Canada, Germany, and elsewhere, is used, this is unlikely to occur,[47] but the possibility does exist that American courts will not interpret proportionality in the way that courts elsewhere have but instead interpret it as "strict proportionality," that is, a surrogate for strict scrutiny.

What difference, if any, would the Canadian version of the proportionality test have on the American "rough proportionality" requirement under *Dolan v. City of Tigard?* Clearly, the analysis would differ. Procedurally, under the proportionality principle the city would not have been given the burden of proving the existence of a "rough proportionality," as it was under the *Dolan* decision, because the court would have undertaken the investigation itself. This change alone might well have changed the result of the case, for the Supreme Court's decision seemed to be based on the city's failure to sustain its burden of proof as much as on any other factor.

Analytically, under the Canadian version of the proportionality test, the first question is whether the city's land-use regulation and exaction had violated Florence Dolan's constitutionally protected property right. The answer clearly seems to be yes. Even under a capacious view of the social-obligation norm, Dolan's ownership interest included the right to exclude the public under the circumstances of the case. Unlike the property in *Penn Central,* there was nothing unique about her property that created a basis for supposing that the public had a prior legitimate reason to gain access to her land. It certainly cannot be argued that the fact that the city found it necessary to impose a restriction on her land is evidence of such a prior public interest. Had Dolan not planned on expanding her business and parking facilities, the city would have taken no action to restrict the use of her property in any way. In a real sense, she, not the city, initiated the land-use restriction.

The second part of the proportionality test then requires that the court address three questions. First, the court investigates the real legislative purpose behind the regulation and asks whether that purpose is legitimate and rationally connected to the regulation.[48] This question would replace the "nexus" requirement that the Court first imposed in the *Nollan* case.[49] Basically, it would replicate the Court's "rational relationship" test that it used in its equal protection jurisprudence and would almost certainly be satisfied on the facts of *Dolan*, given the minimal amount of scrutiny involved under that test. The city sought to maintain the integrity of its drainage system and to minimize parking congestion in its downtown area.[50] These purposes clearly were legitimate, and the even the Court acknowledged that there was a nexus between them and the exactions the city sought from the owner.[51]

The second two questions would track *Dolan*'s idea of moving beyond a mere "nexus" or "rational relationship" requirement to require proportionality. The second question would turn to whether the regulatory limitation impairs the property right as little as possible. As previously indicated, under the Canadian practice this test does not approximate the American "least restrictive alternative" test. Instead, in the more recent cases it has been used as a sliding scale comparing the importance of the governmental interest, the importance of the right, and the degree of intrusion with that right.[52] The facts in *Dolan* ought to satisfy this requirement. The governmental interest was significant. The concern with flooding especially is difficult to minimize, giving the high social costs associated with serious and repeated flooding, particularly in highly populated areas. While the exactions had a high qualitative impact on Florence Dolan's right, the right to exclude—traditionally one of the incidents of private ownership most highly protected[53]—the quantitative impact was not great. Only ten percent of her land was affected by the public dedication. Moreover, while the incident of property that was affected, the right to exclude, is important, the functional type of property involved is less weighty. Under the Canadian approach, judges have assessed the relative value of the property interest involved.[54] Reinforced by a frankly functional method of analyzing the affected property interest, a doctrinal borrowing that I will advocate below, the court should find that Dolan's property interest is not entitled to the same degree of protection as the type of property that immediately affects the owner's personal security or autonomy. It was a commercial interest whose function was strictly economic.

Under the "flexible" sliding scale used by the Canadian courts then, the second of the proportionality principle's three-part test should be found satisfied in *Dolan*. The degree of regulatory impairment of the owner's property interest was justifiable in view of the substantial public concern with health and safety and the relatively lower degree of protection to which a solely commercial interest is entitled.

The third and final inquiry is proportionality in the narrow sense of the term: "are the effects of the measure generally proportional to the objective."[55] This is the inquiry that comes closest to capturing the Court's "rough proportionality" requirement. The problem is that the *Dolan* Court failed to identify what factors were exactly involved in this requirement. To *what* exactly did the development exaction have to be proportional? Professors David Dana and Thomas Merrill have usefully unpacked three values that might be implicated: (1) the social cost attributable to the development; (2) the fair market value of the property interest the government acquires by the exaction; and (3) the reduction in the social cost resulting from the regulatory restriction.[56] While the Supreme Court in *Dolan* appeared to say that the two values that should be compared are those listed in items 1 and 3, in at least one other case the Court seemed to compare 1 and 2.[57] Dana and Merrill argue that on the basis of the theory that the takings clause is aimed at making the government's use of the resource efficient, the relevant comparison should be between 2 and 3.[58] Since the Canadian courts have not made clear exactly what their theory of constitutional protection of property is, we cannot be certain what comparison they would view as the appropriate one. Consequently, it is difficult to know how the third element of the Canadian proportionality principle would be resolved on the facts of *Dolan*. My own sense is that the Canadian courts (like their German counterparts) have not confined the constitutional concern with property solely, or even primarily, to one of economic efficiency or wealth maximization. At least as important to them is the noneconomic interest in maintaining a relationship of mutuality, reciprocity, and respect between individual owners and the communities to which they belong. On that view, proportionality in the narrow sense is not strictly a matter of a cost-benefit calculus to determine whether the market value of what the government obtains equals the reduction of social costs, although that is certainly a relevant aspect of the narrow proportionality requirement. It is a matter of making a normative judgment about whether a degree of parity exists among all three of the factors that Dana and Merrill identify. The issue is not strictly an economic one but a political one as well. Is there a significant imbalance of power between the government and the owner, an imbalance that the more powerful side has exploited? The issue is also relational. Exactions represent adjustments in an ongoing relationship between individual owners and the communities to which they belong. Does the proposed exaction so change the relationship that it is no longer one of reciprocity and mutuality? The third element of the Canadian version of the proportionality test invites this rather more holistic approach to investigating the effect of the regulatory condition on the relationship between owner and community.

Under the circumstances of *Dolan,* there was no evidence that the dedication that the city sought as a quid pro quo for granting the development permit fundamentally altered the nature of their relationship or constituted an abuse of power. The city sought the dedication only in response to Florence Dolan's proposed expansion, a change of her land use that by all accounts would have had a material impact on the community. What the city sought in exchange for permitting her to change her land use certainly was functionally tied to the harmful impacts of her proposed development, and it was not obviously out of scale with those negative effects on the community. There was no abuse of power, no abuse of the individual-community relationship. The exaction would (and should) have been permitted.

Can/Should the Proportionality Doctrine Be Transplanted to American Takings Jurisprudence?

From a strictly doctrinal perspective it would not be difficult for American courts to apply proportionality analysis as a general aspect of takings law. While proportionality as such is not a general principle of American constitutional law, the basic idea behind the proportionality principle—instrumental means/ends rationality—is well-established in many areas of constitutional law, especially free speech[59] and equal protection.[60] The proportionality doctrine that is used elsewhere is little more than a reformulation, a more formally expressed version, of the sort of means/ends rationality review that is so familiar elsewhere in American constitutional law. There is nothing uniquely "foreign" about it.

The real questions are whether the proportionality principle *should* be transplanted to American soil, and if so, in which doctrinal contexts. Several objections and concerns (apart from opposition to the whole notion of comparative borrowing) might be raised to the idea of transplanting the proportionality principle. One is the possibility that, especially in the hands of balancing-loving American judges, proportionality analysis will be reduced to balancing, plain and simple. This possibility cannot be dismissed out of hand, but it is not inevitable. As I have already indicated, there are apparent and important doctrinal differences between proportionality review and balancing, and a court that is open to the idea of borrowing a doctrinal innovation from a non-American jurisdiction is likely to be sensitive to the particular details of the transplanted doctrine. Even the most cursory review of the Canadian cases applying the proportionality principle will reveal the substantial differences between it and pure balancing. The greatest risk is that after the initial borrowing, American courts, especially lower courts, will gradually transform the proportionality doctrine into nothing more than balancing. The risk cannot be ignored. Even if this were to occur, however, the impact on existing takings jurisprudence would be trivial. Balancing is already the dominant methodology in takings cases, and there is nothing in the three-part proportionality test that might exacerbate whatever defects one perceives in the existing version of balancing, the *Penn Central* analysis.[61]

The concern in the opposite direction is that the proportionality principle will import a version of strict scrutiny into takings law.[62] If balancing translates into "the government always wins," then "strict scrutiny" in the takings context would equal "the owner always wins." One commentator has gone so far as to suggest that the necessity requirement can "rais[e] the spectre of subjective substantive due process jurisprudence reminiscent of American *Lochnerism.*"[63] As the courts of those countries have applied it, however, the reality is far less dramatic. Lochnerism does not reign in other countries any more than it does in the United States.

The real risk is not *Lochner,* but *Dolan.* The possibility is that American courts would apply the *Dolan* version of proportionality across the board, basically reversing the Supreme Court's current approach to most takings cases. While this possibility does exist, there are several reasons to believe that it is not inevitable that proportionality analysis will pave the way for general strict scrutiny in takings cases. First, the *Dolan* doctrine[64] applies only in one limited and atypical type of takings case: land-use exactions. Subsequent to *Dolan,* the Court in *City of Monterey v. Del Monte Dunes*[65] explicitly announced that its "rough proportionality" requirement applies only to exactions cases. More recently still, the Court in *Tahoe-Sierra Preservation Council, Inc. v. Tahoe Regional Planning Agency*[66] unambiguously affirmed its commitment to its deferential balancing approach in all takings cases other than exactions challenges and *Lucas* total deprivation cases.[67] Even within the context of exactions cases, there is evidence that some state courts are not applying the *Dolan* "rough proportionality" requirement.[68] There seems no reason to believe that the Court is prepared to abandon its longstanding deferential approach in favor of a general strict scrutiny approach.

The version of proportionality analysis proposed here would not upset this apple cart. Proportionality analysis, as the German and Canadian courts have developed it, is not a surrogate for strict scrutiny. As I have already discussed, proportionality analysis, properly formulated, involves three discrete inquiries. Only the last two of these pose any risk of becoming a wedge for strict scrutiny. The second, which asks whether the regulatory limitation impairs the property right as little as possible, conceivably could be translated into a "least restrictive alternative" requirement, but, as I have indicated, that is not as it has been interpreted by Canadian courts. Rather they have used it in a kind of sliding scale fashion that resembles American takings jurisprudence's multifactor balancing approach that was recently reaffirmed in *Tahoe-Sierra*. The third question, whether the effects of the measure are "generally proportional" to the objective, poses the most serious risk of developing into strict scrutiny. Here again, the Canadian experience undermines this concern. As the Canadian courts have applied it, the crux of this inquiry appears to be whether there is a significant imbalance of power between the government and the owner, an imbalance that the government, as the more powerful side, has exploited. But that inquiry is already a, if not *the*, central focus of American takings doctrine. As Saul Levmore has stated, "[T]akings law protects parties that are least secure in the political process."[69] Takings jurisprudence is all about power imbalance, about perceived imbalances of power between private owners and government regulators.[70] Nothing in the third step of proportionality analysis, as currently practiced by other courts, invites a more stringent form of review than American takings law already involves. On balance, then, the risk of proportionality analysis paving the way for strict scrutiny in takings law seems slight.

One possibility for minimizing the risk of proportionality becoming a basis for general strict scrutiny is to limit proportionality review to specific corners of takings law. Two possible candidates are the public-use[71] and "just compensation" requirements. I will discuss how proportionality might change compensation practices later in this chapter, but for now, a brief discussion of the public-use requirement will illustrate the basic idea of a targeted use of the proportionality principle.

Proportionality can be understood and applied in a way that would implement the approach to the public-use question that I described in chapter 2. Briefly, it could allow the Court to scrutinize the regulatory decision to expropriate the landowner's property in a way that steers a middle course between the Court's currently deferential approach, based on a naively optimistic conception of ordinary democratic politics, and a version of strict scrutiny, based on the equally naive conception of government regulators as wont to engage in "out-and-out plan[s] of extortion"[72] in dealing with landowners. Following Professor Merrill's model, the court would look at such matters as whether the government could have voluntarily purchased the land, whether there is, from a planning perspective, a suitable substitute site for the proposed project, and whether the exercise of the eminent domain power was primarily the product of secondary rent seeking. If the court finds affirmative answers to these questions, then the exercise of the eminent domain power could be found to be unconstitutional as being disproportionate. Used alone or in conjunction with changes in compensation practices, the proportionality principle might enhance both the fairness and the progressive character of takings law.

A final consideration that warrants some hesitation about transplanting the proportionality principle to American takings law is the difference in local legal culture between the United States and Canada. As Vicki Jackson points out, it is plausible to suppose that the framers of the Canadian Charter of Rights, a document of far more recent vintage than the American Constitution, intended the courts to engage in the kind of overtly normative reasoning that has been their practice under the proportionality principle.[73] Unlike in Canada, there has been no recent opportunity in the United States for public deliberation about the judicial power to impede the ordinary processes of democratic politics. Concern with the "countermajoritarian difficulty" appears to be greater in the United States than in Canada, where the need for the constraining effects (or at least the appearance of such effects) of formal rules, especially in constitutional law, seems considerably weaker than it is in the United States. This cultural difference suggests that the legitimacy of any version of the proportionality test in which the courts openly base their decisions on the sort of nonformal factors that Canadian courts emphasize would be problematic, to put it mildly. For all of the arguments about ad hoc balancing, judicial reasoning in American takings cases is still highly formulaic in an effort to maintain the appearance of objectivity and value-neutrality. A legal culture that is still preoccupied with denying that judges make controversial value choices is one in which a general, Canadian-style proportionality principle may not play well.

These concerns are reasons for caution, but they are not reasons for ignorance. At a minimum, American judges ought to become more familiar with the proportionality principle, a principle that is in widespread use throughout the world. Applied tentatively and modestly in the context of takings law, the principle might ameliorate some of takings law's muddled state. It can hardly make things worse.

Purposive Analysis

A second candidate for transplantation to American takings law is a matter of judicial method, not substantive doctrine. It is a purposive approach to analyzing takings claims. Using a purposive approach, courts in many jurisdictions around the world analyze takings cases by explicitly focusing on the core purpose of constitutional protection of property, identifying the central constitutional value that such heightened protection is intended to serve, and asking whether that value is immediately at stake under the circumstances before it. American courts have not generally used this method in takings cases, but they should.

The Current Debate over Judicial Method in Constitutional Adjudication

The case for an overtly purposive approach to judicial takings analysis needs to be situated within a broader American debate over constitutional analysis. Anyone who follows American constitutional law even slightly knows that there is an ongoing debate in American legal circles over the proper method of interpreting all legal texts, but especially the American Constitution. Although this is not the place for a complete account of the current debate over the judicial method in constitutional adjudication, a very brief summary of that debate will help to situate the case for an explicitly purposive approach in American takings law.

The debate over judicial method in constitutional cases, fiercely pursued not only in academic circles but by members of the United States Supreme Court as well,[74] pits two theories against each other. One theory, which I will call "formalist" (it also could be called "textualist" or "categorical"), holds that the only constitutionally legitimate method of interpretation is one that derives the constitution's meaning solely from the express words of the constitution or legal precedents. It favors categorical rules and opposes a more open-ended form of judicial analysis. The competing method is balancing, which we discussed in connection with the proportionality principle. Balancing rejects the use of categories and the strict reliance on text and precedent as the exclusive sources of judicial legitimacy.

The predominance of one method over another may vary according to differences in local legal and political culture. Jurisdictions in which rights consciousness is strong, for example, might be more apt to use a formal, categorical method of judicial analysis, especially in constitutional cases. Critics of balancing often argue that it leaves individual rights too much at risk because of the degree of judicial discretion that balancing is usually thought to involve.[75] This explanation is at best incompletely convincing, however, because balancing is the dominant judicial methodology in some areas of American constitutional law, including, notably, takings. The variation in the courts' use of balancing may indicate that another aspect of local legal culture that affects which analytical method predominates is the specific constitutional right at stake. Balancing may dominate American takings jurisprudence while First Amendment jurisprudence tends to be more categorical in method because of the different weighting that American courts have given property rights and free speech rights.

Yet another aspect of local political and legal culture that may influence the use of one method over another is the prevailing attitude of courts toward other political institutions, especially legislatures. It might be argued, for example, that courts that tend to be skeptical of the legitimacy of legislative processes are more likely to use balancing because that method facilitates judicial intervention (or "activism"). According to this view, using an open-ended multifactored approach, courts can more easily overturn legislative decisions by giving greater weight to some factors than the legislature did.[76] From the perspective of this understanding of balancing, one should not be surprised that balancing is the dominant judicial method in American takings jurisprudence. As I discussed in chapter 1, one of the strongest aspects of American political and legal culture historically has been what I there called "the Madisonian anxiety," that is, the concern that the processes of ordinary majoritarian politics are apt to being taken over by factions that trample upon the property rights of those who are less politically empowered. The Madisonian anxiety should lead courts to be more aggressive in policing legislative restrictions on how property can be used; hence, from this perspective, balancing fits.

But balancing in fact does not fit, or rather this conception of balancing does not fit, takings jurisprudence. The Court has been strongly deferential in the vast majority of takings cases, yet balancing is its dominant method. If one associates balancing with an interventionist stance, then the Court's reliance on balancing in takings cases is anomalous. The anomaly disappears, however, when we uncouple the linkage between balancing and judicial intervention. Balancing is no more a concomitant of judicial "activism" than formalism, that is, reliance on categorical rules, is of judicial deference. There is no necessary alignment between the choice of judicial method and judicial treatment of legislative decisions. Both categorical rules and balancing can be used in a way that is either deferential or nondeferential toward legislative decisions.

The important point is not judicial method but the dominant judicial attitude prevailing toward the legislative process. In the context of takings law, the evidence suggests that this aspect of America's historical political and legal culture has changed. At least within the judiciary, the Madisonian anxiety about the excesses of majoritarian control over property holdings has waned. Courts, especially the Supreme Court, have tended to display a more deferential attitude toward legislative decision making where property rights are concerned.[77] From this perspective, the concern that the critics of American takings law express regarding the use of balancing is misplaced. The issue to which their attention should be directed is not balancing versus categorical rules but judicial deference toward legislative decisions about land use. Nevertheless, for many of these critics, the takings bogeyman remains balancing. It is to balancing that critics attribute the incoherent state of American takings law to the Court's reliance on balancing.

American takings law *is* a muddle but neither in the sense or for the reason that the Court's critics usually cite. The muddle is not unpredictability (for the most part, the outcomes are quite predictable) or normative disagreement (which is true in many other areas of the Court's constitutional jurisprudence). Rather the muddle is a lack of transparency about the real normative underpinnings of the opposing views. A primary reason why the fundamental normative reasons for the Court's decisions are so opaque is the Court's failure to discuss its conceptions of the core purposes of constitutional property in an explicit and systemic way.

This diagnosis of what ails the Supreme Court's takings jurisprudence suggests that the appropriate treatment for recovery is not replacing balancing with categorical rules. Balancing in fact is the methodology best suited to the kind of transparent purposive reasoning that is so lacking in takings opinions. There is little room in the formalist approach for explicit analysis of the purpose of constitutional property and the character of the relevant property interest.[78] Balancing, by contrast, invites an open investigation into and discussion of purpose as one of the most important factors in the balancing calculus. Nevertheless, American courts, especially the United States Supreme Court, practice a form of balancing analysis that ignores or buries the central question of purpose. Almost without exception, they totally fail to ask what is the core purpose of property as a constitutional value. One of the strongest points of contrast between American takings law and its counterparts in Germany and South Africa is that the German and South African courts are consistently and explicitly guided by a purposive approach to analyzing what their constitutions' commitments to property require in the immediate case. In both countries, the courts have developed a clear conception of the main function of property as a constitutional value, and their reliance on that conception adds to their constitutional property the coherence and integrity that ours lacks.

Purposive interpretation will not make takings law more principled in the sense of eliminating or even reducing disagreements about how disputes should be resolved. No amount of doctrinal tinkering or borrowing can do that. Takings law will remain an area of strong disagreements over outcomes because it is the central locus of an ongoing and irreducible tension among different conceptions in American legal thought about the core purpose of property and, even more fundamentally, the proper relationship between the individual and the political community. As Carol Rose has pointed out, the takings problem is so intractable because "[o]ur traditional discourse envisions property as serving quite different purposes." These different conceptions "ultimately suggest different characters and limits for public protection of property ownership."[79]

What purposive interpretation can do is add clarity to takings jurisprudence by making more transparent the real reasons behind the decisions.

A Three-Step Method

The purposive approach that I advocate—for the advocacy of a purposive mode of analysis is one of the normative messages of this book—involves three steps. First, the court identifies and articulates the core purpose of the right of property in its constitutional scheme. Second, the court determines the main purpose served by the particular property interest immediately in question. Third, the court resolves whether the immediate property interest implicates the constitutional right's core purpose so as to decide whether the ascertained interest warrants the strong degree of legal protection that constitutional rights are designed to provide.

This method is essentially the mode of analysis used by the German and South African constitutional courts, although they have not formalized it in these terms. Their method, like the one just stated, explicitly examines and identifies both the central value intended to be served by making property a constitutional right and the nature of the interest immediately at stake. Functional analysis has made constitutional property law in Germany, where it is highly developed, more transparent and more predictable than it is in the United States. As we saw in chapter 3 the German courts recognize that different types of property interests serve different goals and that not all of these possible goals are equally important. The courts have explicitly created a hierarchy of property interests based on their understanding of the core function of constitutional property as promoting human dignity, the transcendent value in the hierarchy of German constitutional values. Property interests that are viewed as serving strictly commercial values are less protected than are interests understood as necessary for human dignity and self-development. Thus, for example, tenants' interests in their housing are given greater weight than interests in commercial investments. One may disagree with the German courts' assessment of the relative importance of various types of property interests, but their explicitly functional mode of analysis at least makes their opinions transparent and their results substantially more predictable than can be said of their American counterparts. The most important of the three steps just outlined is the first one. It merits some elaboration because it implicates what I will call the normative pull of property.

The Normative Pull of Property

By the term "normative pull," I mean a specific conception of the relationship between the individual and the community to which the country's constitution is normatively committed through property as a constitutional right. Property invariably has some substantive normative pull, or force, but the valence of that force, the specific direction of that pull, is not inevitable. It is an interpretive choice. Constitutional property has no single necessary normative pull. In the process of interpreting a constitutional property clause, courts inevitably must choose which of several normative pulls that can reasonably be attributed to constitutional property in liberal democracies and what common good or set of common goods to have the institution of private property pursue whenever they interpret a constitutional property clause. Morris Cohen famously stated that "[a]n adequate theory of private property . . . should enable us to draw the line between justifiable and unjustifiable cases of confiscation."[80] Cohen's statement may have been excessively optimistic, but it is certainly true if we revise it to say, "A normative theory of private property is necessary to allow us to draw the line between compensable and noncompensable government actions affecting property."

The necessity of making a choice of normative direction is obvious where a court has explicitly adopted a purposive approach to interpreting its property clause. A purposive reading of a constitutional property clause obviously involves discerning a commitment to one among several normative meanings that might plausibly be attributed to the property clause. Purposive reasoning is all about making normative choices. Less obviously perhaps but just as necessary, a formalist approach also invokes the idea of property's normative pull. A formalist approach, every bit as much as a purposive approach, involves choosing a conception of property that has normative pull. Courts must, and in fact *do,* always make choices among available normative pulls when deciding constitutional property claims. A critical, perhaps *the* critical weakness of formalism is the fact that it often hides the normative pull of its interpretation of property.[81]

The claim that property has no single inherent normative pull may be surprising to many readers. Some will take it as given that the constitutional property right serves only one goal—individual liberty, particularly political liberty. These readers will assume that property is constitutionally protected in order to create a zone of individual autonomy that substantially immunizes the owner from arbitrary intrusions by the state. They believe that property requires extraordinary legal protection because property is the keystone of the wall between the individual and the state, a wall that is indispensable to the project of protecting the individual's highest interest, personal liberty.

Other readers, especially many American legal commentators, will assume that the compensation clause is about economic efficiency, or wealth maximization. The economic theory that is so influential in American takings scholarship assumes that the fundamental goal of the takings clause is maximizing social wealth. The theory measures social wealth in terms of preference satisfaction. It defines collective welfare as maximizing the satisfaction of aggregate individual preferences, and it considers constitutional protection of property as an effective tool in restraining government interference with preference satisfaction.

Both of these theories of the normative pull of constitutional property are correct and incorrect. They are correct insofar as they are plausible readings of a constitutional property clause in the constitution of a liberal democracy. Liberalism's defining characteristic is its recognition of the individual as a free and autonomous moral agent, and both theories easily fit within the liberal frame of reference insofar as they are concerned with individual preferences.

Where these readings of a constitutional property clause go wrong is their rejection of any common good other than individual liberty or maximizing preference satisfaction.[82] Preference satisfaction is surely one possible purpose of constitutional protection of property, but it does not exhaust the possibilities in liberal theory. Liberalism is pluralistic, and a liberal constitutional property clause is, as Hanoch Dagan points out, "devoted to realizing not only the common good of individual liberty but also other common goods . . ."[83]

One important liberal candidate for property's normative pull beyond preference satisfaction is human dignity. The common good of human dignity is closely associated with individual liberty, but it is not libertarianism. We saw in chapter 3 that human dignity and self-development, not individual liberty as such, are the foundational values associated in German constitutional law with property as a constitutional right. German constitutional law does not protect property for the purpose of creating a zone of immunity from external interference, governmental or otherwise, but in order to promote human dignity and proper development of the self.

In the German scheme, human dignity is less a matter of freedom of the individual to do what she wishes, the core meaning of liberty in American constitutionalism, and more a matter of promoting the fully developed human personality.[84] German constitutionalism stresses the idea that the proper development of the human personality always occurs within the social community. This conception of human dignity provides the basis for the further notion, extremely important in German constitutional property law, of social responsibilities as intrinsic to membership in a social community. Thus, from the German point of view, constitutional freedom is not only "freedom from," but freedom as an enabling condition, enabling the fully developed individual to fulfill her proper social responsibilities. As we have seen, this conception of responsibility as inherent in the constitutional ideal of human dignity provides the basis for restrictions on the property owner's autonomy that are foreign to American ideas and practices.

Another candidate for the constitutional property right's core purpose may be drawn from recent work by the Israeli legal scholar Daphna Lewinsohn-Zamir.[85] Professor Lewinsohn-Zamir has argued that while recent American legal scholarship defines as the core objective of property law the fulfillment of individuals' subjective preferences, property law should instead be understood as aimed at maximizing human welfare, objectively defined. According to her objective theory of well-being, "certain things—such as knowledge of ourselves and the world around us, accomplishment of worthwhile goals, and attainment of deep and meaningful relationships—are intrinsically valuable, and having them makes for a better life."[86] Lewinsohn-Zamir argues that "private property and objectively-defined well-being are intimately connected and . . . the former is essential to achievement of the latter."[87] The mutual interdependence between property and objective well-being provides the basis for a hierarchy of property interest not unlike that recognized in German constitutional law. Lewinsohn-Zamir states, "From an objective perspective, not all objects of property are equally important for the advancement of people's welfare; some are more essential than others."[88]

One possible implication of Lewinsohn-Zamir's theory for constitutional property law is that courts should undertake the kind of functional analysis I have outlined. They should explicitly address the questions of what is the core purpose of the constitutional right of property and what sort of property interest is at stake in the immediate dispute. The theory of property that is based on an objective theory of well-being is inherently functional. Under that theory, property interests are not fungible. Assessing any given interest's constitutional significance requires that we interpret that interest in terms of its social role. Just what does that interest contribute to social well-being? Is that social role one that the interpretation that we have given to the constitutional property clause has assigned great weight, or is the fit tenuous, not sufficiently strong to merit the extraordinary protection of a constitutional right?

Yet another candidate draws on a theory of property that elsewhere I have called "proprietarian,"[89] but that might also be called civic.[90] This theory conceives of property's core mission as providing the material condition for the creation and maintenance of the proper social order, a social order based upon the ideals of self-governance and civic participation. The propriety theory's obvious roots lie in the political tradition of civic republicanism, but it also overlaps with several liberal theories of property, including Lewinsohn-Zamir's theory of property as the foundation of objective well-being. The constitutional implication of the propriety theory is the insight that the central meaning of the constitutional right of property is social and public rather than personal and private. It is to serve the public good, understood as more than just the sum of individual preferences. This conception does not so much socialize ownership as it conceives the ends which property is to serve as being social as well as private. Property *is* individually owned, and the individual owner possesses considerable discretion regarding its uses. But the basic reason why the institution of property is recognized in the first place and why it is elevated to the level of constitutional protection is to advance the collective good of the society that has recognized it. That is, property is privately owned insofar as this serves the common welfare, conceived of as more than simply the satisfaction of subjective individual preferences.

While the social dimension of property is conspicuously emphasized in propriety theory, it is by no means absent from other strands of liberal property theory. Even those theories, like the libertarian theory of property, that do not emphasize the social dimension of private ownership must acknowledge some measure of social responsibility as a common good that inheres in the institution of property. For example, John Locke's account of property, which otherwise places individual autonomy at the center of attention, made individual appropriation of communally owned resources provisional on leaving "enough and as good"[91] remaining for others. While the meaning of the Lockean Proviso has been sharply debated, one possible reading is that individual sovereignty is tempered by social responsibility.[92] Likewise, the common law has always recognized that the individual owner's autonomy is inherently limited by the owner's responsibility to others. This is the meaning of the common law's old maxim *sic utere tuo ut non alienum laedas*—"Use your own property in such a manner as not to harm that of another." The open question is not whether social responsibility is part of a constitutional property clause's normative pull, but how much and to exactly what concrete effect. This leads to the third doctrinal borrowing that a comparative approach to constitutional property suggests: an explicit and well-developed social-obligation norm.

A Social-Obligation Norm

Traces of a Social-Obligation Norm in Takings Jurisprudence

Is there a social-obligation norm in American takings law? Unquestionably, yes. Traces of an implicit social-obligation norm are scattered throughout American takings decisions. It is evident, for example, in the frequent invocation of "reciprocity" as one of the factors to be considered in determining whether a regulation has gone too far.[93] It is evident in the New York Court of Appeals' opinion in *Penn Central Transportation Co. v. City of New York*,[94] where the court relied on reasoning that echoed Henry George's theory that society has a legitimate interest in exploiting that portion of a resource's value that is due to society's contribution.[95]

> It is enough," the court stated, "that the privately created ingredient of property receive a reasonable return. It is that privately created and privately managed ingredient which is the property on which the reasonable return is to be based. All else is society's contribution by the sweat of its brow and the expenditure of its funds. To that extent society is also entitled to its due.[96]

Frank Michelman has accurately expressed how the idea of social obligation undergirds the culture of American constitutional protection of property at its most fundamental level. Michelman's synopsis of our constitutional commitment to property as a tool for the common good is worth quoting in full. He states,

> Our constitutional culture includes a deep and ancient tradition of expected regard, when you make use of your property, for other people's and the public's interest and concerns. It includes a deep and ancient strain that says this expectation of regard for public interest and concerns is subject, when the occasion requires, to legislative definition and regulatory enforcement, a strain that developed early under the law of public nuisance. The tradition, in sum, is one of a law of property *that is functionally oriented to contemporary community goals, as well as to protection of private advantage,* and that relies on the police powers of legislatures, alongside common law adjudication by courts, to negotiate and mediate between the two.[97]

It is one thing, however, to recognize the existence of an implicit social obligation of private ownership; it is another thing to explicitly acknowledge such an obligation as a formal element of takings law. This is what is most lacking in American takings jurisprudence. While American takings jurisprudence does implicitly acknowledge a social-obligation norm, it lacks any systematic development of that norm. Having never explicitly recognized a social-obligation norm as a formal aspect of takings jurisprudence, American courts have never developed the contours of that obligation.

Making the social-obligation norm explicit in takings discourse is important for both expressive and substantive reasons. The takings clause expresses multiple social meanings that go beyond those that courts and commentators conventionally acknowledge, namely, economic efficiency and fairness. The takings clause's pluralistic normative character simply reflects the normatively pluralistic nature of American property law generally, as I and others have shown elsewhere.[98] Beyond individual liberty, fairness, social utility, and wealth maximization, the values that commentators most commonly identify as the normative foundations of American property law, there exists, and has existed since the nation's very beginning, a civic conception of property that emphasizes the property owner's responsibility to the community to use property not solely to realize her personal preferences but also to realize the well-being of the community. Like property law generally, the takings clause "is devoted to realizing not only the common good of individual liberty but also other common goods: social responsibility and equality."[99]

Takings discourse needs more openly to express these multiple common goods, particularly social responsibility. Dagan has eloquently articulated the expressive benefit to be gained by making the takings clause's implicit social-obligation norm explicit. He states, "A progressive takings law is a symbolic public expression of our bonds of concern and solidarity with others, a political reaffirmation of the importance we attach to social responsibility and civic virtue."[100] Dagan goes on to point out that the expressive aspect of the social-obligation norm in turn would reinforce the substantive benefits to be gained by the norm as an openly acknowledged purpose of the takings clause.

In substantive terms the failure to make the social-obligation norm explicit is one of the main reasons why American takings case law is so perplexing. Courts have often made takings doctrine murkier than it needs to be by obscuring their real reasons, reasons that lie in their notions of a social obligation inherent in ownership, behind different discursive terms. Nowhere is this practice more evident than in the history of the noxious-use doctrine in takings case law and the nuisance exception to the *Lucas* categorical takings rule. That doctrine is worth special attention because it illustrates both the existence of an implicit social-obligation norm in takings law and the doctrinal confusion that results from failing openly to acknowledge and develop that norm.

The noxious-use doctrine basically provides that if the regulation in question seeks to abate a noxious use, then no compensation is due the affected owner. Animating the doctrine is the idea that the use that the regulation prohibits was never part of the owner's bundle of rights to begin with; hence, the regulation did not deprive the owner of any aspect of her ownership.[101] Commentators usually locate the doctrine's origins in the famous nineteenth-century case of *Mugler v. Kansas*.[102] The Court in that case upheld a state statute prohibiting the operation of a brewery. Its conclusion that the statute did not effect a taking was based on this central insight: "[A]ll property in this country is held under an implied obligation that the owner's use of it shall not be injurious to the community."[103] This statement might have been the foundation for a fully developed notion of the implied obligation of owners, but that potential was never realized. The Court subsequently applied the doctrine in *Hadacheck v. Sebastian*[104] and other cases following it.[105] Numerous state court decisions have also relied on the doctrine.[106]

The doctrine's status in modern takings law is uncertain. The Supreme Court appeared to affirm it in *Keystone Bituminous Coal Association v. DeBenedictis*,[107] but just a few years later, in *Lucas v. South Carolina Coastal Council*,[108] it severely undermined the doctrine's significance. Seemingly rejecting the conventional view of the doctrine as a categorical rule of no taking in cases where the regulated activity constitutes a public nuisance, the *Lucas* Court relied on an argument that several scholars, especially economists and law and economics scholars, have made over the years.[109] The fundamental problem with the doctrine, as conventionally understood, these scholars have argued, is that it is fatally question-begging.[110] As a test for determining when regulations do not constitute takings, the noxious-use doctrine "will not work unless we can establish a benchmark of 'neutral' conduct which enables us to say where refusal to confer benefits (not reversible without compensation) slips over into readiness to inflict harms (reversible without compensation)."[111]

The point is a clever one, but too clever by half. As economist William Fischel has quipped, "It is cleverness of this sort by which economists read themselves out of the takings debate."[112] Fischel's sensible point is that from the ordinary person's perspective, there is little difficulty in distinguishing between, for example, a regulation restricting the size or location of highway billboards, on the one hand, and another regulation limiting the amount of toxic emissions from factories, on the other. As Fischel pithily states, "'Down' does not become 'up' just because one can invert oneself on a trapeze."[113] From the "Ordinary Observer's"[114] viewpoint, the billboard regulation, as an aesthetic regulation, provides the public with a benefit, while the emissions regulation, as a health measure, prevents a public harm.

There are two ways in which one might respond to the baseline problem and revitalize the noxious-use doctrine. The first is to determine whether the state possessed preexisting rights on the basis of private law. Daniel Cole has suggested just such a strategy for cases involving conflicts between private land rights and public water rights.[115] Noting that the Supreme Court has ignored the possibility that preexisting public water rights might have existed in several of its recent cases, including *Nollan*, *Lucas*, and *Palazzolo*, Cole argues that in cases in which the public-harm doctrine *was* invoked, such as *Just v. Marinette County*, the courts properly framed the dispute as "a boundary conflict between a private property regime and a public property regime."[116] Cole goes on to say that how the balance between the two interests should be struck is an "inevitably contestable issue."[117]

The other strategy for revitalizing the public-harm doctrine is through recognition of an explicit social obligation. The focus here is less on identifying conflicting rights than on defining the parameters of the public dimension of private ownership. It is this strategy that I wish to pursue in this book and will discuss at greater length subsequently.

Nevertheless, Justice Scalia seized upon the now familiar critique in his opinion in *Lucas*, pointing out that "the distinction between 'harm-preventing' and 'benefit-conferring' regulation is often in the eye of the beholder."[118] Unless the Court was prepared to abandon the noxious-use doctrine altogether, it had to find some basis for cabining it, or else, as commentators have noted, the doctrine becomes "coterminous with any legitimate public interest . . . sap[ping] the concept of any meaningful content, and mak[ing] regulatory takings analysis equivalent to due process rationality review."[119] Justice Scalia said that this is indeed the proper interpretation of the noxious-use doctrine.[120] The doctrine, he said, was nothing more than "our early formulation of the police power justification necessary to sustain (without compensation) *any* regulatory diminution in value."[121]

Rather than relying on the noxious-use formulation,[122] Justice Scalia's approach was to develop a narrowly defined "nuisance" exception to the categorical rule that he created in that case. The basic rule is that any land-use regulation whose effect is to deprive the land of "all economically productive or beneficial uses" is, per se, a taking. The exception to this rule is that a regulation that "do[es] no more than duplicate the result that could have been achieved in the courts—by adjacent landowners . . . under the State's law of private nuisance, or by the State under its complementary power to abate nuisances that affect the public generally"[123]—does not constitute a taking. Now, as all lawyers know, nuisance itself is an unruly horse. Defining just what activities fall within its scope is notoriously difficult. Scalia's solution to that problem was to restrict the sorts of nuisances that counted for purposes of taking the case out of the *Lucas* doctrine to those activities that traditional state law defined as nuisances:

> A law or decree with such an effect [that is, prohibiting all economically beneficial use of land] must, in other words, do no more than duplicate the result that could have been achieved in the courts—by adjacent landowners . . . under the State's power of private nuisance, or by the State under its complementary power to abate nuisances that affect the public generally, or otherwise.[124]

Putting aside questions that one might raise regarding the analytical persuasiveness of Justice Scalia's reasoning,[125] the point that I wish to make here is that this nuisance exception reflects a social-obligation norm, however truncated. Scalia's nuisance exception rests on an explicit acknowledgment that landowners are subject to a social duty to share the burden of promoting the common good. For constitutional purposes as well as for private legal purposes, landownership does not confer on individuals a privilege to impose harms on the community of such a nature that, by social consensus, the common good is substantially undermined. That is the whole idea of the social-obligation norm. The norm, then, has implicitly been acknowledged. The serious question is what is its scope. That question can be coherently answered only if the norm is openly acknowledged and then developed as a formal element of American takings law.

Developing an Explicit Social-Obligation Norm in Takings Doctrine

TWO CONCEPTIONS OF THE SOCIAL OBLIGATION OF OWNERSHIP In broad terms, two competing conceptions of the social-responsibility norm can be identified in American private and constitutional property law. The first conception provides a thin understanding of the social-obligation norm of constitutional property law. It is limited to the common law's negative obligation to avoid committing nuisance, captured by the *sic utere tuo* doctrine, and a weak affirmative obligation to contribute toward the provision of public goods, such as national defense or police and fire protection.

The economic version of this same basic view explains which affirmative obligations owners owe to their community on the basis of the familiar problems of free riders and holdouts. Individual owners are obligated to make contributions to the public fisc because voluntary means of financing public goods founder on the shoals of high transaction costs, free riders, and holdouts. What is conspicuously absent from the list of projects to which the individual owner's social-responsibility obligation must contribute is the redistribution of wealth done for the sake of equality of welfare. The purging of wealth redistribution from the scope of legitimate social-responsibility objectives would mean, for example, that the progressive income tax, the Social Security tax, and unemployment benefits taxes are all illegitimate.[126] The thin version of the social-obligation norm requires affirmative action of the owner only for the purpose of providing public goods, narrowly defined.

The thin conception of the social-obligation norm, based on the common law's injunction to "use your property so as to avoid harming others," is not so much wrong as it is radically indeterminate. As Joseph Singer has pointed out, "It is well understood that owners cannot use their property to harm others, but it is not well understood how difficult it is to define what that means."[127] The problem with using the harm principle as the basis for defining the social obligations of ownership is that it misleads owners into believing that Blackstone's description of ownership as conferring on owners "sole and despotic dominion" over their property is accurate. It was not accurate in Blackstone's time,[128] and it certainly is not accurate today. Landlords must act to maintain their buildings in habitable conditions for their tenants, including, perhaps, keeping air-conditioning systems in good repair.[129] Owners of residential real estate must disclose to potential buyers the existence of all known defects in the premises, including, according to one view, neighborhood noise problems.[130] Landowners may not construct buildings on their property in a way that interferes with their neighbors' access to sunlight used for solar power.[131] And the list of legally imposed obligations on owners continues to grow.

The thin version of the social-obligation norm underlies what Frank Michelman calls the "possessive" conception of constitutional property rights. According to the possessive version of the constitutional right of property, Michelman states, "we primarily understand property in its constitutional sense as an antiredistributive principle, opposed to governmental interventions into the extant regime of holdings for the sake of distributive ends."[132] As Michelman points out, the social-obligation norm can thicken even under the aegis of this "possessive" conception of constitutional property. Not only does the conception sometimes accept a surprisingly broad range of regulatory measures undertaken to correct "market failures," it also may tolerate explicitly redistributive acts of the state as in fact necessary health or safety measures.[133] Still, as Michelman notes, on those occasions we are apt to feel (to the extent, that is, that we are under the influence of thin social-responsibility thinking), even if we do not admit, that the regulation has transgressed the boundary between the owner's zone of personal autonomy and the legitimate need of the state to act in the interest of providing public goods.

SOCIAL OBLIGATION, COMMUNITY, AND CITIZENSHIP Justice Scalia's nuisance exception is one approach to developing a social-obligation norm. It has the apparent advantage of making the scope of the social-obligation norm relatively clear and certain by anchoring it to a fixed private law norm. That advantage is only apparent, however. As Justice Blackmun in his *Lucas* dissent[134] and a number of academic commentators[135] have pointed out, Scalia's approach to handling the problem of the scope of the nuisance exception begs many questions. Why should nuisance, for purposes of takings law, be defined on the basis of judge-made law alone rather than on the basis of statutory law as well as common law? Why should federal judges defer to state courts in defining state law for constitutional purposes rather than interpreting state law themselves? Why should the meaning of nuisance be frozen in the nineteenth century? To the extent that the common law controls, what if, as is commonly the case, the background decisions defined nuisance in a dynamic way, creating an evolving body of nuisance law rather than a static one? Even if we assume that it is normatively desirable to restrict the social-obligation norm to traditional nuisance law, á la *Lucas*, that approach will be very difficult to implement in anything like the clear and settled way that Justice Scalia had in mind.

Rather than inquiring, as Justice Scalia does, what limitations are inherent in title to land, one might develop the social-obligation norm by focusing directly on the *obligations* of ownership. The language of obligation has certainly not been absent in American takings jurisprudence. Both the liability of property to condemnation for public use and losses resulting from exercises of the police power are, as Justice Frankfurter stated, "properly treated as part of the burden of common citizenship."[136]

But if American courts occasionally have invoked the language of obligation and duty in takings cases, they have not set about systematically developing a coherent constitutional norm of the social obligation of ownership. They deploy the language of obligation here and there in takings cases, but there has been nothing resembling a sustained account of a constitutional norm predicated on the idea that private ownership entails obligations to act (or refrain from acting) for the purpose of promoting the collective good of the community.

A fully developed social-obligation norm requires some social vision, that is, some substantive conception of the common good that serves as the fundamental context for the exercise of the rights and duties of private ownership. There are, of course, many competing conceptions of the collective good of the community. Precisely for this reason, the substantive scope of the social obligation of ownership is highly and inevitably contestable. As Kevin Gray has pointed out, "At stake are rival views of the political balance to be maintained between individual and community interests."[137] Gray goes on to state that defining exactly what social obligations inhere in private ownership "highlights crucial questions about the implicit content of *citizenship.*"[138]

The first conception is premised on a social vision that, in the words of Hanoch Dagan, "underplays the significance of belonging to a community."[139] Dagan goes on to say that the first conception's social vision "perceives our membership [in a political and social community] in purely instrumental terms, and insists that our mutual obligations as members of such a community should be derived either from our consent or from their being to our advantage."[140]

The second conception of the social-obligation norm is considerably thicker.[141] It picks up where the first conception leaves off. In contrast with the minimalist conception of the social obligation of ownership, the social vision underlying the second conception views membership in or belonging to communities as inherent in the human condition. It builds on the Aristotelian notion that the human being is a social animal, not self-sufficient alone. The nature of the human condition is dependency and interdependency. Membership in political and social communities is an inevitable product of the human condition, rather than solely a volitional act committed for instrumental reasons.[142] Moreover, merely by virtue of our inherent embeddedness in communities, we owe obligations to others. Charles Taylor has expressed this social vision in the following terms:

> [S]ince the free individual can only maintain his identity within a society/culture of a certain kind, he has to be concerned about the shape of this society/culture as a whole. He cannot . . . be concerned purely with his individual choices and the associations formed from such choices to the neglect of the matrix in which such choices can be open or closed, rich or meagre.[143]

In recognition of its origins in the ideas of community and citizenship, let us call this version of the social-obligation norm the "civic" conception.[144]

This civic version of the social-obligation norm is not a theory that turns constitutional property from a negative into a positive right. That is, it does not enable the citizen to stand on a constitutional property clause *as such*[145] and file a legitimate, legally cognizable claim for the state to provide her or him with some particular benefit (housing, say). Its focus is not on a non-owner's right to *receive* but on the owner's duty to *give* (or to act or refrain from acting, as the case may be). Owners are under a continuing duty to give (or at least be prepared to give, if and when the duty is activated) to the society that made their ownership possible in the first place.

The fundamental question, of course, is just what are the parameters of this continuing duty. The best answer that I can give is that the owner must provide the society of which she is a member those benefits that the society reasonably regards as necessary and that have some reasonable relationship with ownership of the affected land. An example might help clarify this thicker, civic conception a bit.

AN EXAMPLE: HISTORIC PRESERVATION AS A SOCIAL OBLIGATION

Many areas of public land-use regulatory law, including zoning and historic preservation law, may be understood as being based on such an implicit civic obligation. When a city's architectural board disapproves plans to build a residence whose style is conspicuously incompatible with that of its neighbors, the board is saying, at a minimum, that the owner owes surrounding owners an obligation to maintain everyone's property values.[146] It may also be saying that the public welfare that justifies exercises of the state's police power includes an obligation to maintain aesthetic values as well as to protect physical safety and health.[147] When the owners of New York City's Grand Central Terminal building, with its incomparable nineteenth-century beaux-arts facade, were denied the legal right to develop the air-space directly atop the building,[148] this was a legal recognition that they were owners of an obviously special, nearly unique building with respect to which they owed the community of which the building was a part an obligation not to use it in ways that would irrevocably destroy its unique architectural status.

The constitutional arrangement involving this civically based social obligation of owners is not one-sided; it is reciprocal. The owner gets in return for what is given. The reciprocity involved in the deal, however, may be attenuated, with no requirement of either immediate in-kind compensation or complete proportionality. To elaborate on an earlier example, one might understand the result in the *Penn Central* case in terms of the reciprocity component of a social-responsibility norm. Penn Central Transportation Corporation was required to give up its right to develop the air-space above Grand Central Terminal, which it owned, by virtue of its responsibility to preserve for the benefit of the entire community an endangered urban architectural species. The building's benefit to the community, its historical importance and aesthetic near-uniqueness, was beyond doubt, and as a member of the very community that would benefit from the deal, Penn Central got in return for giving.[149] True, what it got was not of immediate benefit to Penn Central, nor was the benefit directly or completely proportional to what the owner gave up, the very valuable right commercially to develop the air-space above its building. But it did get something.

One might understandably object that this benefit, which Penn Central obtained as a member of the community at large, is simply too attenuated to create any meaningful reciprocity. In contrast with such an "attenuated" form of reciprocity,[150] Dagan has proposed what he calls an "intermediate conception of long-term reciprocity."[151] Under that theory, the regulatory agency is not required to pay compensation

> if, and only if, the disproportionate burden of the public action in question is not overly extreme and is offset, or is likely in all probability to be offset, by benefits of similar magnitude to the landowner's current injury that she gains from other—past, present, or future—public actions (which harm neighboring properties).[152]

Professor Dagan believes that under this intermediate version of reciprocity no compensation was due to Penn Central. The benefit that he sees as having been provided to Penn Central arose from the various other regulatory measures that protected and enhanced New York City's "tourist attractions, business, and industry,"[153] especially in midtown Manhattan, where Grand Central Terminal is located. Thus, argues Dagan, Penn Central "will benefit directly and proportionately in the long-term from the aggregated benefits of the city's public actions, despite the transient disproportionate burden."[154] Surely there is something to this point. The designation of Grand Central Terminal as a historic landmark in all likelihood made it an even bigger tourist attraction than it already was. More tourists generated more revenue for the owner. The rent that Penn Central received from tenants who run commercial operations, including retail concessions, within the building likely increased as a result of rent-escalation clauses that are common in commercial leases for retail stores. This marginal gain in profit should be seen as the result of the regulatory action of the New York City Historical Landmark Commission, providing exactly the kind of long-term reciprocity of advantage that Dagan has in mind. Once this fact is coupled with the further fact that there was nothing arbitrary about identifying Grand Central Terminal as subject to the restriction (for they were the owner and they were the ones proposing the change in question), the case for a compensation requirement becomes weaker and weaker.

Is a Social-Obligation Norm Feasible for U.S. Takings Law?

Legal, including (perhaps one should say "especially") constitutional, borrowings are not simply a matter of whether the borrowed norm is theoretically sound. There is also the question of feasibility. As I discussed in the introduction, doctrinal borrowings are problematic. The same norm may play out quite differently under different legal, political, or social conditions, frustrating the original purpose of the borrowing and perhaps leading to perverse consequences. In the context of constitutional norms, the risks are even greater. Constitutional norms are, by definition, foundational. Acceptance of any new constitutional norm requires a basic measure of compatibility with the basic background political values and assumptions of the society. Surface similarities between legal systems may obscure differences that make a particular constitutional borrowing unacceptable.

The differences between the American constitutional setting and that of Germany, whose constitutional property clause is the main source of a social-obligation norm in the world today, are formidable. The most apparent difference is textual. As we saw in chapter 3,[155] Article 14(2) of the German Basic Law explicitly states that "[p]roperty imposes duties."[156] There is no counterpart to this language in the American Constitution. One might interpret the express reference in Article 14 to property's obligations as an injunction to the German Constitutional Court to develop in a systematic way a social-obligation norm, an injunction that the court has satisfied. No textual basis for such an injunction exists in the American takings clause.

More telling perhaps is the tradition of the *Sozialstaat* in German law. As I discussed earlier,[157] the basic substantive idea behind the *Sozialstaat* concept is that the government has a responsibility to provide for the basic needs of all its citizens. It is not only the government that has a responsibility for the well-being of others, however. The *Sozialstaat* implies that all members of the community are responsible for everyone's welfare. While the state may be the party immediately responsible for satisfying the minimum subsistence needs of its citizens, ultimately it is the citizens themselves who enable the state to fulfill its duty. The *Sozialstaat* concept, then, provides the foundation for Article 14's social-obligation clause.

There is no comparable tradition in American law or politics. To be sure, there is a long history of state-provided social welfare in the United States, but the United States is not a social welfare state of the sort that Germany is. The lack of such a background tradition in the United States might provide support for those who claim that the social-obligation norm, while congenial to German soil, perhaps, is foreign to America's constitutional commitments.

These differences raise the question whether the social-obligation norm, as recognized in Germany and other legal systems, is one that is fundamentally incompatible with the normative conditions of the American constitutional order, particularly in relation to property rights. Many American lawyers are likely to respond that it is so incompatible. Relying on the familiar theme of the sanctity of property rights as the foundation of the American political-legal order and the caricatured Lockean conception of property, these lawyers will be quick to point out that in the American liberal tradition, constitutional protection of property is all about the individual owner's freedom from the coercive power of the collective and that conceptions of ownership as imposing obligations on individuals, other than the thin duty recognized in the common law's *sic utere tuo* doctrine, are squarely at odds with the most fundamental premises of our system.

That reaction, while predictable, is too quick. The differences between the constitutional texts and the constitutional commitments of the United

States and Germany are certainly challenges to the suggestion that American courts borrow the social-obligation norm, but they do not make that suggestion entirely silly. As I have already indicated, American property law is replete with examples of owner obligations that reflect more than the thin conception of obligation. Joseph Singer is right when he observes, "Owners have obligations; they have always had obligations. We can argue about what those obligations should be, but no one can seriously argue that they should not exist."[158] Collectively, these duties constitute a kind of private law version of a social-obligation norm, a template for the development of an explicit constitutional norm of the social obligation inherent in ownership. The private law social-obligation norm, like the private law meaning of ownership itself, does not control the substantive meaning of the constitutional norm, but it does establish the basic principle that private ownership confers duties as well as rights, a point often lost in discussion about the relationship between individual owners and the state.

Whichever of these two conceptions of the social responsibility of ownership a court ultimately chooses, the point is that it must choose *some* theory of what responsibility individual owners owe to others. That theory will form the core of the normative pull that the court gives to property. The purposive approach that the courts in Germany, South Africa, and elsewhere have used has enabled a more transparent analysis of property's normative pull. With that transparency has come greater transparency in German and South African constitutional property law generally. The same measure of transparency can be achieved in American takings law if courts adopt an openly purposive method and, employing that method, consciously develop a constitutional norm of the social obligation that inheres in private ownership.

Compensation Practices

The final potential area of possible borrowing concerns compensation practices. Here I raise the possibility of borrowing, with adjustments that may be necessary to make them more compatible with American takings law requirements, two doctrinal practices drawn from practices in Germany and South Africa. These practices are, first, the use of "equalization" benefits, which, as I described in chapter 3, certain German courts have used to deal with the problem of regulatory excess. The second is what might be called "proportional compensation," an innovation that I draw, again, from practices of Germany and South Africa.

Equalization Benefits

As I described in chapter 3, German courts have provided "equalization" benefits to owners who were disproportionately saddled with the burdens of some otherwise valid property regulation. The German courts have assiduously emphasized that these benefits, which usually take some nonmonetary form designed to mitigate the harmful effects of a regulation on an individual owner, do not constitute compensation for an expropriation. Rather, the purpose of the benefits is to prevent an otherwise desirable regulation from constitutional invalidity for violating the proportionality requirement. The classic example is a public highway project that generates excessive noise for one or a few nearby property owners. The court may either order the developer to install noise-reducing devices such as walls or, if that is inadequate, order payment to the owner for damage to his property.[159]

This practice implicates the requirement of proportionality insofar as it is based on the fact that an otherwise valid property regulation disproportionately burdens one or a small number of owners and that fact is the reason for conferring the equalization benefit. More specifically, it directly addresses the problem that arises when efficiency considerations suggest that a regulation should be held valid but fairness considerations suggest that at least some degree of compensation, monetary or in-kind, should be awarded to specific owners because the burden of the regulation would otherwise disproportionately fall on them.

Generally, the American takings doctrine currently provides no formal mechanism for mitigating this problem. Its approach is all or nothing: either the regulation is a taking, in which case compensation must be paid or else the regulation is invalid, or the regulation is valid because it is not a taking, in which case no compensation or other benefits will be awarded the affected owner. The German equalization practice might be modified somewhat to adapt to American circumstances. In its modified form, it could be used in circumstances where there are good reasons to hold that the regulation is not a taking but where unfairness exists because the regulation disproportionately burdens one or a small number of owners. Equalization, which could take the form of either monetary compensation or in-kind state-conferred benefits, would eliminate or at least reduce the unfairness by mitigating the regulation's disproportionate effects. In this way, the modified version of equalization would break out of the current all-or-nothing straightjacket.

In doctrinal terms, no modification of the German equalization practice is necessary if American courts accept the proportionality principle. In German law, equalization is a means of ensuring that a validly enacted property regulation is not rendered invalid because it imposes an excessive burden on an owner in violation of the proportionality principle.[160] The requisite predicate is that without equalization, the regulation would likely be held invalid on the basis of disproportionality. Even without the proportionality principle, however, equalization can still be justified on strictly administrative grounds, that is, where the equalization benefit is provided as part of an overall regulatory scheme that anticipates the possibility that the property regulation might impose excessive and unfair burdens of an individual or small number of owners.

In fact, something like this form of equalization practice may already occur in the American regulatory context. For example, one way of understanding the *Penn Central* case, in particular Justice Brennan's reference to the conferral of transferable development rights (TDRs) to the owners of Grand Central Terminal, is in terms of this regulatory version of equalization. As part of his discussion of the adverse impact that the Landmark Commission's building permit denial had on the owners, Justice Brennan, speaking for the majority of the Court, stated, "While these rights [that is, TDRs] may well not have constituted 'just compensation' if a 'taking' had occurred, the rights nevertheless undoubtedly mitigate whatever financial burdens the law has imposed on appellants and, for that reason, are to be taken into account in considering the impact of the regulation."[161] Justice Scalia subsequently criticized this analysis, arguing that

> Putting TDRs on the taking rather than the just-compensation side of the equation . . . is a clever, albeit transparent, device that seeks to take advantage of a peculiarity of our Takings-Clause jurisprudence: Whereas once there *is* a taking, the Constitution requires just (i.e., full) compensation, . . . a regulatory taking generally does not *occur* so long as the land retains substantial (albeit not its full) value. . . . If the money that the government-regulator gives to the landowner can be counted on the question of whether there *is* a taking . . . rather than on the question of whether the compensation for the taking is adequate, the government can get away with paying much less.[162]

Even assuming that "just" compensation means "full" compensation (an assumption that I will challenge later in this chapter), Justice Scalia's criticism misses the point of Justice Brennan's reference to TDRs. Justice Brennan did not view TDRs as compensation for a taking. Nor did he seem to think that there would have been a taking but for the TDRs. Rather, he seemed to be saying that although no compensation was necessary because the regulatory action was not a taking, still the TDRs abated the economic impact of the Commission's action, removing whatever doubt might have existed about the constitutional propriety of the permit denial. On this view, the TDRs were a part of the Commission's overall regulatory program, a program that recognized the possibility that application of that regulatory program might in some instances distribute the burdens of the program disproportionately and that sought to mitigate such "regulatory excesses," as they are called in Germany, by providing in-kind benefits that at least offset the possibility of unfairness.[163]

This reading of the case makes *Penn Central* an unintended illustration of an idea proposed more recently by Professors Michael Heller and James Krier in an imaginative 1999 article.[164] Heller and Krier pointed out that some of the most troublesome regulatory takings cases are those in which the goals of efficiency and fairness are at cross purposes because, as they put it, "justice calls for compensation even though efficiency does not."[165] They cite as examples of this dilemma cases in which courts have held that no taking had occurred because the challenged regulation, which drastically reduced the value of an individual owner's property, was aimed at preventing some public nuisance.[166] Heller and Krier argue that in such cases the regulations are efficient and for that reason should be sustained as regulations rather than struck down as regulatory takings. They continue, "The fact remains, however, that the regulatory programs we have in mind often impose losses that should, as a matter of fairness, fall on broader shoulders than those of the unwittingly offending property owners."[167] The owners, for various reasons, deserved compensation, Heller and Krier conclude. They believe that in a small number of such cases courts could award compensation on the basis of private law doctrines such as the tort doctrine of "coming to the nuisance."[168] In most of the cases that fall within their no-taking/compensation category, however, compensation should be handled by "appropriate legislative measures."[169]

Penn Central can be read as a case in which exactly the result that Heller and Krier propose was achieved. The Court sustained an (arguably) efficient regulation on the ground that it did not effect a regulatory taking, but at the same time, unfairness was mitigated by the award of in-kind benefits to the owners. In this instance, the benefits were not awarded after the fact by the legislature but instead were part of an overall regulatory program. This is precisely the way in which the German Constitutional Court in the *Denkmalschutz* case indicated that equalization should be handled, and it could occur in other cases in this country as well. Such cases should be the exception rather than the rule, just as they are in Germany. Ordinarily, equalization should not be awarded where the regulation was indeed not a regulatory taking, but there may be instances in which regulatory agencies have reason to anticipate the possibility that their otherwise valid land-use measure would generate unfair consequences for individual owners and provide for the possibility than offsetting benefits, in-kind or monetary, might be awarded to such owners. The nuisance-abatement cases that Heller and Krier cite and similar cases appear to be strong candidates for such treatment.

Proportionality of Remedies

One major difference between the American approach to compensation and that of both the German and South African constitutions concerns the measure of compensation where a taking, or expropriation, has occurred. Under both the German and South African constitutions, courts may award compensation at some rate less than complete market value. That is not the case under the existing American compensation doctrine, which has long required compensation for takings at full market value. It is worth exploring, albeit briefly, whether deviations from this practice should be permitted in exceptional cases by applying the proportionality principle to remedies.

The proper starting point for considering such a possibility is the object of the takings clause's protection. The American Constitution shares with the German Basic Law an understanding that the object of constitutional protection is *property,* not *wealth.* As we saw earlier, the American Supreme Court has consistently expressed the understanding that the takings clause does not protect wealth but discrete interests labeled "property."[170] The clause is not primarily aimed at preventing the state from redistributing wealth.[171] Rather, its objective is to secure a realm of personal governance concerning particular assets, not to assure that the level of wealth individuals enjoy is unaffected by governmental action. The same understanding holds under the German Constitution. The property clause, Article 14, does not protect wealth but discrete items of property.

The two constitutions share a further, deeper understanding that explains why wealth, as such, is not the object of constitutional protection. In both cases, the property right is not a material but a personal guarantee. The German Constitutional Court has clearly explained this fundamental point. "[T]he property guarantee," the court has said, "must be seen in relationship to the personhood of the owner—i.e., to the realm of freedom within which persons engage in self-defining, responsible activity."[172] As I have argued here, the same understanding is embedded in the American takings clause, although the American courts have not been as explicit about this as the German courts have. More specifically, the American constitutional right to property is primarily aimed at creating and protecting the ability and opportunity of individuals to develop into citizens, that is, members of their communities, who fulfill their self-defined life plans but to do so in a way that takes into account their responsibilities to the political communities of which they are members.

That understanding of the fundamental purpose of the American constitutional property right provides the basis for discerning a further shared aspect of German and American constitutional property law. The German property clause explicitly provides that the measure of compensation is to be based on an "equitable balance"[173] between the individual's affected interest and the public interest. In striking that balance, the courts must look at the individual interest affected by the expropriation in light of the fundamental purpose of the constitutional property right and determine the appropriate measure of compensation due for the loss of that interest on the basis of the proportionality principle. The result of this approach has been that in the vast majority of cases, the individual is awarded compensation on the basis of the full market value of the affected interest. In extraordinary cases, however, something less than complete market value has been awarded.[174] This has occurred in cases where the public interest involved in the expropriation is very great and, because of the nature of the affected item of property, the expropriation did not substantially jeopardize the fundamental purpose of the constitutional property right. As we have seen, on the basis of their definition of that fundamental purpose, the German courts have given greater weight to interests such as a personal residence than they have to interests such as strictly investment property.

If the same functional understanding applies to the property right under the American takings clause, then there is a basis for using a proportionality approach to the question of the level of compensation where a taking has been found to have occurred. American courts could establish a measure of compensation that is proportional to the individual's loss, defined not in terms of wealth but in terms of the fundamental purpose of the property guarantee, and the public interest involved in the governmental action. In cases where the public interest is especially great and where, conversely, the individual loss is less substantial because the affected interest does not directly or immediately jeopardize the owner's opportunity to experience full self-development as a responsible participating member of her political and social communities, courts might award compensation at a rate less than full market value. Under this approach, the compensation norm would remain the entire fair market value amount, just as it is in Germany. Departures from that norm would occur only in truly exceptional cases.

Suppose, for example, that in response to a recent history of hurricanes occurring with increasing frequency and intensity along a particular stretch of the Atlantic coast in the Southeast, a local government condemned a single offshore island whose risk of being hit by a hurricane is usually high. Suppose further that the island is currently undeveloped and is owned by a development firm. Its market value has steadily and significantly increased in recent years as a result of multiple factors, including not only the residential development of other (but less immediately threatened) islands in the area but especially the availability of public insurance and disaster relief that effectively operate to subsidize residential development in the area.

A plausible argument can be made that in such a situation compensation of something less than the market value of the island immediately prior to the condemnation is warranted. Several factors support such an argument. First, the public interest in the condemnation is very great. This is far from the routine cases of eminent domain, where the government has condemned land for the purpose of some public project such as an airport or highway. The state is acting to protect human lives that would be put at serious risk if the island were residentially developed. Moreover, the nature of the owner's interest does not substantially implicate the fundamental purpose of the constitutional right of property in a way that would be the case if the island were owned by an individual whose personal residence were there. Although the concept of property necessary for the development of "personhood" is problematic and no bright-line test can distinguish what might be called "personal" from "commercial" property, the idea that different forms of property implicate the fundamental purpose of the constitutional right of property to different degrees is neither incoherent nor impossible to implement in a fairly consistent way. The German courts have analyzed various forms of property precisely in these terms for many years, and by and large their conclusions have been consistent.

Finally, a proportional analysis of the compensation question here would take into account the fact that some portion of the island's fair market value is due to public subsidies that create incentives for uses of the island that likely would not be made in the absence of any subsidy. Moral hazard is always a problem in the presence of insurance, but it is especially acute here. But for the public subsidies, the island's fair market value would undoubtedly be less than what it currently is, and this fact ought to affect the amount of compensation that the state must pay. Were government summarily to end all of these subsidies, there would be no basis for the owner to challenge the government's decision on takings or other constitutional grounds, despite the fact that the government's action causes the land's fair market value to decrease, perhaps substantially so. It would be understandable then if the government were to say, "Yes, we have a constitutional obligation to compensate you for your loss that we occasioned, but not an obligation to pay you the full market value." A proportional approach would allow the court to take into account that increment of the property's pretaking fair market value that is due to the government's non-obligated subsidization of investment in such property.[175]

Is compensation at some less than market value rate constitutionally permissible? Nothing in the Constitution forbids it. The term "just" in the phrase "just compensation" is not self-defining. It is defined by the courts, and the courts could, if they saw fit, vary in appropriate cases their practice of awarding complete market value. Commentators have recently recommended that in appropriate cases courts award compensation above the fair market value,[176] and there is no constitutional obstacle to deviating from the fair market value standard in the opposite direction either.

If there is no textual impediment to less than market value compensation, there is no textual foothold for using the proportionality principle as the analytical means for determining how much compensation should be paid. This is an important difference between the German and American compensation clauses. While the German clause textually permits, indeed obligates the court to strike an "equitable balance" between the public and private interests, there is no comparable language in the takings clause. It would hardly be surprising, then, if some, perhaps most, American courts resisted the idea of determining the appropriate compensation due for a taking of property on the basis of a proportional analysis of the individual owner's interest in light of the relevant public interest.

Despite the absence of a textual foothold, however, there is both precedential and analytical basis for such an approach. As I have already indicated, however, there is ample precedent for using proportionality, albeit in a very different form than that suggested here, in analyzing the obligations flowing from constitutional provisions, including the takings clause,[177] whose text seemingly provides no invitation for such a mode of analysis. More fundamentally, the question of compensation cannot be analytically set apart from the question of the character of the constitutional right.[178] The meaning of "just" in the phrase "just compensation" depends upon the strength of the affected constitutional property interest and that, in turn, depends on precisely the type of purposive calculus that proportionality analysis invites.

The opportunity for these four borrowings does exist. Courts are free to accept, reject, or modify any or all of them. The choice is up to them. Even if they choose not to implement any of these doctrinal borrowings, however, they would be well advised to study the doctrines. Knowledge of how other jurisdictions approach the same difficult questions that the American takings clause poses might stimulate courts to find their own way through the takings thicket. Ignorance of alternative possibilities can only further entrench the settled habits of thought that have made takings law a muddle in the first place.

Conclusion

There is no single right answer to the question whether property should be a constitutional right. Nor is there any single best way of formulating a constitutional property clause. Everything depends on context. Attempts to standardize constitutional provisions are fundamentally mistaken for just this reason. Just as mistaken are efforts to block constitutional recognition of property on the ground that doing so will necessarily replicate experiences of other particular legal systems whose constitutions expressly protect property (for example, Canada is not the United States).

Constitutions cannot erase background traditions and culture. The effect of constitutional property clauses on property interests within societies is strongly path dependent. Preexisting legal and political traditions and culture continue strongly to influence the stability and security of property rights even where those traditions and culture seemingly conflict with or are in tension with constitutional expressions.

At the same time, while historical legal traditions and culture exert a strong influence on property, they are not determinative. Constitutions can matter, both substantively and expressively. They can provide the catalyst for changing preexisting legal cultures. This was the hope that attended the adoption of South Africa's constitutional property clause. Whether that hope becomes reality remains to be seen.

One area in which text may matter with regard to the effect that a constitutional property clause has on the relationship between property holdings and society is the question of a social-obligation norm in constitutional property law. Comparing the American and German experiences with constitutional property suggests the importance of constitutional text. Because Germany's constitutional property clause explicitly recognizes a social-obligation inherent in ownership, the German courts have had to develop the substantive dimension of that obligation in an explicit and systematic way. The text of the takings clause, by contrast, has allowed American courts to avoid openly acknowledging what they implicitly do recognize. Keeping the social-obligation norm hidden is one important reason why American takings jurisprudence is so opaque. Although the text of the takings clause does not force American courts openly to acknowledge and develop the social-obligation norm, neither does it prevent American courts from doing so. One of the key lessons to be learned from comparing the German and American approaches to analyzing constitutional property disputes is the benefit to be gained by explicitly recognizing and systemically developing the social obligation of ownership.

This comparative study has revealed the existence of both commonalities and differences among various constitutional property regimes. Key commonalities include the following points. First, all of the regimes studied here deny that the constitutional right of property is absolute. They all expressly empower the state to expropriate private property so long as it is done for the benefit of the public and so long as the state compensates the owner. Second, all of the jurisdictions recognize, implicitly or explicitly, a social obligation of ownership, but they all leave to courts the task of defining the parameters of that obligation. No constitutional property clause purports to specify the substantive content of the social obligation. Third, all of the jurisdictions share the core problem of distinguishing between noncompensable regulations of property and compensable de facto expropriations, a task that every constitution considered here leaves to the courts to sort out. Constitutional texts provide only the most general guidance, if any at all. This third common characteristic leads to a fourth. All of the constitutional regimes struggle with the core dilemma of determining when a government measure that formally is a regulation has gone too far and constitutes a de facto expropriation.

Important differences have been found as well. These include the fact that some regimes explicitly recognize a social obligation while others leave it implicit and unacknowledged. A second difference is that some regimes positively recognize and protect the right of private property while others do not. Third, some constitutional orders allow courts to order compensation while others allocate the power to compensate exclusively to the legislature. Fourth, some but not all explicitly prescribe that the constitutional right of property is subject to legislatively defined limitations. Finally, in some but not all constitutional systems, courts explicitly identify the central purposes of property as a constitutional right and develop their constitutional property jurisprudence around this settled understanding.

Comparative analysis of constitutional property law reveals other insights as well. It reveals, for example, the fact that constitutional protection of property implicates values and concerns that go beyond social utility, economic efficiency, individual liberty, or distributive fairness. Constitutional property is also about internal struggles for power among various governmental institutions. Property clauses, like other constitutional provisions, are about who gets to decide what. The experiences of India and Canada, which led ultimately to a rejection of constitutional property clauses in both countries, illustrate that this institutional consideration in some cases is more decisive than considerations of economic efficiency or distributive fairness. In federal regimes, constitutional property may also be about issues of federalism. Here again, Canada's example illustrates the underappreciated importance of allocations of power between state and national government to understanding what values a constitutional right of property implicates in particular societies.

Comparison also reveals that clarity and principled reasoning are enhanced by a purposive approach to interpreting constitutional property clauses. Where courts openly discuss and debate the central purpose (or purposes) that property serves as a constitutional right within the particular constitutional regime and in the particular context of the case, they are much more apt to reveal the real normative bases for their decisions. As Laura Underkuffler has pointed out, "[T]he constitutionalization of property can present a powerful opportunity for a more direct and honest facing of the question of the meaning of property and its role in contemporary social and political life."[1] Courts in some countries, such as South Africa and Germany, have recognized this point and met the challenge head-on. In other countries, courts have been less apt to face the challenge. Constitutional property law is more likely to be viewed as principled and coherent when courts directly face and positively respond to the challenge. The unsatisfactory state of takings jurisprudence in the United States is due in no small measure to the failure of American courts to do so.

A final, even deeper insight emerges from this comparative study of constitutional property law. No constitutional provision and no judicial method of interpreting a constitutional provision can possibly resolve, once and for all, value conflicts over property. Even in Germany and South Africa constitutional property remains controversial. No constitutional text or judicial method can eliminate disagreements about the appropriate relationship between private property owners and the communities to which they belong. Both as a concept and as an institution, property is inherently controversial, and constitutional provisions protecting property cannot eliminate the conflicting values that are inherent in the idea of private property.[2] Consequently, in the United States and elsewhere in the world, constitutional property law must remain controversial.

NOTES

INTRODUCTION

1. This point is made by Vicki Jackson and Mark Tushnet in the introduction to their recent collection of essays on comparative constitutional law. See Vicki C. Jackson and Mark Tushnet, introduction to Defining the Field of Comparative Constitutional Law, ed. Vicki C.Jackson and Mark Tushnet (Westport, CT: Praeger Publishers, 2002), pp. xi, xiii.
2. Bruce Ackerman, The Rise of World Constitutionalism, 83 Va. L. Rev. 771 (1997).
3. See, for example, Mark Tushnet (ed.), Comparative Constitutional Federalism (New York: Greenwood Press, 1990).
4. This is hardly surprising, as American constitutionalists largely ignore the takings question as a whole. Takings scholarship tends to be the province of property law specialists.
5. See Aeyal M. Gross, The Politics of Rights in Israeli Constitutional Law, 3 Isr. Stud. 80, 92–93, 97–99, 101–106 (Fall 1998).
6. See chapter 1.
7. The seminal work in neoclassical development theory, stressing the necessity of legally secure property rights for economic growth, is by Douglass North. See Douglass C. North, Institutions, Institutional Change, and Economic Performance (New York: Cambridge University Press, 1990); Douglass C. North, Structure and Change in Economic History (New York: W. W. Norton & Co., 1981). The premises of neoclassical development theory have been challenged on several different grounds. See, for example, Carol Jones, Capitalism, Globalization and Rule of Law: An Alternative Trajectory of Legal Change in China, 3 Soc. & Leg. Stud. 195 (1994). For a brief but clear overview of the debate within development theory, focusing on China, see Randall Peerenboom, China's Long March toward Rule of Law (New York: Cambridge University Press, 2002), pp. 450–512.
8. For a modern example of this view, see Samuel Bowles and Herbert Gintis, Democracy and Capitalism: Property, Community, and the Contradictions of Modern Social Thought (New York: Basic Books, 1986).
9. Cass R. Sunstein, On Property and Constitutionalism, 14 Cardozo L. Rev. 907, 908 (1993).
10. See chapter 1.

11. Frank I. Michelman, Possession vs. Distribution in the Constitutional Idea of Property, 72 Iowa L. Rev. 1319, 1320 (1987).
12. This is the conception of the liberal right of property that Jennifer Nedelsky forcefully attacks. See Jennifer Nedelsky, Private Property and the Limits of American Constitutionalism: The Madisonian Framework and Its Legacy (Chicago: University of Chicago Press, 1990).
13. Claus Offe, Modernity and the State, East, West (Cambridge, 1996), p. 154.
14. William Blackstone, Commentaries on the Laws of England, vol. 2 (1765–69; facsimile ed., Chicago: University of Chicago Press, 1979), p. 2.
15. See, for example, Carol M. Rose, Canons of Property Talk, or, Blackstone's Anxiety, 108 Yale L.J. 601 (1998); Joan C. Williams, The Rhetoric of Property, 83 Iowa L. Rev. 277, 280–83 (1998).
16. This theme was especially prominent in the work of Robert L. Hale. See Barbara Fried, The Progressive Assault on Laissez Faire (Cambridge, MA: Harvard University Press, 1998); Gregory S. Alexander, Commodity & Propriety: Competing Visions of Property in American Legal Thought (Chicago: University of Chicago Press, 1997), pp. 335–40.
17. The relational aspect of property has been most forcefully expressed in recent years by Laura S. Underkuffler, The Idea of Property: Its Meaning and Power (New York: Oxford University Press, 2003); Joseph William Singer, Entitlement: The Paradoxes of Property (New Haven, CT: Yale University Press, 2000); and Jennifer Nedelsky, Reconceiving Rights as Relationship, 1 Rev. Const. Stud./Revue d'études constitutionelles 16 (1993).
18. Nedelsky, Reconceiving Rights as Relationship, p. 8.
19. Nedelsky, Private Property and the Limits of American Constitutionalism, p. 1.
20. Laura S. Underkuffler-Freund, Property: A Special Right, 71 Notre Dame L. Rev. 1033, 1038 (1996). Of course, as basic economics teaches us, the recognition of exclusive property rights facilitates the creation of social wealth, from which new property rights may emerge. Underkuffler-Freund's point is that with respect to any existing (nonpublic) asset, the legal recognition of A's right to exclude the rest of world from possession, use, or enjoyment of that asset precludes the simultaneous legal recognition of the same right in B.
21. Underkuffler-Freund, Property: A Special Right.
22. This statement is an appropriate occasion for clarifying exactly what I mean when talking about "property." Throughout most of this book, by that term I mean what one might call "old-style" property, especially land. The vast majority of takings disputes, certainly in the United States, involve land. In linking the right of property with access to food and shelter, I move beyond property as it is conventionally understood to include socioeconomic rights. I am hardly the first to make this linkage. One strategy by which some proponents of so-called positive rights, that is, socioeconomic rights, have sought to gain recognition of such rights as a *constitutional* matter has been to adopt the republican definition of property as the material foundation for personal identity, self-governance, and participation in civic life. Under that definition, socioeconomic rights are a species of, indeed perhaps the most important species of, the right of property. In American constitutional jurisprudence, the foremost exponent of this view is Frank Michelman. (For an early example, see Frank I. Michelman, Welfare Rights in a Constitutional Democracy, 1979 Wash. U.L.Q. 659.) Elsewhere in the world the linkage between property and socioeco-

nomic rights is less controversial than it is in the United States. As I discuss in chapter 4, the South African Constitution is an especially clear example. Immediately following its property clause (sec. 25), the South African Constitution expressly guarantees certain socioeconomic rights, such as housing, food, and health care. S. Afr. Const. 1996, ch. 2, secs. 25–27. Thus, although it does not subsume socioeconomic rights within the meaning of property as such, the constitution clearly does contemplate that a direct linkage between the two exists. Moreover, the property clause itself includes certain positive guarantees, including restitution of land to persons dispossessed by past racially discriminatory laws and legally secure land tenure, that are parts of the same basic framework as the socioeconomic rights.

23. In Olga Tellis v. Bombay Municipal Corp., A.I.R. 1986 S.C. 180, the Supreme Court of India held that the right to life, protected under Article 21 of the Indian constitution, includes the right to livelihood, that is, "a right to the protection of the means by which alone life can be lived." *Tellis* at 184. "That, which alone makes it possible to live," the court said, "must be deemed to be an integral component of the right to life." *Tellis* at 194. At issue in the case were actions taken by the city of Bombay demolishing the crude shelters erected on pavements by slum dwellers. The court held that these eviction actions violated the pavement dwellers' right to life by depriving them of their means of livelihood in an arbitrary and unfair way.
24. See Theunis Roux, Understanding *Grootboom*—A Response to Cass R. Sunstein, 12 Const. Forum 41, 44 (2002).
25. By the term "constitutional property clause," both here and elsewhere in the book, I mean simply an express provision of a constitution that recognizes, directly (as in the case of Germany) or indirectly (as in the case of the United States), property as a constitutionally protected individual right. Some constitutional property clauses, such as Germany's, also expressly recognize and protect the *institution* of private property.
26. The term "expropriate" is far more common than the American Constitution's highly ambiguous term "take."
27. Compensation practices differ, sometimes in very important ways. In the United States, for example, the courts have interpreted the constitutional requirement of "just compensation" as requiring payment to the owner of the full market value for the expropriated asset. In South Africa, on the other hand, the constitution expressly limits the compensation requirement by providing that "[t]he amount of the compensation and the time and manner of payment must be just and equitable, reflecting an equitable balance between the public interest and the interests of those affected, having regard to all relevant circumstances [defined to include not solely market value but also such factors as "the history of the acquisition and use of the property" and "the nation's commitment to land reform"]. S. Afr. Const. ch. 2, sec. 25(3). The South African Constitution clearly contemplates that less than full fair market value may be paid in some cases.
28. Grundgesetz für die Bundesrepublik Deutschland, art. 14, sec. 2.
29. Among the skeptics of the comparative approach generally, William Alford, George Fletcher, and Frederick Schauer have provided thoughtful critiques. See William P. Alford, On the Limits of "Grand Theory" in Comparative Law, 61 Wash. L. Rev. 945 (1986); George P. Fletcher, Constitutional Identity, 14 Cardozo L. Rev. 737 (1993); and Frederick Schauer, Free Speech and the Cultural Contingency of Constitutional Categories, 14 Cardozo L. Rev. 865 (1993). For exceptionally insightful discussions of the current state of comparative law in private, that is, nonconstitutional law, see

Annelise Riles, Wigmore's Treasure Box: Comparative Law in the Era of Information, 40 Harv. Int'l L.J. 221 (1999); and David Kennedy, New Approaches to Comparative Law: Comparativism and International Governance, 1997 Utah L. Rev. 545.

30. See, for example, the majority and dissenting opinions in Stanford v. Kentucky, 492 U.S. 361 (1989), and more recently, in Printz v. United States, 521 U.S. 898 (1997). See also William Rehnquist, Constitutional Courts—Comparative Remarks, in Germany and Its Basic Law: Past, Present, and Future, ed. Paul Kirchhof and Donald P. Kommers (Baden-Baden: Nomos, 1993), p. 412.

31. Some of the standard arguments are given by Donald P. Kommers, The Value of Comparative Constitutional Law, 9 J. Marshall J. Pract. & Proc. 685 (1976). Two particularly valuable recent discussions of comparative constitutional law are Mark Tushnet, The Possibilities of Comparative Constitutional Law, 108 Yale L.J. 1225 (1999); and Sujit Choudhry, Globalization in Search of Justification: Toward a Theory of Comparative Constitutional Interpretation, 74 Ind. L.J. 819 (1999). See also Roger P. Alford, In Search of a Theory for Constitutional Comparativism, 52 UCLA L. Rev. 639 (2005); Ruti Teitel, Comparative Constitutional Law in a Global Age, 117 Harv. L. Rev. 2570 (2004) (book review); Ackerman, The Rise of World Constitutionalism. For a skeptical view of the benefits of the comparative enterprise generally, see Günter Frankenberg, Critical Comparisons: Re-Thinking Comparative Law, 26 Harv. Int'l L.J. 411 (1985).

32. See Choudry, Globalization in Search of Justification, 835–38. On the idea of comparative law as a "distancing" and critical technique, see Frankenberg, Critical Comparisons. See also Mary Ann Glendon, Abortion and Divorce in Western Law (Cambridge, MA: Harvard University Press, 1987); William Ewald, Comparative Jurisprudence (I): What Was It Like to Try a Rat?, 143 U. Pa. L. Rev. 1889 (1995).

33. See Tushnet, The Possibilities of Comparative Constitutional Law, p. 1227.

34. David Schneiderman, Comparative Constitutional Law in an Age of Economic Globalization, in Defining the Field of Comparative Constitutional Law, pp. 237, 244.

35. I discuss this neoliberal claim in chapter 1.

36. See, for example, Jennifer Nedelsky, Should Property Be Constitutionalized?, in Property Law on the Threshold of the 21st Century, ed. G. E. van Maanen and A.J. van der Walt (Antwerp: MAKLU, 1996), pp. 417–32; Matthew Chaskalson, The Problem with Property: Thoughts on the Constitutional Protection of Property in the United States and the Commonwealth, 9 S. Afr. J. Hum. Rights 388 (1993); Alex Frame, Property: Some Pacific Reflections, 1992 New Zealand L.J. 21; Richard W. Bauman, Property Rights in the Canadian Constitutional Context, 8 S. Afr. J. Hum. Rights 344 (1992).

37. See, for example, Society for Democracy, Property—Not a Fundamental Right (Delhi: People's Publishing House, 1970), p. 13. On the Indian experiment with constitutionalizing property, see chapter 1.

38. See Michael A. Heller and James E. Krier, Deterrence and Distribution in the Law of Takings, 112 Harv. L. Rev. 997 (1999) ("[T]he two central concerns of the Takings Clause [are] efficiency and justice.") This conventional wisdom is based on the classic article by Frank I. Michelman, Property, Utility, and Fairness: Comments on the Ethical Foundations of "Just Compensation" Law, 80 Harv. L. Rev. 1165 (1967).

39. Mark Tushnet's typology of three sorts of arguments for doing comparative analysis—"functionalist," "expressive," and "bricolage"—provides a very valuable overview of the benefits and limitations of comparative law, both constitutional and nonconstitutional. See Tushnet, The Possibilities of Comparative Constitutional Law, pp. 1228–30.

40. See Carol M. Rose, *Mahon* Reconstructed: Why the Takings Issue Is Still a Muddle, 57 S. Cal. L. Rev. 561 (1984).
41. See Jackson and Tushnet, Defining Comparative Constitutional Law, pp. 169–73.
42. On the general topic of constitutional borrowing, see Roger P. Alford, In Search of a Theory for Constitutional Comparativism, 52 UCLA L. Rev. 639 (2005); Ruth Bader Ginsburg, Looking beyond Our Borders: The Value of a Comparative Perspective in Constitutional Adjudication, 40 Idaho L. Rev. 1 (2003); Gary Jeffrey Jacobsohn, The Permeability of Constitutional Borders, 82 Texas L. Rev. 1763 (2004). See generally the symposium in 1 Int'l J. Const. L. 177 et seq. (2003).
43. See, for example, Lawrence v. Texas, 539 U.S. 558, 598 (2003) (Scalia, J., dissenting) (rejecting the majority's reference to the decriminalization of sodomy laws by other countries as irrelevant because a right to practice sodomy is not "deeply rooted in this Nation's history and tradition" (quoting Bowers v. Hardwick, 478 U.S. 186, 192 (1986) (quoting Moore v. City of East Cleveland, 431 U.S. 494, 503 (1977)))). But see 539 U.S. at 572–73, 576–77 (Kennedy, J., relying on an international tribunal decision in interpreting individual liberties under the U.S. Constitution). For a direct attack on the suggestion that the U.S. Supreme Court should engage in constitutional borrowing, see John Yoo, Peeking Abroad?: The Supreme Court's Use of Foreign Precedents in Constitutional Cases, 26 U. Haw. L. Rev. 385–404 (2004).
44. For a more sustained discussion of and response to what he calls the "cultural objection," see Jacobsohn, The Permeability of Constitutional Borders, pp. 1814–16.
45. See Frank I. Michelman, Reflection, 82 Texas L. Rev. 1737, 1760–61 (2004).
46. William E. Forbath and Lawrence Sager, Comparative Avenues in Constitutional Law: An Introduction, 82 Texas L. Rev. 1653, 1657 (2004).
47. Legal transparency, I recognize, is not an unqualified good. As Guido Calabresi and Philip Bobbitt have pointed out, sometimes subterfuges may be desirable. What Calabresi and Bobbitt term "tragic choices" involve deep conflicts of fundamental values, and subterfuges are sometimes used in the political process to veil these conflicts. This usually occurs, they argue, when there is some significant advantage to the subterfuge, such as use of a jury to make a tragic choice. Juries do some things better than other institutions. Guido Calabresi and Philip Bobbitt, Tragic Choices (New York: W. W. Norton & Co., 1978), pp. 78–79. In the context of constitutional property, the choices, in my judgment, as sufficiently "tragic" that the benefits of legal subterfuges outweigh the costs. Moreover, transparency is not a binary quality. It is a matter of degree, and few observers of American takings law would assert that modern takings jurisprudence is as transparent as it needs to be.
48. See Donald P. Kommers, Comparative Constitutional Law: Its Increasing Relevance, in Defining Comparative Constitutional Law, pp. 61, 64.
49. See Kommers, Comparative Constitutional Law, p. 62, quoting Giovanni Sartori, Comparative Constitutional Engineering, 2d ed. (New York: New York University Press, 1997), p. 197.
50. Kommers, Comparative Constitutional Law, pp. 62–63.
51. The prime example is Professor Richard Epstein.
52. There is no constitutionally protected right to compensation for expropriation of property in the United Kingdom. However, both the unwritten constitution of England and the written statutes protect against abuses of the state's power to expropriate. See generally Tom Allen, Commonwealth Constitutions and the Right Not to Be Deprived of Property, 42. Int'l & Comp. L.Q. 523 (1993). Moreover, as the United Kingdom is a signatory to the European Convention on Human Rights, which con-

tains a property provision, persons prejudiced by expropriations in the United Kingdom may complain to the European Court of Human Rights. On the European Convention's property clause, see A. J. van der Walt, Constitutional Property Clauses (Cape Town: Juta, 1999), pp. 96–120.

53. For a more extensive list, including relevant texts, see van der Walt, Constitutional Property Clauses, pp. 498–585.
54. Another important difference is textual. Whereas the American constitution protects against "takings," most constitutions identify "expropriations" as the type of act that triggers the compensation requirement. Yet another group of constitutions uses the term "deprivation." The differences, though not necessarily substantive in effect, in practice do tend to yield different results concerning the scope of constitutional protection. Clauses textually protecting only against "expropriations" (or "acquisitions") are limited to eminent domain actions in which the state explicitly takes property away from the owner. Clauses protecting against "deprivations" include police-power regulatory actions as well as eminent-domain actions. Most modern constitutions contain a property clause that includes both limitations. See van der Walt, Constitutional Property Clauses, pp. 12–13, 17–20.
55. See van der Walt, Constitutional Property Clauses, pp. 20–21.
56. David Schneiderman, Comparative Constitutional Law in an Age of Economic Globalization, in Defining Comparative Constitutional Law, pp. 237, 244.
57. Schneiderman, Comparative Constitutional Law in an Age of Economic Globalization.
58. 512 U.S. 374 (1994).
59. The phrase is, famously, from Pennsylvania Coal Co. v. Mahon, 260 U.S. 393, 415 (1922).
60. As I will discuss at greater length elsewhere (chiefly in chapter 5), American takings jurisprudence implicitly embraces a notion of social responsibility within the constitutional concept of ownership. My point is that this notion needs to be brought into the open and debated and developed explicitly. The experience of the German courts and the more limited experience of the South African courts with the constitutional social-obligation norm could guide American courts.
61. See Rose, *Mahon* Reconstructed.
62. Rose, *Mahon* Reconstructed, p. 587. See also Gregory S. Alexander, Takings and the Post-Modern Dialectic of Property, 9 Const. Comm. 259 (1992).
63. Gregory S. Alexander, Commodity & Propriety.
64. See Edward J. Eberle, Human Dignity, Privacy, and Personality in German and American Constitutional Law, 1997 Utah L. Rev. 963, 968.

CHAPTER ONE

1. Free speech and freedom of association are by no means totally exempt from controversy. For example, in debates over human rights in Asian societies like China and Singapore, the status of these interests as constitutional rights has been one of the major issues. See Joanne R. Bauer and Daniel Bell (eds.), The East Asian Challenge for Human Rights (Cambridge: Cambridge University Press, 1999).
2. I discuss the Indian story more fully later in this chapter.
3. See chapter 4.
4. See Kevin Y. L. Tan, Economic Development, Legal Reform, and Rights in Singapore and Taiwan, in The East Asian Challenge for Human Rights, pp. 264, 268.
5. See Andre van der Walt, The Constitutional Property Clause: Striking a Balance be-

tween Guarantee and Limitation, in Property and the Constitution, ed. Janet McLean (Oxford: Hart Publishing Co., 1999), p. 113. On New Zealand's practice of compensated expropriations for public purpose, see Michael Taggart, Expropriation, Public Purpose, and the Constitution, in The Golden Metwand and the Crooked Cord: Essays on Public Law in Honour of Sir William Wade, ed. Christopher Forsyth and Ivan Ware (Oxford: Oxford University Press, 1998), pp. 91, 107–108.

6. I discuss Canada's rejection of a property clause more fully later in this chapter.
7. Franz Wieacker, Foundations of European Legal Culture, 37 Am. J. Comp. L. 1, 29 (1989).
8. There is absolutely nothing unique to the property clause issue in this regard. The formalist trap bedevils all of constitutional law, indeed all written law. For a good response to the formalist trap in the constitutional setting generally, see David A. Strauss, The Role of a Bill of Rights, 59 U. Chi. L. Rev. 539 (1992).
9. Cass R. Sunstein, On Property and Constitutionalism, 14 Cardozo L. Rev. 907, 923 (1993).
10. Cass R. Sunstein, Designing Democracy: What Constitutions Do (New York: Oxford University Press, 2001), p. 223. Commentators have called for explicit constitutional protection of property in Iraq's new constitution. These commentators typically base their call on the argument that a property clause is necessary for both economic and democratic development in Iraq. See Richard W. Rahn, Saving Iraq . . . From the U.N., *Washington Times,* September 17, 2003, p. A18; George Mellon, In Iraqi Oil, Readers Say I Didn't Go Far Enough, *Wall Street Journal,* April 22, 2003, p. A29.
11. The same agenda is also evident in most bilateral investment treaties between major investing countries, especially the United States, and borrowing nations.
12. See Randall Peerenboom, China's Long March toward Rule of Law (Cambridge: Cambridge University Press, 2002), p. 453. The original law and development movement occurred during the 1950s and 60s, when policy makers sought to implement Max Weber's thesis about the relationship among capitalism, rationality, and rule of law in developing countries. Their attempts to use law to produce economic development suffered serious setbacks. See Peerenboom, China's Long March, pp. 451–52. The new law and development movement focuses primarily on the relationship between law and economics, rather than on political development, although it by no means ignores political liberalization. It shares with the original movement a commitment to the idea that institutions, especially legal institutions, matter greatly in the economic development of nations. One of its central tenets is that clear and secure property rights are vitally important, perhaps even necessary, to the process of economic growth. Peerenboom, China's Long March, p. 452. The new law and development movement's claims about the relationship between clear property rights and economic development have certainly not escaped criticisms. See, for example, Carol A. G. Jones, Capitalism, Globalization and Rule of Law: An Alternative Legal Trajectory of Legal Change in China, 3 Soc. & Leg. Stud. 195 (1994) (arguing that China's rapid economic growth, despite the absence of clear property rights, illustrates that in some societies there are substitutes for clear property rights that provide the degree of stability and predictability necessary to attract investment).
13. Stephen Gill, Globalization, Market Civilization, and Disciplinary Neoliberalism, 24 Millenium: J. Int'l Stud. 399 (1995).
14. Gill, Globalization, Market Civilization, and Disciplinary Neoliberalism, 412.
15. See David Schneiderman, Investment Rules and the New Constitutionalism, 25 L. & Soc'y Rev. 757 (2000).

16. James M. Buchanan, The Economics and Ethics of Constitutional Order (Ann Arbor, MI: University of Michigan Press, 1991), p. 104 (emphasis in original).
17. The private law aspect of the rule-of-law orthodoxy's program of standardization has been critiqued by various commentators. See, for example, Katerina Pistor, The Standardization of Law and Its Effects on Developing Countries, G-24 Discussion Paper Series, No. 4 (U.N. Conference on Trade and Development, Harvard Center for International Development, June 2000). Standardization of public law, including constitutional law, has received less attention. See, for example, Schneiderman, Investment Rules and the New Constitutionalism; Ran Hirschl, The Political Origins of the New Constitutionalism, 11 Ind. J. Global Leg. Stud. 71 (2004).
18. See Schneiderman, Investment Rules and the New Constitutionalism; Hirschl, The Political Origins of the New Constitutionalism.
19. See David Schneiderman, Constitutional Approaches to Privatization: An Inquiry into the Magnitude of Neo-Liberal Constitutionalism, 63 Law & Contemp. Probs. 83 (2000) (giving examples from Latin America of how the new (neoliberal) constitutionalism has disciplined domestic constitutional rules).
20. See Schneiderman, Investment Rules and the New Constitutionalism.
21. For a particularly clear expression of the progressive arguments against constitutionalizing property, see Jennifer Nedelsky, Should Property Be Constitutionalized?: A Relational and Comparative Approach, in Property on the Threshold of the 21st Century, ed. G. E. van Maanen and A.J. van der Walt (Antwerp: MAKLU, 1996), p. 417. See also David Schneiderman, Comparative Constitutional Law in an Age of Economic Globalization, in Defining the Field of Comparative Constitutional Law, ed. Vicki C. Jackson and Mark Tushnet (Westport, CT: Praeger Publishers, 2002), pp. 237, 241; Aeyal Gross, The Politics of Rights in Israeli Constitutional Law, 3 Isr. Stud. 80, 98 (1997); Ran Hirschl, The Political Origins of Judicial Empowerment through Constitutionalization: Lessons from Four Constitutional Revolutions, 25 Law & Soc. Inquiry 91 (2000).
22. See Sunstein, On Property and Constitutionalism.
23. The experience of South Africa is especially revealing on the importance of this topic. See chapter 4.
24. Cf. Bruce Ackerman, We, the People: Foundations (Cambridge, MA: Belknap Press, 1991).
25. Andre van der Walt has been the most forceful advocate of this view. See, for example, Andre van Walt, The Constitutional Property Clause: Striking a Balance between Guarantee and Limitation, in Property and the Constitution, p. 109.
26. Zimbabwe is a recent example. Despite the existence of a constitutional provision requiring compensation for government expropriations of property (Constitution of Zimbabwe 1980, sec. 11), in recent years President Robert Mugabe's regime has routinely forced white land owners off their land with no payment of compensation whatsoever. The constitutional provision has played virtually no role in this process of forced removals. It will be interesting to see what effect, including what propaganda effect, China's new constitutional property clause has in future government expropriations of land. Experience with other provisions of China's constitution indicates that the constitution is generally subordinate to party ideology. See Chris Buckley, China Approves Amendments on Property and Human Rights, *New York Times,* March 15, 2004, p. A12.
27. I do not wish to imply that the property right is unique in this respect. My critique could equally be made of every other constitutional right. Indeed, others have made

just that more general point. See, for example, David A. Strauss, The Role of a Bill of Rights, 59 U. Chi. L. Rev. 539 (1992). My aim here is to apply the realist critique to the property right in hopes of shedding a little light on the continuing controversy about constitutional property around the world.

28. van der Walt, Striking a Balance between Guarantee and Limitation, p. 128.
29. Some of the main scholars arguing against a constitutional right of property are Frank Michelman, Jennifer Nedelsky, and Michael Chaskalson. See, for example, Frank I. Michelman, Socio-Political Functions of Constitutional Protection for Private Property Holdings (In Liberal Thought), in Property on the Threshold of the 21st Century, p. 433; Nedelsky, Should Property Be Constitutionalized?; and Michael Chaskalson, The Problem with Property: Thoughts on the Constitutional Protection of Property in the United States and the Commonwealth, 9 S. Afr. J. Hum. Rights 388 (1993).
30. See, for example, Michael Chaskalson, The Problem with Property, pp. 389–408.
31. C. B. MacPherson, Liberal-Democracy and Property, in Property: Mainstream and Critical Positions, C. B. MacPherson (Toronto: University of Toronto Press, 1978), p. 199.
32. See Alan Ryan, Property and Political Theory (Oxford: BaSil Blackwell, 1984), pp. 112, 150.
33. See, for example, Samuel Bowles and Herbert Gintis, Democracy & Capitalism (New York: Basic Books, 1986).
34. See, for example, Gross, The Politics of Rights in Israeli Constitutional Law.
35. Ronald Dworkin, Taking Rights Seriously (Cambridge, MA: Harvard University Press, 1977).
36. Nedelsky, Should Property Be Constitutionalized?, p. 427.
37. Nedelsky, Should Property Be Constitutionalized?, p. 427.
38. Laura S. Underkuffler-Freund, Property: A Special Right, 71 Notre Dame L. Rev. 1033, 1044 (1996).
39. For some examples, see Laurence H. Tribe, American Constitutional Law, 2d ed. (Mineola, NY: Foundation Press, 1988), pp. 568–71; R. W. Bauman, Property Rights in the Canadian Constitutional Context, 8 S. Afr. J. Hum. Rights 344, 355–59 (1992); Chaskalson, The Problem with Property, pp. 395–408.
40. See, for example, Bowles and Gintis, Democracy & Capitalism.
41. See Michelman, Socio-Political Functions of Constitutional Protection for Private Property Holdings, pp. 433, 441–42.
42. William A. Fischel, Regulatory Takings: Law, Economics, and Politics (Cambridge, MA: Harvard University Press, 1995), p. 3.
43. Alexander Bickel, The Least Dangerous Branch (New Haven, CT: Yale University Press, 1962).
44. Bickel, The Least Dangerous Branch, p. 19.
45. Fischel, Regulatory Takings, p. 4.
46. Joel Bakan, Against Constitutional Property Rights, in Constitutional Politics, ed. Duncan Cameron and Miriam Smith (Toronto: Lorimer, 1992), pp. 117, 122.
47. See, for example, Tribe, American Constitutional Law, pp. 568–71.
48. In addressing the argument that constitutionalizing property is antiredistributive, I do not mean to imply that a legal system in which property rights are not constitutionally protected obtains greater flexibility in redistributing wealth but necessarily does so at the expense of economic efficiency. Granting constitutional status to property rights may have inefficient consequences under certain circumstances. If any diminution in the value of property caused by some new legislation gives rise to a

constitutional claim for just compensation, some efficient legislation (gains to winners exceed losses to losers) may become unaffordable given the transaction costs required to find losers, assess their losses, and litigate the size and legitimacy of their claims. See Frank I. Michelman, Property, Utility, and Fairness: Comments on the Ethical Foundations of "Just Compensation" Law, 80 Harv. L. Rev. 1165 (1967).

49. See, for example, Nedelsky, Should Property Be Constitutionalized?, p. 424; Chaskalson, The Problem with Property, p. 389.
50. Pierre-Joseph Proudhon, What Is Property?, trans. Donald R. Kelley and Bonnie G. Smith (Cambridge: Cambridge University Press, 1994; first published 1840).
51. See van der Walt, The Constitutional Property Clause, p. 111.
52. Chaskalson, The Problem with Property, p. 410.
53. Chaskalson, The Problem with Property, p. 2.
54. Chaskalson, The Problem with Property, p. 30.
55. Frank I. Michelman, Possession vs. Distribution in the Constitutional Idea of Property, 72 Iowa L. Rev. 1319 (1987).
56. Michelman, Possession vs. Distribution in the Constitutional Idea of Property, p. 1319.
57. Chaskalson, The Problem with Property, p. 410.
58. See generally Fischel, Regulatory Takings, pp. 100–140 (discussing the problem of majorities in relation to property interests and citing sources).
59. See Forrest McDonald, Novus Ordo Seclorum: The Intellectual Origins of the Constitution (Lawrence, KS: University Press of Kansas, 1985).
60. Mark Kelman, On Democracy Bashing: A Skeptical Look at the Theoretical and "Empirical" Practice of the Public Choice Movement, 74 Va. L. Rev. 199 (1988).
61. See, for example, Peter Aronson, Calhoun's Constitutional Economics, 2 Constitutional Political Economy 31 (1991).
62. See Fischel, Regulatory Takings, pp. 104–107.
63. See Fischel, Regulatory Takings, pp. 104–109.
64. Federalist No. 10 (James Madison), in The Federalist Papers, ed. Clinton Rossiter (New York: Mentor Books, 1961), pp. 77, 79
65. Federalist No. 10 (James Madison), p. 80.
66. Federalist No. 51 (James Madison), in The Federalist Papers, pp. 320, 322.
67. See Laura S. Underkuffler, On Property: An Essay, 100 Yale L.J. 127 (1990).
68. On the similarities between Madison's views and public-choice theory, see Bernard Grofman and Donald Wittman (eds.), The Federalist Papers and the New Institutionalism (New York: Agathon Press, 1989).
69. But see Daryl J. Levinson, Making Government Pay: Markets, Politics and the Allocation of Constitutional Costs, 67 U. Chi. L. Rev. 345, 373–77 (2000).
70. Public-choice theory and its relationship to law is well-discussed in Daniel A. Farber and Philip P. Frickey, Law and Public Choice: A Critical Introduction (Chicago: University of Chicago Press, 1991).
71. Gary Becker, A Theory of Competition among Pressure Groups for Political Influence, 98 Quarterly Journal of Economics 371, 373–74 (1983).
72. For a good account of this argument, see James L. Kainen, The Historical Framework for Reviving Constitutional Protection for Property and Contract Rights, 79 Cornell L. Rev. 87 (1993).
73. William H. Riker and Barry R. Weingast, Constitutional Regulation of Legislative Choice: The Political Consequences of Judicial Deference to Legislatures, 74 Va. L. Rev. 373 (1988).

74. Riker and Weingast, Constitutional Regulation of Legislative Choice, p. 373; Richard A. Epstein, Takings: Private Property and the Power of Eminent Domain (Cambridge, MA: Harvard University Press, 1985).
75. See Jon R. Elster, Ulysses and the Sirens (Cambridge: Cambridge University Press, 1979).
76. On constitutions as precommitment devices, see Stephen Holmes, Precommitment and the Paradox of Democracy, in Constitutionalism and Democracy, ed. Jon Elster and Rune Slagstad (Cambridge: Cambridge University Press, 1988).
77. 483 U.S. 825 (1987).
78. *Nollan* at 837 (quoting J.E.D. Assocs. v. Atkinson, 432 A.2d 12, 14–15 (N.H. 1981)).
79. Fischel, Regulatory Takings, p. 1.
80. Fischel, Regulatory Takings, p. 5.
81. See James E. Krier, Takings from Freund to Fischel, 84 Geo. L.J. 1895, 1902 (1996).
82. Fischel, Regulatory Takings, p. 107.
83. Krier, Takings from Freund to Fischel, p. 1902 (footnote omitted).
84. William M. Treanor, The Original Understanding of the Takings Clause and the Political Process, 95 Colum. L. Rev. 782, 863–64 (1995); Daniel A. Farber, Economic Analysis and Just Compensation, 12 Int'l Rev. L. & Econ. 125, 130 (1992).
85. Treanor, The Original Understanding, pp. 868–69.
86. Krier, Takings from Freund to Fischel, p. 1910.
87. Richard A. Posner, The Constitution as an Economic Document, 56 Geo. Wash. L. Rev. 4, 23 (1987).
88. See, for example, Michael Les Benedict, Laissez-Faire and Liberty: A Reevaluation of the Meaning and Origins of Laissez-Faire Constitutionalism, 3 Law & Hist. Rev. 293 (1985); Alan Jones, Thomas Cooley and Laissez-Faire Constitutionalism: A Reconsideration, 53 J. Am. Hist. 751 (1967); Charles W. McCurdy, Justice Field and the Jurisprudence of Government-Business Relations: Some Parameters of Laissez-Faire Constitutionalism, 1863–1897, 61 J. Am. Hist. 970 (1975).
89. See William J. Novak, The People's Welfare: Law and Regulation in Nineteenth-Century America (Chapel Hill, NC: University of North Carolina Press, 1996).
90. Quebec's legal system, of course, is based on the civil law rather than the common law.
91. The possibility that courts will read such protection into the Charter cannot be ruled out. The likely locus for the change is the Charter's analogue to the American due process clause, section 7, which states, "Everyone has the right to life, liberty and security of person and the right not to be deprived thereof except in accordance with the principles of fundamental justice." Part 1 of Constitution Act, 1982, sec. 7. The two textual ambiguities of the clause where traction might be found for substantive protection of property are the references to "fundamental justice" and to "liberty." See Sujit Choudhry, The *Lochner* Era and Comparative Constitutionalism, 2 Int'l J. Const. L. 1, 27–42 (2004). The supreme court in fact adopted a substantive interpretation of "fundamental justice" in Re BC Motor Vehicle Act, [1985] 2 S.C.R. 486, but thus far the decision has not been used to extend substantive protection to economic interests. Indeed, in Attorney-General of Quebec v. Irwin Toy Ltd., [1989] 1 S.C.R. 927, the court held that section 7 does not protect property. Nevertheless, as Professor Choudhry points out, "Attempts to protect economic liberty by means of section 7 have continued." Choudry, Comparative Constitutionalism, p. 39. These attempts have primarily been through the "liberty" prong of section 7, and they have had limited success in the lower courts. One set of cases involved challenges to regulations of professions, such as geographic restrictions on physicians' right to prac-

tice under provincial health care plans. See, for example, Mia v. British Columbia (Medical Serv. Comm'n), [1985] 61 B.C.L.R. 273 (Sup. Ct.); and Wilson v. Medical Servs. Comm'n, [1985] 30 B.C.L.R.2d 1 (Ct. App.). The other set of cases involved challenges to suspensions of motor vehicle licenses on the grounds that driving privileges were necessary to earn a livelihood. See, for example, R. v. Robson, [1984] 56 B.C.L.R. 194 (Sup. Ct.), *appeal dismissed,* [1985] 28 B.C.L.R.2d 8 (Ct. App.); R. v. Sengara, [1988] 26 B.C.L.R.2d 71 (Sup. Ct.).

92. Whether the 1946 Japanese constitution protects private property is somewhat debatable. Several scholars have stated that it does not do so. See, for example, Mary Ann Glendon, Rights in Twentieth-Century Constitutions, 59 U. Chi. L. Rev. 519, 528, n. 34 (1992); Akira Osuka, Welfare Rights, 53 Law & Contemp. Probs. 13, 15–16 (1990). Glendon's and Osuka's statements, however, are probably based on the fact that although property is guaranteed in Article 29, it is absent from the due process clause of Article 31. Property was intentionally omitted from the due process clause because the American drafters of the Japanese constitution were well aware of the whole *Lochner* debacle, which they wished to avoid. Their intention was "to incorporate the fruits of the New Deal . . ." Osuka, Welfare Rights, p. 16. Professor Nakamura affirms that Article 29 of the Japanese constitution protects the right of property, specifically against uncompensated expropriations. See Mutsuo Nakamura, Freedom of Economic Activities and the Right to Property, 53 Law & Contemp. Probs. 1, 8–11 (1990). Professor van der Walt also treats Article 29 as a constitutional property clause, which, he points out, has a "unique structure and phraseology." van der Walt, Constitutional Property Clauses, p. 256. See also Nobushige Ukai and Nathaniel L. Nathanson, Protection of Property Rights and Due Process of Law in the Japanese Constitution, in The Constitution of Japan: Its First Twenty Years, 1947–67, ed. Dan Fenno Henderson (Seattle: University of Washington Press, 1968), p. 239.
93. See Sunstein, On Property and Constitutionalism.
94. For helpful discussions of Canada's experience with the constitutional status of property, see Alexander Alvaro, Why Property Rights Were Excluded from the Canadian Charter of Rights and Freedoms, 24 Can. J. Pol. Sci. 309 (1991); Richard W. Bauman, Property Rights in the Canadian Constitutional Context, 8 S. Afr. J. Hum. Rights 344 (1992); Joel Bakan, Against Constitutional Property Rights, in Constitutional Politics, ed. Duncan Cameron and Miriam Smith (Toronto: Lorimer, 1992).
95. Bruce Ziff, "Taking" Liberties: Protections for Private Property in Canada (2004) (unpublished manuscript) (on file with author), p. 1.
96. See Bauman, Property Rights in the Canadian Constitutional Context, p. 361.
97. See Munro v. National Capital Comm'n, [1966] S.C.R. 663.
98. It does so by virtue of the second part of section 1(a) of the Bill of Rights ("the right not to be deprived thereof except by virtue of due process of law"), which effectively functions as a regulation clause.
99. See Constitution Act of 1982, sec. 92(13).
100. See, Re Upper Churchill Water Rights, [1984] 1 S.C.R. 297. The Newfoundland statute in question expropriated all of the assets and water rights of a Newfoundland company generating hydroelectricity in Newfoundland and also Quebec. The supreme court struck down the statute on the ground that it was an invalid attempt to impair a civil right (a contract right) outside the enacting province. The court rejected an attack on the statute based on the ground that it effectively sterilized a federal

company. The statute, the court said, did not deny the company's status or its essential powers. See Peter W. Hogg, Constitutional Law of Canada, looseleaf ed. (Scarborough, Ont.: Carswell, 2004), sec. 28.5(d), p. 28–13.

101. See Bauman, Property Rights in the Canadian Constitutional Context, p. 351.
102. For example, Canada Expropriation Act, R.S.C., ch. E-21 (1985); Ontario Expropriation Act, R.S.O., ch. E-26 (1990); Alberta Expropriation Act, R.S.A., ch. E-13 (2000); Nova Scotia Expropriation Act, R.S.N.S., ch.156 (1989). For further examples, see the Web site of the Expropriation Law Centre: http://www.expropriationlaw.ca/expro005.asp.
103. See Ziff, "Taking" Liberties, p. 11. See generally Eric C. E. Todd, The Law of Expropriation and Compensation in Canada, 2d ed. (Toronto: Carswell, 1992).
104. See R. J. Bauman, Exotic Expropriations: Government Action and Compensation, 52 Advocate 561 (1994); Ziff, "Taking" Liberties, p. 12.
105. Mariner Real Estate Ltd. v. Nova Scotia (Attorney General), [1999] 68 L.C.R. 1 (N.S. Ct. App.) (rejecting the American takings doctrine of Lucas v. South Carolina Coastal Council, 505 U.S. 1003 (1992), that a total taking occurs when development restrictions have the effect of eliminating all economic value of the property).
106. For example, The Queen (B.C.) v. Tener, [1985] 1 S.C.R. 533; Casamiro Resource Corp. v. British Columbia, [1991] 80 D.L.R.4th 1 (B.C. Ct. App.).
107. The important decision on this issue is Manitoba Fisheries Ltd. v. The Queen, [1978] 88 D.L.R.3d 462 (Sup. Ct.).
108. In Attorney General v. De Keyser's Royal Hotel, Ltd., [1920] A.C. 508 (H.L.).
109. Attorney General v. De Keyser's Royal Hotel at 508.
110. See Thomas Allen, Commonwealth Constitutions and the Right Not to Be Deprived of Property, 42 Int'l & Comp. L.Q. 523, 524–25 (1993).
111. [1978] 88 D.L.R.3d 462 (Sup. Ct.)
112. See Hogg, Constitutional Law of Canada, sec. 32.1, p. 32-2.
113. See P. W. Hogg, Canadian Law in the South African Constitutional Court, 13 S. Afr. Pub. L. 1, 16 (1998); Bauman, Property Rights in the Canadian Constitutional Context, p. 351. A lower federal court has expressed the view that section 1(a) of the Bill of Rights provides only the conventional procedural forms of protection, such as a hearing, and no substantive protection. Archibald v. The Queen [1997] 146 D.L.R.4th 499, 531 (Fed. Ct. Trial Div.). Moreover, and more recently, the supreme court has indicated that the Bill of Rights does not provide substantive protection against confiscation. Authorson v. (Canada) Attorney General, [2003] 227 D.L.R.4th 385 (Sup. Ct.). Neither of these rulings, however, is definitive.
114. See Ziff, "Taking" Liberties, p. 9.
115. See F. L. Morton, Provincial Constitutions in Canada (2004) (unpublished paper) (on file with author), p. 1. See also Nelson Wiseman, Clarifying Provincial Constitutions, 6 Nat. J. Const. L. 269 (1996). In recent years Quebec and Alberta have shown interest in developing modern written constitutions. Morton, Provincial Constitutions in Canada, p. 2.
116. Bauman, Property Rights in the Canadian Constitutional Context, p. 351. Professor Bauman cites Alberta as an example. See R.S.A., ch. A-16, sec. 1(a) (1980).
117. Bauman, Property Rights in the Canadian Constitutional Context, p. 351.
118. See Alvaro, Exclusion of Property Rights from the Charter, pp. 319–21.
119. The debate over substantive constitutional protection of property continues in Canada. See Bauman, Property Rights in the Canadian Constitutional Context, pp. 344–

45. There have been no major initiatives to include a property clause in the Canadian Charter since 1992. See Choudhry, The *Lochner* Era and Comparative Constitutionalism, p. 25, n. 107.

120. See Hogg, Constitutional Law of Canada, sec. 28.5(a), n. 34. The federal government does have expropriation power, however, under a number of enumerated federal powers. For example, the federal power over navigation and shipping permits the federal government to expropriate property for the purpose of erecting works to facilitate navigation. Hogg, Constitutional Law of Canada, pp. 28-7 to 28-8. Moreover, provincial legislatures, unlike the federal parliament, do have a general expropriation power by virtue of their legislative power over "property and civil rights in the province." Constitutional Act of Canada, 1867, sec. 92(13). See Hogg, Constitutional Law of Canada, sec. 28.5(b).
121. Bauman, Property Rights in the Canadian Constitutional Context, p. 350.
122. For an interesting and revealing account, see Alvaro, Exclusion of Property Rights from the Charter.
123. Shaping Canada's Future Together: Proposals (Ottawa: Minister of Supply and Services 1991).
124. Pierre E. Trudeau, The Constitution and the People of Canada (Ottawa: The Queen's Printer, 1969), pp. 50, 52.
125. Trudeau, The Constitution and the People of Canada, p. 52. See Government of Canada, The Constitutional Amendment Bill: Text and Explanatory Notes (Bill C-60) (Ottawa, July 1978), p. 36; Mark MacGuigan, in Canada, House of Commons Debates, April 29, 1983, p. 25004; Pierre E. Trudeau, in Canada, House of Commons Debates, January 27, 1981, p. 6595.
126. See, for example, Joel Bakan, Against Constitutional Property Rights, in Constitutional Politics, pp. 117, 118; Michael Mandel, The Charter of Rights and the Legalization of Politics in Canada (Toronto: Thompson Educational Publishers, 1994), p. 308.
127. See Alvaro, Exclusion of Property Rights from the Charter, pp. 321–22.
128. Christina McCall and Stephen Clarkson, volume 2 of Trudeau and Our Times (Toronto: McClelland & Stewart, 1994), pp. 2, 11.
129. McCall and Clarkson, Trudeau and Our Times, vol. 2, p. 86; see also Kevin J. Christiano, Pierre Elliott Trudeau: Reason before Passion (Toronto: ECW Press, 1994), p. 81.
130. See Patrick Monahan, Politics and the Constitution (Toronto: Carswell, 1987), pp. 103–106; Alvaro, Exclusion of Property Rights from the Charter, p. 310.
131. See Alvaro, Exclusion of Property Rights from the Charter, pp. 322–23.
132. See Mandel, The Charter of Rights and the Legalization of Politics in Canada, p. 308
133. See Alvaro, Exclusion of Property Rights from the Charter, p. 322.
134. See Mandel, The Charter of Rights and the Legalization of Politics in Canada, p. 308; Alvaro, Exclusion of Property Rights from the Charter, pp. 319–21.
135. See Clarkson and McCall, vol. 1 of Trudeau and Our Times, p. 106.
136. See Alvaro, Exclusion of Property Rights from the Charter, p. 323.
137. Choudhry, The *Lochner* Era and Comparative Constitutionalism, p. 15. Professor Choudhry points out that within Canadian constitutional jurisprudence, *Lochner* has stood for three distinct lessons, laissez-faire constitutionalism being only one of them. The others are judicial activism and constitutional crisis. All three of *Lochner*'s lessons, Choudhry argues, have influenced Canadian constitutionalism. While all three concerns were evident in debates of protection of property under the Charter

of Rights, the one that was most conspicuous was the fear of laissez-faire constitutionalism. The *Lochner* Era and Comparative Constitutionalism, pp. 16–27.

138. See, for example, Hogg, Constitutional Law of Canada, sec. 44.7(b).
139. Bauman, Property Rights in the Canadian Constitutional Context, p. 355.
140. [1997] 146 D.L.R.4th 499 (Sup. Ct.).
141. [1997] 146 D.L.R.4th at 530.
142. Choudhry, The *Lochner* Era and Comparative Constitutionalism, pp. 15–42.
143. See Alvaro, Exclusion of Property Rights from the Charter, pp. 317, 321–22,
144. Alvaro, Exclusion of Property Rights from the Charter, 310.
145. Alvaro, Exclusion of Property Rights from the Charter, 310. This use of the term "proprietarian" is strikingly different and in basic respects incompatible with an older meaning of the term. It is this older tradition of proprietarian thinking that I have in mind when I used the term "propriety" in my book *Commodity & Propriety.* It is important that the two different usages of the term be kept in mind.
146. Alvaro, Exclusion of Property Rights from the Charter, p. 310.
147. Alvaro, Exclusion of Property Rights from the Charter, p. 317.
148. Alvaro, Exclusion of Property Rights from the Charter, p. 321.
149. Alvaro, Exclusion of Property Rights from the Charter, p. 318.
150. Alvaro, Exclusion of Property Rights from the Charter, p. 319.
151. Alvaro, Exclusion of Property Rights from the Charter, pp. 320–21.
152. Alvaro, Exclusion of Property Rights from the Charter, pp. 320–21.
153. Again, it is necessary to emphasize that this argument is not unique to the property right.
154. See Krystyna Daniel, Private Farm Ownership in a Changing Poland: Myth and Reality, in A Fourth Way: Privatization, Property, and the Emergence of New Market Economies, ed. Gregory S. Alexander and Grażyna Skąpska (New York: Routledge, 1994), pp. 138, 139–40.
155. See Hugh Spall, The Development of Private Property Rights in Communist Hungary and the Theory of Path Dependent Institutional Change, in Global Jurist Topics, http://www.bepress.com/gj, p. 7.
156. Bela C. Maday, The Changing Image of the Hungarian Agriculturalist, in New Hungarian Peasants: An East Central European Experience with Collectivization, ed. Marida Hollos and Bela C. Maday (New York: East European Monographs, 1983), p. 315.
157. See Misha Glenny, The Balkans: Nationalism, War and the Great Powers, 1804–1999 (New York: Viking, 1999), pp. 549–56.
158. P. Ishwara Bhat, Tracing Right to Property in the Bosom of Right to Life and Personal Liberty: Comparative Reflection on Recent Constitutional Developments in America, Canada and India, 38 Journal of the Indian Law Institute 13, 25–26 (1996).
159. The following sources are valuable guides to understanding the story of constitutional property in India: M. Hidayatullah, Right to Property and the Indian Constitution (New Delhi: Arnold-Heinemann Publishers, 1983); A. J. van der Walt, Constitutional Property Clauses (Cape Town: Juta, 1999), pp. 188–228 (1999); John Murphy, Insulating Land Reform from Constitutional Impugnment: An Indian Case Study, 8 S. Afr. J. Hum. Rights 362 (1992).
160. The Constitution of India (1950), provided, in relevant part, as follows:
Article 19(1):

> All citizens shall have the right—
> (f) To acquire, hold and dispose of property . . .

Article 31:

> (1) No person shall be deprived of his property save by authority of law.
> (2) No property, movable or immovable, including any interest in, or in any company owning, any commercial or industrial undertaking, shall be taken possession of or acquired for public purposes under any law authorising the taking of such possession or such acquisition, unless the law provides for compensation for the property taken possession of or acquired and either fixes the amount of compensation, or specifies the principles on which the compensation is to be determined and given.

A superb and brief account of the battle over property rights under Articles 19(1) and 31 of the 1950 Indian Constitution is provided in van der Walt, The Constitutional Property Clause, in McLean, pp. 117–23. See also Murphy, Insulating Land Reform from Constitutional Impugnment.

161. Golak Nath v. State of Punjab, A.I.R. 1967 S.C. 1643.
162. Vajravelu v. Special Deputy Collector, A.I.R. 1965 S.C. 1017.
163. R. C. Cooper v. Union of India (the "Bank Nationalization" Case), A.I.R. 1970 S.C. 564.
164. K. N. Goyal, Compensation: Down but Not Out, 38 J. Ind. L. Inst. 1, 2 (1996).
165. Constitution (Forty-Fourth Amendment) Act of 1978, removing Articles 19(1)(f) and 31 of the 1950 Constitution of India.
166. Subhash C. Jain, The Constitution of India (New Delhi, 2000), p. 229.
167. See van der Walt, The Constitutional Property Clause: Striking a Balance between Guarantee and Limitation, p. 123.
168. See John Murphy, Insulating Land Reform from Constitutional Impugnment, pp. 362, 382–83.
169. The success of these programs, however, is a very different question, one that is beyond the scope of this study.
170. van der Walt, The Constitutional Property Clause: Striking a Balance between Guarantee and Limitation, pp. 118–19.
171. See Dhavan, The Supreme Court of India (Bombay, 1977), p. 129.
172. Raghubir Singh v. Court of Wards Amjer, A.I.R. 1953 S.C. 373; State of Bihar v. Kameshwar Singh, A.I.R. 1952 S.C. 252.
173. The *zamindari* system is explained in H. C. L. Merillat, Land and the Constitution in India (New York, 1970), pp. 13–15.
174. Murphy, Insulating Land Reform from Constitutional Impugnment, p. 378.
175. Murphy, Insulating Land Reform from Constitutional Impugnment, p. 378.
176. Merillat, Land and the Constitution in India, p. 55.
177. See S. S. Sharma, Property in Indian Law, in van Maanen and van der Walt, Property Law on the Threshold of the 21st Century, pp. 345, 349.
178. Sharma, Property in Indian Law, 345, 349. In addition, compensation was paid in bonds, not cash, and was spread over a number of years. Sharma, Property in Indian Law, 345, 349.
179. Merillat, Land and the Constitution in India, p.55.
180. Dhavan, The Supreme Court of India and Parliamentary Sovereignty (New Delhi, 1976), p. 196–97; Granville Austin, The Indian Constitution: Cornerstone of a Nation (London, 1966), p. 88.
181. Merillat, Land and the Constitution in India, pp. 55–56.

182. See Tom Allen, The Right to Property in Commonwealth Constitutions (Cambridge: Cambridge University Press, 2000), pp. 48–50; Dhavan, The Supreme Court of India, pp. 146–49.
183. 1951 A.I.R. 91 (Patna) 38.
184. Murphy, Insulating Land Reform from Constitutional Impugnment, pp. 378–81.
185. Kameshwar Singh v. State of Bihar, A.I.R. 1952 S.C. 252. The colorable legislation doctrine is a matter of legislative competence. The constitution expressly specifies the scope of the federal and state legislature's power. Under the colorable legislation doctrine, the court reviews legislation to determine whether a legislative act, appearing to be competent in form, substantively exceeds the prescribed scope of the legislation's authority. The term "colorable legislation" applies to action that indirectly or covertly exceeds legislative competence. See Murphy, Insulating Land Reform from Constitutional Impugnment, p. 381, n. 68.
186. For a critical appraisal of the court's reliance on the colorable legislation doctrine, see Dhavan, The Supreme Court of India, p. 153–54.
187. van der Walt, Constitutional Property Clauses, pp. 195–96.
188. Murphy, Insulating Land Reform from Constitutional Impugnment, p. 381. Professor Rajeev Dhavan has also expressed a skeptical attitude about the degree to which the court's property decisions reflected political bias. See Dhavan, The Supreme Court of India, p. 129.
189. See Mohammad Ghouse, Nehru and Agrarian Reforms, in Nehru and the Constitution, ed. Rajeev Dhavan and Thomas Paul (New Delhi: N. M. Tripathi, 1992), pp. 77, 91.
190. See M. V. Pylee, India's Constitution (Bombay: Asia, 1979), p. 153.
191. See Paras Diwan and Peeyushi Diwan, Amending Powers and Constitutional Amendments, 2d ed. (New Delhi: Deep & Deep Publications, 1997), pp. 112–19.
192. For example, Kochuni v. States of Madras and Kerala, A.I.R. 1960 (47) S.C. 1080 (holding that the Fourth Amendment did not remove the court's power to review the reasonableness of "deprivations" of property under Article 19 of the constitution); Vajravelu v. The Special Deputy Collector, A.I.R. 1965 (52) S.C. 1017 (reclaiming jurisdiction to decide whether compensation was "reasonable," although not whether compensation was adequate).
193. A.I.R. 1967 (2) S.C. 1643.
194. A.I.R. 1970 (57) S.C. 564.
195. A.I.R. 1973 (60) S.C. 1461.
196. The court's turnabout seems to be most clearly attributable to the results of the 1971 election campaign, in which the Congress Party, which campaigned against the court and in support of land reform, won a sweeping victory in both houses of the parliament.
197. Murphy, Insulating Land Reform from Constitutional Impugnment, p. 385.
198. See Francine R. Frankel, India's Political Economy, 1947–1977: The Gradual Revolution (Princeton: Princeton University Press, 1978), pp. 156–200.
199. Murphy, Insulating Land Reform from Constitutional Impugnment, p. 387.
200. For an account, see D. R. Mankekar and Kamla Mankekar, Decline and Fall of Indira Gandhi (New Delhi: Vision Books, 1977).
201. Indira Nehru Gandhi v. Raj Narain, A.I.R. 1975 S.C. 2299.
202. See Upendra Baxi, The Indian Supreme Court and Politics (Lucknow: Eastern Book Co., 1980), p. 64.
203. Baxi, The Indian Supreme Court and Politics, p. 167.

204. Baxi, The Indian Supreme Court and Politics, p. 167.
205. Baxi, The Indian Supreme Court and Politics, p. 167.
206. van der Walt, Constitutional Property Clause, p. 128.
207. For a trenchant critique of the claim that constitutional property law can effectively serve a politically progressive agenda of distributive justice, see Hanoch Dagan, Takings and Distributive Justice, 85 Va. L. Rev. 741 (1999). See also Molly McUsic, The Ghost of *Lochner:* Modern Takings Doctrine and Its Impact on Economic Legislation, 76 B.U.L. Rev. 605, 665 (1996).
208. For a discussion of why the Progressive no-compensation approach harms the poor and other disadvantaged groups, see Dagan, Takings and Distributive Justice, pp. 761, 778.
209. See Epstein, Takings.
210. For an example of such a pluralist theory of constitutional property, see Stephen P. Munzer, A Theory of Property (Oxford: Oxford University Press, 1990), pp. 442–69.
211. See Thomas W. Merrill, The Landscape of Constitutional Property, 86 Va. L. Rev. 885 (2000).
212. The reference is, of course, to A. Douglas Melamed and Guido Calabresi, Property Rules, Liability Rules, and Inalienability: One View of the Cathedral, 85 Harv. L. Rev. 1089 (1972).
213. A. J. van der Walt, Dancing with Codes—Protecting, Developing and Deconstructing Property Rights in a Constitutional State, 118 S. Afr. L.J. 258, 297 (2001).
214. I discuss the German constitutional property clause in detail in chapter 3 and South Africa's constitutional property clause in chapter 4.
215. This was the animating concern for John Hart Ely's famous process theory of judicial review. See John Hart Ely, Democracy and Distrust: A Theory of Judicial Review (Cambridge, MA: Harvard University Press, 1980).

CHAPTER TWO

1. I will confine my attention to the Supreme Court's takings cases, although some very interesting and significant takings decisions have emerged from state courts and lower federal courts (particularly the United States Court of Appeals for the Federal Circuit).
2. Readers, both American and non-American, who are not thoroughly familiar with American takings law may wish to consult other sources to provide a more comprehensive study of the doctrinal landscape of takings law. An especially good place to start is David A. Dana and Thomas W. Merrill, *Property: Takings* (New York: Foundation Press, 2002).
3. The takings clause does not create the power of eminent domain; it only confirms it. It is, as the Supreme Court has said, "a tacit recognition of a preexisting power." United States v. Carmack, 329 U.S. 230, 241–42 (1946). From early times, American practice regarding eminent domain was heavily influenced by English law, including the practice of compensating for expropriation despite the fact that no nonstatutory basis for such an obligation existed. See William M. Treanor, The Original Understanding of the Takings Clause and the Political Process, 95 Colum. L. Rev. 782 (1995).
4. See Lawrence Berger, The Public Use Requirement in Eminent Domain, 57 Oregon L. Rev. 203, 205 (1978).
5. Thomas W. Merrill, The Economics of Public Use, 72 Cornell L. Rev. 61 (1986).
6. The Court's deferential approach has been the subject of considerable criticism, the most withering of which is Professor Epstein's. See Richard A. Epstein, Takings: Pri-

vate Property and the Power of Eminent Domain (Cambridge, MA: Harvard University Press, 1985), pp. 161–81.

7. 348 U.S. 26 (1954).
8. 348 U.S. at 32.
9. 467 U.S. 229 (1984).
10. Haw. Rev. Stat. secs. 516-22 to -23 (1976).
11. 467 U.S. at 242.
12. 467 U.S. at 241.
13. Merrill, The Economics of Public Use, p. 70.
14. No. 04-108, 545 U.S. — (2005) (5-4 vote).
15. No. 04-108, 545 U.S., slip op. at 13.
16. No. 04-108, 545 U.S., slip op. at 18.
17. No. 04-108, 545 U.S., slip op. at 12 (O'Connor, J., dissenting).
18. No. 04-108, 545 U.S., slip op. at 16 (Stevens, J.). The Court emphasized that its deferential approach to the public-use requirement applied only for purposes of the federal takings clause. Nothing prevents individual states from adopting more stringent approaches, reining in the exercise of eminent domain. Several states have done precisely that, either by way of eminent domain statutes that restrict economic development condemnation to blighted areas (for example, Cal. Health & Safety Code secs. 33030–33037 (West 1997)) or as a matter of state constitutional law. The most important recent state court decision to limit the exercise of eminent domain for economic development purposes is County of Wayne v. Hathcock, 684 N.W.2d 765 (Mich. 2004). That case reversed the widely criticized decision in Poletown Neighborhood Council v. City of Detroit, 304 N.W.2d 455 (Mich. 1981). In *Poletown,* the Michigan Supreme Court sustained as a permissible use of the eminent domain power the city of Detroit's condemnation of a residential neighborhood (not a slum or blighted area) for purposes to reconveying the land to General Motors, which wanted to build an assembly plant on that site. The Michigan court held that the public benefit of creating new jobs was sufficient to satisfy the public-use requirement. The *Hathcock* decision squarely reversed *Poletown* and severely limited the exercise of eminent domain for economic development purposes.
19. Merrill, The Economics of Public Use, p. 61.
20. For a particularly clear example of secondary rent seeking by a private firm, see Southwestern Ill. Dev. Auth. v. Nat'l City Envtl., LLC, 768 N.E.2d 1 (Ill. 2002).
21. For an analysis of the problems inherent in the fair market value standard, see Christopher Serkin, The Meaning of Value: Assessing Just Compensation for Regulatory Takings, 99 Nw. U.L. Rev. 677 (2005).
22. The Court's fair market value approach to defining "just compensation" was recently put in doubt by the Supreme Court's analysis of the issue in the *Brown* case. I discuss that development later in this chapter.
23. Coniston Corp. v. Village of Hoffman Estates, 844 F.2d 461, 464 (7th Cir. 1988).
24. See United States v. 564.54 Acres of Land, 441 U.S. 506, 511 (1979).
25. See, for example, Merrill, The Economics of Public Use, pp. 82–85, 90–92; Robert C. Ellickson, Alternatives to Zoning: Covenants, Nuisance Rules, and Fines as Land Use Controls, 40 U. Chi. L. Rev. 681, 736–37 (1973).
26. See James E. Krier and Christopher Serkin, Public Ruses, 4 Mich. St. L. Rev. 859 (2004).
27. See Michael A. Heller and James E. Krier, Deterrence and Distribution in the Law of Takings, 112 Harv. L. Rev. 997 (1999).
28. For example, United States v. Willow River Power Co., 324 U.S. 499, 511 (1945).

29. For example, United States v. Virginia Elec. & Power Co., 365 U.S. 624 (1961) (flowage easement); United States v. Gen. Motors Corp., 323 U.S. 373 (1945) (leasehold); Pennsylvania Coal Co. v. Mahon, 260 U.S. 393 (1922) (mining interest); United States v. Sec. Indus. Bank, 459 U.S. 70 (1982) (security interest).
30. Flemming v. Nestor, 363 U.S. 603 (1960) (future Social Security interests); *Willow River Power Co.*, 324 U.S. 499 (head of water in river).
31. Board of Regents v. Roth, 408 U.S. 564, 577 (1972). *Roth* was a procedural due process case, but the Court has approvingly cited it in takings cases as well. See, for example, Webb's Fabulous Pharmacies v. Beckwith, 449 U.S. 155, 161 (1980).
32. Dana and Merrill, Property: Takings, pp. 62–63.
33. Dana and Merrill refer to these approaches as the "pure positivism" and "patterning" approaches, respectively. Property: Takings, p. 63. They endorse the latter.
34. See Palazzolo v. Rhode Island, 533 U.S. 606 (2001) (holding that state law does not control whether the owner's bundle of rights is qualified by development restrictions); Keystone Bituminous Coal Ass'n v. DeBenedictis, 480 U.S. 470 (1987) (holding that the right of support is only an incident of property despite the fact that state law defined it as a separate estate in land). I discuss *Palazzolo* at greater length later in this chapter.
35. Dana and Merrill, Property: Takings, pp. 68–72.
36. See Bruce A. Ackerman, Private Property and the Constitution (New Haven, CT: Yale University Press, 1977).
37. See Penn Cent. Transp. Co. v. City of New York, 438 U.S. 104, 124 (1978); Dana and Merrill, Property: Takings, p. 69. Moreover, in Eastern Enters. v. Apfel, 524 U.S. 498 (1998) (challenge to a federal statute that retroactively increased coal mine operators' liability for health care benefits for retired employees), five members of the Court affirmed the view that property, for purposes of the takings clause, is limited to discrete assets. In their view, the takings clause did not apply to the statute, as it created only a general financial liability rather than affecting a discrete asset.
38. The Court has not confined its understanding of discrete assets to tangible "things." For example, it seems to be of the view that interest paid from a sum of money on deposit is a separate item of property for takings purposes. See Phillips v. Wash. Legal Found., 524 U.S. 156 (1998) (holding that interest earned on money held by attorneys for clients constitutes a separate item of property); *Webb's Fabulous Pharmacies*, 449 U.S. 155 (holding that interest earned from money deposited with a court as an interpleader fund is separate property). I discuss *Phillips* at greater length later in this chapter.
39. For example, Andrus v. Allard, 444 U.S. 51 (1979); Penn Cent. Transp. Co., 438 U.S. 104.
40. For example, College Sav. Bank v. Florida Prepaid Postsecondary Educ. Expense Bd., 527 U.S. 666, 673 (1999); Kaiser Aetna v. United States, 444 U.S. 164, 176, 179–80 (1979). On the centrality of the right to exclude to the concept of property in general, see Thomas W. Merrill, Property and the Right to Exclude, 77 Neb. L. Rev. 730 (1998).
41. Hodel v. Irving, 481 U.S. 704, 705 (1987) (holding that a federal statute that totally abrogated descent and devise of small fractional interests in tribal Indian land violated the takings clause). Importantly, however, the Court did not hold that these interests themselves constituted property for takings purposes.
42. *Andrus*, 444 U.S. at 51.
43. The term was first coined in Margaret Jane Radin, The Liberal Conception of Prop-

erty: Cross Currents in the Jurisprudence of Takings, 88 Colum. L. Rev. 1667, 1676 (1988).

44. 260 U.S. 393 (1922).
45. For a contrary view, see Robert Brauneis, The Foundation of Our "Regulatory Takings" Jurisprudence: The Myth and the Meaning of Justice Holmes's Opinion in *Pennsylvania Coal Co. v. Mahon,* 106 Yale L.J. 613 (1996).
46. *Mahon,* 260 U.S. at 415.
47. 438 U.S. 104 (1978).
48. See 438 U.S. at 124, 131.
49. Joseph William Singer, Property Law: Rules, Policies, and Practices (Boston: Aspen Law & Business, 1993), p. 1228. For a thorough analysis of the "character of the government action" factor, see Jeremy Paul, The Hidden Structure of Takings Law, 64 S. Cal. L. Rev. 1393, 1433–92 (1991).
50. See *Penn Cent. Transp. Co.,* 438 U.S. at 134.
51. See Michelman, Property, Utility, and Fairness, p. 1213.
52. See, for example, Connolly v. Pension Benefit Guar. Corp., 475 U.S. 211 (1986); Ruckelshaus v. Monsanto Co., 467 U.S. 986 (1984); *Kaiser Aetna,* 444 U.S. 164.
53. For a thorough discussion of these problems, see Carol M. Rose, *Mahon* Reconstructed, 561, 566–69.
54. Jesse Dukeminier and James E. Krier, *Property,* 3d ed. (Boston: Little, Brown, & Co., 1993), p. 1198, n. 29.
55. 447 U.S. 255 (1980).
56. 447 U.S. at 260.
57. As we will see, however, the Court has relied on this language in its exactions decisions, Nollan v. California Coastal Comm'n, 483 U.S. 825 (1987), and Dolan v. City of Tigard, 512 U.S. 374 (1994). In *Nollan,* the Court, citing *Agins,* stated, "We have required that the regulation substantially advance the legitimate state interest sought to be achieved . . . , not that the State could rationally have decided that the measure adopted might achieve the State's objective." 483 U.S. at 825, n. 3.
58. No. 04-163, 544 U.S. — (2005).
59. Chevron U.S.A. Inc. v. Cayetano, 198 F. Supp. 2d 1182 (D. Haw. 2002).
60. 363 F.3d 846 (9th Cir. 2004).
61. 544 U.S. at —, slip. op. at 10.
62. 544 U.S. at —, slip. op. at 10.
63. The Court also noted that although the "substantially advances" language was used in *Nollan* and *Dolan,* in neither of those cases did it actually apply the substantially advances test. In both cases, the Court said, the question was whether the exactions were so onerous as to amount to a taking. There was never any question that the exaction advanced some legitimate objective. 544 U.S. at —, slip. op. at 17.
64. See Marcia Coyle, Court's Takings Hat Trick, *National Law Journal,* June 27, 2005, pp. 1, 10 (quoting John Echeverria as saying, "The interesting constitutional [property-rights] challenges to come are going to focus on the equal protection and due process clauses.").

    The incentive to bring federal takings claims in federal court was reduced by a third decision of the U.S. Supreme Court in its 2005 term. In San Remo Hotel v. City and County of San Francisco, No. 04-340, 545 U.S. — (2005), the Court held that it would not create an exception to the full faith and credit statute, 28 U.S.C. sec. 1738, to open federal courts to takings claims where the federal constitutional issue had already been decided by a state court.

65. *Penn Cent. Transp. Co.*, 438 U.S. at 124.
66. Allison Dunham, *Griggs v. Allegheny County* in Perspective: Thirty Years of Supreme Court Expropriation Law, 1962 Sup. Ct. Rev. 63.
67. Joseph L. Sax, Takings and the Police Power, 74 Yale L.J. 36, 37 (1964).
68. Jeremy Paul, The Hidden Structure of Takings Law, p. 1524.
69. See, for example, Susan Rose-Ackerman, Against Ad Hocery: A Comment on Michelman, 88 Colum. L. Rev. 1697 (1988).
70. In a famous dissent, Justice Brandeis strongly challenged this analysis, saying that the relevant asset for diminution-in-value purposes is the whole land, not simply some segment of the property. From that perspective, the degree of diminution in value was likely not very great. The question of the relevant asset is sometimes referred to as the "denominator problem."
71. Brandeis challenged this point as well. He viewed the statute as aimed at abating a public nuisance.
72. 260 U.S. at 414.
73. 438 U.S. at 137. In dissent, Chief Justice Rehnquist vigorously challenged that assertion. In his view, TDRs have relevance only as compensation for a taking, and as compensation they were inadequate because they are not "'a full and perfect equivalent for the property taken.'" 438 U.S. at 150 (quoting Monogahela Navigation Co. v. United States, 148 U.S. 312, 326 (1893)). I discuss the possibility of viewing the TDRs as a tacit form of equalization benefits, analogous to those used in Germany, in chapter 5.
74. 458 U.S. 419 (1982).
75. 447 U.S. 74 (1980).
76. See, for example, Miller v. Schoene, 276 U.S. 272 (1928); Hadacheck v. Sebastian, 239 U.S. 394 (1915); Just v. Marinette County, 201 N.W.2d 761 (1972).
77. The classic discussion of this dilemma remains Michelman, Property, Utility, and Fairness, pp. 1196–97.
78. Michelman, Property, Utility, and Fairness, p. 1197.
79. Michelman, Property, Utility, and Fairness, p. 1197.
80. 480 U.S. 470 (1987).
81. 505 U.S. 1003 (1992).
82. 505 U.S. at 1023–24 (quoting *Nollan*, 483 U.S. at 834) (internal quotation omitted).
83. Underkuffler, The Idea of Property, p. 145.
84. See, for example, Singer, Entitlement, pp. 9–13; Craig Anthony (Tony) Arnold, The Reconstitution of Property: Property as a Web of Interests, 26 Harv. Envtl. L. Rev. 281, 284–316 (2002); J. E. Penner, The "Bundle of Rights" Picture of Property, 43 UCLA L. Rev. 711 (1996); Jeanne L. Schroeder, Chix Nix Bundle-o-Stix: A Feminist Critique of the Disaggregation of Property, 93 Mich. L. Rev. 239 (1994).
85. See, for example, *Keystone Bituminous Coal Ass'n*, 480 U.S. at 470; *Andrus*, 444 U.S. at 51.
86. Arnold, The Reconstitution of Property, p. 282.
87. See William Blackstone, vol. 2 of Commentaries on the Laws of England (Chicago: University of Chicago Press, 1979; originally published in London, 1765–1769), p. 2.
88. On the historical origins of the bundle-of-rights metaphor in American law, see Alexander, Commodity & Propriety, pp. 319–23.
89. See, for example, Tahoe-Sierra Preservation Council, Inc. v. Tahoe Regional Planning Agency, 535 U.S. 302 (2002).

90. Radin, The Liberal Conception of Property, p. 1676.
91. See Joan C. Williams, The Rhetoric of Property, 83 Iowa L. Rev. 277 (1998); Leif Wenar, The Concept of Property and the Takings Clause, 97 Colum. L. Rev. 1923 (1997).
92. See, for example, *Andrus*, 444 U.S. at 51; *Penn Cent. Transp. Co.*, 438 U.S. at 104.
93. See 480 U.S. at 470.
94. 480 U.S. at 497 (quoting *Andrus*, 444 U.S. at 65–66) (internal quotations omitted).
95. 481 U.S. 704 (1987).
96. The purpose of this statute was to facilitate prudent leasing and management of Indian land by reconsolidating multiple small fractionated interests. Without such reconsolidation, Congress felt, efficient management and use of the land would likely be frustrated by coordination problems.
97. 480 U.S. at 716 (quoting *Kaiser Aetna*, 444 U.S. at 176).
98. 482 U.S. 304 (1987).
99. See 482 U.S. at 318–19.
100. Frank Michelman, Takings, 1987, 88 Colum. L. Rev. 1600, 1617–18 (1988).
101. See 480 U.S. at 496–98.
102. Michelman, Takings, 1987, pp. 1619–21.
103. Michelman, Takings, 1987, 1619.
104. On exactions, both generally and in relation to the *Nollan-Dolan* doctrine, see Douglas T. Kendall and James E. Ryan, "Paying" for the Change: Using Eminent Domain to Secure Exactions and Sidestep *Nollan* and *Dolan*, 81 Va. L. Rev. 1801 (1995); Stewart E. Sterk, *Nollan*, Henry George, and Exactions, 88 Colum. L. Rev. 1731 (1988).
105. See 483 U.S. at 825.
106. See 512 U.S. at 374.
107. See Note, Municipal Development Exactions, the Rational Nexus Test, and the Federal Constitution, 102 Harv. L. Rev. 992, 992–93 (1989).
108. Michelman, Takings, 1987, p. 1608.
109. See Eric T. Freyfogle, The Owning and Taking of Sensitive Lands, 43 UCLA L. Rev. 77, 87, n. 41 (1995).
110. 503 U.S. 519 (1992).
111. 503 U.S. at 532.
112. 503 U.S. at 527 (quoting FCC v. Florida Power Corp., 480 U.S. 245, 252 (1987)).
113. See Hadacheck v. Sebastian, 239 U.S. 394 (1915) (regulation prohibiting operation of brickyard within city limits); Miller v. Schoene, 276 U.S. 272 (1928) (regulation requiring destruction of diseased cedar trees); Goldblatt v. Hempstead, 369 U.S. 590 (1962) (prohibition of quarry in residential area).
114. 505 U.S. at 1019.
115. 505 U.S. at 1027.
116. For trenchant criticisms of *Lucas*, see Freyfogle, The Owning and Taking of Sensitive Lands, pp. 118–27; William W. Fisher III, The Trouble with *Lucas*, 45 Stan. L. Rev. 1393 (1993); John A. Humbach, Evolving Thresholds of Nuisance and the Takings Clause, 18 Colum. J. Envtl. L. 1 (1993).
117. Rose-Ackerman, Against Ad Hocery, p. 1700.
118. Underkuffler, The Idea of Property, p. 154. See also Dana and Merrill, Property: Takings, p. 59.
119. See Thomas W. Merrill, The Economics of Public Use, pp. 95–96 (finding that ninety-nine percent of appellate takings cases involved land).

On the question whether land should be treated with more solicitude than personal property, see Eduardo M. Peñalver, Is Land Special?, 31 Ecology L.Q. 227 (2004).

120. See, for example, *College Savings Bank,* 527 U.S. at 672.
121. 524 U.S. 156 (1998).
122. 533 U.S. 606 (2001).
123. In addition to *Phillips* and *Palazzolo,* other recent Supreme Court decisions that bear on the problem of defining constitutional property include *Eastern Enterprises,* 524 U.S. 498, where the Court held unconstitutional a scheme under which coal operators had to make payments into a fund for health care benefits for retirees and which assigned retirees to companies for purposes of the obligation to make payments. A plurality of the Court based the decision on the takings clause and expressed the view that the takings clause applies only where identifiable assets, rather than a general financial liability, is at stake. Also included is *Webb's Fabulous Pharmacies,* 449 U.S. 155, in which the Court held that interest earned on an interpleader fund deposited with the court is property.
124. If the amount of the client's fund is sufficiently large that the client would earn net interest (that is, total interest minus the costs of keeping track of the interest and distributing it to the client), the lawyer must distribute the interest to the client or establish a separate term account rather than an IOLTA account.
125. 524 U.S. at 164, n. 4 (quoting petition for certiorari).
126. 538 U.S. 216 (2003).
127. 524 U.S. at 164 (quoting *Roth,* 408 U.S. at 577).
128. See the discussion in the section entitled "What Counts as Property?".
129. As Professor Merrill has pointed out, it is odd that the Court in *Phillips,* having decided that the source of constitutional property is to be found in nonconstitutional sources, looked only to the common law, ignoring the state's IOLTA rules. See Merrill, The Landscape of Constitutional Property, p. 897. See also Michael A. Heller and James E. Krier, Making Something out of Nothing: The Law of Takings and *Phillips v. Washington Legal Foundation,* 7 Sup. Ct. Econ. Rev. 285 (1999).
130. Valuable pre-*Palazzolo* discussions of the problems include Gregory M. Stein, Who Gets the Takings Claim? Changes in Land Use Law, Pre-Enactment Owners, and Post-Enactment Buyers, 61 Ohio St. L.J. 89 (2000); and Lynn E. Blais, Takings, Statutes, and the Common Law: Considering Inherent Limitations on Title, 70 S. Cal. L. Rev. 1 (1996).
131. 533 U.S. at 616.
132. 533 U.S. at 626.
133. 533 U.S. at 627.
134. 538 U.S. at 216.
135. 538 U.S. at 234.
136. 538 U.S. at 235.
137. The Court said that "the overall, dramatic success of [IOLTA programs] in serving the compelling interest in providing legal services to literally millions of needy Americans certainly qualifies the Foundation's distribution of these funds as a 'public use' within the meaning of the Fifth Amendment." 538 U.S. at 232.
138. 538 U.S. at 235.
139. *Phillips,* 524 U.S. at 170.
140. See, for example, United States v. 50 Acres of Land, 469 U.S. 24, 29 (1984); Kirby Forest Indus., Inc. v. United States, 467 U.S. 1, 10 (1984): United States v. Miller, 317 U.S. 369, 374 (1943); *Coniston Corp.,* 844 F.2d at 464. See generally Philip Nichols, vol. 4 of Nichols' The Law of Eminent Domain, 3d ed., ed. Julius L. Sackman (New York: Matthew Bender, 1964), vol. 4, sec. 12.02[1].

141. On this indemnification standard, see Dana and Merrill, Property: Takings, pp. 173–75.
142. Ronald D. Rotunda, Found Money: IOLTA, *Brown v. Legal Foundation of Washington,* and the Taking of Property without the Payment of Compensation, 2003 Cato Supreme Court Review 245, 258.
143. John D. Echeverria, Regulatory Takings after *Brown,* 33 Envtl. L. Rep. 10626, 10631 (2003).
144. 535 U.S. at 302.
145. The relevant time period was the subject of some debate. The Court based its view on the court of appeals' determination that the relevant time frame lasted only from August 1981 until April 1984, the period when the two moratoria were in effect. Chief Justice Rehnquist, in dissent, argued that the Court should also take into account the period through 1987, when the petitioners were still not permitted to develop their land as the result of regional development plans adopted in 1984 and 1987 by the TRPA. In his view, then, the relevant period is six years, the period during which the petitioners were actually unable to develop their land. The Court believed that the period of nonuse after April 1984 was not before the Court because the petitioners had not challenged the court of appeals' holding that the petitioners' post-1984 alleged injuries were caused by the district court's injunction against implementation of the 1984 plan, rather than the plan itself. (The effect of the injunction was to prohibit the petitioners from developing their land until a revised plan was adopted in 1987). Consequently, the Court said, the validity of the 1984 plan was not before the Court.
146. 535 U.S. at 321 n. 16.
147. The TRPA was created in 1968 by the joint actions of the California and Nevada legislatures through the Tahoe Regional Planning Compact, which Congress approved the same year. The compact established goals for the protection of Lake Tahoe and created the TRPA, which was charged with the task of "coordinat[ing] and regulat[ing] development in the [Lake Tahoe] Basin and . . . conserv[ing] its natural resources." 535 U.S. at 309 (quoting Lake Country Estates, Inc. v. Tahoe Regional Planning Agency, 440 U.S. 391, 394 (1979)).
148. Sean Whaley, Clinton Pledges Tahoe Aid, *Las Vegas Review Journal,* July 27, 1997, p. 1A.
149. Mark Twain, Roughing It, ed. Shelley Fisher Fishkin (New York Oxford University Press, 1996), p. 169.
150. Twain, Roughing It, pp. 174–75.
151. Tahoe-Sierra Preservation Council, Inc. v. Tahoe Regional Planning Agency, 34 F. Supp. 2d 1226, 1231 (D. Nev. 1999).
152. *Tahoe-Sierra* at 1226, 1231.
153. *Tahoe-Sierra* at 1226, 1231.
154. The district court found that it was "unsurprising" that the TRPA was unable to meet the deadline, given the complexity of the task of defining "environmental threshold carrying capacities." *Tahoe-Sierra* at 1235.
155. More specifically, Ordinance 81-5, the first of the two, prohibited construction of new residences on so-called Stream Environment Zone (SEZ) lands in either California or Nevada and on class 1, 2, or 3 lands in California. SEZ lands were lands near streams or wetlands, and class 1, 2, and 3 lands were lands classified as "high-hazard" lands based on the risk of runoff, due largely to steepness. Resolution 83-21, the second of the two challenged TRPA actions, imposed an eight-month morato-

rium on all construction on high-hazard lands in either state. A new regional plan was supposed to be adopted in 1984. Although the TRPA in fact adopted the 1984 plan, the state of California sued to enjoin its implementation on the ground that the plan was insufficiently stringent. The district court granted the injunction, which remained in effect until 1987, when a new plan was adopted.

156. *Tahoe-Sierra,* 535 U.S. at 313 (quoting appendix at 34).
157. *Tahoe-Sierra,* 34 F. Supp. 2d at 1245.
158. 535 U.S. at 328.
159. The Court divided 6-3. Justice Stevens wrote the majority opinion, supported by Justices Breyer, Ginsburg, Souter, O'Connor, and Kennedy, while Chief Justice Rehnquist dissented, along with Justices Scalia and Thomas.
160. 535 U.S. at 330 (quoting *Lucas,* 505 U.S. at 1019).
161. 535 U.S. at 330.
162. 535 U.S. at 331 (citation omitted). The phrase "the denominator question" refers back to the diminution-in-value factor, which was first mentioned by the court in *Penn Coal Co. v. Mahon.* To determine the diminution in value, one must compare the value of what has been lost as a result of the regulation (the numerator) with the value of what the owner had prior to the regulation (the denominator). The same problem arose in *Penn Central,* where the Court also rejected conceptual severance, but in that case the severance was of the physical variety rather than temporal, as in *Tahoe-Sierra.*
163. See United States v. Petty Motor Co., 327 U.S. 372 (1946); *General Motors Corp.,* 323 U.S. 373.
164. *Tahoe-Sierra,* 535 U.S. at 335.
165. *Tahoe-Sierra,* 535 U.S. at 338.
166. *Tahoe-Sierra,* 535 U.S. at 340.
167. *Tahoe-Sierra,* 535 U.S. at 340–41.
168. For a similar judgment, and an excellent analysis of the case, see Laura S. Underkuffler, *Tahoe*'s Requiem: The Death of the Scalian View of Property and Justice, 21 Const. Comment. (in press).
169. More recent signals from the Court have clouded somewhat the issue of the Court's preferred method of analysis. In Brown v. Legal Foundation of Washington, 538 U.S. 216 (2003), the Court appeared to apply a per se taking rule. However, the Court's opinion was narrowly written and appears to assume, without definitively deciding, that a per se approach applied. Moreover, the facts of that case are highly unusual and unlikely to be replicated.
170. For clarifying discussions of the various forms of conceptual severance, see Michael A. Heller, The Boundaries of Private Property, 108 Yale L.J. 1163, 1207–17 (1999); Henry A. Span, Public Choice Theory and the Political Utility of the Takings Clause, 40 Idaho L. Rev. 11 (2003).
171. Dana and Merrill, Property: Takings, pp. 105–106.
172. Dana and Merrill, Property: Takings, p. 106.
173. See Dana and Merrill, Property: Takings, p. 106. In *Palazzolo,* the Court provided only slightly more guidance as to what constitutes a total taking for *Lucas* purposes. It stated that "[a]ssuming a taking is otherwise established, a State may not evade the duty to compensate on the premise that the landowner is left with a token interest." 533 U.S. at 631. Such was not the case on the facts before the Court, however. The Court concluded that because the development regulation permitted the owner to construct a "substantial residence" on an eighteen-acre parcel, he was not forced

to leave his property "'economically idle'" within the meaning of *Lucas*. 533 U.S. at 631.

174. The example is drawn from the facts of *Andrus*, 444 U.S. 51. The Court in that case rejected the conceptual severance argument.
175. See Wenar, The Concept of Property and the Takings Clause, p. 1928.
176. See Span, Public Choice Theory and Political Utility of the Takings Clause, p. 87.
177. 444 U.S. at 65–66.
178. 481 U.S. at 704.
179. 481 U.S. at 716 (quoting *Kaiser Aetna*, 444 U.S. at 176).
180. See, for example, *Nollan*, 483 U.S. 825; *Loretto*, 458 U.S. 419.
181. Merrill, The Landscape of Constitutional Property, p. 900.
182. See, for example, Dana and Merrill, Property: Takings, p. 103.
183. Dana and Merrill, Property: Takings, p. 103.
184. 505 U.S. at 1007, 1009.
185. Dana and Merrill, Property: Takings, p. 104.
186. See, for example, Frank I. Michelman, A Skeptical View of "Property Rights" Legislation, 6 Fordham Envtl. L. Rev. 409 (1995).

CHAPTER THREE

1. Address by Bundespräsident Walter Scheel to U.S. Congress, quoted in Rudolf Dolzer, Property and Environment: The Social Obligation Inherent in Ownership (Morges, Switzerland: International Union for Conservation of Nature and Natural Resources, 1976), p. 59, n. 6.
2. The full text of Article 14, the property clause, reads as follows:

> Article 14 [Property, inheritance, expropriation]
>
> (1) Ownership and the right of inheritance shall be guaranteed. Their substance and limits shall be determined by law.
>
> (2) Ownership entails obligations. Its use should also serve the public interest.
>
> (3) Expropriation shall only be permissible in the public interest. It may only be ordered by or pursuant to a law that determines the nature and extent of compensation. Compensation shall reflect a fair balance between the public interest and the interests of those affected. In case of a dispute regarding the amount of compensation recourse may be had to the ordinary courts.

Basic Law for the Federal Republic of Germany (1995), p. 18. This is the official translation. The translation of *Eigentum* in section 2 as "ownership" is accurate as far as it goes, but it is potentially misleading. As we will see, the Federal Constitutional Court has extended it beyond ownership interests, strictly so-called. So a better term to express what Article 14 protects and what it is about might be "property."

Some other translations differ from the official translations. They too create problems. Both Currie and Finer, Bogdanor, and Rudden translate *Wohle der Allgemeinheit*, the term officially translated for purposes of Article 14(2) as "public interest," as " public weal." See David P. Currie, The Constitution of the Federal Republic of Germany (Chicago: University of Chicago Press, 1994), pp. 343, 349; S. E. Finer, Vernon Bogdanor, and Bernard Rudden, Comparing Constitutions (Oxford: Oxford University Press, 1995), pp. 127, 134. The term is used in two places in Article 14, in sections 2 and 3, and it has two quite different purposes in those provisions. As we shall see, in Article 14(2), the social-obligation provision, it is intended to protect the public interest by placing a limit on the individual right. In its second use, in Article 14(3), it is intended to protect the individual right by placing restrictions on the state's expropriation power. See A. J. van der Walt, Constitutional Property Clauses (Cape Town: Juta, 1999), p. 121, n. 1.

3. Other provisions in the *Grundgesetz* concerning property do not deal with the scope of individual ownership rights. Articles 134 and 135, for example, are transitional provisions affecting property other than that of individuals. Article 134 deals with the status of property under the Third Reich and provides that Reich property becomes federal property. Article 135 concerns the status of property owned by the several states, or *Länder.*
4. See generally Thomas W. Merrill, The Landscape of Constitutional Property, 86 Va. L. Rev. 885 (2000).
5. See Dolzer, Property and Environment, p. 59, n. 6.
6. Entscheidungen des Bundesverfassungsgerichts [BVerfGE] [Federal Constitutional Court] 1968, 24, 367 (389) (F.R.G.) (*Deichordnung* or *Hamburg Flood Control Case*).

   Unlike American practice, the official reports of the Federal Constitutional Court do not give official names to the cases. The names that I provide in parentheses are based either on common German references or on the names provided in the two leading English language books on German constitutional law, Donald P. Kommers, The Constitutional Jurisprudence of the Federal Republic of Germany, 2d ed. (Durham, N.C.: Duke University Press, 1997), and Currie, The Constitution of the Federal Republic of Germany.
7. Currie, The Constitution of the Federal Republic of Germany, p. 290 (footnote omitted). Some commentators have taken the view that the Supreme Court in fact has been quite protective of property interests, using the First Amendment and other provisions that protect ostensibly political rights rather than the takings or due process clauses. See John B. Attanasio, Personal Freedoms and Economic Liberties: American Judicial Policy, in Germany and Its Basic Law, ed. Paul Kirchhof and Donald P. Kommers (Baden-Baden: Nomos, 1993), p. 221.
8. BVerfGE 50, 290 (339) (*Mitbestimmung* or *Codetermination Case,* 1979).
9. 300 U.S. 379 (1937).
10. See James W. Ely, Jr., The Guardian of Every Other Right: A Constitutional History of Property Rights (New York: Oxford University Press, 1992), p. 127.
11. Accord Ronald J. Krotoszynski, Jr., Fundamental Property Rights, 85 Geo. L.J. 555, 560 (1997) ("[P]laintiffs who wish to assert that the deprivation of a particular property interest violates substantive due process have had difficulty getting the contemporary Supreme Court's attention.").
12. In the lower federal courts, a split has emerged over whether substantive due process protects property interests at all. Compare Sinaloa Lake Owners Ass'n v. City of Simi Valley, 882 F.2d 1398 (9th Cir. 1989) (holding that substantive due process protects all property rights, fundamental and nonfundamental alike), *cert. denied,* 494 U.S. 1016 (1990), *overruled by* Armendariz v. Penman, 75 F.3d 1311 (9th Cir. 1996) (en banc), and Moore v. Warwick Pub. School Dist. No. 29, 794 F.2d 322 (8th Cir. 1986) (same), with Local 342, Long Island Pub. Serv. Employees v. Town Bd., 31 F.3d 1191 (2d Cir. 1994) (holding substantive due process does not protect nonfundamental property interests), and Charles v. Baesler, 910 F.2d 1349 (6th Cir. 1990) (same).
13. Richard A. Epstein, Takings, p. 143.
14. Dolan v. City of Tigard, 512 U.S. 374, 392 (1994).

15. See William W. Fisher III, The Trouble with *Lucas*, 45 Stan. L. Rev. 1393, 1398 (1993).
16. Franz Wieacker, A History of Private Law in Europe, trans. Tony Weir (Oxford: Oxford University Press, 1995), p. 485.
17. On the fuller meaning of the *Rechtsstaat* principle, see the discussion later in this chapter.
18. H. W. Koch, A Constitutional History of Germany in the Nineteenth and Twentieth Centuries (London: Longman, 1984), p. 26.
19. Koch, A Constitutional History of Germany, p. 26.
20. Article 79(3) provides that "the principles laid down in Article . . . 20" are protected against constitutional amendment.
21. See Roman Herzog, Article 20, in Theodor Maunz, Günter Dürig, and Roman Herzog, Grundgesetz Kommentar, 28th ed., pt. 7, Randnummer 30–42 (Munich: C. H. Beck Verlag, 1990) (generally known as Maunz/Dürig) [hereinafter Maunz/Dürig].

    The Federal Constitutional Court once denied that Article 20 implicitly adopted the *Rechtsstaat* principle. See BVerfGE 30, 24–25 (1970). However, this view is not accepted today. See generally Philip Kunig, Das Rechtsstaatsprinzip: Überlegungen zu seiner Bedeutung für das Verfassungsrecht der Bundesrepublik Deutschland (Tübingen, Germany: Mohr Siebeck, 1986), pp. 49–110.
22. Art. 20(1) GG.
23. Art. 28(1) GG. During the first decade after the adoption of the Basic Law, there was some controversy regarding whether the *Sozialstaat* principle could aptly be classified as a constitutional value since it is not reflected in a single constitutional provision. See Philip Kunig, The Principle of Social Justice, in The Constitution of the Federal Republic of Germany–Essays on the Basic Rights and Principles of the Basic Law, ed. Ulrich Karpen (Baden-Baden: Nomos, 1988), pp. 188, 193. However, the Federal Constitutional Court has expressly recognized the existence of the principle. See, for example, BVerfGE 1, 97 (105) (1951); BVerfGE 3, 377 (381) (1954).
24. See, for example, Gottfried Dietze, Liberalism and the Rule of Law, 25 Jahrbuch des öffentlichen Rechts der Gegenwart (Neue Folge) 221, 237 (1976).
25. See Duard Kleyn, The Constitutional Protection of Property: A Comparison between the German and the South African Approach, 11 SA Publiekreg/SA Public Law 402, 406 (1996).
26. Kleyn, The Constitutional Protection of Property, pp. 402, 406.
27. Klaus Stern, vol. 1 of Das Staatsrecht der Bundesrepublik Deutschland (Munich: C. H. Beck Verlag, 1977), p. 602.
28. See Leonard Krieger, The German Idea of Freedom: History of a Political Tradition (Chicago: University of Chicago Press, 1957), pp. 252–61.
29. Theodor Maunz, Deutsches Staatsrecht, 20th ed. (Munich: C. H. Beck Verlag, 1975), pp. 72–74. See generally Loammi C. Blaau [sic], The Rechtsstaat Idea Compared with the Rule of Law as a Paradigm for Protecting Rights, 107 S. Afr. L.J. 76, 81 (1990).
30. See Krieger, The German Idea of Freedom, pp. 252–67; Kunig, Das Rechtsstaatsprinzip, passim.
31. Michael John, Politics and the Law in Late Nineteenth-Century Germany (Oxford: Oxford University Press, 1989), p. 89.
32. Hanri Mostert, The Constitutional Protection and Regulation of Property and Its Influence on the Reform of Private Law and Landownership in South Africa and Germany (Berlin: Springer, 2002), p. 139.
33. Mostert, The Constitutional Protection and Regulation of Property, p. 140.
34. See Finer, Bogdanor, and Rudden, Comparing Constitutions, p. 37

35. Wieacker, A History of Private Law in Europe, pp. 432–38. As Wieacker points out, the social state idea was especially prominent in the context of land law. He describes a "certain dualism" in land law: private law regulates the individual's ownership of her plot of land, while public law regulates land in general. A History of Private Law in Europe, p. 436.
36. See Kommers, The Constitutional Jurisprudence of the Federal Republic of Germany, p. 35.
37. On the Prussian Code, see Wieacker, A History of Private Law in Europe, pp. 260–66.
38. See Gerhard Casper, Changing Concepts of Constitutionalism: 18th to 20th Century, Sup. Ct. Rev. 311, 321 (1989).
39. See Ulrich Karpen, Soziale Marktwirtschaft and Grundgesetz. Eine Einführung in die rechtlichen Grundlagen der sozialen Marktwirtschaft (Baden-Baden: Nomos, 1990), p. 14.
40. Ulrich Karpen, The Constitution in the Face of Economic and Social Progress, in New Challenges to the German Basic Law, ed. Christian Starck (Baden-Baden: Nomos, 1991), pp. 87, 90 (footnote omitted).
41. See Kommers, The Constitutional Jurisprudence of the Federal Republic of Germany, pp. 35–36.
42. Compare, for example, Ernst Forsthoff, Begriff und Wesen sozialen Rechtsstaates, in Rechtsstaat im Wandel (Stuttgart: W. Kohlhammer, 1964), p. 27, with Ernst Benda, Werner Maihofer, and Han-Jochen Vogel, Handbuch des Verfassungsrechts der Bundesrepublik Deutschland, vol. 1 (Berlin: de Gruyter, 1984), pp. 509–12.
43. See Hans Huber, Rechtstheorie, Verfassungsrecht, Völkerrecht (Bern: Stämpfli, 1971), p. 36.
44. Ernst-Wolfgang Böckenförde, State, Society, and Liberty, trans. J. A. Underwood (New York: Berg, 1991), p. 67.
45. See Blauu [sic], The Rechtsstaat Idea Compared with the Rule of Law, pp. 76, 85.
46. David J. Gerber, Constitutionalizing the Economy: German Neo-Liberalism, Competition Law and the "New" Europe, 42 Am. J. Comp. L. 25, 31, n. 25 (1994).
47. See, for example, Jan Tumlir, Franz Böhm and the Development of Economic-Constitutional Analysis, in German Neo-Liberals and the Social Market Economy, ed. Alan Peacock and Hans Willgerodt (New York: Palgrave MacMillan, 1989), pp. 125, 135–40; Philip Alston, Resisting the Merger and Acquisition of Human Rights by Trade Law: A Reply to Professor Petersmann (NYU. School of L., Symposium: Trade and Human Rights, Jean Monnet Working Paper No. 12/02, 2002, p. 38, n. 116).
48. This distinction is explained in Norman P. Barry, Political and Economic Thought of German Neo-Liberals, in German Neo-Liberals and the Social Market Economy, pp. 105, 111–13.
49. Alan Peacock and Hans Willgerodt, Overall View of the German Liberal Movement, in German Neo-Liberals and the Social Market Economy, pp. 1, 3.
50. Gerber, Constitutionalizing the Economy, p. 36.
51. The term was apparently first coined by Armack-Müller. See Konrad Zweig, The Origins of the German Social Market Economy (Adam Smith Institute, unpublished manuscript, 1980), p. 18.
52. Gerber, Constitutionalizing the Economy, p. 32.
53. Zweig, The Origins of the German Social Market Economy, p. 5.
54. Quoted in Zweig, The Origins of the German Social Market Economy, p. 9.
55. See Heinz Rieter and Matthias Schmolz, The Ideas of German Ordoliberalism 1938–

45: Pointing the Way to a New Economic Order, 1 Eur. J. Hist. Econ. Thought 87, 104–105 (1993).

56. Walter Eucken, Grundsätze der Wirtschaftspolitik (Bern: A. Francke, 1952), p. 1. Eucken gave the term "social" a special meaning. "For Eucken, 'social' was the equivalent of 'independent,' that is, to live in a world without monopolies and without power." Schlecht, Macht und Ohnmacht der Ordnungspolitik—Eine Bilanz nach 40 Jahren Sozialer Marktwirtschaft, 40 ORDO 303, 309 (1989).
57. See Gerber, Constitutionalizing the Economy, p. 44.
58. See Sylvain Broyer, The Social Market Economy: Birth of an Economic Style (Wissenschaftszentrum Berlin, Discussion Paper FS I 96–318, 1996, p. 13).
59. Gerber, Constitutionalizing the Economy, pp. 36–37.
60. Gerber, Constitutionalizing the Economy, pp. 45–49.
61. Broyer, The Social Market Economy, p. 9.
62. Gerber, Constitutionalizing the Economy, p. 58.
63. Gerber, Constitutionalizing the Economy, p. 60.
64. See Broyer, The Social Market Economy, p. 14.
65. The literature on the German *Menschwürdigkeit* principle is vast. A good starting point is Christoph Enders, Die Menschenwürde in der Verfassungsordnung (Tübingen: Mohr, 1997).
66. Art. 1(1) GG.
67. See van der Walt, Constitutional Property Clause, p. 125.
68. Compare Walter Leisner, Eigentum, in Handbuch des Staatsrechts, ed. Josef Isensee and Paul Kirchhof (Heidelberg: C. F. Mueller, 1989), pp. 1025 [3], 1032 [18] et seq. (arguing that the Basic Law ranks fundamental rights hierarchically), with Klaus Stern, Das Staatsrecht des Bundesrepublik Deutschland (Munich: C. H. Beck, 1994), pp. 561, 614, 677, 827. (denying that the Basic Law creates a general hierarchy of rights). For a general discussion of this debate, see Loammi Blaauw-Wolf and Joachim Wolf, A Comparison between German and South African Limitation Provisions, 113 S. Afr. L.J. 267, 282–83 (1996).
69. See, for example, Stern, Das Staatsrecht der Bundesrepublik Deutschland.
70. Art. 79(3) GG: "Amendments of this Basic Law affecting the division of the Federation into *Länder,* the participation in principle of the *Länder* in legislation, or the basic principle laid down in Articles 1 and 20 shall be inadmissible."
71. See, for example, BVerfGE 6, 32 (36, 41) (1957); BVerfGE 27, 1 (6) (1969); BVerfGE 45, 187 (227) (*Mikrozeusus* case, 1977). Whether human dignity is also a subjective right is unsettled and hotly debated among German commentators. See Dierk Ullrich, Concurring Visions: Human Dignity in the Canadian Charter of Rights and Freedoms and the Basic Law of the Federal Republic of Germany, 3 Global Jurist Frontiers 1, 78 (2003).
72. Indeed, Article 79 of the Basic Law provides that these two provisions are immune from any constitutional amendment.
73. Kurt Sontheimer, Principles of Human Dignity in the Federal Republic, in Germany and Its Basic Law, p. 215.
74. BVerfGE 4, 7 (15–16) (*Investment Aid Case,* 1954).
75. The Federal Constitutional Court is divided into two eight-member panels, called senates. These have mutually exclusive jurisdiction and membership. In cases of jurisdictional conflict, the two senates meet together as a single plenum. Each senate is headed by the equivalent of a chief justice; traditionally, the president heads the First Senate, while the vice president heads the Second Senate. The two-senate structure

represents a compromise of an old debate over the character of the court as a legal or a political institution. See generally Kommers, The Constitutional Jurisprudence of the Federal Republic of Germany, pp. 16–18.

76. Ernst Benda, Werner Maihofer, and Hans-Jochen Vogel, Die Menschenwürdige, vol. 1 of Handbuch des Verfassungsrechts der Bundesrepublik Deutschland (Berlin: de Gruyter, 1984), pp. 110, 117.
77. For a rich discussion of the Kantian roots and communitarian character of the German constitutional "image of man," see George P. Fletcher, Human Dignity as a Constitutional Value, 22 U. W. Ont. L. Rev. 171, 178 (1984).
78. See Kommers, The Constitutional Jurisprudence of the Federal Republic of Germany, p. 241. Professor Winfried Brugger refers to the communitarian dimension of the Basic Law as "liberal communitarianism." Winfried Brugger, Communitarianism as the Social and Legal Theory behind the German Constitution, 2 Int'l J. Const. L. 431 (2004). The communitarian theories that seem most compatible with the Basic Law's "image of man" idea are those of Michael Sandel and Charles Taylor.

    There are also parallels between the German conception of the relationship between the self and property and the role of property in civic republican thought. Republican theory, like German constitutional theory, does not treat property as an end in itself. Property is an epiphenomenal right. It is valued insofar as it facilitates the development of the self as a responsible entity capable of contributing to the well-ordered society. See generally Gregory S. Alexander, Commodity & Propriety.
79. See Hans-Jürgen Papier in 2 Maunz/Dürig, Art. 14, para. 1–5; Otto Kimminich, Art. 14, in Bonner Kommentar zum Grundgesetz, 75th ed., ed. Rudolf Dolzer (Heidelberg: C. F. Mueller, 1995), para. 31.
80. BVerfGE 24, 367 (1968).
81. The standard datum cited to evidence the weakness of the public-use requirement under the Fifth Amendment's takings clause is Hawaii Hous. Auth. v. Midkiff, 467 U.S. 229 (1984).
82. BVerfGE 24 at 389 (emphasis added).
83. BVerfGE 24 at 389. In the immediate case, the court decided that the compensated expropriation of dikelands did not violate the owners' basic rights because it satisfied the requirement of Article 14(3)(i) that expropriations be made only for "the public weal" ("*Wohle der Allgemeinheit*"). More specifically, it was not a redistribution of land made for general reasons but an appropriate response to a particular problem of affecting the public good.
84. See C. Edwin Baker, Property and Its Relation to Constitutionally Protected Liberty, 134 U. Penn. L. Rev. 741, 746–47 (1986); Margaret Jane Radin, Property and Personhood, 34 Stan. L. Rev. 957 (1982).
85. Radin, Property and Personhood, p. 957.
86. See generally Alan Ryan, Property and Political Theory (Oxford: Basil Blackwell, 1984).
87. See Jean-Jacques Rousseau, The Social Contract, and Discourses (New York: Dutton, 1950) (the essay entitled "Discourses on the Origin of Inequality" is especially relevant in this connection).
88. See generally Isaiah Berlin, Two Concepts of Liberty (Oxford: Clarendon Press, 1958) passim.
89. Social security interests are protected in Germany today only if these accrue by virtue of employment. See Fritz Ossenbühl, Festschrift für Wolfgang Zeidler, Band 1 (Berlin: de Gruyter, 1987), p. 625.

90. See van der Walt, Constitutional Property Clauses, p. 124.
91. Art. 14(1)(i) GG.
92. See van der Walt, Constitutional Property Clauses, p. 124.
93. BVerfGE 50, 290 (*Mitbestimmung* case, 1979). See van der Walt, Constitutional Property Clauses, p. 127.
94. See Walter Leisner, Eigentum, in Handbuch des Staatsrecht, pp. 1023, 1026[26] (citing cases).
95. See Leisner, Eigentum, p. 1027[8].
96. See van der Walt, Constitutional Property Clauses, pp. 128–30.
97. BVerfGE 24, 367 (419) (*Deichordnung* case, 1968).
98. BVerfGE 24, at 420–22.
99. See Hans-Jürgen Papier, Art. 14, in 2 Maunz/Dürig, pt. 4, para. 642–43.
100. Art. 14(3) GG.
101. The term comes from the fact that the proceeding is the reverse of the usual expropriation proceeding. The claimant is the property owner, rather than the government, and the claimant seeks damages. See Dukeminier and Krier, Property, p. 1219.
102. First English Evangelical Lutheran Church v. County of Los Angeles, 482 U.S. 304 (1987). For a discussion of state court decisions, see Gene R. Rankin, The First Bite at the Apple: State Supreme Court Takings Jurisprudence Antedating First English, 22 Urb. Law. 417 (1990).
103. BVerfGE 58, 300 (322–24) (*Naßauskiesung* case, 1981). The Federal Constitutional Court recently affirmed its position in the *Monument Protection Case*, BVerfGE 100, 226 (*Denkmalschutz* case, 1999). I discuss this case infra.
104. Article 14(3) provides that "[i]n case of dispute regarding the amount of compensation, recourse may be had to the ordinary courts." The effect of this provision has been to grant jurisdiction to the civil courts to determine the amount of compensation and to order payment of compensation. These courts do not have jurisdiction to declare legislation invalid for constitutional reasons. Only the Federal Constitutional Court may do so. The highest civil ("ordinary") court is the Federal Court of Justice (*Bundesgerichtshof*, or BGH). The highest administrative court is the Federal Administrative Court (*Bundesverwaltungsgericht*, or BVerwG).
105. The civil (or "ordinary") courts have jurisdiction over compensation. The administrative courts have jurisdiction over the administrative aspects of expropriation.
106. See, for example, Entscheidungen des Bundesgerichtshofes in Zivilsachen [BGHZ] 83, 61 (1982); BGHZ 64, 220 (1975); BGHZ (Supreme Court en banc to resolve conflicts among the senate for civil cases) 83, 61 (1982).
107. Where the unusual sacrifice was the result of an excessive but otherwise valid (that is, properly authorized) regulation, that is, a regulatory taking, the action was known as "expropriatory infringement" (*enteignender Eingriff*). Where it was the result of an action that was not properly authorized (that is, no proper statutory basis), it was known as "expropriatory-like infringement" (*enteignungsgleicher Eingriff*). For a valuable discussion of this distinction, see Andreas von Arnauld, Enteignender und Enteignungsgleicher Eingriff Heute, 93 Verwaltungs-Archiv 394 (2002).
108. For example, BGHZ 91, 20 (1984); Entscheidungen des Bundesverwaltungsgerichts [BVerwGE] [Federal Administrative Court] 84, 361 (1990).
109. BGHZ 64, 220 (1975).
110. On the proportionality principle in German constitutional law, see the discussion later in this chapter.
111. The Federal Constitutional Court also uses the doctrine of unusual sacrifice in its

analysis of regulatory excess (*Übermaßverbot*), that is, to determine whether a regulation is unconstitutional (and therefore invalid) on the basis of disproportionality.

112. BVerfGE 58, 300 (*Naßauskiesung* case, 1981), discussed in detail infra.
113. For example, BGHZ 90, 17 (1984); BGHZ 91, 20 (1984). For a critical analysis of the post-*Naßauskiesung* developments in German constitutional property law, see Joachim Lege, Eigentumsdogmatik un Umweltrecht, 83 Jahrbuch des Umwelt- und Technikrechts 7 (2005).
114. Where the regulation was not lawfully authorized, it is invalid and no compensation is awarded by any court.
115. BVerfGE 100, 226 (*Denkmalschutz* case, 1999).
116. See BVerfGE 100, at 287.
117. See, for example, BVerfGE 104, 1 (*Baulandumlegung* case, 2001) (emphasizing difference between regulation and expropriation).
118. In this aspect of the case the Court's reasoning resembled that of the United States Supreme Court in *Lucas*. As we saw in chapter 2, under *Lucas*, where the effect of a land-use regulation is to deprive the owner of all economically viable use, there is per se a taking.
119. See Hanri Mostert, Recent Developments in the Jurisprudence of Art. 14 GG (unpublished manuscript 2004) (on file with author at Stellenbosch University, South Africa), p. 6.
120. The term is borrowed, of course, from Clifford Geertz. See Clifford Geertz, The Interpretation of Cultures: Selected Essays (New York: Basic Books, 1973), pp. 3–30.
121. See David M. Beatty, The Ultimate Rule of Law (Oxford: Oxford University Press, 2004).
122. See van der Walt, Constitutional Property Clauses, p. 26.
123. See Bruce A. Ackerman, Private Property and the Constitution (New Haven, CT: Yale University Press, 1977), pp. 100–103.
124. The distinction between the institutional and individual guarantees of property in Article 14 is relevant here. The *institutional* guarantee restricts the legislature's power to define the *content* (*Inhalt*) of property rights, while the *individual* guarantee restricts the legislative determination of the *limits* (*Schranken*) of property. With respect to definition of the contents, the institutional guarantee means that the legislature must preserve traditional property institutions and establish new property institutions as they become necessary. See, for example, BVerfGE 24, 367 (*Deichordnung* case, 1968). With respect to limitations on property, the individual guarantee means that the legislature must protect existing individual property rights, as distinguished from institutions. This guarantee, however, has to read in connection with the social-obligation clause of Article 14(2). Basically, this means that the Court must decide whether the legislature has maintained an equitable balance between the interests of the individual owner and those of society. A substantial part of the analytical work in making this determination is done by the proportionality principle, which I discuss subsequently. See generally van der Walt, Constitutional Property Clauses, pp. 132–34.
125. Art. 19(1) GG: "[A statute restricting a fundamental right] shall apply generally and not solely to an individual case. Furthermore, such statute shall name the fundamental right, indicating the Article concerned."]
126. Art. 19(2) GG.
127. Currie, The Constitution of the Federal Republic of Germany, pp. 306–307. Accord, Blaauw-Wolf and Wolf, A Comparison between German and South African Limita-

tion Provisions, 113 S. Afr. L.J. 275 (1996).

128. See the discussion of proportionality later in this chapter.
129. See van der Walt, Constitutional Property Clauses, p. 158.
130. See the discussion later in this chapter.
131. Art. 14(1)(ii) GG.
132. See the discussion later in this chapter.
133. See, for example, BVerfGE 58, 300 (*Naßauskiesung* case, 1981), discussed later in this chapter.
134. BVerfGE 24, 367 (*Deichordnung* case, 1968).
135. For a lucid and insightful discussion of the muddled state of American constitutional doctrine on this question, see Thomas W. Merrill, The Landscape of Constitutional Property, 86 Va. L. Rev. 885 (2000). The difference between the American and German experiences may be due in part to the fact that the German Basic Law has a single property clause and a single property-dependent doctrine, while the American Constitution has two property clauses (the Fifth and Fourteenth Amendments) and three property-dependent doctrines (the takings doctrine of the Fifth Amendment and the procedural due process and substantive due process doctrines of the Fourteenth Amendment). Of course, the mere existence of multiple references to property in the American Constitution does not necessitate multiplicity of meanings.
136. See the discussion earlier in this chapter.
137. Section 90 of the BGB provides that only corporeal interests can qualify as "things" (*Sachen*) for the purposes of section 903 BGB, the provision that specifies the rights of owners. Corporeal interests include movables as well as immovables.
138. See Leisner, Art. 14, p. 1025 [4].
139. BVerfGE 51, 193 (218) (*Warenzeichen* case, 1979).
140. van der Walt, Constitutional Property Clauses, p. 151.
141. BVerfGE 89, 1 (*Besitzrecht des Mieters* case, 1993). The name *Landlord-Tenant Case* comes from Kommers, The Constitutional Jurisprudence of the Federal Republic of Germany, p. 255.
142. See, for example, Otto Depenheuer, Entwicklungslinien des Verfassungsrechtlichen Eigentumsschutzes in Deutschland 1949–2001, in Bericht zur Lage des Eigentums, ed. Thomas von Danwitz, Otto Depenheuer, and Christoph Engel (Berlin: de Gruyter, 2002), pp. 109, 124–26, 129–30; Matthias Ruffert, Vorrang der Verfassung und Eigenständigkeit des Privatrechts (Tübingen: Mohr, 2001), pp. 366–92.
143. BGB section 903.
144. Civil law theory views ownership as unitary rather than as a bundle of rights, as American property theory does. See Reinhard Riegel, Das Eigentum im europäischen Recht (Berlin: de Gruyter, 1975), pp. 25–26.
145. BVerfGE 89 at 6.
146. A. J. van der Walt, Property Theory and the Transformation of Property Law, pt. 1, 2005 S. Afr. L. J. (forthcoming).
147. For a penetrating critique of the court's reasoning in the case, see A. J. van der Walt, Ownership and Eviction: Constitutional Rights in Private Law, 9 Edinburgh L. Rev. 32 (2004).
148. See BVerfGE 74, 129 (148) (1987); BVerfGE 24, 367 (400) (*Deichordnung* case, 1968); see generally Papier, Art. 14, in 2 Maunz/Dürig, para. 8 et seq., 150 et seq.; Otto Kimminich, Art. 14, para. 50 et seq.
149. Article 153 of the 1919 Weimar Constitution was the basis for some aspects of Article 14 of the post–World War II Basic Law. A number of important differences ex-

isted, however, between the treatment of property under the two constitutions, including the fact that, by not allowing compensated expropriations to be judicially challenged, the Weimar Constitution did not protect the institution of property as such. Compensation was always an adequate substitute for the thing itself. See Papier, Art. 14, in 2 Maunz/Dürig, para. 18–23.

On the weakness of basic rights under the Weimar Constitution generally, see Volkmar Götz, Legislative and Executive Power under the Constitutional Requirements Entailed in the Principle of the Rule of Law, in New Challenges to the German Basic Law, pp. 141, 150–52.

Analyzing the ostensible weakness of the Weimar Constitution, Michael Stolleis has expressed a view that is quite consistent with the basic premise of this book, namely, the importance of background traditions and culture. Stolleis argues that the weakness of the Weimar Constitution was not inherent in the text but lay elsewhere. He writes, "What [the Weimar Constitution] lacked was not better constitutional mechanics, but a web of unwritten rules by which a political class, split by concrete issues yet self-confident and sustained by a basic consensus, could have bridged possible weaknesses in the structure of the constitution." Michael Stolleis, A History of Public Law in Germany, 1914–1945, trans. Thomas Dunlap (Oxford: Oxford University Press, 2004), p. 60.

150. BVerfGE 24 at 389 (emphasis added).
151. 198 U.S. 45 (1905).
152. Art. 14(3)(i) GG.
153. The same is true for the U.S. Constitution under the takings clause's public-use requirement.
154. Charles A. Reich, The New Property, 73 Yale L.J. 733 (1964).
155. BVerfGE 53, 257 (1980).
156. BVerfGE 69, 272 (*Eigenleistung* case, 1985), discussed infra.
157. BVerfGE 72, 9 (1986).
158. See, for example, Walter Leisner, Eigentum, in Handbuch des Staatsrechts, pp. 1023, 1069; Helmut Rittstieg, Art. 14 (Eigentum, Erbrecht und Enteignung), in Kommentar zum Grundgesetz für die Bundesrepublik Deutschland, Luchterhand Band I (Neuwied: Luchterhand, 1989), p. 1098; Badura, Eigentum, p. 349.
159. BVerfGE 42, 263 (*Contergan* case, 1976). See Rudolf Wendt, Art. 14 [Eigentum, Erbrecht und Enteignung], in Grundgesetz Kommentar, ed. Michael Sachs (Munich: C. H. Beck, 1996), pp. 482, 491.
160. BVerfGE 69 at 302.
161. BVerfGE 69 at 302.
162. See BVerfGE 78, 232 (1988).
163. See BVerfGE 39, 169 (1975).
164. BVerfGE 69, 272 (*Eigenleistung* case, 1985).
165. BVerfGE 69, 272.
166. BVerfGE 69 at 304 (citations omitted).
167. BVerfGE 69 at 302.
168. Charles A. Reich, The New Property, 73 Yale L.J. 733 (1964).
169. It is important to bear in mind, however, that the mere fact that an interest counts as "property" under Article 14 does not necessarily mean that it is not subject to regulations that are constitutionally justifiable. The *Eigenleistung* case illustrates the fact that a substantively protectable interest is nevertheless subject to reasonable regulation.

170. Hanoch Dagan, Takings and Distributive Justice, 85 Va. L. Rev. 741, 772 (1999).
171. Currie, The Constitution of the Federal Republic of Germany, p. 295.
172. Currie, The Constitution of the Federal Republic of Germany, p. 295 (citing cases).
173. BVerfGE 89, 1 (5) (*Besitzrecht des Mieters* case, 1993). See the discussion of this case in A. J. van der Walt, Ownership and Eviction: Constitutional Rights in Private Law, 9 Edinburgh L. Rev — (2005).
174. According to the protective duties (*Schutzpflichten*) theory, however, fundamental rights, including property, contain both negative defensive rights and positive values that form the basis of positive rights of protection against the legislature. The theory of protective duties holds that the constitution imposes obligations (as opposed to only allowing obligations) upon the legislature to impose negative restrictions on owners. See BVerfGE 7, 198 (*Lüth* case, 1958).
175. The *Sozialstaatsprinzip* (principle of social justice) of Articles 20 and 28 does not create subjective rights, but instead establishes a goal for the state to pursue through the legislature. See BVerfGE 1, 91 (105) (1951); BVerfGE 27, 253 (283) (1969); BVerfGE 40, 121 (133) (1975).
176. See van der Walt, Constitutional Property Clauses, p. 139.
177. This is referred to as the *Sozialbindung* or *Sozialverpflichtung*. See Rudolf Dolzer ed., Bonner Kommentar zum Grundgesetz, para. 153.
178. Quoted in Dolzer, Property and Environment, p. 17.
179. Article 153(1) of the Weimar Constitution read, "Ownership entails a social obligation. Its use shall also be a service to the public good." See Dolzer, Property and Environment. See generally Peter Badura, Eigentum, in Handbuch des Verfassungsrechts des Bundesrepublik Deutschland (1994), para. 608.
180. See Currie, The Constitution of the Federal Republic of Germany, p. 294, n. 143.
181. Currie, The Constitution of the Federal Republic of Germany, p. 21. See generally Hans F. Zacher, Das soziale Staatsziel, in vol. 1 of Handbuch des Staatsrecht, p. 1045.
182. Ernst Benda, The Constitutional and Legal Situation of German Industrial Society and the Historical Development of Social Change, in German and American Constitutional Thought: Context, Interactions, and Historical Realities, ed. Hermann Wellenreuther (New York: Berg Publishers, 1990), pp. 477, 483.
183. See Kommers, The Constitutional Jurisprudence of the Federal Republic of Germany, p. 242.
184. In the context of determining the limits of the individual's property right, this principle is referred to as the prohibition against regulatory excess (*Übermaßverbot*).
185. van der Walt, Constitutional Property Clauses, p. 135.
186. One prominent commentator, Günter Dürig, attributed the modern origin of the proportionality principle to Article 19.2, which states, "In no case may the essence of a fundamental right be encroached upon." See Günter Dürig, Art. 2(1) GG, in 1 Maunz/Dürig, Randnummer 31–32, 62–63. That view was not widely accepted, and today nearly all agree that the principle derives from Article 20's *Rechtsstaat* concept. See Loammi Blauuw-Wolf, The "Balancing of Interests" with Reference to the Principle of Proportionality and the Doctrine of *Güterabwägung*—A Comparative Analysis, 14 SA Publiekreg/SA Public Law 178, 193 (1999).
187. See Currie, The Constitution of the Federal Republic of Germany, p. 309. As Currie notes, the earliest cases in which the Federal Constitutional Court relied on the proportionality principle made no attempt to explain the source of the principle within the Basic Law. See, for example, BVerfGE 2, 266 (280–81) (1953); BVerfGE 3, 383 (399) (1954); BVerfGE 7, 377 (407) (1958).

188. For a good summary of its origins and role, see Currie, The Constitution of the Federal Republic of Germany, 307–310.
189. Versions of the proportionality principle are used in many other countries, especially in Europe, but also in all such Commonwealth countries as Canada and Australia. They differ in some details from the German version, but the fundamentals are the same. See generally Nicholas Emiliou, The Principle of Proportionality in European Law: A Comparative Study (London: Springer, 1996); Vicki C. Jackson, Ambivalent Resistance and Comparative Constitutionalism: Opening Up the Conversation on "Proportionality," Rights and Federalism, 1 U. Pa. J. Const. L. 583 (1999). I discuss the proportionality principle further in chapter 5.
190. This is basically the same three-part approach used by the Canadian courts. See R. v. Oakes, [1986] S.C.R. 103.
191. See, for example, BVerfGE 78, 232 (245–47) (1988).
192. For example, BVerfGE 78 at 245.
193. For example, BVerfGE 7, 377 (1958).
194. See Blaauw-Wolf, The Balancing of Interests, Proportionality and *Güterabwägung*, p. 194. The difference between proportionality in the broader sense—*Verhältnismäßigkeit*—and the narrow sense—*Angemessenhei*—is subtle but important. The broader sense of the term is a matter of adjusting the general relation between the affected private party(ies) on the one hand and the public on the other hand. In the narrow sense, the term refers to the relation between the specific restriction and the immediate purpose.
195. In fact, there is some disagreement among commentator about the number of factors involved in proportionality review. Bernard Schlink, for example, argues that there really are only two factors, suitability and necessity, with the latter factor encompassing the Federal Constitutional Court's second two factors. See Bernard Schlink, Freiheit durch Eingriffsabwehr—Rekonstruktion der klassischen Grundrechtsfunktion, 11 Europäische Grundrechte Zeitschrift 457, 460, 462 (1984).
196. See the discussion earlier in this chapter.
197. See van der Walt, Constitutional Property Clauses, p. 162; Blaauw-Wolf, The Balancing of Interests, Proportionality and *Güterabwägung*, pp. 197–99.
198. van der Walt, Constitutional Property Clauses, p. 162.
199. See, for example, T. Alexander Aleinikoff, Constitutional Law in the Age of Balancing, 96 Yale L.J. 943 (1987); Paul W. Kahn, The Court, the Community and the Judicial Balance: The Jurisprudence of Justice Powell, 97 Yale L.J. 1 (1987).
200. See Mostert, The Constitutional Protection and Regulation of Property, p. 296.
201. Van der Walt, Constitutional Property Clauses, p. 135 (citing sources). See generally Martin Thormann, Abstufung in der Sozialbindung des Eigentums (Stuttgart: Boorberg, 1996), pp. 211–25.
202. Konrad Hesse, Grundzüge des Verfassungsrechts der Bundesrepublik Deutschland, 20th ed. (Heidelberg, 1995), p. 192.
203. BVerfGE 52, 1 (1979).
204. BVerfGE 50, 290 (*Mitbestimmung* case, 1979).
205. James M. Buchanan and Gordon Tullock, The Calculus of Consent (Ann Arbor, MI, 1965).
206. Vol. 2 of European Commercial Cases, p. 366.
207. Other grounds for the challenge included interference with the rights of occupation (Article 12) and association (Article 9). There is a substantial degree of interrela-

tionship between Articles 12 and 14. For a lucid discussion, see Fritz Ossenbühl, Economic and Occupational Rights, in Germany and Its Basic Law, p. 251.

208. Vol. 2 of European Commercial Cases, p. 361.
209. Vol. 2 of European Commercial Cases, 359.
210. See generally Badura, Eigentum, in Handbuch des Verfassungsrechts, p. 653.
211. Vol. 2 of European Commercial Cases, p. 360.
212. Vol. 2 of European Commercial Cases, pp. 364–65.
213. See, for example, BVerfGE 58, 300 (*Naßauskiesung* case, 1981); BVerfGE 21, 73 (*Grundstückverkehrsgesetz* case, 1967); BVerfGE 37, 132 (*Wohnraumkündigungsschutzgesetz* case, 1985).
214. BVerfGE 58, 300 (1981). Kommers refers to the case as the *Groundwater Case*. See Kommers, The Constitutional Jurisprudence of the Federal Republic of Germany, pp. 257–61.
215. For a sampling of views about the case, see Joachim Lege, Der Rechtsweg bei Entschädigung für "enteignende Eingriff" Wirkungen, 42 Neue Juristische Wochenschrift 2745 (1995); Ingo Kraft, System der Klassifizierung eigentumsrelevanter Regelungen, Bayerische Verwaltungsblätter, February 15, 1994, p. 97; Martin Burgi, Die Enteignung durch "teilweisen" Rechtsentzug als Prüfstein für die Eigentumsdogmatik, Neue Verwaltunge Zeitschrift, p. 527 (1994).
216. The case was actually a series of cases that were litigated through various courts, including the Federal Court of Justice (*Bundesgerichtshof*) as well as the Federal Constitutional Court.
217. Schriftlicher Bericht des 2. Sonderausschusses—Wasserhaushaltsgesetz—BtDrs. II/3536 (1953) [Record of the Parliamentary Debates of the Federal Water Resources Law].
218. Neue Juristische Wochenschrift (1978), p. 2290.
219. BGB section 905: "The right of the owner to a piece of land extends to the space above the surface and to the terrestrial body under the surface . . ." This doctrine, which derives from Roman law, is the same as the common law's *ad coelum* doctrine: *Cujus est solum, ejus est usque ad coelum et ad infernos* (to whomsoever the soil belongs, he owns also to the sky and to the depths).
220. BVerfGE 58, 300 (1981).
221. BVerfGE 58 at 345.
222. BVerfGE 58 at 339.
223. BVerfGE 58, at 339.
224. This statement requires an important caveat: as we have already discussed, under Article 14(2), the legislature and only the legislature has competence to define the "contents and limits" (*Inhalt und Schranken*) of ownership, but Article 19(2) requires that the Federal Constitutional Court define the essence of the constitutionally protected property right.
225. BVerfGE 58 at 340.
226. On the modern regulation of water in German and Austrian law, see Franz Merli, Öffentliche Nutzungsrechte und Gemeingebrauch, pp. 140–75 (Vienna: Springer, 1995).

For a recent discussion of the dominant role that materialist rhetoric has played in American discussions about natural resources, see Holly Doremus, The Rhetoric and Reality of Nature Protection: Toward a New Discourse, 57 Wash. & Lee L. Rev. 11, 19–23 (2000).

227. Merli, Öffentliche Nutzungsrechte und Gemeingebrauch, p. 341, citing BVerfGE 10, 113.
228. See the excellent discussion in Barton H. Thompson, Tragically Difficult: Overcoming Obstacles to Governing the Commons, 30 Envtl. L. 241, 249–53 (2000). See generally National Research Council, Water Transfers in the West: Efficiency, Equity, and the Environment (Washington, D.C.: National Academy Press, 1992).
229. Eric T. Freyfogle, Water Rights and the Common Wealth, 26 Envtl. L. 27, 31 (1996).
230. Freyfogle, Water Rights and the Common Wealth, p. 32.
231. On the topic of ecological interdependence and its implication for property law, see Lynda L. Butler, The Pathology of Property Norms: Living within Nature's Boundaries, 73 S. Cal. L. Rev. 927 (2000).
232. BVerfGE 58 at 345.
233. BVerfGE 58 at 345. ("*Aus der verfassungsrechtlichen Garantie des Grundeigentums läßt sich nicht ein Anspruch auf Einräumung gerade der jenigen Nutzungsmöglichkeit herleiten, die dem Eigentümer den größmöglichen wirtschaftlichen Vorteil verspricht.*")
234. On the topic of the relationship between legal transitions and takings, see Holly Doremus, Takings and Transitions, 19 J. Land Use & Envtl. L. 1 (2003).
235. BVerfGE 58 at 350–51.
236. BVerfGE 58.
237. See, for example, Keystone Bituminous Coal Ass'n v. DeBenedictis, 480 U.S. 470 (1987); Penn Cent. Transp. Co. v. City of New York, 438 U.S. 104 (1978).
238. See Margaret Jane Radin, The Liberal Conception of Property: Cross Currents in the Jurisprudence of Takings, 88 Colum. L. Rev. 1667 (1988).
239. See chapter 2.
240. This includes the *Landlord-Tenant* (*Besitz des Mieters*) *Case,* which I do not read as adopting the Anglo-American bundles-of-rights conception of ownership.
241. Carol Rose, The Comedy of the Commons: Custom, Commerce, and Inherently Public Property, 53 U. Chi. L. Rev. 711 (1986).
242. See Barton H. Thompson, Water Law as a Pragmatic Exercise, 25 Ecology L.Q. 363 (1998); Carol M. Rose, Property as the Keystone Right? 71 Notre Dame L. Rev. 329, 351 (1996).
243. See generally Butler, The Pathology of Property Norms.
244. For a rich discussion of the legal status of water rights from a similar perspective, see Joseph L. Sax, The Constitution, Property Rights and the Future of Water Law, 61 U. Colo. L. Rev. 257 (1990); Joseph L. Sax, The Limits of Private Rights in Public Waters, 19 Envtl. L. 473 (1989).
245. BGH. DVBl. 1984, 391, reported in Neue Juristische Wochenschrift (1984), p. 1169.
246. What was really going on here was a tug-of-war game between the Federal Constitutional Court and the Federal Court of Justice, with the latter taking a more expansive view of the state's obligation to compensate private owners for governmental encroachment of their property interests. In American terms, the conflict is somewhat analogous to the difference between the views of Justice Brennan and Chief Justice Rehnquist in the *Penn Central* case.

    Professor Ossenbühl has expressed the interesting idea that the alternative, nonconstitutional basis for compensation in cases of regulatory takings should be customary law. That is, the concept of *enteigungsgleicher Eingriff* should be separated from Article 14 of the Basic Law and treated as a matter of customary law. See Ossenbühl, *Staatshaftungsrecht,* pp. 185–87.
247. Hanoch Dagan, Takings and Distributive Justice, 85 Va. L. Rev. 741, 772, 744 (1999).

CHAPTER FOUR

1. The property clause of the 1996 South African Constitution is section 25. It provides as follows:

(1) No one may be deprived of property except in terms of law of general application, and no law may permit arbitrary deprivation of property.

(2) Property may be expropriated only in terms of law of general application—

a. for a public purpose or in the public interest; and

b. subject to compensation, the amount of which and the time and manner of payment of which have either been agreed to by those affected or decided or approved by a court.

(3) The amount of the compensation and the time and manner of payment must be just and equitable, reflecting an equitable balance between the public interest and the interests of those affected, having regard to all relevant circumstances, including—

a. the current use of the property;

b. the history of the acquisition and use of the property;

c. the market value of the property;

d. the extent of direct state investment and subsidy of the acquisition and beneficial capital improvement of the property; and

e. the purpose of the expropriation.

(4) For purposes of this section—

a. the public interest includes the nation's commitment to land reform, and to reforms to bring about equitable access to all South Africa's natural resources; and

b. property is not limited to land.

(5) The state must take reasonable legislative and other measures, within its available resources, to foster conditions which enable citizens to gain access to land on an equitable basis.

(6) A person or community whose tenure of land is legally insecure as a result of past racially discriminatory laws or practices is entitled, to the extent provided by an Act of Parliament, either to tenure which is legally secure or to comparable redress.

(7) A person or community dispossessed of property after 19 June 1913 as a result of past racially discriminatory laws or practices is entitled, to the extent provided by an Act of Parliament, either to restitution of that property or to equitable redress.

(8) No provision of this section may impede the state from taking legislative and other measures to achieve land, water and related reform, in order to redress the results of past racial discrimination, provided that any departure from provisions of this section is in accordance with the provisions of section 36(1).

(9) Parliament must enact the legislation referred to in subsection (6).

2. Several provisions of the 1996 constitution create socioeconomic rights. Among the most important of these are the following:

Section 26. Housing

(1) Everyone has the right to have access to adequate housing.

(2) The state must take reasonable legislative and other measures, within its available resources, to achieve the progressive realization of this right.

(3) No one may be evicted from their home, or have their home demolished, without an order of court made after considering all the relevant circumstances. No legislation may permit arbitrary evictions.

Section 27. Health Care, Food, Water, and Social Security

(1) Everyone has the right to have access to

a. health care services, including reproductive health care;

b. sufficient food and water; and

c. social security, including, if they are unable to support themselves and their dependants, appropriate social assistance.

(2) The state must take reasonable legislative and other measures, within its available resources, to achieve the progressive realization of each of these rights

(3) No one may be refused emergency medical treatment.

Section 28. Children

(1) Every child has the right . . .

c. to basic nutrition, shelter, basic health care services and social services;

d. to be protected from maltreatment, neglect, abuse or degradation;

e. to be protected from exploitative labour practices . . .

(3) In this section "child" means a person under the age of 18 years.

Section 29. Education

(1) Everyone has the right

a. to a basic education, including adult basic education; and

b. to a further education, which the state, through reasonable measures, must make progressively available and accessible.

3. Cass R. Sunstein, Designing Democracy: What Constitutions Do (New York: Oxford University Press, 2001), p. 261.
4. For a valuable historical discussion of the preapartheid-era practices that paved the way for legal apartheid, see Leonard Thompson, A History of South Africa (New Haven, CT: Yale University Press, 2000), pp. 154–87.
5. S. Afr. Const. ch. 2, sec. 36(1).
6. "Homelessness" is an amorphous and unhelpful concept in any society, but especially so in South Africa. There, hundreds of thousands of people live in informal (and illegal) squatter settlements. See Michael Aliber, Overview of the Incidence of Poverty in South Africa for the 10-Year Review (paper prepared for the Human Sciences Research Council, November 2002), p. 12. These people do live in homes in a sense, but the homes are grossly inadequate. Some are former farmworkers who migrated to urban areas. Some are urban wage earners who cannot afford decent housing. Most are unemployed.

   Land redistribution in South Africa has occurred at a frustratingly slow pace. The maldistribution of landownership continues to follow racial lines. When apartheid ended, the new, democratically elected government promised that it would transfer thirty percent of white-owned farmland to nonwhites in five years. Ten years later, only two percent had been transferred. More than ninety percent of all of South Africa's commercial farmland remains in the hands of just 50,000 white farmers. Land invasions by squatters are still a common occurrence today. See Sharon LaFraniere and Michael Wines, Africa Puzzle: Landless Blacks and White Farms, *New York Times*, January 6, 2004, p. A1.

7. Much of the current insecurity of land tenure was the direct result of lingering effects of the past, including not only apartheid but also conquest. See Geoff Budlender, The Constitutional Protection of Property Rights, in Juta's New Land Law, ed. Geoff Budlender, Johan Latsky, and Theunis Roux (Cape Town: Juta, 1998), pp. 1–70. For an excellent overview of the historical practices that have made black land tenure commonly insecure, see Charles van Onselen, The Seed Is Mine: The Life of Kas Maine, A South African Sharecropper 1894–1985 (New York: Hill and Wang, 1996), pp. 3–11.
8. Port Elizabeth Municipality v. Various Occupiers, 2005 (1) SA 217 (CC); Mkontwana v. Nelson Mandela Metropolitan Municipality and Others, 2005 (1) SA 530 (CC); Jaftha v. Schoeman, 2005 (2) SA 140 (CC); In re Certification of the Constitution of the Republic of South Africa, 1996 (4) SA 744 (CC); First National Bank SA Ltd t/a Wesbank v. Commissioner, 2002 (4) SA 768 (CC) (*FNB Case*); Phoebus Apollo Aviation CC v. Minister of Safety and Sec., 2003 (2) SA 34 (CC); President of the Repubic of South Africa v. Modderklip Boerdery (Pty) Ltd., CCT 20/04 (CC) (2005); DuToit v. Minister of Transport, CCT 22/04 (CC) (2005). Of these, the *FNB Case* is the most doctrinally significant. It and several other of the most recent cases will be discussed later in this chapter.
9. See Lebowa Mineral Trust Beneficiaries Forum v. President of the Republic of South Africa, 2002 (1) BCLR 23 (T); Nhlabathi v. Fick, 2003(2) All SA 323 (LCC); Geyser v. Msunduzi Municipality, 2003 (5) SA 18 (N).
10. Harksen v. Lane NO, 1998 (1) SA 300 (CC). Section 28 of the interim constitution continues be very relevant even after the final constitution's adoption. It determines the validity of all laws in force prior to adoption of the final constitution (February 4, 1997). See Ferreira v. Levin NO, 1996 (1) SA 984 (CC). In the interest of keeping this chapter as brief as possible, I will limit my discussion to the property clause of the final constitution.
11. In the context of South Africa, the term "common law" has a special meaning, unfamiliar to most Anglo-American lawyers. The term refers to the largely uncodified system of rules received from Roman-Dutch civil law as well as case law that interprets and analyzes those rules. Some aspects of the English common law were transplanted to South Africa, however, and the result is a mixed legal system that is distinguished from both English common law and from European civil law. For an introduction to South African common law and references to further literature, see Reinhard Zimmermann and Daniel P. Visser, Introduction: South Africa as a Mixed Legal System, in Southern Cross: Civil Law and Common Law in South Africa, ed. Reinhard Zimmermann and Daniel P. Visser (Oxford: Oxford University Press, 1996), p. 1.
12. For a similar view, see Dennis Davis, Democracy and Deliberation: Transformation and the South African Legal Order (Cape Town: Juta, 1999), pp. 99–101.
13. S. Afr. Const. 1996.
14. Karl Klare, Legal Culture and Transformative Constitutionalism, 14 S. Afr. J. Hum. Rights: 146, 152 (1998).

15. 1995 (3) SA 391 (CC).
16. 1995 (3) SA 391 (CC), at 262.
17. See the discussion of the theory of a "protective duty" and the *Modderklip* case later in this chapter.
18. See The Social and Economic Rights Action Centre and the Centre for Economic and Social Rights v. Nigeria, Comm. 155/96 (October 2001), African Commission on Human and People's Rights at para. 46.
19. For a fuller discussion of the content of the "duty to fulfill," see UN Committee on Economic, Social and Cultural Rights (UNCESCR) General Comment (GC) 12 (19th session, 1998), UN doc.E/1999/22, para. 15; GC 14, para. 37; GC 15, para. 25.
20. S. Afr. Const. 1996, ch. 2, secs. 26(2), 27(2).
21. See the discussion of horzontality later in this chapter.
22. Government of the Republic of South Africa v. Grootboom, 2001 (1) SA 46 (CC), discussed later in this chapter.
23. Ex parte Chairperson of the Constitutional Assembly: In re Certification of the Constitution of the Republic of South Africa, 1996 (4) SA 744 (CC).
24. 1996 (4) SA 744 (CC) at para. 76.
25. 1996 (4) SA 744 (CC) at para. 76.
26. See Sandra Liebenberg, The Interpretation of Socio-Economic Rights, in Constitutional Law of South Africa, 2d ed., ed. Stuart Woolman et al. (Cape Town: Juta, 2004), pp. 33-i, 33-5.
27. S. Afr. Const. ch. 2, sec. 39(1)(c).
28. Section 173 complements this provision by giving all high courts, including the Constitutional Court, "the inherent power . . . to develop the common law, taking into account the interests of justice."
29. The well-known case on this topic is Carmichele v. Minister of Safety and Sec., 2001 (4) SA 938 (CC). I discuss this case later in this chapter.
30. S. Afr. Const. ch. 2, sec. 167(3). The Constitutional Court consists of a president, a deputy president, and nine other judges. S. Afr. Const. ch. 2, sec. 167(1). Members of the court are appointed by the president of the republic in consultation with a judicial service commission and leaders of the political parties represented in the National Assembly. S. Afr. Const. ch. 2, sec. 174. Members of the court are appointed for a nonrenewable term of 12 years. There is a mandatory retirement age of 70. S. Afr. Const. ch. 2, sec. 176.
31. S. Afr. Const. ch. 2, sec. 167(3)(b).
32. S. Afr. Const. ch. 2, sec. 168(3).
33. S. Afr. Const. ch. 2, sec. 169. There are certain constitutional matters that the constitution assigns exclusively to the Constitutional Court, such as disputes between national or provincial organs of state regarding their constitutional powers or functions. See S. Afr. Const. ch. 2, sec. 167(4).
34. S. Afr. Const. ch. 2, secs. 166, 170.
35. See Budlender, The Constitutional Protection of Property Rights, pp. 1–3 ("The question of property rights was one of the most controversial issues in the constitutional negotiations over the bill of rights.").
36. For a brief but helpful account of how apartheid law contributed to the gross inequality of distribution of land in South Africa, see Heinz Klug, Constituting Democracy: Law, Globalism and South Africa's Political Reconstruction (Cambridge: Cambridge University Press, 2000), pp. 41–44.
37. See Hund, A Bill of Rights for South Africa, 34 Am. J. Juris. 23, 31 (1989); Albie

Sachs, Toward a Bill of Rights in a Democratic South Africa, 6 S. Afr. J. Hum. Rights 1, 4, 6–8 (1990); John Dugard, A Bill of Rights for South Africa?, Cornell Int'l L.J. 459–60 (1990).

38. See Andre van der Walt, Property Rights, Land Rights, and Environmental Rights, in Rights and Constitutionalism: The New South African Legal Order, ed. in Dawid van Wyk, John Dugard, Bertus de Villiers, and Dennis Davis (Cape Town: Juta, 1994), pp. 455, 479.
39. To be sure, voices were raised in opposition to any property clause in the new Constitution. See, for example, A. J. van der Walt, Toward the Development of Post-Apartheid Land Law: An Exploratory Survey, De Jure 1, 43 (1990). Professor van der Walt states that he subsequently changed his mind when he realized "that it was possible actually to use the constitutional property clause to *promote* land reform and the redistribution process." A. J. van der Walt, The Constitutional Property Clause (Cape Town: Juta, 1997), p. 2, n. 5.
40. See, for example, Hugh Corder et al., A Charter for Social Justice: A Contribution to the South African Bill of Rights Debate (Cape Town: Juta, 1992), pp. 60–65.
41. Corder et al., A Charter for Social Justice, pp. 60–61.
42. Corder et al., A Charter for Social Justice, pp. 63–64.
43. John Dugard, A Bill of Rights for South Africa?, 29 Cornell Int'l L.J. 460 (1990).
44. Matthew Chaskalson, Stumbling towards Section 28: Negotiations over the Protection of Property Rights in the Interim Constitution, 11 S. Afr. J. Hum. Rights 222, 224 (1995).
45. Clause 18, Government's Proposals on a Charter of Fundamental Rights of February 3, 1993, reproduced in 19 Recht en kritiek 339 (1993).
46. Under apartheid, eighty percent of the South African population was prohibited from owning or leasing land in over eighty percent of the country, which was held by the government for its white citizens. Michael de Klerk, ed., A Harvest of Discontent: The Land Question in South Africa (Cape Town: Juta, 1991); Annika Claassens; Ownership and Tenure, Institute for a Democratic Alternative for South Africa (Cape Town: Juta, 1991), p. 23. Only thirteen percent of the country's land area was certified for black occupation. Annika Claassens, For Whites Only—Land Ownership in South Africa, Institute for a Democratic Alternative for South Africa (Cape Town: Juta, 1991), p. 43.
47. Chaskalson, Stumbling towards Section 28, p. 224.
48. See Article 13(1), ANC Draft Bill of Rights, 19 Recht en kritiek 328–30 (1993).
49. See Article 12(2), ANC Draft Bill of Rights, 19 Recht en kritiek 328–30 (1993).
50. Chaskalson, Stumbling towards Section 28, p. 226.
51. See Doreen Atkinson, Insuring the Future? The Bill of Rights, in vol. 7 of South African Review, ed. Steven Friedman and Doreen Atkinson (1994); The Small Miracle: South Africa's Negotiated Settlement (Johannesburg: Ravan Press, 1994), p. 136.
52. See Clause 18, Government's Proposals on a Charter of Fundamental Rights of February 3, 1993.
53. Atkinson, Insuring the Future, p. 129.
54. See A. J. van der Walt, The Constitutional Property Clause, in Property and the Constitution, ed. Janet MacLean (Oxford: Hart Publishing, 1999), p. 112.
55. Chaskalson, Stumbling towards Section 28, p. 231.
56. Chaskalson, Stumbling towards Section 28, p. 231.
57. Chaskalson, Stumbling towards Section 28, p. 231.
58. Interim Constitution secs. 121, 122, 123.

59. Chaskalson, Stumbling towards Section 28, p. 232.
60. Doreen Atkinson, Insuring the Future?, p. 135.
61. Chaskalson, Stumbling towards Section 28, pp. 14–15.
62. Chaskalson, Stumbling towards Section 28, 232.
63. Chaskalson, Stumbling towards Section 28, 233.
64. Chaskalson, Stumbling towards Section 28, 233, 234.
65. Interim Constitution sec. 28(3).
66. See Chaskalson, Stumbling towards Section 28, pp. 234–35.
67. Budlender, The Constitutional Protection of Property rights, pp. 1-5–1-6.
68. See Dene Smuts, Etienne Mureinik's Contribution to Property Rights, 14 S. Afr. J. Hum. Rights 197 (1998).
69. See Smuts, Etienne Mureinik's Contribution to Property Rights; Cyril Ramaphosa, Negotiating a New Nation: Reflections on the Development of South Africa's Constitution, in Post-Apartheid Constitutions: Perspectives on South Africa's Basic Law, ed. Penelope Andrews and Stephen Ellman (Johannesburg: Witwatersrand University Press, 2001), pp. 71, 83.
70. See Budlender, The Constitutional Protection of Property Rights.
71. Smuts, Etienne Murenik's Contribution to Property Rights, p. 199.
72. First National Bank of SA Ltd. t/a Wesbank v. Commissioner, 2002 (4) SA 768 (CC).
73. Theunis Roux, The Arbitrariness Vortex: Constitutional Property Law after *FNB* (presentation, Conference on Property Law, University of Reading, Reading, UK, March 26, 2004). Roux points out that in this respect, the court's section 25 mode of analysis is similar to the analysis it has used in its socioeconomic rights jurisprudence. Theunis Roux, The Constitutional Protection of Property Rights, in Constitutional Law of South Africa, pp. 46-1, 46-3.

    Some indication that lower courts have interpreted *FNB* in just this way, directly concentrating on the arbitrariness inquiry, is provided in two cases: Nhlabathi v. Fick, 2003 (2) All SA 323 (LCC), paras. 30–31 (S. Afr.); Geyser v. Msunduzi Municipality, 2003 (5) SA 18 (N) at 36J-39A(S. Afr.).
74. The significance of an institutional guarantee is that it prevents the legislature from abolishing or undermining the institution of private ownership of property by, for example, removing certain categories of property, like subsurface water or minerals, from the realm of private ownership unless there is a substantial state interest in doing so. See van der Walt, Constitutional Property Clauses, p. 326.
75. See chapter 3 supra.
76. See van der Walt, Constitutional Property Clauses, pp. 325–27. Professor van der Walt points out that although the land-reform parts of section 25 are positively stated, they do not establish a limited institutional guarantee but rather are akin to positive claim rights.
77. Section 25(4). This has already been done with respect to water under the National Water Act 36 of 1998 and with respect to minerals under the Mineral and Petroleum Resources Development Act 28 of 2002.
78. These three "pillars" of land reform are identified as such in the Reconstruction and Development Programme. For a general overview of the Programme, see Andre van der Walt, Land Reform in South Africa since 1990—An Overview, 10 S. Afr. Pub. L 1 (1995).
79. See A. J. van der Walt, Striving for the Better Interpretation—A Critical Reflection on the Constitutional Court's *Harksen* and *FNB* Decisions on the Property Clause (2003), 121 S. Afr. L.J. 854 (2004).

80. 2002 (4) SA 768 at paras. 38–39.
81. The court's six-stage method of analysis has been termed a "true algorithm." Johan de Waal, Iain Currie and Gerhard Erasmus, The Bill of Rights Handbook, 5th ed. (Cape Town: Juta, 2004). As Roux points out, however, it is not a true algorithm because in one situation a court can skip one stage. If the answer to question c is "yes," then the court should skip question d and proceed directly to e. Roux, The Constitutional Protection of Property Rights, p. 46-4. Roux helpfully depicts the court's mode of analysis as a decision tree. Roux, The Constitutional Protection of Property Rights, p. 46-5.
82. 2002 (4) SA 768 at para. 46.
83. 2002 (4) SA 768 at para. 51.
84. 1996 (10) BCLR at 1288G-1289B [75], 1288F [74] (S. Afr.). Strangely, a lower court subsequently interpreted the court's statement as indicating that mineral rights are *not* constitutional property. See Lebowa Mineral Trusts Beneficiaries Forum v. President of the Republic of South Africa, 2002 (1) BCLR 23 (T) at 28E-G (S. Afr.). This conclusion is surely wrong. See Roux, Property, at 46-13, n.1. van der Walt suggests that this holding was "possibly inspired by old-fashioned privatist orthodoxy about the restricted scope of property in Roman-Dutch law." van der Walt, Overview, p. 8. He further points out that what makes the decision even more puzzling is the fact that mineral rights are considered property in modern South African private law. I discuss the question of the influence of the traditional South African private law *mentalitè* on its constitutional jurisprudence later in this chapter.
85. 2002 (4) SA 768 at para. 52 (quoting van der Walt, The Constitutional Property Clause, p. 11).
86. Roux, Property, p. 46-16.
87. See the discussion of the constitutional conception of property in German constitutional law in chapter 3.
88. See Reinhard Zimmermann and Daniel Visser, South Africa as a Mixed Legal System, in Zimmermann and Visser, Southern Cross, pp. 659, 696–97.
89. Transkei Public Servants Ass'n v. Government of the Republic of South Africa, 1995 (9) BCLR 1235 (Tk).
90. 1995 (9) BCLR at 1246–47.
91. See Roux, Property, p. 46-17.
92. See chapter 2.
93. 2002 (4) SA 768 para. 100(f) (S. Afr.).
94. See van der Walt, Overview, p. 10.
95. 2002 (4) SA 768 at para. 61.
96. 2002 (4) SA 768 at para. 57.
97. Roux, Property, p. 46-18.
98. 2005 (1) SA 530 (CC).
99. Local Government: Municipal Systems Act sec. 118(1) provided in relevant part as follows:

> A registrar of deeds may not register the transfer of property except on production to that registrar of deeds of a prescribed certificate—
>
> a. issued by the municipality or municipalities in which that property is situated; and
>
> b. which certifies that all amounts that became due [by the owner] in connection with that property for municipal service fees, surcharges on fees, property rates and other municipal taxes, levies and duties dur-

ing the two years preceding the date of application for the certificate have been fully paid.

100. 2005 (1) SA 530 at para. 32.
101. 2005 (1) SA 530 at paras. 32–33.
102. 2002 (4) SA 768 at para. 57.
103. 2002 (4) SA 768 at para. 58.
104. van der Walt, Striving for a Better Interpretation, p. 14. Professor van der Walt points out that in this respect *FNB* departs from the court's earlier approach taken in the *Harksen* case.
105. Theunis Roux argues that this approach may have the unintended and undesirable consequence of introducing a degree of inflexibility into the property clause analysis. Once it is determined that a law is arbitrary and not justified under section 36, it cannot be saved on the basis of the fact that it provides for payment of just and equitable compensation under section 25(2). The arbitrariness analysis will swallow up the section 25(2) inquiry into provision of adequate compensation. This effectively precludes a court from sustaining a law by reading into it a requirement that the state pay adequate compensation, a result that might have been be the most desirable solution. Roux, Property, pp. 46-19 to -20.
106. See for example, Geoff Budlender, The Constitutional Protection of Property Rights: Overview and Commentary, in Budlender et al., The New Land Law, 1st ed. (Cape Town: Juta), pp. 1-34 to -36.
107. See A. J. van der Walt, The Limits of Constitutional Property, 12 S. Afr. Pub. L. 275 (1997).
108. 2002 (4) SA 768 at para. 65.
109. 2002 (4) SA 768 at para. 100.
110. 2002 (4) SA 768 at para. 100.
111. 2002 (4) SA 768 at para. 108.
112. Roux, Property, p. 46-24.
113. This observation was confirmed by the Constitutional Court's subsequent decision in the *Mkontwana Case.* The court there held that while the statute did effect a "deprivation," the deprivation was not arbitrary. The court emphasized the difference between the two cases in the connection between the affected property and the debt. In *FNB,* it said, the automobile had nothing whatsoever to do with the customs debt. In *Mkontwana,* on the other hand, the utility consumption charge, even though based on consumption by an occupant who was not the owner, was connected with both the property and the owner. "[T]he supply of electricity and water to property," the court reasoned, "ordinarily increases its value; the consumption of electricity and water enhances its use and enjoyment." 2005 (1) SA 530 at para. 40. And with respect to the owner, "there is a level at which the owner and the debt are usually connected or related regardless of the nature of the relationship between the owner and the occupier and of whether the property is lawfully occupied. This is because the owner is bound to the property by reason of the fact of ownership which . . . entails certain rights and responsibilities." 2005 (1) SA 530 at para. 41. The court's willingness to find that the deprivation was nonarbitrary despite the slender relationship between the charges and the property and its owner seems likely to be due to the facts that the statute at issue in the case burdened fewer incidents of ownership than did the statute in *FNB* and that the deprivation was only temporary. The *Mkontwana* Court explicitly pointed to the fact that the statute deprived the owner of only a sin-

gle incident of ownership, leaving the owner free to enjoy the property in other important respects. 2005 (1) SA 530 at paras. 45–46.

114. S. Afr. Const. sec. 36(1).
115. 2002 (4) SA 768 at para. 110.
116. See, for example, Roux, Property, p. 46-27; van der Walt, Striving for the Better Interpretation, p. 19; de Waal et al., The Bill of Rights Handbook, p. 422.
117. More recently, the Constitutional Court decided the question whether a statute provided for the constitutionally correct approach to the issue of compensation. See Du-Toit v. Minister of Transport, — SA — (decided September 8, 2005). The court made no reference to *FNB*.
118. See van der Walt, An Overview of Developments, p. 28; Roux, Property, p. 46-31.
119. 1998 (1) SA 300 at para. 32.
120. For a general discussion of the doctrine of constructive expropriations in South Africa, see A. J. van der Walt, Moving toward Recognition of Constructive Expropriation?, 65 Tydskrif vir Hedendaagse Romeins-Hollandse Reg 459 (2002).
121. See Steinberg v. South Peninsula Municipality, 2001 (4) SA 1243 (SCA). The court there, while refusing to find a constructive expropriation on the instant facts, said in dicta that "there may be room" for the development of [the constructive eviction] doctrine in South Africa.
122. Accord Roux, Property, p. 46-32; van der Walt, An Overview of Developments, p. 31.
123. But see DuToit v. Minister of Transport, — SA — (September 8, 2005) (deciding compensation issue without referring to *FNB* analysis).
124. See, for example, Khumalo v. Potgieter, 2000 (2) All SA 456 (LCC); Ex parte Former Highland Residents; In re Ash v. Department of Land Affairs, 2000 (2) All SA 26 (LCC).
125. See van der Walt, An Overview of Developments, p. 34.
126. In DuToit v. Minister of Transport, — SA — (decided September 8, 2005), the Constitutional Court gave some indication of the approach it will take to compensation issues. By a divided vote, the court concluded that it will use a two-step analysis. The first step is to consider what compensation is payable under the Expropriation Act of 1975, which was the primary statutory instrument for compensation for expropriations in South Africa prior to adoption of the constitution. The Act basically adopts a market value standard of compensation. The second step is to determine whether the amount established under the Act is "just and equitable" under section 25(3) of the constitution. In dissent, Justice Langa stated that this two-step approach "would continue to privilege market value at the expense of other considerations relevant to justice and equity which are expressly advocated by the Constitution." In his view, analysis of the adequacy of compensation should involve only one inquiry, namely, what compensation is required in light of justice and equity.
127. As commentators have noted, the familiar distinction between so-called positive and negative rights is highly problematic. See, for example, Cass R. Sunstein, The Second Bill of Rights: FDR's Unfinished Revolution and Why We Need It More Than Ever (New York: Basic Books, 2004). I use the term here simply as a convenient heuristic.
128. Inclusion of socioeconomic rights in the constitution was highly controversial. Among the objections was the concern that because of their positive character they are not justiciable. The Constitutional Court held otherwise in the important case of Ex parte Chairperson of the Constitutional Assembly: In re Certification of the Constitution of the Republic of South Africa, 1996 (4) SA 744 (CC). The court there held that socioeconomic rights are "at least to some extent, justiciable." At a minimum they can be negatively protected against improper invasion.

129. See Sandra Liebenberg, The Interpretation of Socio-Economic Rights, in Woolman et al., Constitutional Law of South Africa, pp. 33-i, 33-1.
130. 2001 (1) SA 46 (CC).
131. 2005 (1) SA 217 (CC).
132. As the court stated in *Port Elizabeth Municipality,* "The term 'land invasion' . . . must be used with caution." The term, Sachs pointed out, "can be stretched to cover widely dissimilar cases, [such as] where a relatively small number of people have erected shacks and lived on undeveloped land for relatively long periods of time, or the situation in *Grootboom* where although a thousand desperate people occupied a hillside due to be developed for low-cost housing, no intent to jump the queue was shown and a remedy was not refused, or [where] there had been a deliberate and premeditated act culminating in the unlawful invasion and occupation of a large tract of land." 2005 (1) SA 217 n. 22.
133. 2005 (1) SA 217 at para. 27-29.
134. 2005 (1) SA 217 at para. 9.
135. Under the Natives Land Act 27 of 1913 and the Natives Land Act 18 of 1936, thirteen percent of all of South Africa's land was designated for occupation by the black majority, while the remaining eight-seven percent was available for minority whites, Indians, and so-called coloreds. 2005 (1) SA 217 at para. 9, n. 4. See generally Klug, Constituting Democracy, pp. 41–44.
136. See Leonard Thompson, A History of South Africa, 3d ed. (New Haven, CT, 2000), p. 178.
137. 2005 (1) SA 217 at para. 10, n.7.
138. Thompson, A History of South Africa, pp. 192–93.
139. See Kate O'Regan, No More Forced Removals? An Historical Analysis of the Prevention of Illegal Squatting Act, 5 S. Afr. J. Hum. Rights 361 (1989).
140. 2001 (1) SA 46 at para. 8. Wallacedene was located in the far eastern part of the Cape Town metropolitan area. According to the court, a quarter of the households in Wallacedene had no income whatsoever. About half were children. All of the residents lived in shacks that had no water, sewage, or garbage services. Only five percent of the shacks had electricity. 2001 (1) SA 46 at para. 8.
141. 2001 (1) SA 46 at para. 66.
142. 2001 (1) SA 46 at para. 34 (emphasis added).
143. 2001 (1) SA 46 at para. 30. The notion of a "minimum core obligation" originated in the interpretive comments on the International Covenant on Economic, Social, and Cultural Rights, by the United Nations Committee on Economic, Social, and Cultural Rights. See 2001 (1) SA 46 at para. 30.
144. 2001 (1) SA 46 at para. 33.
145. 2001 (1) SA 46 at para. 33. The court's rejection of a minimum core obligation has been strongly criticized. See Sandra Liebenberg, The Right to Social Assistance: The Implications of *Grootboom* for Policy Reform in South Africa, 17 S. Afr. J. Hum. Rights 232 (2001); David Bilchitz, Giving Socio-Economic Rights Teeth: The Minimum Core and Its Importance, 118 S. Afr. L.J. 484 (2002); Theunis Roux, Understanding *Grootboom*—A Response to Cass R. Sunstein, 12 Const. Forum 41 (2002).
146. 2001 (1) SA 46 at para. 63.
147. 2001 (1) SA 46 at para. 77.
148. 2001 (1) SA 46 at para. 78.
149. 2001 (1) SA 46 at para. 79.
150. 2001 (1) SA 46 at para. 71.

151. Cass R. Sunstein, Designing Democracy, p. 233.
152. 2001 (1) SA 46 at para. 71.
153. Sunstein, Social and Economic Rights?, p. 130.
154. 2001 (1) SA 46 at para. 66.
155. See Sandra Liebenberg, The Interpretation of Socio-Economic Rights, pp. 33–51.
156. See, e.g., Roux, Property, p. 46-19.
157. 2005 (1) SA 217 at para. 12.
158. For an illuminating discussion of these changes, see A. J. van der Walt, Ownership and Eviction: Constitutional Rights in Private Law, 9 Edinburgh L.J. 32 (2005).
159. See, for example, Cheety v. Naidoo, 1974 (3) SA 13 (A).
160. 2005 (1) SA 217 at para. 29, n. 29.
161. 2005 (1) SA 217 at para. 14.
162. 2005 (1) SA 217 at paras. 18–19.
163. 2005 (1) SA 217 at paras. 18–19.
164. 2005 (1) SA 217 at paras. 19–20.
165. 2005 (1) SA 217 at para. 23.
166. Eviction at the hands of a private individual is regulated by section 4 of PIE and, according to the court, involves a somewhat different analysis.
167. 2005 (1) SA 217 at paras. 35–36.
168. 2005 (1) SA 217 at para. 36.
169. 2005 (1) SA 217 at para. 43.
170. There is a nontrivial risk that the process of mediation may become intensely fact-specific and require a substantial investment of time. Any assessment of mediation in this context has to weigh those costs against its benefits, which would seem to include reducing what Frank Michelman, in a different context, has called "demoralization costs."
171. Bishop Tutu has defined the notion of *ubuntu*, a word that derives from the Zulu and Xhosa languages, in these terms: "A person with ubuntu is open and available to others, affirming of others, does not feel threatened that others are able and good, for he or she has a proper self-assurance that comes from knowing that he or she belongs in a greater whole and is diminished when others are humiliated or diminished, when others are tortured or oppressed." Desmond Tutu, No Future without Forgiveness (New York: Doubleday, 1999). The interim constitution identified it as one of the foundational values of the new Republic of South Africa, and the final constitution's replacement concept, human dignity, needs to be understood in relation to the indigenous notion of *ubuntu*.
172. 2005 (1) SA 217 para. 10.
173. 2005 (1) SA 217at para. 23 (emphasis added).
174. See, for example, *Grootboom*, 2001 (1) SA 47 (CC); Soobramoney v. Minister of Health, Kwazulu-Natal, 1998 (1) SA 765 (CC); Minister of Health v. Treatment Action Comm., 2002 (5) SA 721 (CC).

In *Grootboom* the court did make reference to the negative aspects of the section 26 housing rights provision, but it did not develop the point. More recently, in Jaftha v. Schoeman, 2005 (2) SA 140 (CC), the court did hold that section 26(1) ("Everyone has the right to have access to adequate housing") imposes a negative obligation on the state. The court stated, "[A]ny measure which permits a person to be deprived of existing access to adequate housing, limits the right protected in section 26(1)." 2005 (2) SA 140 (CC) at para. 34.
175. See Johan Neethling, A Vision of the Future of South African Private Law—Full or

Reconciliatory Synthesis?, in The Future of South African Private Law, ed. Annél van Aswegen (Pretoria: University of South Africa).

176. See, for example, Derek van der Merwe, Constitutional Colonization of the Common Law: A Problem of Institutional Integrity, 2000 J. S. Afr. L. 1, 12.
177. See, for example, Davis, Democracy and Deliberation, pp. 127–63; A. J. van der Walt, Tradition on Trial: A Critical Analysis of the Civil-Law Tradition in South African Property Law, 11 S. Afr. J. Hum. Rights 169 (1995); Un-Doing Things with Words: The Colonization of the Publlic Sphere by Private Property Discourse, 1998 Acta Juridica 235.
178. For a good overview, see Derek van der Merwe, Ramus, Mental Habits, and Legal Science, in Essays on the History of Law, ed. Daniel P. Visser (Cape Town: Juta, 1989), p. 32.
179. The system of private rights was subsequently refined by the nineteenth-century German Pandectists, particularly Bernhard Windscheid (1817–92), who introduced a strongly subjectivist dimension to this system of rights. Windscheid derived his subjectivist approach from Kant and Friedrich von Savigny (1779–1861). See A. J. van der Walt, Ownership and Personal Freedom: Subjectivism in Bernhard Windscheid's Theory of Ownership, 56 J. Contemp. Roman-Dutch L. 569 (1993).
180. The felicitous term is Professor van der Walt's.
181. Colonization, in the view of self-described private-law proponents, comes in the form of the horizontal application of the Bill of Rights, a topic that we will take up subsequently.
182. See, for example, P. J. Visser, Some Remarks on the Relevance of the Bill of Rights in the Field of Delict, 1998 J. S. Afr. L. 529, 535–36.
183. Johan Neethling, A Vision of the Future of South African Private Law—Full Co-Existence or Reconciliatory Synthesis?, in The Future of South African Private Law, ed. Annél van Aswegen (Pretoria: University of South Africa, 1994), pp. 1, 3.
184. For a representative sampling of writings making more or less this same argument, see J. M. Potgieter, The Role of the Law in a Period of Political Transition: The Need for Objectivity, 54 J. Contemp. Roman-Dutch L. 800 (1991); T. J. Scott, The Future of Our Roman-Dutch Law: Reflections and a Suggestion, 26 De Jure 394 (1993); M. M. Corbett, Trust Law in the 90s: Challenges and Change, 56 J. Contemp. Roman-Dutch L. 262 (1993).
185. On the three pillars of South African land reform, see van der Walt, Land Reform in South Africa since 1990—An Overview.
186. Evictions may be brought under land-reform statutes that amended and restricted the common law of eviction, particularly PIE and the Extension of Security of Tenure Act of 1997, or, where those statutes are inapplicable, under common law.
187. 2000 (4) SA 468 (W). Contrast *Betta Eiendomme* with Ross v. South Peninsula Municipality, 2000 (1) SA 589 (C) (holding that section 26(3) of the constitution amended and restricted the common law of eviction).
188. For example, the court might obtain guidance from section 25(3) of the constitution, which specifies circumstances to be taken into account in determining the amount of compensation to be paid in an expropriation.
189. Both the Extension of Security of Tenure Act (1997) and PIE (1998), for example, specify a number of factors that the court is required to take into account in determining whether eviction is appropriate. For discussion of these statutes and cases interpreting them, see A. J. van der Walt, Exclusivity of Ownership, Security of Tenure, and Eviction Orders: A Model to Evaluate South African Land-Reform Legislation,

2002 J. S. Afr. L. 254; A. J. van der Walt, Exclusivity of Ownership, Security of Tenure and Eviction Orders: A Critical Evaluation of Recent Case Law, 18 S. Afr. J. Hum. Rights 372 (2002).

190. In the argot of modern constitutional law, the court rejected a "horizontal" application of section 26.

191. See 2000 (4) SA 468 at para. 10.1.

192. 2000 (4) SA 468 at para. 7.2.

193. Davis, Democracy and Deliberation, p. 133.

194. 2000 (4) SA 468 at para. 10.1.

195. 2000 (4) SA 468 at para. 102.

196. Stephen Gardbaum, The "Horizontal Effect" of Constitutional Rights, 102 Mich. L. Rev. 387, 395 (2003).

197. This conventional wisdom is challenged in Gardbaum, "Horizontal Effect," p. 387.

198. I put to one side for the moment the possibility, famously recognized in American constitutional law in Shelley v. Kraemer, 334 U.S. 1 (1948), that the constitution may provide a private individual who has been harmed in some way an owner's use of her property with the means to prevent or redress that harm. I discuss this possibility in connection with the South African Constitutional Court's analysis of the "horizontality" doctrine.

199. Klaus Stern, vol. 3, pt. 1 of Das Staatsrecht der Bundesrepublik Deutschland (Munich: C. H. Beck Verlag, 1988), p. 1553.

200. An indirect version of horizontality is sometimes called *Ausstrahlung*, or "radiation effect." See Ralf Brinktrine, The Horizontal Effect of Human Rights in German Constitutional Law, 6 Eur. Hum. Rights L. Rev. 421, 424 (2001).

The *locus classicus* on the German doctrine of horizontality is the famous *Lüth* case, BVerfGE 7, 198 (1958). That case is the origin of the established principles that constitutional rights form an "objective order of values" and that the state has a positive duty to promote those objective values. According to the Federal Constitutional Court, that value system affects the entire legal system. It influences private law as well as public law, and private law rules must be construed consistently with its spirit. This means that private law rules are invalid if they conflict with constitutional values. Thus, while constitutional rights provisions do not have a direct impact on private actors, they do have a direct effect on private law. See Gardbaum, Horizontal Effect, p. 404.

In recent years, the theoretical framework for analyzing the relationship between constitutional law and private litigation has shifted from horizontality to the state's duty to protect constitutional values. See Matthias Ruffert, Vorrang der Verfassung und Eigenständigkeit des Privatrechts: eine Verfassungsrechtliche Untersuchung zur Privatrechtswirkung des Grundgesetzes (Tübingen, Germany: Mohr Siebeck Verlag, 2001), pp. 10–12, 13–14, 20–21. German constitutional law recognizes the state's positive duties, known as "protective duties" (*Schutzpflichten*), to promote certain constitutional values. These duties affect private law and private individuals in various ways. For example, the constitution (Basic Law) can impose a duty on legislatures to create or change private law statutes in such a way as to protect fundamental constitutional values. Moreover, some constitutional provisions are capable of directly affecting private law relations. See Stern, Das Staatsrecht der Bundesrepublik Deutschland, p. 1563. The shift from a focus on horizontality to protective duties is connected with the core distinction in German constitutional theory between fundamental rights as *subjective* rights, on the one hand, and the *objective content* of fundamental rights provisions. (I am grateful to Andre van der Walt for emphasizing this point to me.)

201. Elsje Bonthuys, The South African Bill of Rights and the Development of Family Law, 119 S. Afr. L.J. 748, 749 (2002). The South African literature on horizontality is quite large. Interesting examples include Johan van der Walt, *Progressive* Indirect Horizontal Application of the Bill of Rights: Toward a Co-Operative Relation between Common-Law and Constitutional Jurisprudence, 17 S. Afr. J. Hum. Rights 341 (2001); Lorraine Wolhuter, Horizontality in the Interim and Final Constitutions, 11 S. Afr. Pub. L. 512 (1996).
202. Gardbaum, Horizontal Effect, p. 389.
203. 1996 (3) SA 850 (CC). In that case the court held that the 1993 constitution's Bill of Rights "does not have general direct horizontal application, but that it may and should have an influence on the development of the common law as it governs relations between individuals." 1996 (3) SA 850 (CC) at 887 (footnote omitted). The textual basis for this holding was section 7, which provided,

    > (1) This Chapter shall bind all legislative and executive organs of the state at all levels of government; (2) This Chapter shall apply to all law in force and all administrative decisions taken and acts performed during the period of operation of this Constitution.

    S. Afr. Const. 1994, ch. 3, sec. 7. The exclusion of the judiciary from section 7(1) seemed to the court to preclude an inference of direct horizontal application. At the same time, the court in effect affirmed an indirect version of horizontal application.
204. S. Afr. Const. ch. 2, sec. 8.
205. 2001 (1) SA 489 (CC).
206. 2001 (1) SA 489 (CC) at para. 39.
207. 2001 (1) SA 489 (CC) at para. 54.
208. See the subsequent discussion of the protective duty theory in connection with the *Modderklip* case.
209. Danie Smit, Integration or Integrity? Private Law, Constitutionalism and the Rule of Values in South Africa (unpublished manuscript, Harvard Law School 2004), p. 20. See Bernhard Schlink, German Constitutional Culture, in Constitutionalism, Identity, Difference, and Legitimacy–Theoretical Perspectives, ed. Michel Rosenfeld (Durham, NC, 1994), p. 197.
210. Gardbaum, The "Horizontal Effect" of Constitutional Rights, p. 390, n.10. As Professor Gardbaum observes, in the United States, the answer to that question generally is no.
211. This is not to say that the protective duty theory and indirect horizontal application are identical. In German constitutional law, an important difference exists between the two. The duty to protect places constitutional duties on both courts and legislatures to amend private law to conform to and promote fundamental rights. Indirect horizontal application (*mittelbare Drittwirkung*), on the other hand, applies only to judge-made law. The theory of indirect horizontal application is that preexisting legal norms are affected by the radiation effect (*Ausstrahlungswirkung*) of the Basic Law's scheme of objective values. See Robert Alexy, A Theory of Constitutional Reights, trans. Julian Rivers (Oxford: Oxford University Press, 2004), pp. 351–65. It remains to be seen how the South African courts will develop the theory of the state duty to protect.

212. The same reasoning may lead the court to find that the state is under a duty to take preventive measures to ensure that other private actors do not encroach upon the fundamental rights of individuals.
213. See A. J. van der Walt, Transformative Constitutionalism and the Development of South African Property Law, pt. 1, 2005 J. S. Afr. L — (forthcoming); pt. 2, 2005 J. S. Afr. L. — (forthcoming).
214. 2004 (8) BCLR 821 (SCA), aff'd on other grounds, CCT 20/04 (CC) (decided May 13, 2005).
215. The settlement had just one water tap, and the only facilities were rudimentary pit toilets.
216. R1.8 million (approximately $275,000).
217. 2004 (8) BCLR 821 at para. 16.
218. 2004 (8) BCLR 821 at para. 52(b)(I).
219. The court based its conclusion on the *Grootboom* decision, but the implications of that decision on the instant case are rather more complex than the court allowed. Among other concerns is the possibility that queue jumping, which the *Grootboom* court clearly stated must not be permitted or encouraged, might be encouraged under the court's view. The court concluded that because the occupants had mistakenly believed that the land was municipal land no queue jumping was involved in the case. 2004 (8) BCLR 821 at 832.
220. 2004 (8) BCLR 821 at para. 30.
221. 2004 (8) BCLR 821 at para. 16, n. 17, citing X & Y v. The Netherlands, 8 Eur. H.R. Rep. 235 (Eur. Ct. H.R. 1985); Union des Jeunes Avocats v. Chad, 9th Annual Activity Report 72 (African Commission); The Social and Economic Rights Action Center and the Center for Economic and Social Rights v. Nigeria, 15th Annual Activity Report 30 (African Commission); and Velàsquez Rodriguez v. Honduras, 28 ILM 291 (1989) (Inter-American Court of Human Rights).
222. Section 1 refers to the "[s]upremacy of the constitution and the rule of law" as among the values that are foundational to the constitutional order. Section 34 reads, in relevant part, "Everyone has the right to have any dispute that can be resolved by the application of law decided in a fair public hearing before a court or, where appropriate, another independent or impartial tribunal or forum."
223. Modderklip, CCT 20/04 (CC) at para. 43.
224. The court's unwillingness to reach this matter was due to the fact that there was no indication whether or not the state owned other land to which it could have relocated the occupiers. Were such land available to the state, the court said, it would not be just and equitable for the court to order the state to acquire specific land on Modderklip's farm. CCT 20/04 (CC) at para. 64.

CHAPTER FIVE

1. For an explicit endorsement of constitutional borrowing, see United States v. Then, 56 F.3d 464, 468–69 (2d Cir. 1995) (Calabresi, J., concurring). For a more skeptical view, see A. E. Dick Howard, The Indeterminacy of Constitutions, 31 Wake Forest L. Rev. 383 (1996).
2. See Carol M. Rose, *Mahon* Reconstructed.
3. 521 U.S. 507 (1997).
4. 521 U.S. at 530.
5. See, for example, John T. Noonan, Jr., Religious Liberty at Stake, 84 Va. L. Rev. 459, 470–71 (1998). See generally Vicki C. Jackson, Ambivalent Resistance and Compar-

ative Constitutionalism: Opening Up the Conversation on "Proportionality," Rights and Federalism, 1 U. Pa. J. Const. L. 583, 602–34 (1999).

6. Jackson, Ambivalent Resistance and Comparative Constitutionalism, p. 603.
7. 512 U.S. 374 (1994). I discuss the *Dolan* case in light of the Canadian version of the proportionality principle later in this chapter in the section titled "Would a Proportionality Principle Make Any Difference in Takings Law?"
8. 512 U.S. at 375.
9. 512 U.S. at 375.
10. See City of Monterey v. Del Monte Dunes, 526 U.S. 687, 702 (1999). See Lee Anne Fennell, Hard Bargains and Real Steals: Land Use Exactions Revisited, 86 Iowa L. Rev. 1 (2000).
11. See Jackson, Ambivalent Resistance and Comparative Constitutionalism, p.604 ("proportionality is a widespread concept in European law"); Nicholas Emiliou, The Principle of Proportionality in European Law: A Comparative Study (London: Springer, 1996), p. xi (to the same effect); David M. Beatty, Constitutional Law in Theory and Practice (Toronto: University of Toronto Press, 1995); Jeremy Kirk, Constitutional Guarantees, Characterisation and the Concept of Proportionality, 21 Melbourne U. L. Rev. 1, 4 (1997) ("Proportionality has been . . . applied in public law around the world."). On the growth of proportionality in Europe, see Alec Stone Sweet, Governing with Judges: Constitutional Politics in Europe (Oxford: Oxford University Press, 2000), pp. 97–99, 114–24.
12. In European Community law, the proportionality principle is used primarily in two substantive areas: the law of common agricultural policy and the law of the free movement of goods. See Emiliou, The Principle of Proportionality, pp. 1–2.
13. Jackson, Ambivalent Resistance and Comparative Constitutionalism, p. 605 (discussing Canadian cases); Kirk, Constitutional Guarantees, p. 2 (discussing the Australian proportionality principle).
14. See R. v. Oakes, [1986] 1 S.C.R. 103, 138–40.
15. The Australian Commonwealth Constitution (1900) does not include a conventional bill of rights. See Van der Walt, Constitutional Property Clauses, p. 39. However, the courts treat Section 51(xxxi) of the Australian Commonwealth Constitution as the equivalent of a constitutional property provision. They have developed a proportionality principle that works as outlined above.
16. See, for example, BVerfGE 21, 150 (154–55).
17. See S. v. Makwanyane, 1995 (3) SA 391 (CC).
18. See Mostert, The Constitutional Protection and Regulation of Property, p. 134.
19. Section 36 of the final version of the South African Constitution, the general limitation provision, is basically a codification of the analysis followed by the South African Constitutional Court in the *Makwanyane* case. The court's analysis in that case, in turn, was premised on the reasoning in the Canadian cases, especially *Oakes*. See van der Walt, Constitutional Property Clauses, p. 95, n. 60; Stuart Woolman, Out of Order? Out of Balance? The Limitation Clause of the Final Constitution, 13 S. Afr. J. Hum. Rights 102 (1997). Mostert argues that although "the roots of the South African proportionality test are mostly sought in its Canadian counterpart, the German Basic Law remains the best comparative agent as far as the content and nature of the proportionality test in South Africa is concerned." Mostert, The Constitutional Protection and Regulation of Property, pp. 135–36 (footnote omitted).
20. This version of the proportionality test was initially developed by the Canadian Supreme Court in R. v. Oakes, [1986] 1 S.C.R. 103.

21. See Jackson, Ambivalent Resistance and Comparative Constitutionalism, pp. 606–607. This is essentially the same set of requirements used in German constitutional law as well. See Currie, The Constitution of the Federal Republic of Germany, pp. 309–310.
22. Jackson, Ambivalent Resistance and Comparative Constitutionalism, p. 615 (citing R. v. Keegstra, [1990] 3 S.C.R. 697, as illustrative).
23. Jackson, Ambivalent Resistance and Comparative Constitutionalism, 608.
24. Jackson, Ambivalent Resistance and Comparative Constitutionalism, pp. 610, 616, 617.
25. See R. v. Keegstra, [1990] 3 S.C.R. 697, 744–58.
26. Jackson, Ambivalent Resistance and Comparative Constitutionalism, pp. 613–14.
27. Jackson, Ambivalent Resistance and Comparative Constitutionalism, p. 616.
28. See, for example, RJR MacDonald v. Canada, [1995] 3 S.C.R. 199, 268–78 (LaForest, J., dissenting).
29. See the discussion later in this chapter in the section titled "Can/Should the Proportionality Doctrine Be Transplanted to American Takings Jurisprudence?"
30. See, for example, Kirk, Constitutional Guarantees, p. 5.
31. See Woolman, Out of Order? Out of Balance?, p. 111.
32. Henk Botha, Metaphoric Reasoning and Transformative Constitutionalism, part 2, J. S. Afr. L.20, 30 (2003).
33. See Mostert, The Constitutional Protection and Regulation of Property, pp. 294–95.
34. See Loammi Blaauw-Wolf, The "Balancing of Interests" with Reference to the Principle of Proportionality and the Doctrine of *Güterabwägung*—A Comparative Analysis, South African Publiekreg/Public Law 178, 198–201 (1999).
35. 341 U.S. 494, 525–26 (1951) (Frankfurter, J., concurring).
36. See, for example, T. Alexander Aleinikoff, Constitutional Law in the Age of Balancing, 96 Yale L.J. 943 (1987); Mark Tushnet, An Essay on Rights, 62 Texas L. Rev. 1363 (1984); Laurent B. Frantz, The First Amendment in the Balance, 71 Yale L.J. 1424 (1962).
37. See Aleinikoff, Constitutional Law in the Age of Balancing, p. 993.
38. 438 U.S. 104 (1978).
39. See the discussion of the Court's methodology in chapter 2.
40. See Penn Central, 438 U.S. at 124.
41. See the discussion of functional analysis later in this chapter in the section titled "A Social-Obligation Norm."
42. See, for example, Susan Rose-Ackerman, Against Ad-Hocery: A Comment on Michelman, 88 Colum. L. Rev. 1697 (1988).
43. 505 U.S. 1003 (1992).
44. Jackson, Ambivalent Resistance and Comparative Constitutionalism, p. 622.
45. See the discussion in the section titled "Can/Should the Proportionality Doctrine Be Transplanted" later in this chapter.
46. Epstein, Takings, passim.
47. Cases from Canada and Germany using proportionality have not resulted in a libertarian requirement of full compensation for owners every time the burden of a property regulation is not immediately and completely compensated by in-kind benefits.
48. See Mostert, The Constitutional Protection and Regulation of Property, p. 289.
49. See Nollan v. California Coastal Comm'n, 483 U.S. 825 (1987).
50. Dolan, 512 U.S. at 374.
51. 512 U.S. at 386–87.

52. See Jackson, Ambivalent Resistance and Comparative Constitutionalism, p. 608.
53. See Thomas W. Merrill, Property and the Right to Exclude, 77 Neb. L. Rev. 730 (1998).
54. See Jackson, Ambivalent Resistance and Comparative Constitutionalism, p. 616.
55. Jackson, Ambivalent Resistance and Comparative Constitutionalism, pp. 606–607.
56. David A. Dana and Thomas W. Merrill, Property: Takings (New York: Foundation Press, 2002), pp. 223–24.
57. See City of Monterey, 526 U.S. at 702.
58. Dana and Merrill, Property: Takings, p. 224.
59. See, for example, Ward v. Rock against Racism, 491 U.S. 781, 796–802 (1989); Central Hudson Gas & Elec. Co. v. Public Service Comm'n of N.Y., 447 U.S. 557, 565 (1980).
60. See Geoffrey R. Stone et al., Constitutional Law, 3d ed. (Boston: Little Brown, 1996), pp. 567–68.
61. The Supreme Court recently reaffirmed its use of the *Penn Central* analysis in Tahoe-Sierra Preservation Council, Inc. v. Tahoe Regional Planning Agency, 535 U.S. 302 (2002).
62. Hanoch Dagan has raised this concern, arguing that a "strict proportionality rule" "undermin[es] social responsibility." Hanoch Dagan, Just Compensation, Incentives, and Social Meanings, 99 Mich. L. Rev. 134, 136 (2000). As my description of proportionality should indicate, however, the version of proportionality that I discuss is not the "strict proportionality" principle that Dagan rejects.
63. Van der Walt, Constitutional Property Clauses, p. 85.
64. On the *Dolan* doctrine, see the discussion earlier in this chapter in the section titled "Would a Proportionality Principle Make Any Difference in Takings Law?"
65. 526 U.S. at 702–703.
66. 535 U.S. 302 (2002).
67. For criticisms of the Court's bifurcated approach, see Mark Fenster, Takings Formalism and Regulatory Formulas: Exactions and the Consequences of Clarity, 92 Calif. L. Rev. 609 (2004); Lee Anne Fennell, Hard Bargains and Real Steals: Land Use Exactions Revisited, 86 Iowa L. Rev. 1 (2000).
68. Lambert v. City & County of San Francisco, 67 Cal. Rptr. 2d 562 (Ct. App. 1997), *cert. denied,* 529 U.S. 1045 (2000). See Ronald H. Rosenberg, The Non-Impact of the United States Supreme Court Regulatory Takings Cases on the State Courts: Does the Supreme Court Really Matter?, Fordham 6 Envtl. L.J. 523, 555–56 (1995) (collecting earlier state court cases ignoring *Nollan, Dolan,* and *Lucas*). But see Town of Flower Mound v. Stafford Estates Ltd. P'ship, 135 S.W.3d 620 (Tex. 2004).
69. Saul Levmore, Takings, Torts, and Special Interests, 77 Va. L. Rev. 1333, 1334–35 (1991).
70. See Gregory S. Alexander, Takings, Narratives, and Power, 88 Colum. L. Rev. 1752 (1988).
71. I am indebted to Hanoch Dagan for making this point to me.
72. J.E.D. Assocs. v. Town of Atkinson, 432 A.2d 12, 14 (N.H. 1981).
73. Jackson, Ambivalent Resistance and Comparative Constitutionalism, p. 618.
74. In its current incarnation, the debate is between Justice Antonin Scalia, who has long staked out a strongly literalist view of constitutional interpretation, and Justice Stephen Breyer, who has more recently developed what he calls a "pragmatic," theory. Compare Antonin Scalia, The Rule of Law as a Law of Rules, 56 U. Chi. L. Rev. 1175 (1989), with Stephen Breyer, Our Democratic Constitution, 77 N.Y.U. L. Rev.

245 (2002). See generally, Kathleen M. Sullivan, Foreword: The Justices of Rules and Standards, 106 Harv. L. Rev. 22 (1992).

75. See, for example, Aleinikoff, Constitutional Law in the Age of Balancing, p. 943.
76. Jackson and Tushnet, Comparative Constitutional Law, p. 1329.
77. Justice Stevens' opinion for the Court in *Tahoe-Sierra* is perhaps the best example of this attitude. He there stated, "The interest in facilitating informed decision-making by regulatory agencies counsels against adopting a *per se* rule that would impose such severe costs on their deliberations." 535 U.S. at 339.
78. Little, but not none. Determining whether the instant case fits within this or that categorical rule inevitably requires some attention to purposes, but the reliance on categories mutes the discussion of purposes. Furthermore, some categorical rules, like the sort the Court developed in the *Lucas* case, include exceptions, and these exceptions themselves typically require investigation into purpose.
79. Rose, *Mahon* Reconstructed, p. 594. The same view is expressed in Gregory S. Alexander, Takings and the Post-Modern Dialectic of Property, 9 Const. Comm. 259 (1992).
80. Morris R. Cohen, Property and Sovereignty, 13 Cornell L.Q. 8, 26 (1927).
81. The failure of formalist judges to explicitly identify the core normative message that they attribute to property is ironic since one reason for formalism's appeal is its ostensible clarity.
82. As Carol Rose has nicely put it, "[B]oth libertarian and neo-utilitarian [that is, economic] scholars . . . often give the impression of an almost defiantly exuberant celebration of individual self-interest, with a concomitant rejection of common interests as anything other than the sum of individual preference satisfactions." Carol M. Rose, Property and Persuasion: Essays on the History, Theory, and Rhetoric of Ownership (Boulder, CO: Westview Press, 1994), p. 3.
83. Hanoch Dagan, Just Compensation, p. 149.
84. See Edward J. Eberle, Dignity and Liberty: Constitutional Visions in Germany and the United States (Westport, CT: Praeger, 2001), p. 7.
85. Daphna Lewinsohn-Zamir, The Objectivity of Well-Being and the Objectives of Property Law, 78 N.Y.U. L. Rev. 1669 (2003).
86. Lewinsohn-Zamir, The Objectivity of Well-Being, pp. 1672–73.
87. Lewinsohn-Zamir, The Objectivity of Well-Being, p. 1674.
88. Lewinsohn-Zamir, The Objectivity of Well-Being, p. 1717.
89. Gregory S. Alexander, Commodity & Propriety: Competing Visions of Property in American Legal Thought, 1776–1970 (Chicago: University of Chicago Press, 1997).
90. Elsewhere, I have labeled this theory "communitarian." See Gregory S. Alexander, Takings and the Post-Modern Dialectic of Property, p. 259.
91. John Locke, The Second Treatise of Government, ed. J. W. Gough (Oxford: Oxford University Press, 1976), p. 15.
92. Such a reading is rejected by Robert Nozick, Anarchy, State, and Utopia (New York, 1974), pp. 175–82. Nozick's reading is rejected in turn by Jeremy Waldron. See Jeremy Waldron, The Right to Private Property (Oxford: Oxford University Press, 1988), pp. 280–83. For further debate about the meaning of the Lockean Proviso, see, for example, John Stick, Turning Rawls into Nozick and Back Again, 81 Nw. U. L. Rev. 363 (1987); Carol M. Rose, 'Enough and As Good' of What?, 81 Nw. U. L. Rev. 417 (1987).
93. The first case explicitly to refer to reciprocity as relevant in drawing the regulation/

takings line is Pennsylvania Coal Co. v. Mahon, 260 U.S. 393 (1922), where Justice Holmes spoke of "an average reciprocity of advantage."

94. 42 N.Y.2d 324, 366 N.E.2d 1271 (1977).
95. See generally Henry George, Progress and Poverty (New York: Robert Schalkenbach Foundation, 1955; first published in 1879). For a more comprehensive application of George's "single-tax" idea to modern takings law, see T. Nicolaus Tideman, Takings, Moral Evolution, and Justice, 88 Colum. L. Rev. 1714 (1988).
96. Penn Central, 42 N.Y.2d at 328.
97. Frank I. Michelman, A Skeptical View of "Property Rights" Legislation, 6 Fordham Envtl. L.J. 409, 416 (1995) (emphasis added) (footnotes omitted).

    It is worth noting that Michelman distinguishes between "contemporary community goals" and "private advantage." Similarly, in distinguishing between "proprietarian" and "commodity" conceptions of property, I have argued that the commodity, or market conception, which is aimed at providing private advantage, cannot be reduced to the proprietarian conception by supposing that the maximum fulfillment of private advantage constitutes a normatively coherent vision of the proper social order, or common weal. See Alexander, Commodity & Propriety, pp. 1–3.
98. See Alexander, Commodity & Propriety; Gregory S. Alexander, Property as Propriety, 77 Neb. L. Rev. 667 (1998); Alexander, Takings and the Post-Modern Dialectic of Property, p. 259; Hanoch Dagan, The Craft of Property, 91 Calif. L. Rev. 1517 (2003); Frank I. Michelman, Possession vs. Distribution in the Constitutional Idea of Property, 72 Iowa L. Rev. 1319 (1987); Carol M. Rose, Property and Persuasion (Boulder, CO, 1994), pp. 58–65; Rose, *Mahon* Reconstructed, p. 561; Joseph William Singer, Entitlement: The Paradoxes of Property (New Haven, CT: Yale University Press, 2000); Gary Minda, The Dilemmas of Property and Sovereignty in the Postmodern Era: The Regulatory Takings Problem, 62 U. Colo. L. Rev. 599 (1991).
99. Dagan, Just Compensation, Incentives, and Social Meanings, p. 149.
100. Dagan, Just Compensation, Incentives, and Social Meanings, p. 149. (footnote omitted).
101. See Lucas, 505 U.S. at 1027.
102. 123 U.S. 623 (1887).
103. 123 U.S. at 665.
104. 239 U.S. 394 (1915).
105. See Miller v. Schoene, 276 U.S. 272 (1928); Goldblatt v. Town of Hempstead, 369 U.S. 590 (1962).
106. See, for example, Graham v. Estuary Properties, Inc., 399 So. 2d 1374 (Fla. 1981) (ordinance prohibiting development of wetlands sustained); Just v. Marinette County, 201 N.W.2d 761 (Wis. 1972) (same); Sibson v. State, 336 A.2d 239 (N.H. 1972) (same).
107. 480 U.S. 470 (1987).
108. 505 U.S. 1003.
109. As far as I am aware, the argument was first made in Frank I. Michelman, Property, Utility, and Fairness: Comments on the Ethical Foundations of "Just Compensation" Law, 80 Harv. L. Rev. 1165 (1967). While Professor Michelman's more recent work certainly places him outside the ranks of law and economics scholars, his earliest work was among the first generation of economics-influenced legal scholarship, a point that I made in Gregory S. Alexander, The Concept of Property in Private and Constitutional Law: The Ideology of the Scientific Turn in Legal Analysis, 82 Colum. L. Rev. 1545 (1982).

110. See, for example, Glynn S. Lunney, Jr., Responsibility, Causation, and the Harm-Benefit Line in Takings Jurisprudence, 6 Fordham Envtl. L.J. 433 (1995).
111. Michelman, Property, Utility, and Fairness, p. 1197.
112. William A. Fischel, Regulatory Takings: Law, Economics, and Politics (Cambridge, MA: Harvard University Press, 1995), p. 354.
113. Fischel, Regulatory Takings, p. 354.
114. The term "Ordinary Observer" was first coined by Bruce Ackerman in his influential 1977 book. Bruce A. Ackerman, Private Property and the Constitution (New Haven, CT: Yale University Press, 1977).
115. Daniel H. Cole, Pollution and Property: Comparing Ownership Institutions for Environmental Protection (Cambridge: Cambridge University Press, 2002).
116. Cole, Pollution and Property, p. 171.
117. Cole, Pollution and Property, p. 171. Laura Underkuffler has recently suggested a useful means of analyzing how the balance *should* be struck in such conflicts. See Laura S. Underkuffler, The Idea of Property: Its Meaning and Power (Oxford: Oxford University Press, 2003), pp. 775–803.
118. 505 U.S. at 1024.
119. Dana and Merrill, Property: Taking, p. 150.
120. The Court itself had previously adopted that view in *Penn Central.* See 438 U.S. at 134, n. 30. The Court subsequently retreated from that position and once again relied on the harm-abatement/benefit-conferring distinction in Keystone Bituminous Coal Ass'n. v. DeBenedictis, 480 U.S. 470, 489–92 (1987).
121. 505 U.S. at 1026–27 (emphasis in original).
122. As David Dana has pointed out, however, Scalia himself was guilty of relying on the harm-prevention/benefit-conferring distinction in *Lucas.* Scalia expressed the view that the preservation law in that case secured a benefit for the public, for which the public should be required to pay. 505 U.S. at 1028. See David A. Dana, Natural Preservation and the Race to Develop, 143 U. Penn. L. Rev. 655, 665 (1995).
123. 505 U.S. at 1029.
124. 505 U.S. at 1029 (footnote omitted).
125. See, for example, Fischel, Regulatory Takings, pp. 61, 355; William W. Fisher III, The Trouble with *Lucas,* 45 Stan. L. Rev. 1393 (1993); Joseph L. Sax, Property Rights and the Economy of Nature: Understanding *Lucas v. South Carolina Coastal Council,* 45 Stan. L. Rev. 1433 (1993).
126. See Epstein, Takings, pp. 295–303, 309–12.
127. Singer, Entitlement, p. 16.
128. For an account of Blackstone's actual views, see Carol M. Rose, Canons of Property Talk, or Blackstone's Anxiety, 108 Yale L.J. 601 (1998).
129. See, for example, Park Hill Terrace Assocs. v. Glennon, 369 A.2d 938 (N.J. App. Div. 1977).
130. See Alexander v. McKnight, 7 Cal. App. 4th 973, 9 Cal. Rptr. 2d 453 (1992).
131. See Prah v. Maretti, 321 N.W.2d 182 (Wis. 1982).
132. Michelman, Possession vs. Distribution, p. 1319.
133. Michelman, Possession vs. Distribution, pp. 1319–20.
134. See Lucas, 505 U.S. 1003.
135. See, for example, Dana and Merrill, Property: Takings, pp. 106–110; Lynn E. Blais, Takings, Statutes, and the Common Law: Considering Inherent Limitations on Title, 70 S. Cal. L. Rev. 1 (1996); Fisher, The Trouble with *Lucas,* pp. 1406–408.
136. Kimball Laundry Co. v. United States, 338 U.S. 1, 5 (1949).

137. Kevin Gray, Land Law and Human Rights, in Land Law: Issues, Debates, Policy, ed. Louise Tee (Cullumpton, UK: Willan Publishing, 2002), pp. 211, 240.
138. Gray, Land Law and Human Rights, pp. 211, 240 (emphasis in original).
139. Hanoch Dagan, Takings and Distributive Justice, 85 Va. L. Rev. 741, 771 (1999).
140. Dagan, Takings and Distributive Justice, pp. 771–72 (footnote omitted).
141. For examples of such a conception see, Dagan, Takings and Distributive Justice, pp. 771–74; Joseph William Singer and Jack Beerman, The Social Origins of Property, 6 Can. J.L. Juris. 217, 241–48 (1993); Singer, Entitlement, pp. 197–216.
142. For an elaboration of this idea, see Gregory S. Alexander, Dilemmas of Group Autonomy: Residential Associations and Community, 75 Cornell L. Rev. 1, 21–28 (1989).
143. Charles Taylor, Atomism in Charles Taylor, vol. 2 of Philosophy and the Human Sciences: Philosophical Papers (Cambridge: Cambridge University Press, 1985), pp. 187, 207.
144. The civic understanding of the social obligation norm is essentially what I have called the "proprietarian" theory of property. See Alexander, Commodity & Propriety, passim.
145. The emphasis in the text is intended to indicate that states are free to tailor constitutional property clauses as they wish, explicitly adding, for example, a positive constitutional right to basic and adequate housing. Most—nearly all, in fact—do not.
146. See State ex rel. Stoyanoff v. Berkeley, 458 S.W.2d 305 (Mo. 1970).
147. See Berman v. Parker, 348 U.S. 26, 33 (1954).
148. Penn Central, 438 U.S. 104.
149. This argument is a version of what Hanoch Dagan calls the "attenuated conception of reciprocity." Dagan, Takings and Distributive Justice, p. 769.
150. See Dagan, Takings and Distributive Justice, p. 769.
151. Dagan, Takings and Distributive Justice, p. 769.
152. Dagan, Takings and Distributive Justice, pp. 769–770 (footnote omitted).
153. Dagan, Takings and Distributive Justice, p. 797.
154. Dagan, Takings and Distributive Justice, p. 798.
155. See chapter 3.
156. Art. 14(2) (GG).
157. See chapter 3, the section titled "Some Background on the German Basic Law."
158. Singer, Entitlement, p. 18.
159. For example, Entscheidungen des Bundesgerichtshofes in Zivilsachen [BGHZ] 64, 220 (1975).
160. French law also provides for something quite similar, but the compensation is justified in different terms. In French administrative law, owners can claim compensation for loss caused by some regulatory measure on the basis of the equality principle, even when the regulatory measure is not deemed an expropriation, for which the French Constitution requires compensation. The basic idea is that the burden of valid regulatory measures should be spread equally, and when it is not, compensation should be paid. The equality principle is implicitly recognized in American law as well. It is reflected in the famous injunction of the Supreme Court in Armstrong v. United States, 364 U.S. 40, 49 (1960), that individual owners should not be forced by the state to "bear public burdens which, in all fairness and justice, should be borne by the public as a whole."
161. Penn Central, 438 U.S. at 137. The Court's allusion to the possible inadequacy of TDRs as "just compensation" refers to criticisms of TDRs as having uncertain value.

See, for example, John J. Costonis, The Chicago Plan: Incentive Zoning and the Preservation of Urban Landmarks, 85 Harv. L. Rev. 574, 585–89 (1972).

162. Suitum v. Tahoe Regional Planning Agency, 520 U.S. 725, 747–48 (1997) (Scalia, J., concurring).

163. American land-use regulators have used other measures for precisely the same purpose. See Windfalls for Wipeouts: Land Value Capture and Compensation, ed. Donald G. Hagman and Dean J. Misczynski (Chicago: American Society of Planning Officials, 1978).

Another way of understanding TDRs and other such "equalization" benefits is as a kind of "reverse exaction." Exactions, which we previously encountered in connection with the discussion of the *Nollan* and *Dolan* cases, are "various types of fees or . . . goods in kind [that developers must pay] in order to get permission to do their projects." Fischel, Regulatory Takings, p. 341. That is, in standard exaction practice, a desired development permit is granted, but a (public) benefit is extracted from the developer. TDRs and similar harm-mitigation devices reverse this alignment of permits and benefits: a development permit is *denied,* but a (private) benefit is *conferred.*

164. Michael A. Heller and James E. Krier, Deterrence and Distribution in the Law of Takings, 112 Harv. L. Rev. 997, 1009 (1999).

165. Such cases constitute what they call "Box 3" cases. See Heller and Krier, Deterrence and Distribution in the Law of Takings, pp. 1009–13. That term is based on a grid of takings cases they construct on the basis of the two goals they associate with the takings clause, efficiency and fairness. See Heller and Krier, Deterrence and Distribution in the Law of Takings, p. 1002.

166. Heller and Krier, Deterrence and Distribution in the Law of Takings, p. 1002 (citing Hadacheck v. Sebastian, 239 U.S. 394 (1915); Miller v. Schoene, 276 U.S. 272; and Just v. Marinette County, 201 N.W.2d 761).

167. Heller and Krier, Deterrence and Distribution in the Law of Takings, 1011 (footnote omitted).

168. Heller and Krier, Deterrence and Distribution in the Law of Takings, p. 1012.

169. Heller and Krier, Deterrence and Distribution in the Law of Takings, p. 1013. That solution echoes the German constitutional requirement of *Junktim Klausel,* which I discussed in chapter 3. As I indicated there, in its most recent pronouncement on the subject (the *Denkmalschutz* case), the German Constitutional Court cryptically indicated that the legislature should "anticipate" the possible need for equalization. Pointedly, however, it did not hold that equalization benefits may be awarded only with express legislative authorization. Equalization is usually handled at the administrative level, through administrative agencies and administrative courts.

170. See, for example, Penn Central, 438 U.S. at 124.

171. See Dana and Merrill, Property: Takings, p. 69.

172. BVerfGE 24, 367 (*Deichordnung* or *Flood Control Case,* 1968).

173. Art. 14(3) (GG).

174. For example, Art. 14(3) (GG).

175. This hypothetical also illustrates a possible incidental benefit of awarding less than full market value in exceptional cases. The current rule of full market value creates perverse incentives for government agencies. Under the existing doctrine, government agencies have strong incentives to try to achieve the ends through regulation rather than through exercises of eminent domain, even though eminent domain may be the more obvious means to the end. If they choose the eminent domain route, it is certain that they must pay full market value. On the other hand, they will be able

completely to avoid a compensation obligation if they adopt regulatory measures that basically achieve the same ends (assuming that the regulation is not later held to be a regulatory taking). Members of the Supreme Court have objected to government regulations in some cases on precisely this ground. (The most notable example is Justice Scalia's majority opinion in Nollan, 483 U.S. 825). This perverse incentive might be mitigated somewhat if the current all or nothing approach were abandoned. To be sure, significant incentives to regulate rather than condemn would still remain under a proportional approach to compensation, but at least in some cases the regulatory authority might prefer a straightforward condemnation proceeding rather than risking invalidation of a regulation whose validity it has reason to believe is questionable. Compensation at less than full market value might be a price that the regulator is willing to pay to obtain the assurance that what it considers a vitally necessary governmental objective is achieved. I stress, however, that deviations from the current practice would not occur in routine condemnation actions under the proportional analysis that I propose, drawing on the German practice.

176. See James E. Krier and Christopher Serkin, Public Ruses, 4 Mich. St. L. Rev. 859, 866 (2004).

177. I refer, of course, to the "rough proportionality" requirement announced in Dolan, 512 U.S. at 374.

178. See Christopher Serkin, The Meaning of Value: Assessing Just Compensation for Regulatory Takings, 99 Nw. U. L. Rev. 677, 679 (2005).

CONCLUSION

1. Underkuffler, The Idea of Property, p. 160.
2. See Singer, Entitlement, passim.

INDEX

DATE DUE